THE NATIONAL INSTITUTE OF
ECONOMIC AND SOCIAL RESEARCH

Economic and Social Studies
XXXVI

MACROECONOMIC POLICY
IN BRITAIN
1974–87

MACROECONOMIC POLICY
IN BRITAIN
1974–87

ANDREW BRITTON

The right of the
University of Cambridge
to print and sell
all manner of books
was granted by
Henry VIII in 1534.
The University has printed
and published continuously
since 1584.

CAMBRIDGE UNIVERSITY PRESS
CAMBRIDGE
NEW YORK PORT CHESTER MELBOURNE SYDNEY

Published by the Press Syndicate of the University of Cambridge
The Pitt Building, Trumpington Street, Cambridge CB2 1RP
40 West 20th Street, New York, NY 10011-4211, USA
10 Stamford Road, Oakleigh, Melbourne 3166, Australia

First published 1991

Printed in Great Britain at the University Press, Cambridge

British Library cataloguing in publication data

Britton, Andrew *1940*–
    Macroeconomic policy in Britain 1974–1987 – (Economic and
    social studies v. 36).
    1. Great Britain. Macroeconomic policies
    I. Title II. Series
    339.0941

Library of Congress cataloguing in publication data

Britton, Andrew (Andrew J.)
    Macroeconomic policy in Britain, 1974–87 / by Andrew Britton.
        p. ca. – (Economic and social studies ; 36)
    Includes bibliographical references (p.337) and index.
    ISBN 0-521-41004-5 (hardback)
    1. Great Britain–Economic policy–1945– I. Title. II. Series.
HC256.6.B7653 1991
339.5'0941'09047–dc20
90-24759
CIP

ISBN 0 521 41004 5

CONTENTS

Contents

Contents

LIST OF TABLES

LIST OF CHARTS

PREFACE

I could never have written this book on my own. For all those sections which required substantial new research, I had the very able help of a succession of members of the Institute staff. Howard Picton prepared the calendar of events and helped with the bibliography; Mark Minford did much of the statistical analysis of monetary policy in Part 4; Paul Gregg did the work using the Institute's model for Parts 4 and 5; Alan Shipman did the analysis of inflation and the cross-industry comparisons in Part 5; Rebecca Dutton completed the work on monetary policy, did much of that on fiscal policy, and checked a large number of calculations in all Parts of the book; my secretary, Ann Wright, typed the whole of the text (at least once); Frances Robinson compiled the index and prepared the text for publication. I am very grateful to them all.

In writing this history I am conscious that I could be said to have played a part, a very small one, in the events I describe. Until 1982 I was at the Treasury, as a Senior Economic Adviser and then as an Under Secretary. I hope that this has not influenced in any way the objectivity of my account of that period. I have not relied in any important way on my own memories of events, and I trust I have not broken any confidences.

Since 1982 I have been Director of the Institute, and as such have taken part in the continuing debates over the conduct of macroeconomic policy, when commenting on events in the Institute's *Review* or elsewhere. In writing this book I have not felt committed to any particular line that we have taken at the Institute in the past; on the contrary I have seen it as an opportunity to look again at the experience of the recent past to see whether, on second thoughts, a different interpretation would be better.

I am most grateful to the Institute, its Governors and business supporters, for making it possible for me to undertake this study, also the Economic and Social Research Council who made a grant to the Institute in support of the research needed for it. I would like to thank all those who have commented on the text in draft, especially Michael Artis, Charles Goodhart, Simon Wren-Lewis and Huw Evans. I would also like to thank all my friends and colleagues on the staff of the Institute who have helped, directly or indirectly, consciously or unconsciously. But responsibility for the results (including any errors or eccentricities) is mine alone.

INTRODUCTION

The National Institute has already produced two studies of economic policy in Britain. The first, Dow (1964), covering the fifteen years from 1945 to 1960, became a standard work of reference, as well as making a significant original contribution to the interpretation of economic behaviour. The second, Blackaby (1978), was designed to be a sequel in that it covered a similar span of years, 1960–74, but it was more ambitious in that it dealt extensively with a wider range of policies, industrial and commercial for example as well as fiscal and monetary. For that reason it was a group rather than an individual enterprise. The present volume is intended as a third in the series.

The task facing the historian of economic policy from the mid-1970s is a daunting one, more daunting surely than that which faced the authors of studies covering earlier postwar periods. It seems as if there have been more 'events' per year; and the volume of statistics and commentary referring to the period far outweighs that inviting analysis by historians of any earlier period. The task, if it is to be manageable at all, has to be narrowed down.

This is a book about macroeconomic policy, a term which is to be defined more precisely below. It is about the ways in which governments have tried to contain or reduce inflation, to influence the growth of output and employment. It concentrates on the use made, for these purposes, of monetary and fiscal policy. It has very little to say about other aspects of economic policy, such as industrial policy, trade relations, the structure of taxes and public spending; and it has relatively little to say about incomes policy under Labour and the special labour market measures used by governments of both parties to limit unemployment.

Another problem faces the author of this study more acutely than his predecessors. It has become much more difficult than it was, in the 1960s at least, to present the 'facts' of monetary and fiscal policy actions in a neutral and uncontroversial way, let alone to give an account of their consequences which would be generally acceptable to economists. Macroeconomics is not that kind of subject any more, and has not been for twenty years. For this reason alone this is not an easy book to write. It is written, however, in the strong belief that objective analysis is possible even in areas highly charged with political emotion, as well as by the value judgements of economists themselves. That said, it would be a dull book which tried only to present facts, without any new interpretation. The aim is not only to chronicle events, describe policy and the ideas which inspired it, but also to draw certain conclusions about what was achieved by policy in this particular period. What is more, the book is written in the belief that historical studies of this kind are a necessary step on the way to useful generalisations about macroeconomic policy as it can or should be conducted.

THE CHARACTER OF THE PERIOD

Not only in Britain, but in all the major industrial countries, economic performance since 1974 has been very disappointing by comparison with earlier postwar years. The growth rate of output has slowed down in almost all countries. In Britain this deceleration was very marked indeed during the later 1970s, but there was some catching up in the 1980s not seen elsewhere.

The deterioration in economic performance is even more obvious in relation to unemployment and inflation – the two variables for which macroeconomic policy is traditionally responsible. Full employment (in the proper sense of the term) was maintained continuously in Britain from the war until the early 1970s; in the period covered by this study it was *never* achieved. The 1950s and 1960s were characterised by persistent inflation, but inflation at a moderate rate that most found acceptable, if not actually desirable; the 1970s and early 1980s twice saw inflation in Britain at over 20 per cent a year, a rate at which it comes to dominate economic policy and to interfere considerably with the lives of most citizens. This book therefore must be mainly about the earnest struggles of macroeconomic policymakers, not about their triumphant successes. The best that could be said of them would be that they did well 'in the circumstances'; some did better than others, but none had much cause for satisfaction or self-congratulation.

It would be good to offer some all-embracing and cogent explanation of what went wrong, but historical studies, especially studies of economic history, seldom produce clearcut conclusions of that kind. It would in any case be necessary to extend the study to the world economy as a whole, before those features of economic performance which Britain shared with other industrial countries could be accounted for convincingly. All that can be done here is to point to some attendant circumstances which characterise the period, and may help to account for the failures of macroeconomic policy and performance.

The oil price increases of 1973 and 1979 undoubtedly caused major upheavals in the world economy and were widely blamed for the ills of the industrial world. They added to inflation by raising costs, and they depressed output by cutting the real value of incomes. They created an unfamiliar pattern of payments balances between countries which may have upset financial markets. Even so it is surely too convenient an explanation for the finance ministers and central bankers of the world to say that the *main* reason for the poor performance of the world economy was the actions of oil producers. The system should have been able to cope with disturbances of this kind and scale.

A more profound change, between the 1960s and the 1970s, was the move from fixed to floating exchange rates. As later sections of this book will describe, this changed profoundly the nature of macroeconomic policy in all the major industrial countries, including Britain. At this stage we should simply note that the rules of the game had changed, making the conduct of policy altogether more difficult, at least while practitioners were trying to find out what the new rules were.

Britain was more exposed than most countries to the new international financial environment, especially after the abolition of exchange control in 1979, because of the importance of sterling as a currency in world markets, and because of the decision not to join in the exchange rate mechanism of the European Monetary System. We shall have occasion to refer to exchange rate movements in almost every section of this book.

It might be expected that the effects of Britain's entry into the European Economic Community (EEC) in 1973 would provide another recurrent theme for the study. In fact it will hardly be mentioned. In macroeconomic policy, as distinct from commercial policy, competition policy, regional policy and so on, Brussels did not have a great influence on the British authorities at this time. There were attempts to 'coordinate' policy within the Monetary Committee, but these were no more significant than the attempts to cooperate worldwide through the International Monetary Fund (IMF) and the Organisation for Economic Cooperation and Development (OECD). Indeed the views of the American authorities mattered more in London at most times than the views of Paris or Bonn. Very gradually the influence of EEC directives and laws touched more and more facets of life in Britain, so that by the end of our period the issue of sovereignty was becoming one of real political significance. But, strangely enough, macroeconomic policy was still one of the issues *least* affected by entry into the EEC.

In economics generally, and in the debate over macroeconomic policy in particular, British opinion was conditioned by events and ideas in America, not in Europe. The debate in Britain, as we shall see, was especially lively because the economic doctrine of monetarism came to be loosely identified with the Conservative Party whilst the Labour Party remained more or less faithful to Keynes. This is a crude and misleading simplification, but it is just the sort of crude and misleading simplification that often colours public debate. The period of this study was characterised in Britain by a debate over macroeconomic policy which was unusually bitter and contentious. There had been a broad agreement between political parties from the war until the early 1970s about the general lines on which macroeconomic policy should be conducted. When that consensus broke down, opinion in Britain went to extremes. The intellectual opinions adopted and the policies actually put in place on the basis of them were more dogmatic, less pragmatic, than those found in most of Continental Europe. It will be argued that the oddities of British thought and practice may have contributed to our relatively poor performance. The British are not usually thought of as volatile, argumentative or passionate people, but in matters of macroeconomic policy in the 1970s and 1980s that was the way we behaved.

The approach of the Labour government from 1974 to 1979 was broadly an attempt to keep the old style of economic policy in being (despite some important changes of tactics and despite growing doubts as to its efficacy). Government was expected still to direct the economy in all strategic, and in many particular, respects. Exchange controls remained; bank credit was rationed; industrial and regional policy was still active; above all prices and incomes policy negotiated with national trade union leaders was more crucial than ever to attempts to contain inflation.

The approach of the Conservatives after 1979 was, by contrast, revolutionary. Incomes policy was scrapped; exchange control was scrapped; direct regulation of the banks was scrapped as well. Little remained of industrial and regional policy. Firms and individual workers were told to serve their private economic interests, with no guidance from on high, and only the minimum of regulation by law. The decisions of bureaucrats were replaced by the market mechanism. The speed and thoroughness of the reforms, popularly called 'Thatcherism', were watched with awe by the outside world, mixed either with admiration or with dismay.

This book, however, is about macroeconomic policy, not about economic reform in this much broader sense. The conduct of macroeconomic policy, and of monetary policy in particular, was central to the rhetoric of Thatcherism, but it will be argued that in this area there was less discontinuity than elsewhere. The way in which the Bank of England and the Treasury set interest rates day by day or month by month was not vastly different in 1987 from the way they set them in 1974, or indeed twenty years before that. Against the background of economic upheaval and the clash of opinion, the routine work of the monetary authorities was surprisingly little affected.

The same might even be said of fiscal policy. The use of the budget as an instrument of macroeconomic policy never was as active in practice in the 1950s and 1960s as economic textbooks would have one believe. Throughout the 1970s and 1980s the Treasury went on making short-term economic forecasts, and using them to advise the Chancellors what they could 'afford' by way of tax cuts or public spending. The Chancellors, as always, took the advice with scepticism, but did not ignore it altogether. Here too there was some continuity between the period of this study and that of its two predecessors.

So much for the overture! It remains, before embarking on the first act of the performance, to identify rather more precisely what the title means. The word 'macroeconomic' as applied to policy is intended in a limited and rather precise sense, which must now be carefully defined.

MACROECONOMIC POLICY

Paradoxically, macroeconomic policy consists typically of *small* decisions, nudging interest rates up or down by a percentage point or so, whilst microeconomic policy includes momentous strategic choices like joining the EEC or reforming trade union law. The borderline is not always clearcut or undisputed, so it is necessary before embarking on a history of macroeconomic policy to adopt a working definition of it, and to reflect for a moment on what macroeconomic policy thus defined might reasonably be expected to achieve.

The aims of macroeconomic policy concern the behaviour of the economy as a whole, not that of particular industries, regions or social groups. Indeed, the great merit of macroeconomic policy is that it enables the government to take responsibility for some aspects of aggregate performance without needing the information, or the legal powers, to intervene in the affairs of particular parts of the economy. It can be conducted impersonally, apolitically and decisively, by means of a limited set of instruments which have a pervasive effect on the working of the entire economic system. It is common ground to economists of widely differing views that the conduct of macroeconomic policy with sufficient skill and determination is a necessary condition for the well-being of society. It provides the framework, to use a familiar metaphor, within which the private sector – and indeed the public sector as well – can take decisions about the allocation and use of resources. Suggestions have been made that macroeconomic policy should be put in some sense 'above politics', by handing it over to officials or experts who might be more farsighted, less partisan, than the government of the day. Such suggestions have not been put into practice, but the possibility of making them says something about the character of macroeconomic policy, and about the ideals of many of those involved in its conduct.

The aims of macroeconomic policy are usually said to be full employment and price stability. Few would quarrel with that as an ideal; the practical difficulty is that the two aims may be incompatible. The actual experience of the period covered by this study is one of high and rising unemployment together with persistent, volatile and often alarming inflation. If price stability was attainable at all, it was so only at the cost of yet higher unemployment, for all or much of the time. Thus a prior choice had to be made as to the rate of inflation which was considered tolerable, a choice which officials and experts on their own were hardly entitled to make, but which politicians were reluctant to make explicitly. Yet the day-to-day or year-to-year conduct of macroeconomic policy has always to be predicated on a choice of that kind.

The choice is made more difficult because we are ignorant of the 'trade-off' between unemployment and inflation. Many economists would indeed deny that such a trade-off exists in the long run; they would say that the choice is between a temporary fall in unemployment and a permanent fall in inflation – the debate continues. If politicians are reluctant to make explicit choices between inflation and unemployment it is partly because economists cannot tell them with confidence which combinations are possible, and which are not. Moreover it is possible, indeed likely, that the nature of the trade-off that exists between inflation and unemployment itself depends on the way in which macroeconomic policy is conducted.

Within any given overall strategy the routine conduct of macroeconomic policy could be described as demand management. This term, although it went out of vogue in the 1970s, still described rather well what the Treasury and the Bank of England were trying to do. They tried to prevent aggregate demand in the economy rising above, or falling below, the level compatible with the combination of inflation and unemployment which was found to be the least unacceptable. 'Management' is a better word than 'control' because the precision with which demand can be maintained and influenced has never been high – so-called fine-tuning of demand was always an unrealistic aim.

It may seem odd to equate the routine of macroeconomic policy with demand management when the presentation of policy for many years was in terms of monetary control. But the difference in theory is not as great as the heat of controversy between monetarists and Keynesians would suggest; and the difference in practice is even less. In theory monetary control ensures control of inflation because an excess or deficiency of money adds to or substracts from demand for goods and services. The precise mechanism is open to question, but most theoretical accounts of a monetarist regime imply some sort of automatic regulation of aggregate demand. The way monetary control was attempted in Britain was extraordinarily similar to demand management, since the operational decisions were about the level of interest rates and the size of budget deficit necessary to hit the monetary target. There was no attempt to control the money supply *directly*; what the authorities tried to manage was the demand for money, a close relation, as it happens, of aggregate demand for goods and services, expressed at current prices.

Nevertheless, to talk of demand management in the 1970s and 1980s without qualification *would* be somewhat anachronistic, because the floating of the exchange rate introduced a new and very important element into the calculations of policymakers. Monetary policy was dominated by exchange market pressures for much of the period covered by this book. On occasion fiscal policy had to be used as well to 'defend the pound'. The first requirement to be met by a set of macroeconomic policy measures often was that it should be well-received by international bankers, not that it should be appropriate to the pressure of demand in the domestic economy.

Sir Peter Middleton (1989) has suggested that the need to keep the confidence of financial markets was recognised by the Treasury as the essential first requirement of a sound macroeconomic policy some time in the 1970s. 'Confidence and expectations in financial markets are crucial to policymaking in today's world of global markets. It is no use thinking that those involved in financial transactions will take the trouble to understand the nuances of domestic economic policy'. The chronicle of events in Part 1 will include many events which serve well to illustrate that text. It may not give a complete account of the substance of macroeconomic policy, but it is a necessary corrective to those who think that demand management can continue unchanged in exactly the same way as it was conducted when Butler or Gaitskell was Chancellor of the Exchequer.

Even under the new rules of the game appropriate to a world of floating exchange rates, however, the old, hard choice between inflation and unemployment still had to be made. The authorities had to decide what level of the exchange rate they would try to defend: a high exchange rate helps reduce inflation, but a low exchange rate makes industry more competitive. There is still a trade-off, although its nature may not be the same as that available in a closed economy.

To achieve their preferred combination of output and inflation the Treasury and the Bank of England have two instruments at their disposal. They can, within limits, decide the rate of interest at the short end of the market, day by day and month by month. That is the main way in which monetary policy operates. The government can also decide year by year roughly what the level of public sector borrowing shall be. That for present purposes summarises fiscal policy.

The system is a good deal more complicated in practice, so that the two levers of macroeconomic policy could easily be described as two dozen. In the case of monetary policy, decisions have also to be taken about operations in gilt-edged markets, about purchases and sales of foreign exchange, about regulation of the banking system, in the past, about hire purchase control and about a host of other things. In the case of fiscal policy the mix between different kinds of public spending matters as well as its overall level; the rates of taxation matter for their effects on private sector behaviour as well as for the revenue they raise.

The choice between fiscal and monetary measures, when it is thought necessary to expand or contract demand, was not always taken in a systematic way. In the Spring action might be in the budget, at other times of year it was interest rates that changed. In an emergency, such as characterised much of the 1970s, action had to be taken on both fronts, even at the 'wrong' time of year. The possibility of using the two arms of policy in a more constructive way than this was often discussed. It is an issue we shall take up later in this study.

The hint was dropped a few pages back that the nature of the trade-off between inflation and unemployment might be changed by the way in which macroeconomic policy is conducted. If that is true, it is obviously a consideration of the first importance. The routine of macroeconomic policy may be aptly described as demand management even in the 1970s and 1980s, but the term does much less than justice to the ambitions of governments in that period, and it gives much too narrow an account of the issues covered by the concurrent debate about the way in which macroeconomic policy should be conducted.

Demand management was once seen by economists as an essentially technical exercise, what used to be called 'steering the economy'. But all the theory of macroeconomic policy was rewritten in the 1970s to take account of the way in which expectations are influenced by the conduct of policy. (The fact that floating exchange rates respond to expectations very sensitively may be of importance to the timing of this intellectual revolution.) Macroeconomic policy is a matter of political leadership, credibility and reputation as well as a technical matter of economic forecasting and modelbuilding. Politicians may feel that they have known this all along, but since the 1970s economists have incorporated a more rigorous use of this language into their debate and policy recommendations. The interesting policy choices were not seen so much in terms of one year's budget or one week's interest rate change, but in terms of alternative rules or regimes that might be put into operation and govern policy responses for the foreseeable future.

The attempt to influence expectations was one way of addressing the central problem of economic policy, that of combining an 'acceptable' rate of inflation with an 'acceptable' rate of unemployment. The other way was to call in aid additional arms of policy which could as easily be called microeconomic as macroeconomic, and which *did* involve detailed intervention by government in the working of the economy.

Prices and incomes policies were intended to act on inflation directly – to suppress it, rather than to cure it, a critic would say. A more sophisticated way of putting it would be that they were an attempt to reduce the level of unemployment that was compatible with constant inflation. Special employment measures tackle the same problem from the other end. They act directly on unemployment – to disguise it, a critic would say, not to eliminate it. They too may shift the trade-off between unemployment and inflation. Less obviously and directly many kinds of economic policy initiatives may have an influence, for good or ill, on the sustainable level of economic activity and the degree to which the system is prone to inflation. A case could be made, for example, for including trade union legislation and competition policy in a book on macroeconomic policy; but a line must be drawn somewhere.

OUTLINE OF THE BOOK

The earlier parts of the book are mainly descriptive, the later parts more analytical. There are no footnotes, but each part is provided with bibliographic notes and a list of references at the end of the book. Part 1 is a chronological account of macroeconomic policy actions and their setting. The topics covered during the periods of Labour and Conservative governments necessarily differ a little: for example the description of successive phases of incomes policy from 1974 to 1979 has no parallel in the later sections. A calendar of events is provided at the end of the book, as well as charts of the main economic indicators.

This is followed in Part 2 by a history of ideas about macroeconomic policy and its effects. This describes some of the most influential writings of economists in Britain during the period, throwing light on the reasons given for policy actions by ministers and by officials. Given the intellectual ferment of this period, it is not possible to include all the significant ideas that have been given an airing. It is hoped that the themes which are developed are reasonably representative.

The influence of the world economy on Britain was not the subject of special attention by Dow or by Blackaby, but it has now become so pervasive that it calls for a Part of its own. Part 3 gives a necessarily brief account of the developments in the major economies and compares their experience with that of Britain.

Part 4 contains the main analysis of monetary and fiscal policy. This is of broadly two kinds. The first considers how policy instruments were used in response to different indicators, such as inflation, unemployment, the exchange rate or interest rates abroad. In the case of interest rate movements econometric estimation is possible, showing for example how the reactions of the authorities differed before and after 1979. The second kind of analysis uses the National Institute's macroeconomic model of the United Kingdom economy, and compares the course of events with what might have happened if macroeconomic policy had been different in several carefully defined ways.

Part 5 is concerned with the consequences of macroeconomic policy, that is with what actually happened to inflation, unemployment, the external balance and the rate of growth. The issues addressed include the following: the consequences of a floating exchange rate; the reasons for the upward trend in unemployment; the relationship between inflation and the pressure of demand; and the effects of demand management on growth potential in the long run.

The conclusions drawn in Part 6 contrast the rhetoric of policy with what was actually done, and the claims made for policy with what was in fact achieved. We try to give a brief summary of 'what actually happened'. After that we try to draw out some lessons from history. It is necessary to come to terms with the events and ideas of the past before prescribing policies for the future.

PART 1

NARRATIVE OF EVENTS

2

PRELUDE: THE LAST YEARS OF THE HEATH GOVERNMENT

In the early months of 1974 Britain was in an acute crisis, that was both political and economic. The world's major oil producers had raised fourfold the price of crude oil. The coal miners in Britain then voted for an all-out strike, having previously almost exhausted coal stocks by banning overtime. The prospect facing the country was one of accelerating inflation, growing balance of payments deficit and recession. In these circumstances the Prime Minister, Edward Heath, called a general election, and lost.

To understand how this situation came about it is necessary to go back at least two years, to look briefly at the policies followed by the Heath government in its last two years and the boom conditions that ensued. This episode is crucial to the understanding not only of the situation in 1974, but of much that was said and done about economic policy in Britain for at least a decade thereafter. It is described in some detail in Blackaby (1978), so only an outline of events will be given here.

During 1972 economic policy became exceptionally expansionary, arguably more so than at any time since the war. The stated aim was to raise the growth rate of gross domestic product (GDP) to 5 per cent a year. This was higher than the 4 per cent aim of the 1964 National Plan, higher again than the average growth rate, about 3 per cent, actually achieved during the 1960s. As a short-term objective it was perceived as bold; as a medium-term objective it was criticised as unrealistic. The fact that unemployment at the beginning of 1972 was over 800,000 (compared with only 300,000 in 1966) encouraged many to see a period of rapid expansion as both possible and highly desirable. It was also believed by influential economists that a period of faster growth, by satisfying aspirations for real income increase, would make it easier to persuade trade unionists to be moderate in their wage claims.

The 1972 budget cut taxes substantially, mainly by increasing personal allowances against income tax. The effect of the budget on GDP was officially estimated at 2 per cent. Increases were also planned in public spending, especially public sector fixed investment, although the subsequent shortfall from plan shows that they were not fully implemented, or implemented much later than intended.

At the same time monetary policy was also relaxed, although the motives in this case were only in part to do with the expansion of demand. A new method of operating monetary policy had been announced by the Bank of England in 1971, described as 'Competition and Credit Control'. It replaced the old system of direct quantitative restriction on the lending of each bank, which restricted competition, by a new system relying on control (direct or indirect) of short-term interest rates. The banks responded to the change by increasing their lending dramatically, competing energetically amongst themselves as well as bidding funds away from other financial institutions. The result was a very rapid rise in the broad monetary aggregate M3.

The monetary authorities viewed this expansion with some concern but did not want to do anything that would frustrate the government's aim of expanding demand and output. Interest rates were kept relatively low, rising a little in the latter part of 1972, but falling back again in the first half of 1973.

Another ingredient of the policy package was the decision in June 1972 to allow the exchange rate to float in the foreign exchange markets. The Chancellor had said in his budget speech that a fixed exchange rate would not be allowed to stand in the way of economic expansion. Even so the announcement came as a surprise. The decision was announced as temporary and was taken in order to avoid raising interest rates at a time when sterling was under pressure. It meant abandoning the dollar rate agreed at the Smithsonian in the previous December and also the agreement as recent as 1 May to join the other European exchange rates in the 'snake in the tunnel'. Year-on-year, between 1972 and 1973 the sterling effective exchange rate index fell by about 10 per cent.

These expansionary measures contributed to the strength of what is known as the 'Barber boom'. The Central Statistical Office, in its charts of cyclical indicators, identifies February 1972 as the lower turning point. (The timing is obscured by an earlier miners' strike which lasted from early January to the end of February.) From then until May 1973, the upper turning point, demand and output rose very fast indeed. The rise in the output index of GDP between the second quarters of 1972 and 1973 was 5½ per cent. (Between the first quarters it was 9½ per cent, but that surely exaggerates the underlying rate of increase.) Unemployment peaked in the first quarter of 1972 and fell 200,000 over the next twelve months. In that respect at least the expansionary policy had an immediate success.

The miners' strike of 1972, as well as distorting the economic indicators and raising fears of industrial anarchy, also had an effect on subsequent wage claims. The shift to more expansionary policies, and more expansionary conditions, seemed to do little to moderate these claims. After earnest attempts to secure a voluntary incomes policy the government was obliged instead to impose a freeze on both prices and incomes in November 1972.

This is not the place to describe in detail the successive phases of incomes policy in 1973, nor the long and painful attempts to secure trade union agreement with them. The main point to make is that these attempts were in the end frustrated by the renewed militancy of the miners. That in the end was what brought the government down. On the way to that downfall, however, the government put in place a form of incomes policy which was to prove exceedingly inappropriate to the circumstances in which it came into operation.

As part of incomes policy Stage 3, which was announced in November 1973, earnings were to be increased automatically to compensate fully for any increase in the rate of inflation above 7 per cent. The intention was to bring home to union negotiators the way in which wage restraint by any one group would reduce the overall rate of price inflation and hence reduce the case for wage increases for other groups. Unfortunately there are other reasons for price increases apart from increases in unit labour costs, as the oil producers' cartel (OPEC) was about to demonstrate.

Well before the oil price 'hike' the prices of imports were rising sharply. This was partly a reflection of the fall in sterling following the decision to float. It was also a reflection of world inflation, especially the rise in raw material prices. The years 1972 and 1973 were years of exceptional expansion not just in this country, but also in the world generally. It was indeed the first occasion since the Korean War boom of the early 1950s when demand in the industrialised world was so closely synchronised. Demand pressure in world markets was one reason for the commodity price boom, although no doubt special factors also contributed to the increase in many particular cases.

One consequence of the rise in import prices was the deterioration of the balance of payments. The current account had been in modest surplus in 1972, but during the next year it crossed over into deficit for the first time since 1968. Another consequence was an increase in the rate of inflation. Year-on-year the retail prices index rose about 7 per cent in 1972, but about 9 per cent in 1973. As so often, it was difficult to tell to what extent the balance of payments deficit and the rise in inflation was the result of world events, to what extent of 'overheating' in the United Kingdom itself.

Whatever the correct diagnosis may be, the conclusion drawn by the authorities during 1973 was that expansion had gone far enough, indeed by the end of the year they decided it had gone a long way too far. The budget of 1973 was broadly neutral and notable mainly for the introduction of VAT (following the accession of Britain to the EEC at the beginning of the year). The switchover to VAT was well publicised and there was widespread purchasing of consumer goods in the first quarter of the year in anticipation. This gave a final upward impetus to economic activity. The upper turning point of the cycle is now put at May 1973.

By May policy was already becoming contractionary: public spending cuts were announced, mainly affecting 1974/5. Further cuts were announced in October. Meanwhile the Bank of England was struggling to regain control of the money supply. Attempts had already been made to curb its growth by calling special deposits, but they had met with little success. In September the banks were asked to restrict lending to consumers and property speculators. More significantly perhaps, interest rates began to rise substantially. Minimum lending rate rose from 7½ per cent to 13 per cent between June and November. The period of expansionary monetary policy was at an end. The stock market price index, which had been drifting down gradually ever since 1972, now fell sharply in November and especially in December of 1973.

The mini-budget of 17 December 1973 was the last major act of economic policy under the Heath government, and it put into reverse the strategy of expansion that had characterised the previous two years. Further and much larger cuts in public spending were announced for 1974/5, hire purchase controls were reintroduced and a new method was adopted for the control of the banking system. By this time crisis point had already been reached for the world as a whole through the action of the oil producers, and for the United Kingdom in particular through the action of the miners. The December mini-budget, however, was not a response to OPEC or to the miners, but to the economic indicators, especially the balance of payments and the rate of inflation. The 'experiment' of the Heath government with expansion was seen to have failed. The reasons for that failure were debated again and again for much of the period with which this book is concerned.

The new method of controlling the banking system, the Supplementary Special Deposits Scheme or 'corset', was a return to direct quantitative intervention. The steep increases in interest rates had not had the desired effect of reducing bank lending and the growth of bank deposits. The scheme introduced as 'Competition and Credit Control' was shown to be technically defective. Its replacement was known as the 'corset' and it did indeed reduce the unhealthy-looking bulges in the monetary statistics.

Initially the action of Middle-Eastern oil producers threatened the availability of oil to the West, but by the end of the year this threat had been replaced by the shock of an unheard-of increase in the price of oil. The price of oil had already doubled in response to cutbacks in supply when they were redoubled by OPEC from 23 December. The effect on the world economy is described in Part 3 below. In common with other oil-importing countries the United Kingdom was faced with a change rather similar to an increase in indirect taxation. Oil was so widely used in production that the general level of prices was bound to rise. To the extent that the rise was limited, for example by price controls, company profits and liquidity would suffer; to the extent that prices did rise the real value of personal income would fall, depressing demand for consumer goods and stimulating demand for higher wage increases.

The oil crisis may also have encouraged the militancy of the coal miners and it certainly strengthened their bargaining position. Their overtime ban began on 8 November, the day after Stage 3 of the incomes policy was announced. By 13 December it was clear that coal stocks were dangerously low and a three-day working week for British industry was announced to take effect from 1 January 1974. Further meetings failed to break the deadlock. The government refused to break its own incomes policy and the miners voted by a large majority in favour of a strike. The Prime Minister then called a general election for 28 February, but the strike went ahead nonetheless.

The complete breakdown of incomes policy on this occasion was another failure of the Heath government that left its mark on subsequent events. Some drew the conclusion that incomes policies would never work and that a quite different approach was needed to the problem of inflation, and hence to economic policy generally. Others saw the miners' action as more overtly political and concluded that incomes policies might still be available but only to governments that had the political support of trade unionists. After the fall of the Heath government the debate over economic policy became much more explicitly party-political and it became much more difficult to discuss economics at all in a politically neutral way. It is quite difficult to do so even today.

3

THE LABOUR GOVERNMENT 1974–9

The result of the general election on 28 February 1974 was not decisive. The Labour Party had the largest number of seats, but no absolute majority. They were able to form a minority government, but it was clear that the political crisis was not over: there would have to be another election, and another electoral campaign, before the new government was to become fully effective. Thus the seven months from March to October 1974 were a period of transition, a period of political weakness exceptional in postwar British history. The circumstances in which the Labour government came to power further reduced their freedom of action. They owed, or seemed to owe, their electoral success, such as it was, to militant industrial action by the miners. This was an embarrassment to the new government, especially its more moderate members, and it further inhibited their actions especially in the field of economic policy.

The new government was headed by Harold Wilson, with Denis Healey as Chancellor. The new cabinet had many other members with experience of, or interest in, economic policy. The two ex-Chancellors, James Callaghan and Roy Jenkins, who were Foreign and Home Secretaries respectively, were both regarded as moderates. But there were others in the cabinet with a reputation as radicals in economic policy, such as Michael Foot at the Department of Employment and Tony Benn at the Department of Industry.

The Labour government of the 1960s had set out with the intention of recasting economic policy within the framework of a National Plan. The aim had been to increase the influence of government on economic development, and to mobilise private sector resources for a consistent set of national economic objectives. The plan had also been meant to ensure that the behaviour of government itself was consistent over time, rather than lurching from one direction of policy to another in the notorious cycle of 'stop' and 'go'. That aim had not been achieved. On the contrary, the 1967 devaluation had been followed by an exceptionally severe 'stop' period when the balance of payments proved slow to respond.

Recollection of these events of some years previously was important to the approach to economic policy adopted by Labour leaders when they regained office in 1974. They did not write another National Plan, neither did they recreate the Department of Economic Affairs. The Treasury's leading role in economic policymaking was not challenged in the same way again. On the other hand economic policy was not seen simply in traditional Treasury terms. The crucial issue in 1974 and for several years thereafter was seen as pay, and hence economic policy was seen quite largely as a process of negotiation with the leaders of the TUC. In the circumstances of 1974 it is perhaps understandable that no clear medium-term framework for policy emerged from these negotiations. It was more a matter of trying to limit the immediate damage to the economy from the critical situation in which the new government took over. Having failed, for that reason, to provide a clear framework for policy at the outset, the subsequent moves made by the Labour government during its whole term of office gave the impression of responses to short-term expediency.

The first action of the new government was to pay off the miners with an increase in wages more than double that available to them under Stage 3 of the Heath government's income policy. Full working on the coalfields was resumed. They were also quick to repeal the previous government's Industrial Relations Act and even cancelled the tax debts of the unions which had refused to register under that Act. It remained to be seen, however, whether these moves to restore good relations between government and the unions would result in a more moderate rate of wage increase.

Statutory control of pay came to an end in July with the abolition of the Pay Board and the National Industrial Relations Court. Reliance was placed instead on the voluntary agreement of unions to comply with a new 'social contract' agreed at national level by the TUC. Pay settlements were not to be more frequent than annual and they were to provide only for compensation for increases in the cost of living. There were to be special provisions for raising the pay of women and lower-paid workers. The Price Code was to remain in being, and it was expected that price moderation would ensure wage moderation in a self-reinforcing spiral of disinflation. Meanwhile the threshold agreements which were part of the 1973 Stage 3 incomes policy remained operative, and were triggered each month after April 1974.

The close linkage of pay and prices, which was a feature of both the threshold agreements and the social contract, proved disastrous. The system which was intended to produce a downward spiral of inflation in fact produced an upward spiral. One upward impetus was given by the rise in fuel prices and another by the lagged effects of the increases in the prices of other imports during the previous year. Food prices were rising particularly fast. By the second quarter of the year the retail price index was nearly 16 per cent up on a year earlier; by the third it was up about 17 per cent and still accelerating.

At the same time as inflation was spiralling upwards the economy was moving into recession. The level of output in the first quarter of 1974 was reduced by perhaps 3 per cent as a direct result of the miners' strike and the three-day week, as stocks were run down. Some bounce-back might have been expected in the second quarter to make good lost production and rebuild stocks. In the event total output was a little lower in the second quarter of 1974 than it had been in the fourth quarter of 1973. Exports did well, but consumer spending was well down, as was also fixed investment. Within fixed investment the most obvious casualty was housebuilding. By the second quarter private sector housing starts were only half as many as they had been a year before. Industrial investment in new building and works was also falling.

The labour market was also affected. At the end of 1973 unemployment was still falling fast, lagging about six to nine months behind the output cycle. In the fourth quarter the number wholly unemployed (excluding school-leavers) fell below half a million for the first time since 1968. That proved to be the lower turning point and unemployment has never again been so low. The number of unemployed rose in the first quarter of 1974, partly as a result of three-day working. Instead of falling back when normal working was resumed in March, unemployment continued to rise at an accelerating pace. Unfilled vacancies also remained well below their 1973 peak. It was evident by the summer of 1974 that the economy was in recession, but it was very difficult, in the circumstances of that year, for the government to take measures to expand demand on anything like a commensurate scale.

There was disagreement amongst Treasury ministers and amongst their advisers as to what should be done, but the main line of policymaking might, at this period and for some years thereafter, be described as 'frustrated Keynesianism'. Policymakers saw a need for counter-cyclical fiscal policy, but were inhibited from taking decisive action by fears of yet-faster inflation and yet-wider deficits on the balance of payments.

The British situation was not very different from that of most other industrial countries. The move into large balance of payments deficit resulted from the oil price increases at the end of 1973. These affected all oil-importing countries, and all, to a greater or lesser extent, saw their balance of payments position as limiting the growth of domestic demand that could reasonably be expected for the next year or two. All, moreover, experienced accelerating inflation and a downturn in output, also in part as a consequence of the same oil price increases.

The first budget of the minority Labour government was introduced on 26 March, less than a month after the election. It was announced at the time that there would be another budget in the autumn. This March budget was described as broadly neutral in its effect on aggregate demand, if anything slightly contractionary. Both expenditure and taxation were increased, and the main effect of the changes was to redistribute to the relatively poor from companies and from the relatively well-off. Although food subsidies were substantially increased, other measures largely offset the effect of this on the general level of prices.

The second budget of the year came in July. The main change was a reduction in the rate of VAT from 10 per cent to 8 per cent, with a direct effect on retail prices calculated at 1 per cent. In a small way the British Treasury was trying to put into reverse the effects on prices and output of the OPEC oil price increases, which could themselves be likened to a tax on the rest of the world. The tax cut should also be seen in the context of the social contract which had just been agreed with the TUC. Cutting indirect taxes held back the rate of price increase, limiting the extent of the 'triggering' under the old threshold agreements, and satisfying some of the demand for increases in the real value of wages. Compared with the rate of price increase by then building up, however, it was at best only a small abatement of inflationary pressure. Compared with the mounting signs of recession, the reflationary effect of the July budget was also small. Meanwhile the Chancellor was planning his November budget in which more fundamental tax changes were to be made. That, however, had to await the achievement of a majority for Labour in Parliament after the October general election.

If minimum lending rate is used as a measure of monetary policy, that, as well as fiscal policy, was broadly neutral throughout 1974. There had been a sharp rise of interest rates in the latter half of the preceding year, and its lagged effects may have been felt during 1974, for example in the housing market. Real interest rates, as conventionally measured, on the other hand fell sharply. Nominal interest rates (on Treasury bills) fell gradually from $12\frac{1}{4}$ in the first quarter to $11\frac{1}{4}$ in the fourth, whilst inflation, measured over the preceding twelve months, rose from 13 per cent to 18 per cent. Real interest rate on this or any other likely definition became substantially negative.

The failure of interest rates to rise sufficiently to offset inflation was not an altogether new phenomenon, neither was it confined to this country. But it raises some profound questions to which we shall return at a later stage of this study. For the present, we shall simply remark that it created considerable confusion in the minds of those concerned with monetary policy as to whether that policy was very lax (as measured by real interest rates) or broadly neutral (as measured by nominal interest rates). Indeed it was also possible to argue that policy was very tight, if it was measured by the growth of the monetary aggregates.

The Supplementary Special Deposits Scheme introduced at the end of 1973 seems to have done what it was intended to do, by slowing down the growth of bank deposits and bank lending to the private sector. The broad aggregate £M3 rose by 11 per cent between the fourth quarters of 1973 and 1974, compared with 27.1 per cent over the preceding four quarters. In real terms £M3 was falling fast. The corresponding changes in the 'counterparts' to the growth of the money supply were an increase in non-bank purchases of public sector debt, a fall in sterling lending to the United Kingdom private sector and an outflow corresponding to the deficit on the balance of payments. The public sector borrowing requirement, on the other hand, rose substantially, as would be expected when the economy was moving into recession. Ironically this period of abrupt slowdown in the growth of the monetary aggregates was one of the few periods in recent history when the authorities had no declared objective for those aggregates to meet. But, given the size of the increase that had taken place over the two previous years, it may have been a case of 'closing the stable door after the horse had bolted'.

The visible trade balance was in unprecedented deficit: in 1974 almost £5½ billion, compared with £2½ billion in 1973. But this was explained, and to some extent excused, by the increase in the price of oil. The oil-producing countries had large surpluses to dispose of, and in 1974 they devoted substantial sums to the purchase of sterling assets. This was important because it helped to hold up the sterling exchange rate despite accelerating inflation and a severe imbalance of trade. Between 1974 and 1973 the exchange rate index fell by only about 3 per cent.

One reason for the relative strength of sterling in the aftermath of the oil price increase may have been the knowledge that the United Kingdom was itself potentially a rather large-scale oil producer. Certainly this factor played a part in calculations of the size of balance of payments deficit it would be (in some sense) appropriate for it to maintain. The United Kingdom, unlike other oil consuming countries, might reasonably plan to borrow on the strength of future oil revenues, even though oil production in the North Sea did not in fact get under way until 1977.

The stability of sterling in 1974 implied some loss of cost and price competitiveness vis-à-vis other industrial countries. Between the fourth quarters of 1973 and 1974 the loss was only about 3½ per cent as measured by relative export prices, but as much as nearly 10 per cent on the IMF index of relative unit labour costs. Export prices were lagging behind the acceleration of wage inflation, thus adding to the pressure on the profit margins of manufacturers.

The pressure on profit margins was a matter of wider concern as domestic prices were constrained by the Price Code. For some time a risk had been identified that inadequate company liquidity would force de-stocking and a labour shake-out, and would result in widespread bank-ruptcy. That would deepen the recession and prolong it into 1975. The obvious palliative was to loosen the Price Code, but that would add to inflation. The problem was put off until the General Election was out of the way.

That election was held on 10 October. The Labour Party gained eighteen seats, enough to give it a working majority, although not an overall one. This was the second defeat of the year for Edward Heath and was followed, early the next year, by his replacement as leader of the Conservative Party by Margaret Thatcher. Even before the election of October 1974, leading Conservatives, most notably Keith Joseph, were changing quite profoundly their ideas about economic policy. They were publicly and explicitly disowning the policies of the Heath government and blaming them for the subsequent inflation. As early as 1974 the ideas which guided the next Conservative government were taking shape.

FASTER INFLATION, DEEPER RECESSION:
OCTOBER 1974–DECEMBER 1975

The second general election of 1974 resolved the political crisis and provided an opportunity for a firmer and more consistent approach to economic policy. Although its majority was small and dependent on support from minor parties, the Labour Party was able to retain office for almost the maximum five-year life of a Parliament.

At the end of 1974, however, one political problem remained outstanding. The Labour Party had promised to hold a referendum on the continuation of British membership of the EEC. The Labour Party, and even the government, were divided on this central issue of foreign and economic policy. It was believed moreover that this referendum was to be interpreted as a vote of confidence by the public in the management of the economy by the Prime Minister and the Chancellor. The actual outcome was not in much doubt as most Conservative Party supporters would vote for continued membership. Nevertheless, the prospect of facing the electorate again on the issue of economic policy may have been a constraint on the government's freedom to take necessary but unpopular policy action. In the event the referendum held in June 1975 went two-thirds in favour of membership and one-third against, a sufficient endorsement of EEC membership, if not an enthusiastic one.

The economic situation confronting the government after the October election was extremely worrying, even though the subsequent depth of the recession was not foreseen at the time. Inflation was running at over 15 per cent and rising, the balance of payments was in deep deficit and unemployment had turned decisively up. The social contract negotiated with the unions in the summer was not working as intended. With wage costs accelerating and import prices still rising fast whilst output prices were constrained by the Price Code, the corporate sector was heading for financial crisis. The stock market, which had been falling gradually through 1973 and in the early part of 1973, dropped sharply at the end of the year to a low point in December, lower (in nominal terms) than at any time since the early 1950s.

Insofar as the policies followed for the next few years were not constrained by other considerations, they were governed by the cautiously Keynesian approach that had evolved in the Treasury and the Bank over the preceding 30 years. The Chancellor's principal official advisers were the Permanent Secretary, Sir Douglas Wass, and the Chief Economic Adviser, Sir Bryan Hopkin, both appointed in 1974, while the Governor of the Bank of England was advised by Kit MacMahon and Christopher Dow. All these belonged, with various degrees of qualification, to the same school of thought. A rather different tradition, which was undoubtedly Keynesian but less cautious, was represented at the Treasury by Lord Kaldor and more briefly by Wynne Godley. The monetarists were winning over the press, the city and the Conservative Party but they had as yet scarcely a toe-hold either in the Treasury or in the Bank.

In November 1974 the fourth budget within twelve months was introduced. Its main purpose was to ease the pressure on the profits and liquidity of the company sector. Relief was given from the burden of taxation on stock appreciation arising from accelerating inflation. The Price Code was eased to allow firms to pass on most of the increase in labour costs, and to pass on more if they were increasing investment. Subsidies to nationalised industries were to be limited and VAT on petrol was raised to 25 per cent. The measures may not have seemed helpful, in that they would raise prices and cut consumer demand, as well as raising public sector borrowing. They were seen, however, as a response to a crisis for the company sector, which required urgent relief. Indeed the action taken could be criticised as 'too late', delayed solely so as to get the election out of the way; it could also be criticised as 'too little' in view of the behaviour of companies the following year.

The deepening of recession in 1975 was not generally expected at the time. The average estimate of GDP now shows a fall of 0.8 per cent year-on-year. As late as Easter 1975, however, the Treasury, the National Institute and the London Business School all expected rises year-on-year of about 1–1½ per cent. The depth of the recession was unprecedented since the war, and in other ways it did not conform to the pattern of earlier downturns. Recession was not confined to the United Kingdom; one component of *our* recession therefore was the fall in exports, after a rather good year in 1974. Fixed investment, on the other hand, considering that this was the second year of a recession, held up rather well, showing only a 2 per cent fall year-on-year. The personal sector savings ratio rose to the record level of 12 per cent (compared with 11 per cent in 1974). This was variously explained by the rise in inflation, the fall in asset values and the restriction of credit.

Another major contribution to the fall in expenditure was a turn-round from positive to negative stockbuilding. It was not unexpected to see some destocking in the latter part of a recession. There was destocking, for example, in the first half of 1972, around the lower turning point of the preceding recession. But the rundown of stocks in 1975 was on a quite different scale and more widespread across industries. For manufacturing industry alone the turn-round in stocks between 1974 and 1975 amounted to over £5 billion (at 1985 prices) or 2.1 per cent of GDP. With hindsight this could be explained in a variety of ways, but one possibility must be that the pressure on company liquidity, despite the November budget, had had the feared result of prolonging and deepening the recession.

Despite the recession and the financial pressure on companies, employment held up reasonably well in 1975, falling less than ½ per cent year-on-year. That was enough, however, to produce a steep rise in unemployment. In the fourth quarter of 1974 the number wholly unemployed, excluding school-leavers and seasonally adjusted, was just under 600,000; a year later it had passed the million mark. The lower turning point of the cycle is identified by the CSO as falling in August 1975. The complete cycle, trough to trough, since February 1972, was only 3½ years in length, short compared with the typical postwar cycle and much shorter than the two cycles that followed. It was also exceptionally steep, both in the upturn and in the downturn. Between 1973 and 1975 the economy moved from euphoria to despair, from possible triumph to obvious disaster.

Despite all this the 1975 budget was mildly contractionary. Its purpose was not to 'manage' total demand, but to shift resources from domestic demand to the improvement of the balance of payments and to reduce the size of the public sector borrowing requirement. Income tax, VAT and specific duties were all raised. Public spending was cut, especially spending on subsidies. On the other hand tax relief on stock appreciation and relief from the Price Code for purposes of investment were extended. A temporary employment subsidy was announced to encourage companies to defer redundancies. The estimated overall effect of the budget was to reduce demand and employment whilst raising the price level by more than 2½ per cent. In the circumstances it was a very un-Keynesian budget. Priority was given to reducing two deficits which were seen as closely related: the fiscal deficit and the deficit on the balance of payments.

The public sector borrowing requirement (PSBR) was hardly a concern of policymakers at all until the mid-1970s. The expansionary policies of the Heath government had started from a position close to balance on the PSBR. In successive years the requirement grew, but it was the combination of recession and inflation in 1974, and especially in 1975, that produced an unplanned and unexpected figure of over £10 billion for the PSBR, about 10 per cent of GDP. It was widely feared that the finances of the public sector were out of control.

Despite this worrying development in the public sector, the growth of the money supply in 1975 slowed down. Year on year the rise in £M3 was less than 6 per cent, far less than the rate of inflation. Sales of public sector debt to the non-bank private sector rose strongly and the current account deficit contributed to another negative adjustment for external financial flows. But the most dramatic change was in bank lending to the private sector which was actually negative in 1975. The 'corset' was no longer in place, having been suspended by the Bank of England in February, so the reason for the contraction in credit may have been as much on the side of demand as of supply. But the banks may have also been wary of lending, as the recession was accompanied by a rise in bankruptcy, most notoriously amongst speculative builders. For whatever reason, it was another example of monetary restraint successfully maintained at a time when no special efforts were being made to that end.

The other worrying deficit, the deficit on the current account of the balance of payments, was reduced, but not eliminated, in 1975. This improvement was entirely in the visible balance, in which the value of imports rose year-on-year by only 4 per cent, whilst that of exports rose by 18 per cent. The volume of imports fell sharply as industry ran down its stocks of materials and as consumer spending fell. The terms of trade moved in favour of the United Kingdom because the domestic rate of price inflation was faster than that of the rest of the world. Neither of these considerations suggested that the improvement in the balance of payments would last long; on the other hand there was reason to hope that a higher level of world activity would, sooner or later, provide a better market for British goods. One aim of the budget policy was to keep resources available to meet such demand, should it emerge; another was to prevent imports from rising too fast.

The exchange rate for sterling was weak throughout 1975 and the fall, year-on-year, was about 8 per cent. However, given the rate of inflation actually being experienced in the United Kingdom, relative to inflation abroad, it should be said rather that the exchange rate was strong. The real exchange rate, that is the ratio of producer prices in the United Kingdom to those of major competitors converted into sterling, rose by about 3 per cent. The index of relative export price competitiveness showed a change of similar magnitude. This development threatened to reduce the share that British industry could actually win of world markets, when the upturn in the world economy eventually came.

The relative strength of sterling in 1975 may have owed something to the movement of interest rates abroad. The three-month eurodollar deposit rate fell abruptly at the beginning of the year from about 10 per cent to about 7½ per cent and for the rest of the year fluctuated at about that level, or rather below. Sterling interest rates also eased, but less sharply. The uncovered differential on three-month deposits favoured sterling against the dollar throughout the year by a margin of about 3 percentage points. This differential may not, however, have been wide enough to compensate for the expected depreciation of the pound or for differences in the expected rates of inflation in Britain and the United States. Sterling was also helped by the traditions of some Middle East oil producers who were accustomed to keep their financial wealth in London. Moreover the United States was regarded as an ally of Israel, so the alternative of placing the new oil wealth in dollars seemed less attractive.

In 1975 most countries experienced rapid inflation, but inflation at a slower rate than in the preceding year. In the United States for example the inflation rate fell from 11 per cent to about 9 per cent, whilst in Japan it fell from nearly 25 per cent to nearly 12 per cent. The United Kingdom was an exception, in that inflation rose, and rose markedly, from 16 per cent in 1974 to over 24 per cent in 1975. At the beginning of 1975 the retail prices index was 20 per cent up on a year earlier. That percentage continued to climb through the spring and the summer, helped by the budget changes, reaching a peak of 26.9 per cent in August.

The British public had no experience of rates of inflation like this and they were not well-prepared to cope with them. Insurance contracts for example were not indexed, neither were many private pension schemes. Inflation, therefore, had a redistributive effect between individuals which was arbitrary and inequitable. Lenders generally lost and borrowers, especially the public sector, gained. The experience of the mid-1970s led, over the years that followed, to a much wider adoption of index-linking in a variety of contracts and other financial arrangements. The government itself acknowledged the problem as early as January 1975 by introducing index-linked National Savings contracts, although they were at first restricted to small savers and those over pensionable age. The Sandilands Committee prepared a report on the inflation adjustment of company accounts which was published in September.

Few countries had experienced inflation continuing for more than a year at around 20 per cent. The main precedents were for 'creeping' inflation, about 5 or 10 per cent a year, on the one hand and 'hyper inflation' on the other. There was therefore a real fear at the time that inflation would rise explosively. This influenced even those who would have been quite prepared to tolerate inflation at 5 or even 10 per cent in perpetuity. It made trade unionists in particular more ready to accept, even to welcome, the substitution of a much tighter form of incomes policy for the social contract which had failed in its purpose.

On 11 July the government published a White Paper, 'The Attack on Inflation'. This set a maximum pay rise of £6 per week, with no increase at all for those earning more than £8,500 a year. The flat-rate limit was deliberately chosen to favour the lower paid, narrowing differentials and making for a more equal distribution of earned income. This helped to win the support of some large trade unions, and was welcomed by many in the Labour Party. Its effect on incentives and the efficiency of the labour market was relatively little discussed at the time. The policy was backed up by reserve powers making it illegal for employers to exceed the pay limit.

The growth rate of average earnings did indeed slow down markedly after this new policy was introduced. The earnings index compiled at that time for all production industries and some services showed a rise of 26½ per cent in the year to the third quarter of 1975, but only 13½ per cent in the next twelve months. The rate of price inflation also gradually began to abate. By the end of the year it was below 25 per cent and falling significantly each month. Those who feared hyper-inflation could begin to hope that the country was pulling back from the brink.

As soon as inflation began to abate, or perhaps even before, the focus of attention shifted to the alarming rise in the level of unemployment. The 'headline total', not seasonally adjusted, first exceeded a million when the school-leavers joined the register at the end of the summer. Little could be given by way of conventional demand stimulus, although the Chancellor, in yet another package of measures just before Christmas, eased the restrictions on consumer credit. For the time being at least the policy response was directed rather to measures which would now be called micro-economic.

These were of two kinds. The first was characterised by the Industry Act which became law in November. This introduced a mild form of indicative planning and established the National Enterprise Board to take a public stake in industry and help to turn round ailing businesses. There was provision for direct help to firms on a variety of grounds or pretexts and in subsequent years quite significant sums of public money were spent.

The other kind of initiative was a more direct response to unemployment and consisted of special measures designed to create or preserve jobs at a cost to the exchequer far lower than that of a conventional reflation. In August the Temporary Employment Subsidy came into effect, giving help to employers for up to six months if they would reverse or delay plans to make workers redundant. The extent of employment subsidies was widened by further measures announced in September and again in the December package.

This was the beginning of an approach to employment policy that proved far from temporary. It was the result of a political and social need for government to do something about unemployment, even though its hands were tied for the present on macroeconomic policy. But this turned out to be a continuing, or at least a recurrent, situation and the need for special measures became greater, not less. They were never designed as a coherent strategy; they rather emerged as a series of stop-gaps, more or less hastily conceived and put in place. In the event they were to become a major element, even *the* major instrument, of policy to promote employment. At the end of 1975, however, the issue was not seen that way. It was still a question of waiting for the appropriate moment to bring in the general reflation, the major reflation, that would restore full employment in the sense of the 1950s and 1960s. This was the prelude to the dramatic events of 1976.

THE YEAR OF STERLING CRISIS, JANUARY—DECEMBER 1976

The economic recovery which began in the latter half of 1975, continued quite briskly through 1976. Year-on-year the rise in the average estimate of

GDP was 2½–3 per cent. Through the year, fourth quarter to fourth quarter, the rise in the output estimate, the best for short-term comparisons, was over 4 per cent.

Stockbuilding became positive during the year, reversing some of the heavy destocking that had deepened and prolonged the recession. This could be seen as part of a normal bounce-back in the recovery stage of the trade cycle. Exports also made an important contribution to the recovery; the volume of goods and services combined rose by 10 per cent fourth quarter on fourth quarter. The personal sector savings ratio fell back a little.

This rise in output was enough to hold back the increase in unemployment, but not to reverse its trend. This was disappointing, since vacancies turned up again from their low point in the first quarter of the year and were rising quite sharply by the end. Moreover, the fall in employment also came to an end in the second quarter, to be followed by a slow recovery.

The rate of inflation was still very high at the beginning of the year, but falling significantly each month. From 23.4 per cent in January it came right down to 12.9 per cent in July before turning up again, for reasons to be discussed below. The £6 pay policy worked well, and the virtuous circle of disinflation that had proved impossible to initiate since the days of the Heath government seemed at last to be getting under way. The current account of the balance of payments was actually in surplus in the first quarter of the year, a very welcome improvement from the yawning deficits that had followed the oil price increase at the end of 1973. Later in the year there were deficits to follow, but they were on quite a modest scale, such as one might well expect to be financed easily enough by a country now preparing to be a significant producer of oil.

Another encouraging sign was the reduction in public sector borrowing, although that admittedly was slower than had been hoped. The PSBR in 1976 was £9 billion compared with £10 billion the year before. This fall in public sector borrowing was nevertheless accompanied by a recovery in the growth of £M3 to about 9 per cent in 1976, although even that figure was well below the rate of inflation, implying a fall in the real value of the stock of monetary assets outstanding.

This acceleration of monetary growth was made possible by the absence of any direct controls on bank lending, the Supplementary Special Deposits Scheme having been suspended in the early months of 1975. Interest rates were being continuously reduced at the beginning of 1976. By a succession of quarter and half-point reductions, minimum lending rate crept down from its high point of 12 per cent in October 1975 to 9 per cent in March the following year. Eurodollar rates meanwhile were much lower, about 5½ per cent and also falling a little. Looking at all these indicators many years after the event it is not at all obvious why this was to be the year of the great sterling crisis.

The Labour government up to this point had been wary of adding to the level of domestic demand and activity, because inflation was so fast and because the balance of payments was in large deficit. Now in the early part of 1976, for the first time, the opportunity seemed to be there to revert to something like the policies of 1972. Although output was now recovering, and although unemployment was hardly rising any more, the case for expansion was bound to be considered seriously. The level of unemployment, well over a million, still seemed inexcusably high. The Keynesian tradition, to which most ministers and officials still subscribed, told them that their duty was to seize the first opportunity to reflate. The policies of 1972 did not just involve tax cuts; they also meant allowing the exchange rate to fall so that the current account would correct itself, and so that export demand could add to the growth of output. (It was reasonable to hope, by 1976, that the fall in the exchange rate need only be quite modest, since the prospect for the balance of payments in the late 1970s would be much better when North Sea oil production came on stream.) To contain the inflationary effects of depreciation and demand pressure in the domestic economy the package had also to include restraint on pay.

Policies of this sort might appeal to the government, but they had lost any appeal they might once have had in the City or in other international financial centres. The press would also be unsympathetic. Most of the ills that had fallen on the economy since 1972 were widely attributed to the rashness of the Heath government. Similar policies followed by a Labour government would be met with even more scepticism and suspicion. The government did not actually need to do or say very much to produce a financial crisis. The level of mutual trust was so low between the authorities, the press and the markets that a crisis could arise on almost any pretext.

In February the Chancellor announced extra public spending mainly designed to increase employment. The package included several of the ingredients already becoming familiar: more assistance for industrial investment, more training places, more job creation, an extension of the Temporary Employment Subsidy. The public spending plans for 1975/6 and 1976/7 were both being exceeded, but cuts were announced in the February White Paper affecting plans for subsequent years and proposing that the total volume of spending be held flat for several years.

The budget introduced in April proposed quite substantial cuts in income tax, but made them conditional on agreement by the TUC to a low pay norm for the next stage of incomes policy. This made explicit the idea of a macroeconomic bargain that was already implicit in earlier attempts to combine incomes policies with reflation. The government's contribution to the deal could be interpreted either as the creation of extra employment or as higher take-home pay for the workers. Whatever the political implications of allowing the unions to influence taxation in this way, the economic effects of the deal seemed to benefit everyone.

There was another way of looking at the proposed deal, however, which made it look much less attractive. The Chancellor's approach to reducing inflation involved increasing the pressure of demand in the domestic economy and hence, presumably, increasing the deficit in the balance of payments. It also involved raising public sector borrowing and hence, presumably, the growth of the money supply. This did not look like orthodox economics to the city, the press or foreign bankers, least of all to those recently converted to the ideas of the monetarists.

This was not the only problem with the proposed deal over the budget. The TUC failed to deliver their side of the bargain. The Chancellor had over-played his hand. Scarcely a week after the budget was presented, the TUC leaders rejected his proposal of a 3 per cent norm, although they said they would continue their discussions with the government. The Incomes Policy White Paper, which was published in June, set out a 5 per cent norm but gave less to higher paid workers and more to lower paid. There were also modifications to the Price Code allowing prices to rise a little faster. In the event, the rise in the earnings index slowed down to under 10 per cent over the next twelve months, compared with nearly 14 per cent in the twelve months before.

Meanwhile sterling was showing signs of serious weakness. Early in March its value fell below two dollars for the first time. The authorities did little or nothing to stop its fall. On the contrary minimum lending rate edged down to 9 per cent and the yield on three-month inter-bank deposits suggested that a further fall was expected. Later in the same month the French effectively devalued the franc by leaving the 'snake', that is the joint EEC currency alignment against the dollar. There was a suspicion in the markets that the British authorities would welcome a similar depreciation of the pound. That suspicion was indeed well-founded, although it would be wrong to say that a definite decision had been taken in the Treasury that the pound should be devalued.

Between the first and second quarters of the year the effective sterling exchange rate index fell by 9 per cent. The dollar rate, which was still much more widely quoted, fell to $1.81, down nearly 10 per cent in the quarter. The authorities' attempts to limit the fall of the pound were soon reflected in the balance of payments statistics. In the first quarter the reserves actually increased, although this was made possible only by drawing on IMF loan facilities. In the second quarter, large-scale official borrowing was not enough to prevent a fall in the reserves.

Interest rates were raised sharply in April and again in May. There then followed a period of relative calm in the foreign exchange markets. About the same time, however, the stock market turned down. It had recovered well from the very depressed levels reached at the end of 1974. For much of the subsequent year it was on an upward trend, which accelerated as interest rates came down towards the end of 1975 and in the early months of 1976. When interest rates were raised again in March the stock market turned down.

The markets, and the press, were not to be satisfied by increases in interest rates. They believed that the government's whole strategy was rash and ill-conceived. In particular they thought that it paid too little attention to the size of the PSBR, and they were worried that public spending was out of control. In July, partly in response to this pressure, public spending cuts of £1 billion for 1977/8 were announced. It was impossible at this stage to get ministerial agreement to a larger package. At the same time the Chancellor gave a forecast of the money supply growth for the current financial year. It was a forecast, not a target, but still represented a significant concession to public demand for a new way of conducting and presenting monetary policy.

These concessions were not enough. As sterling continued to fall the range of options open to the government narrowed. The scale of the depreciation was already affecting the rate of inflation: from its low point of 12.9 per cent in July the rate (measured over the preceding twelve months) was rising again, to reach 15 per cent by November. The exchange rate could not simply be left to find its own level.

In October alone sterling fell by more than 5 per cent on the effective exchange rate index. By then it was 23 per cent down on the same period of the preceding year. Official intervention continued on a considerable scale and minimum lending rate was raised, to 13 per cent in September, and to 15 per cent in October. It was all in vain. There seemed to be no limit to the fall in sterling that the market might dictate.

The pressure from the press and in the markets could be satisfied if the government applied to the IMF for a loan. The loan itself would provide funds to continue intervention in the foreign exchange markets. More importantly the terms on which a loan could be made available would require a change in the direction of economic policy. It would limit the freedom of action of the government, and that was precisely what the markets and the press needed as reassurance.

The only other option open to the government was to cut itself off from dependence on financial opinion altogether. To do this it would have to impose tighter exchange control and probably restrict trade as well. Some saw a strategy of this kind, if only for a short period, as the only way of pursuing an independent economic policy, and the only way of managing the level of output or employment in the domestic economy. Perhaps British industry would only flourish under protection. The new Prime Minister, James Callaghan, who had succeeded Harold Wilson earlier in the year, presided over a very divided Cabinet at this stage.

The terms proposed by the IMF, when negotiations for a loan were eventually completed, were not as onerous as might have been feared. As with all loans of this kind they required a commitment to a target path for Domestic Credit Expansion (DCE). This hybrid was neither a monetary aggregate nor a measure of fiscal policy, but it was convenient from the IMF's point of view as it put pressure on borrowing countries both to slow down the growth of the money supply and to improve their balance of payments position. By accounting identities, to which British financial experts were now getting accustomed, DCE was approximately equal to the growth of £M3 plus official financing of the balance of payments. The numbers chosen for the Letter of Intent signed by the British government were not intended to be very difficult to achieve, but they were a binding commitment. There were further commitments to a progressive reduction in the PSBR and cuts were made in public spending plans both for 1977/8 and 1978/9. An increase was also made in rates of indirect taxation on tobacco and alcohol. The credibility of these commitments had been increased in November by the reimposition of direct controls on bank lending to the private sector by means of the SSD scheme (the corset). The government undertook to keep the scheme in being at least for the immediate future.

The market response to the negotiation of an IMF loan on these terms was immediate and favourable. Sterling stabilised at $1.65 and soon the authorities were intervening to rebuild their foreign exchange reserves. The questions in the following year were to be whether the exchange rate should be allowed to rise again and how far interest rates should fall. The turn-round of sentiment seems out of proportion to the policy measures actually announced. But more had changed than the public spending plans for the late 1970s. The plans for a protectionist strategy had been decisively rejected. Moreover the 'cautious' Keynesians themselves had also suffered a severe setback. The combination of reflation and incomes policy with a permissive attitude to depreciation had been shown to be potentially unstable, at least if it was rejected by market sentiment and the press.

The 'cautious' Keynesians, both ministers and officials, remained in power for a few years yet, and the approach to economic policy which they supported was not altogether abandoned. But their intellectual position was much weakened by the events of 1976 and quite different ideas about the aims and instruments of policy were becoming influential even in the Treasury and the Bank. Moreover, so long as the country was in debt to the IMF the intellectual position of the Fund staff (and of the governments of the member countries which ultimately controlled the IMF) mattered as much as the views of ministers and officials in London.

FOLLOWING THE LETTER OF INTENT,
JANUARY–DECEMBER 1977

The economic policies recommended to the British government by the staff of the IMF centred on the achievement of export-led growth. In this they were not very different from the policies recommended to other member countries who found it necessary to borrow from the Fund. The first priority was that the borrowers should put themselves in a position to repay the Fund; the second was that the level of domestic activity in the borrowing country should not be made to suffer unnecessarily. Since direct controls on imports were anathematised, the only way to reconcile these requirements was export-led growth. Happily from this point of view in the case of the United Kingdom at the end of 1976, the exchange rate had fallen so low that the prospects for an increasing share in world trade seemed very good.

On the IMF's index of normalised relative unit labour costs (1985=100) in the fourth quarter of 1976 the United Kingdom stood at 68.1, the lowest level recorded since the series began in 1963. It was lower, for example, than it had been in the aftermath of the 1967 devaluation, when at its low point it was still 75.1 on the same scale, or after the Heath government let sterling float in 1972 when it fell to 75.8 at the end of the subsequent year. The aim of policy in 1977 was to maintain that competitive advantage by preventing the exchange rate from rising, whilst keeping down the growth of domestic costs.

The policies of 1977 were not Keynesian, in that domestic demand was constrained by the need to meet a DCE objective, and specifically by the need to cut public spending. On the other hand they were also very different from the policies followed later under the Conservatives, in that the exchange rate was kept low to help exports even though this meant that import price rises were adding to the rate of inflation. Moreover, incomes policy retained its central place in the strategy, as the published Letter of Intent itself required.

Keeping the exchange rate down proved no easy task. International confidence in Britain returned with a rush. In January the Bank of England was able to sign the Basle Agreement with the BIS under which the official sterling balances held in London by members of the old sterling area were protected by a medium-term credit facility. These balances were seen as a source of embarrassment, not a source of strength, to the authorities in the management of sterling. The return of confidence in sterling was to be used as the occasion for an orderly running down of the balances, not for their rebuilding.

On the other hand the official foreign currency reserves were themselves severely depleted and the Bank was relieved in the early months of 1977 to be able to rebuild them by selling sterling in the market. It was also a relief to be able to reduce short-term interest rates from the very high levels (up to 15 per cent for MLR) seen in the last quarter of 1976. By the end of March 1977 MLR was down to 9½ per cent.

Meanwhile the events of 1976 were having their effect on the state of the economy. Inflation (measured over the preceding twelve months) had turned up in the latter half of 1976 as the exchange rate fell. This acceleration, at a time when inflation was abating in most other countries, continued until the summer of 1977 peaking at 17.7 per cent in June. Had the exchange rate been allowed to rise as confidence returned the rate of inflation presumably would have come down rather sooner.

The path of output through the early part of 1977 is also of some interest. All three measures of GDP show a sharp rise in the fourth quarter of 1976, followed by slower growth or even a fall in the first half of 1977. The fall in the expenditure measure is quite marked, reflecting falls in most categories, including both public and private consumption. This would be in line with the strategy of the Letter of Intent and also a natural consequence of the deterioration in the terms of trade as the exchange rate fell. The CSO index of coincident cyclical indicators shows an unusual pause in the midst of an upswing, lasting about a year, from late 1976 to early 1978. Meanwhile the labour market indicators gave an uncertain or ambiguous reading with unemployment almost flat in the first quarter of 1977 and unfilled vacancies still rising.

It soon became clear that the painfully negotiated figures for DCE in the Letter of Intent were even less of a constraint on fiscal policy than had been expected, or intended. The figures for government borrowing in 1976/7 were revised down significantly, as often happens to these notoriously unreliable estimates. Moreover the return of market confidence and the expectation of falling interest rates made it very easy indeed to sell government debt outside the banking system. The risk of rapid money supply growth arose from the external component, that is from official intervention to hold down the pound in the foreign exchange market. But that intervention did not raise DCE.

The background to the 1977 budget therefore was not quite as worrying as it seemed likely to be six months earlier. Even so the Chancellor could not afford to relax as long as inflation continued at such an alarming rate. Consistently with the strategy agreed with the IMF, his main aim in the budget was the same in 1977 as in the preceding year: he wanted to use such tax concessions as he could afford to 'buy' the agreement of the TUC to another year of wage restraint. This time he overplayed his hand more seriously. He proposed a cut in the basic rate of income tax from 35 to 33 per cent, but that proposal was made conditional on agreement to a new pay limit. That agreement was impossible to obtain.

The pay limits agreed in 1975 and 1976 had been reasonably well observed and had had a visible effect on the rate of price inflation. The consequence, in 1976 and 1977, was that the growth of wages slowed down sharply. In 1976 up to the third quarter this involved little change in the real value of earnings, as price inflation slowed down more or less in line. In 1977, however, as inflation reaccelerated, real wages fell sharply. Between the third quarters of 1976 and 1977 the index of basic wage rates rose only 5 per cent, in line with Stage 2 of the incomes policy, and the old earnings index rose 8.7 per cent. The rise in the retail price index over the same period was over 16 per cent. Some re-acceleration of earnings was surely unavoidable.

What eventually emerged from negotiation was a norm of 10 per cent for wage increases and a renewed commitment to annual settlements. This was a weak form of incomes policy and it did not command much support from individual unions. Over the next twelve months the rise in both wages and earnings was in fact over 16 per cent. The strain put on the incomes policy framework following the substantial exchange rate depreciation of 1976 and the subsequent price inflation proved too great. The system of cooperation which had worked well for about two years broke down; it has not been repaired since. The Chancellor partly acknowledged his failure when he announced that only 1p of the proposed 2p cut in the basic rate of income tax was to be implemented.

The budget ran into some difficulty on other fronts as well. The government lacked a clear majority in the Commons and was obliged to change its proposals in response to backbench pressure. A proposed increase in petrol duty had to be abandoned. Of more lasting significance was the Rooker-Wise Amendment which required governments to raise personal tax allowances each year in line with inflation, except when specific exceptions are made in the Finance Act.

Despite the government's problems in relation to Parliament and to the trade unions, confidence in sterling remained strong; indeed the strength of sterling was becoming a source of considerable embarrassment to the monetary authorities. Throughout the first half of 1977 the exchange rate was held below $1.72 which was only a little above its low point in the fourth quarter of 1976. The official reserves, which had fallen to only a little over $4 billion at the end of 1976, were rebuilt to over $11 billion by June 1977 and over $20 billion by December.

Concern was being expressed that official intervention in the foreign exchange markets was adding to the growth of the domestic money supply. In the first quarter of the year DCE (seasonally adjusted) was negative for the first time in five years. Despite a positive external adjustment M3 rose quite slowly. In the second quarter, however, less debt was sold to the non-banking sector at home and, as the external adjustment was still adding to monetary growth, the increase in M3 looked more threatening. In the third quarter the external adjustment became very large indeed and M3 growth was again substantial, although DCE was again negative.

Even so the growth of M3 was still well below the rate of inflation and slower than it had been in 1976. In August the Bank of England suspended the Supplementary Special Deposits Scheme, which had been reactivated at the time of the IMF agreement and renewed in May. Clearly the growth of M3 was not a matter of overriding concern to the authorities. Interest rates continued to fall.

Minimum lending rate (MLR) had been reduced in easy stages from 15 per cent to 9½ per cent by March. The falls continued for most of the year in an attempt to stem the unwanted inflow of foreign money. By October MLR was as low as 5 per cent, the lowest level since 1964, having fallen 10 percentage points in twelve months. It was very difficult to see how a fall of this magnitude could be appropriate to domestic economic conditions, especially as inflation was about 14 per cent both in October 1976 and in October 1977. One did not need to take 'new-fangled' monetary statistics like M3 altogether seriously to believe that the attempt to hold down the pound was leading the authorities to behave in an otherwise inappropriate way.

The purpose of holding down the pound was to preserve relative cost competitiveness and promote export-led growth. Relative inflation rates, even at a constant exchange rate, were eroding that cost advantage. Between the fourth quarters of 1976 and 1977 the IMF index for normalised relative unit labour costs in the United Kingdom rose by 10 per cent, of which about half was due to exchange rate movements and about a half to relative inflation rates. Meanwhile the growth rate of exports of goods and services was actually slowing down. This may seem to show that the strategy for export-led growth was unsuccessful, but it did not mean that the gain in competitiveness was ineffective. World trade growth in 1977 slowed down from 11 per cent to under 5 per cent; exports of goods and services from the United Kingdom slowed down from 9 per cent to 7 per cent. Our performance certainly improved relative to that of other exporters, and in the year after the exchange rate fell our share of world trade rose.

This export performance, coupled with the slow growth in spending on imports (and improving terms of trade), turned the current account of the balance of payments from deficit in the first half of the year to surplus in the second. Thus one of the principal aims of the strategy agreed with the IMF was satisfactorily achieved. But it was achieved more by curtailing the growth of output, less by transferring resources to meet external demand, than had been hoped at the beginning of the year.

The extraction of oil and gas from the North Sea fields was, in 1977, for the first time making a useful contribution to the trade balance. The value of production in 1976 (mainly gas) was £0.6 billion; in 1977 it was £2.1 billion. Almost all of that increment could be seen as a direct contribution to the improvement of the trade balance. Meanwhile the slow growth of, or even stagnation in, output was having a perceptible effect on the labour market. The vacancy statistics still showed a slight rise, but this may have been due to an increase in the proportion of vacancies covered. Unemployment, which had been almost unchanged for nine months, began to rise worryingly again in the latter part of 1977.

Special attention was being paid by government to the problem of youth unemployment, which had risen disproportionately. The youth opportunities programme (YOP) was approved at the end of June. Although relatively cheap in terms of gross public spending (and even cheaper in terms of net effect on the exchequer) it was designed to help almost ¼ million young people. It was an important further step in the slow evolution of special employment measures, which were to play an increasing part in the response of successive governments to unemployment.

With the total register well over the million mark, however, it was still believed by many economists that the pressure of demand in the economy was low, giving ample room for macroeconomic expansion, if the situation on the balance of payments and inflation made it possible. The mini-budget of October could be seen as a modest step in that direction. There were further income tax cuts, backdated to April; pensioners got a Christmas bonus; there were additions to public spending concentrated on construction. The effect on the PSBR was comparable in scale to that of the package agreed with the IMF a year earlier, but in the opposite direction.

So long as the authorities were intervening energetically to hold sterling down, the market was willing to buy apparently unlimited amounts of the currency. This was especially true after July when the Bank of England switched its tactics from stabilising the sterling–dollar rate to stabilising the effective exchange rate index. The markets believed throughout the year that the policy would sooner or later be abandoned, that sterling would then rise and that they could then sell it back to the Bank of England at a profit.

They were right, eventually, on the first count. At the end of October the Bank announced that the rate would be allowed 'for the time being' to find its own level; the 'cap' was removed, and the expectation was that the rate would gush up like oil from a well. In the event it hardly rose at all. Once the one-way option was removed the speculators lost interest and so, as a group, they made little profit.

The experience of exchange market policy in 1977 was important for the future. It was widely perceived as unsuccessful, in that the authorities had to abandon it by the end of the year, and it was said to have undermined monetary control. Two further lessons drawn were that the strategy necessitated too sharp a fall in interest rates, and that the cost of its success was faster inflation at a crucial time for the development of incomes policy.

At the end of the year the Chancellor wrote another letter to the IMF. This time there was no need for protracted negotiation or Cabinet room confrontations. The promises made this time were (like most international agreements on economic policy) promises to do what he had intended to do anyway. The United Kingdom was in a strong position. It was being asked not to draw as much credit from the IMF as it was entitled to, because the IMF needed all its own resources for other purposes elsewhere in the world. So far as the IMF was concerned the problems of the British economy were, for the present at least, solved. So far as the United Kingdom was concerned, however, that was far from the case, as subsequent events were to show.

THE LAST STAGE OF THE LABOUR GOVERNMENT, JANUARY 1978–APRIL 1979

The aims of macroeconomic policy, and its basis in an understanding of the way the economy works, were particularly unclear in the final phase of the

Labour government. The immediate need to follow the lead given by the IMF had receded during 1977. There could, however, be no explicit going back to traditional Keynesian policies of reflation as exemplified by the later Heath years; the experience of 1976 was still very recent and very chastening. On the other hand ministers and top officials at the Treasury and the Bank were not intellectually converted to the approach of the monetarists. They now treated it with far more respect than they would have done a year or two previously, but with the detached respect of non-believers. It was a period of intellectual confusion, or perhaps of transition, which some of the official publications of the period betray. Most of the senior officials were still unsympathetic to monetarism: Sir Douglas Wass was still Permanent Secretary and the new Chief Economic Adviser, Sir Fred Atkinson, was another 'cautious' Keynesian. Others in influential positions, like Ken Couzens, Peter Middleton and Geoffrey Maynard at the Treasury, were not precommitted; Charles Goodhart and others at the Bank were closely in touch with monetarist economists outside the official institutions and helped to promote the exchange of ideas.

Increasingly the conduct of policy was affected by the difficulty of maintaining a Parliamentary majority. Proposals for tax changes during 1978 had to be modified several times in order to keep the support of Liberal MPs. (Support from the Scottish and Welsh Nationalists depended mainly on the preparations for legislation and constitutional change.) The possibility of an early general election was given increasing weight in the conduct of economic policy and the way it was discussed. In this context the most difficult problem was the negotiation of an acceptable deal with the trade unions on pay and prices.

In one respect at least 1978 might be deemed a satisfactory year: a good rate of economic growth was resumed after the 'pause' of 1977. Year on year the average of the three measures of GDP shows a rise of 3 per cent. The main demand stimulus came from consumer spending, which rose by as much as 5½ per cent year on year. This in turn was the result of resumed, and rapid, growth in real personal incomes, especially real wages. The savings ratio actually rose. The later stages of incomes policy under Labour allowed, or failed to stop, wage increases far in excess of the current rate of inflation. The sacrifice of real incomes in Phases 1 and 2 was swiftly reversed. Tax cuts reinforced the stimulus. The result was a consumer boom. Government current spending on goods and services was up by 2.3 per cent roughly reversing the fall of the previous year. Fixed investment also recovered and stockbuilding remained substantial. Export growth, however, was slowing down and resources were shifting out of the balance of payments.

Unemployment which had risen to 1.2 million in the fourth quarter of 1977 fell steadily, if slowly, through 1978 to 1.1 million a year later. The Conservatives might claim in the 1979 election campaign that 'Labour isn't working' but this was in fact the last time that a fall in unemployment was to be recorded for eight years.

Unemployment certainly remained very high relative to the experience of previous upturns, but unfilled vacancies had risen to over a quarter of a million, a level higher than the peak in 1969, although still some way below the exceptional level of 1973. It had become very difficult to read the indicators of aggregate pressure of demand and the margin left for further expansion was much disputed.

The budget of April 1978 was moderately expansionary, adding to the stimulus already given in the previous October. The main innovation was the introduction of a lower rate of tax, 25 per cent on an initial tranche of taxable income. An opposition amendment forced a cut of 1p in the standard rate as well. The problems faced by government are even better illustrated by events that followed. Market concern about the loss of revenue during the progress of the Finance Bill obliged the government to announce an increase of 2½ percentage points in the National Insurance Surcharge. Political pressure from the Liberals then forced the government to cut that increase back to 1½ percentage points. It is difficult to say whose views were really effective in the conduct of fiscal policy at this stage.

The conduct of monetary policy was also running into difficulties, but of a different kind. Towards the end of the preceding year interest rates had risen again when the 'cap' was taken off the exchange rate, but they remained relatively low. 1978 was a year of continuous rise in interest rates with minimum lending rate at 6½ per cent in January, but 12½ per cent in November. Thus the long decline of 1977 was largely reversed. This was reflected in share prices which had risen strongly in 1977 but showed no change between January and December of 1978.

The progressive rise in interest rates through the year was not only the result of concern about the exchange rate. There was a period of weakness in the second quarter, but the sterling index in the first quarter of 1979 was back to the level at which intervention had been abandoned more than a year previously. The rise in interest rates was rather the result of growing concern about the accelerating increase in the money supply, M3, caused by expansionary fiscal measures, and a lower level of debt sales to the non-banks, which prompted talk in the summer months of a 'gilts strike' by the institutions. On the other hand the Bank no longer needed to finance foreign exchange market intervention on anything like the same scale as in the preceding year. Thus DCE rose much more sharply between 1977 and 1978 than did the growth of the money supply.

The progress of M3 was now being monitored against official projections for its growth. The 9–10 per cent range given in the 1977 Budget Statement for the year to April 1978 had been called an 'estimate' not a 'target'. In the event it was exceeded by 3 percentage points. In the 1978 Budget Statement the range was lowered to 8–12 per cent for the following year, starting from the new base, and the word 'target' was used. The targets were to be reassessed every six months.

In order to control the money supply it was necessary to sell gilts to the non-banks, and in order to sell gilts it was necessary to demonstrate that the money supply was under control. So that the authorities should have a greater assurance of hitting their targets the 'corset' or Supplementary Special Deposits Scheme was reactivated in June. The rise in interest rates which continued throughout the year was believed to help on both fronts, selling gilts and restraining the demand for credit. For the present all turned out well enough. The growth of M3 from April 1978 to April 1979 was 11 per cent, happily inside the target range.

The adoption of six-monthly 'rolling' targets for M3 was one momentous decision in the field of monetary policy taken by the Labour government in its closing stages. An equally important choice was made when the United Kingdom decided not to become a full member of the new European Monetary System. Thus two of the main elements of the so-called 'Thatcher experiment' were inherited from her predecessor.

Jim Callaghan and Denis Healey were not averse to international cooperation in economic policy as such. On the contrary they were enthusiastic supporters of the strategy of coordinated expansion adopted at the Bonn Summit meeting in July 1978, after extensive discussion at many meetings of the OECD. The central idea was that those countries with strong balance of payments positions should expand domestic demand and thus act as 'locomotives' pulling along their less fortunate neighbours and stimulating economic growth everywhere. Coordinated economic expansion is an idea with perennial appeal to 'cautious' or 'frustrated' Keynesians in this country.

Close cooperation with France and Germany in the EMS was less appealing. A Green Paper, published by the Treasury in November 1978, gave some of the pros and cons. To do so with clarity would have required an unambiguous statement of the government's attitude to the exchange rate as an instrument of policy and of the priority to be given to money supply targets. The paper is a good example of the difficulty the monetary authorities had at this time in formulating or describing their monetary policy at all. The great majority of economists in the United Kingdom came out against the EMS for a variety of mutually contradictory reasons. It would have required a very strong lead from the government to overcome public suspicion. Another set of arguments about EMS membership, not elaborated in the Green Paper, related to politics rather than economics. The attitude of the Labour Party to Europe was still (at best) ambivalent, and there was no enthusiasm in the British electorate for a commitment which might restrict the freedom of action of British governments.

There was also some real disagreement as to the design of the EMS. The British authorities wanted a system in which the obligations of surplus and deficit countries, lenders and borrowers, were symmetrical. This was not just a disinterested preference, as experience suggested that sterling would be weak most of the time against the mark, if not against the franc or the lira. They did not want to join a DM zone, in which it would have been their responsibility alone to keep sterling in line. It proved difficult enough to get agreement on this, and related points, between the rest of Europe whilst Britain remained on the periphery of the EMS. The time for full United Kingdom membership, it was said, was not ripe. The case for procrastination was to be argued again and again, in good times and bad, for the next decade.

The assumption sometimes made, tacitly or openly, in the debate about EMS membership in 1978 was that sterling would soon be weak again, and that a fall could not, or should not, be resisted. Continuing inflation was again eroding the competitive position of British industry; the level of the index of relative unit labour costs at the end of 1978 was in fact much the same as it had been towards the end of 1975, in the run up to the last great sterling crisis. Export growth was slowing down and Britain's share of world trade was again being reduced. Imports on the other hand were growing fast thanks to the very rapid rise in consumer spending. The balance of payments on current account was close to balance, but that was thanks to rising oil production in the North Sea and an improvement in the terms of trade. Unless inflation could swiftly be brought under control it was difficult to see how another sterling crisis could be avoided.

This was the background to the last act in the drama of incomes policy in the 1970s. The policy, as we have seen, was already in severe trouble in 1977; indeed it is hard to say whether the Phase 3 norms, in operation from July 1977 to July 1978, actually held back earnings growth at all. There were, however, innumerable groups, many of them relatively well-paid, many of them in the public sector, who believed that they had been unfairly treated and who now wanted 'catching up' settlements. The TUC did not want to be committed to any kind of Phase 4 which it knew it would be unable to enforce.

The government nevertheless went ahead in July 1978 and published a White Paper called 'Winning The Battle Against Inflation' which included a 'guideline' of just 5 per cent. Inflation at that time was running at about 7½ per cent, so it appeared that another cut in real wages was being demanded. There were to be exceptions, it is true, but they were meant, in the main, to be self-financing. It may well be true that a level of settlements of this kind was what was necessary to secure a further reduction in inflation, but the framework of incomes policy was not strong enough to secure it. Like the Heath government before it, the Callaghan government was drawn into a conflict it could not win. Wages in the twelve months from July 1978 rose over 12½ per cent, earnings by 16½ per cent. Inflation was up to 15½ per cent. The conflict this time was of two kinds. One was with firms who accepted pay deals outside the pay limits and who were supposed to be penalised in a variety of ways. The other kind of conflict, which was more damaging politically, was with public sector unions that called strikes or took other forms of industrial action. The months prior to the general election of 1979 were called the 'Winter of Discontent', a time of troubles, when the news was all of disruption or of inflationary wage settlements; often of both. It did not perhaps feel as dangerous to society as the events that precipitated the fall of the Heath government five years earlier, but there were similarities nevertheless.

Another parallel with 1974 was the behaviour of oil prices. Early in 1978 the prospect seemed to be for a fall in oil prices rather than a rise, but by November OPEC members reached an agreement to restrict production and in December they announced a series of phased price increases for the next year. Also in December oil exports from Iran came to a standstill during the agitation against the Shah. In the early part of 1979 a steep rise in prices began which was ultimately to increase the cost to oil importers by as much as had the first price 'hike' of 1973 and 1974. That, amongst other things, falsified all expectations that sterling would be weak in 1979. This process, however, was only just beginning at the time of the general election in Britain, so its effects belong to the next chapter.

The Labour Party surrendered power in economic circumstances rather similar to those in which it had gained it five years earlier. The cycle in output and employment in May 1979 was not as far advanced as it had been in February 1974, but even in the first quarter of 1979 growth was faltering and the fall in unemployment was levelling off. Inflation in the second quarter of 1979 was 10½ per cent and rising, compared to nearly 13 per cent and rising in the first quarter of 1974.

Like the Conservatives before them, the Labour Party left office convinced that it was a failure of economic policy above all that had secured their defeat. In opposition they were also to change leaders and to disown the policies they had pursued in power. The divisions within the Labour Party after 1979, however, were deeper than those in the Conservative Party after 1974 and were not confined to economic policy. They had therefore to wait longer for another chance to govern.

4

THE CONSERVATIVE GOVERNMENT 1979–83

The Conservatives won the general election of May 1979 with a majority of 43 seats. The new government, unlike its predecessor, had no need to bargain with other parties in order to secure the passage of legislation. It was also, especially in the area of economic policy, a government that knew its own mind, and was prepared to take decisive action. On occasion it chose to highlight the elements of continuity between its policies and those of the Callaghan government post-1976, and this was indeed justified to some degree, as has already been suggested above. Nevertheless, there was a fresh start after the election, as the new Chancellor claimed in his first budget speech. 'The British people are convinced', he said, 'that it is time for a new beginning'.

The 1979 election campaign did not take the form of a contest between monetarism and Keynesianism. The Conservative party itself was still divided on economic policy between those who wholeheartedly embraced the new philosophy and those who merely respected it, whilst retaining the party's traditional scepticism concerning dogmatic beliefs of any kind. The new Prime Minister was undoubtedly an enthusiast, and the new Chancellor, Sir Geoffrey Howe, in his quieter way, was also prepared to make radical changes. A wide range of opinion was represented in the Cabinet, from Sir Keith Joseph, the most zealous champion of monetarism, as Secretary of State for Industry, to Jim Prior, well-known as a moderate, as Secretary of State for Employment. Dissent within the ranks of the Cabinet did influence the conduct of policy under this, as most other governments, but it was of least influence in precisely those areas where the monetarists wished above all to see changes, that is the conduct of monetary policy and the budget judgement. So far as monetary policy was concerned the attitude of the Bank of England, the necessary instrument of policy, mattered more than that of any minister. At no time could the philosophy of the Bank possibly be described as monetarist (in the same sense as that of the government) although its officials no doubt were loyal, at all times, to the government and tried to be as sympathetic as they could. The Governor, Sir Gordon Richardson, and others at the Bank, were attracted to a much more pragmatic version of monetarism of the kind long familiar to most central banks – but that was not the same species of monetarism at all.

The proposition that 'money matters' was by this time common ground for most commentators, for the Treasury, the Bank and backbench MPs. But for the first twelve or fifteen months of the new government, economic policy was governed by the far stronger proposition that 'only money matters'. Incomes policy was abandoned, not just because it was counter-productive or unenforceable, but because it was redundant. The recommendations of the Clegg Commission on Pay Comparability for the public sector, set up by the previous government, were to be honoured in full. This was done to fulfil a pledge made during the election campaign, but it was defended on the grounds that inflation was a monetary disorder which would be treated by monetary means. One of the first acts of the new government was to abolish the Price Commission.

The budget was introduced little more than a month after the election. The principal changes in taxation were a cut in the basic rate of income tax from 33p to 30p in the pound and an increase in the rates of Value Added Tax from 8 and 12½ per cent to a unified rate of 15 per cent. The effect of this tax-switch on the retail prices index was estimated at 3½ per cent.

The case for raising indirect taxes and cutting direct taxes rests either on their different incidence, or on their different effects on incentives. So far as macroeconomic policy is concerned the main danger of such a reform must be that of setting off an inflationary spiral. Workers may perceive a need to compensate for rises in prices however caused, but take little or no account of their income tax position. The new government consciously ignored this argument on the grounds that inflation depends on the growth of the money supply, not (except briefly) on changes in the rate of indirect taxes. Few commentators supported the tax-switch; it was strongly criticised, for example, by the international monetarists at the London Business School.

At the time of the general election the rate of inflation (measured over the preceding twelve months) was 10.3 per cent and rising. It went on rising until the following May, by which time it had reached nearly 22 per cent. Throughout the latter part of 1979 the policies of the new government were making no demonstrable improvement, although they had identified the control of inflation as their main, their overriding, priority. Success in this campaign was to be much slower in coming, and more costly than they, or the economists whose advice they followed, had expected.

Measured by its effect on public sector borrowing the 1979 budget was moderately contractionary. Cuts amounting to almost £1½ billion were announced in public spending for the year ahead. They were concentrated on industrial support, energy and the Department of the Environment. The aim from now on was to be to 'roll back the boundaries of the public sector'. One means of doing this was privatisation and the sale of public sector assets. The PSBR for the coming financial year was estimated at £8¼ billion, compared to £9¼ billion in the preceding year. The target range for £M3 was reduced from 8–12 per cent to 7–11 per cent, a modest reduction but an ambitious one given the acceleration of inflation already under way. The main onus for achieving this monetary target fell on interest rates and the SSD scheme which had already been in operation for nearly a year. At the time of the budget, minimum lending rate was raised from 12 to 14 per cent and it was announced that the SSD scheme would remain in operation for the time being.

In the second quarter of 1979, the target monetary aggregate was 13 per cent up on a year earlier, the increase in the second quarter itself (seasonally adjusted) being particularly large. The increases in the third and fourth quarters added about 6 per cent, which (at an annual rate) was just above the top end of the target range. Even a small overshoot was thought to threaten the credibility of the government's economic strategy. No effort was to be spared therefore to demonstrate the authorities' determination and ability to exercise monetary control.

The main difficulty arose from the growth of bank lending to the private sector, which was rising rapidly throughout 1979 despite successive increases in interest rates. Sales of public sector debt were running at a very high level in the first half of the year, but moderated in the third quarter. The difficulty may have been that the June increase in minimum lending rate came to be seen as insufficient, and the market for gilt-edged securities went quiet as investors waited for the authorities to make the next move. Operations in the gilts markets did not provide a system of monetary control which could be used with any precision.

In order to be sure of reviving the market for debt, and also in the hope of reining back the demand for bank lending, the authorities decided to give a clear, even a dramatic, signal. On 15 November minimum lending rate was raised by 3 percentage points to 17 per cent. This was the largest one-day rise on record and it produced the highest level ever of short-term interest rates in this country. It produced a sharp fall in the stock market. It did not, however, stop, or even much slow down, the growth of £M3.

The increase in interest rates during 1979 was not confined to the United Kingdom. In June, Eurodollar deposits paid 10½ per cent, well below the return on similar sterling deposits after the budget day increase in MLR. The United States authorities, however, were also concerned about monetary growth and began experimenting with a new approach to the setting of interest rates, allowing them to be more volatile in the hope of thereby achieving better control of the monetary aggregates. As a result Eurodollar deposits in October were paying more than 15 per cent, nearly 1 per cent more than sterling certificates of deposit. The United Kingdom authorities at this time had no explicit objective for the exchange rate, so there was, strictly, no need to follow the lead set by the United States. There can be little doubt, however, that they would have been very worried by anything that threatened to precipitate a sharp fall in sterling.

Sterling had in fact strengthened considerably in the early months of 1979. In the second quarter the exchange rate index was about 9 per cent up on the same quarter of 1978. This was believed to result from the Conservative election victory and the prospect of a tough anti-inflationary stand, as well as the increases in the price of oil. (We shall try to provide our own explanation in Parts 4 and 5 of this study). The cost of this appreciation was a loss of competitiveness which industry found very worrying.

In the second quarter of 1979 (about the time of the election), the IMF index of relative unit labour costs was 17 per cent up on the preceding year. The new government thus inherited an exchange rate which was already well out of line with domestic costs. Since domestic costs were rising at a fast, even an accelerating, pace, the misalignment could only get worse if sterling did not depreciate. The new government chose to turn a blind eye to this problem and followed a monetary policy determined exclusively by their target for £M3. Foreign exchange intervention was foresworn and interest rates, as we have seen, were dramatically raised. The immediate effect on the exchange rate was not great, partly because interest rates were rising in other countries as well. Sterling rose significantly in the third quarter, but then fell back a little in the fourth. The effect of the November rise was to be felt in 1980, rather than in 1979.

The strength of sterling provided the right environment for a major reform, the abolition of exchange control. Since the war the Bank of England had operated a set of restrictions on the foreign exchange transactions of United Kingdom residents, which, despite some easing over the years, still had an important effect on the market for sterling. The magnitude of that effect was necessarily unknown before the event, so the total abolition of control in a few months was itself an act of faith. It was clear, from the experience of 1976 for example, that exchange control could not prevent a run on sterling in the right circumstances. 'Leading and lagging' trade-related payments was enough to outweigh the scale of the market intervention that the authorities could command. Controls were more effective in determining the composition of assets held by large British institutions, especially pension funds. The extent to which they would diversify into foreign assets if permitted was unknown before the event. It was assumed that 'long-term' capital flows of this kind would result in some downward pressure on sterling, perhaps over a protracted period, as portfolios were adjusted. Such downward pressure was, on balance, thought to be welcome at the time. In the event there was a quite substantial effect on capital flows, especially portfolio outflows, in subsequent years, but no discernible downward pressure on sterling at the time that the controls were removed.

The other effect of exchange control abolition was to undermine the SSD scheme as a method of monetary control. The scheme was already somewhat discredited by the growing practice of 'disintermediation'. This involved banks acting, in effect, as agents arranging borrowing and lending between their customers, without recording assets or liabilities on their own balance sheets. Freedom for United Kingdom banks to operate in the euromarkets provided them with another back door through which to conduct business for their customers that the SSD scheme did not restrict. This was not regarded as a serious argument for retaining exchange controls. The SSD scheme was in any case being retained only as a temporary expedient until a better method of effective monetary control could be devised. The November announcements included the promise of a consultative document on monetary control early in the new year.

Meanwhile the strength of sterling relative to domestic costs was contributing to a pause in the growth of output and to mounting pressure on the finances of the company sector. In the Financial Statement issued at budget time, the Treasury for the first time published an official forecast that output would fall. 'The prospect is for economic activity to decline slightly over the next year or so.' This view, which was proved substantially correct, was rather more pessimistic than that of most independent forecasters, including those at the National Institute. In his budget speech the Chancellor, with less candour, spoke of a period of 'no growth' and expressed doubts as to the reliability of the forecasts he was obliged by law to publish. He added however that an easier stance of fiscal policy would make matters worse, not better.

As the year progressed it became clear that the rise in output was over. The upper turning point in the cycle is identified by the CSO as May 1979. From the second quarter peak (caused by anticipation of a higher rate of VAT), consumer spending fell back in the third and remained roughly constant thereafter. There was a rise in the savings ratio, possibly resulting from the higher rate of inflation. Public expenditure also levelled off, thanks in part to more effective control by central government. As is common at the top of the cycle, fixed investment continued to rise for a few more quarters and stockbuilding remained positive up to the end of the year. There was a sharp burst of growth in imports, possibly as a result of capacity constraints in some sectors of British industry at a time when consumer spending was still buoyant. There were signs that export volume was beginning to suffer from the loss of international competitiveness.

The fall in unemployment continued until the autumn, bringing the total (seasonally adjusted and excluding school-leavers) down to just under 1.1 million. The rise in employment also levelled off and vacancies began to fall. The signs of a downturn were easy to read, and evident to commentators at the time. What was not so evident was the scale of the recession that was to follow.

The economic situation was in some respects similar to that of 1974. Output growth was faltering; oil prices had been raised very sharply and wages were accelerating. As in 1974, the pressure was quickly felt by the company sector, unable to pass on its costs in full. This time the restraint on prices was not the price code, but international competition and a firm exchange rate. The rise in interest rates in 1979 (which had no parallel in 1974) added to the financial pressure on the sector. Industrial and commercial companies in aggregate (including oil companies) were roughly in financial balance in the first half of 1979, after recording healthy surpluses in the preceding two years. In the latter half of 1979 the sector moved into deficit, a position which prevailing conditions made difficult to finance.

The Chief Economic Adviser to the Treasury, Sir Fred Atkinson, was due to retire at the end of 1979. The question of the succession was naturally regarded as an important one and was widely discussed beforehand in the press. The job could only be done effectively by someone who sympathised with the new beginning initiated after the election, but who at the same time understood the methods used by the large team of macroeconomists at the Treasury and could command their respect. Fortunately such a person was found in Terry Burns of the London Business School, whose relative youth was decided to be, in these special circumstances, no disqualification.

TWO MILLION UNEMPLOYED, JANUARY – DECEMBER 1980

The recession began in earnest in the first quarter of 1980 and continued throughout the year. The output measure of gross domestic product, usually regarded as the most reliable, at least for short-period comparisons, fell by nearly 6 per cent between the fourth quarters of 1979 and 1980; manufacturing output, which was especially hard-hit in this recession, fell by 15 per cent over the same period. Unemployment, which was 1.3 million at the end of 1979 (seasonally adjusted and on the definition then in use) had risen by the end of 1980 to over 2.1 million.

The fall in output was considerably sharper than that experienced in 1975 and the effect on unemployment was more pronounced. The initial level of output, relative to the potential of the economy, was probably lower in 1979 than it had been after the boom of 1973; certainly the starting level of unemployment at the end of 1979, before the second great recession, was far higher than that in 1973 or 1974 when the first great recession began. The upward trend of unemployment through the 1970s and much of the 1980s, however, is difficult to interpret and it would probably be wrong to regard it as a straightforward indicator of the slack in the labour market. The issue was naturally a crucial one for the design of macroeconomic policy throughout the period covered by this study. (It is addressed again in Part 5 below). However that trend is interpreted, there can be no doubt that the economy suffered a major setback in 1980, from which it took many years to recover.

If the path of output is to be explained by that of the different categories of expenditure, then the origin of the 1980 recession is to be found principally in the course of stockbuilding. There was an abrupt turnround from positive stockbuilding worth some 1¼ per cent of gross domestic product in 1979, to negative stockbuilding of similar, or a little greater, magnitude in 1980. This is a pattern familiar from previous cycles, although not previously seen on the same scale. It is possible that firms, on this occasion, concluded that output would not be sustained as it had been sometimes in the past by a deliberate counter-cyclical use of macroeconomic policy, and accordingly cut back their level of stocks to one more appropriate to a permanently lower level of production and sales. It is clear that some firms at least had little choice in the matter, but shed stocks as fast as they could to stave off bankruptcy. For similar reasons fixed investment in the private sector turned down in the course of the year.

Public sector investment had been falling for some years, as the previous government found it easier to cut capital budgets than to hold back the growth of current spending. This trend continued after the election with a fall in general government fixed investment (excluding sales of existing assets) of 6 per cent in 1980 alone. The volume of government current spending on goods and services, however, showed a small rise.

Private consumption fell fractionally in 1980, as the savings ratio remained at the high level reached in the latter part of the preceding year. At nearly 14 per cent, the savings ratio in 1980 is the highest recorded for any year, attributable perhaps to rapid inflation and an exceptionally high level of interest rates.

Both imports and exports of goods and services were falling for most of the year. The fall in imports reflected the fall in output, the rising production of North Sea oil and negative stockbuilding. The fall in exports may be explained by the very high exchange rate of the pound relative to domestic costs. The world economy was still expanding, although at a much reduced pace compared with 1979. The onset of the 1980 recession cannot credibly be blamed in any large part on the slowdown in world economic activity following the second oil price shock, although clearly this was one of the many contributory factors.

The scale of the recession was not foreseen, still less intended, by policymakers at the time. As we have seen in the previous section, the origins of the recession can be traced back to the situation inherited by the Conservatives when they came into office in May 1979: the consumer-led upswing had already spent its force, inflation was already dangerously high and the real exchange rate was already misaligned. The measures taken by the new government, however – public spending cuts, an increase in indirect taxation, and two sharp increases in interest rates – must have contributed substantially to the scale of the fall in output which followed. As the extent of that fall became evident during the course of the year, the stance of policy was, gradually and reluctantly, changed. Having begun by making a virtue of inflexibility, the government learnt from the experience of 1980 that some degree of pragmatism was indispensable.

In the Financial Statement and Budget Report presented in March, the Chancellor set out a Medium-Term Financial Strategy (MTFS). This was intended to provide a framework within which macroeconomic policy would be conducted over a period of four years. The conduct of both fiscal and monetary policy in the past was criticised, with some justice, as being a matter of short-term expediency, lacking a clear vision of objectives and of the constraints to be overcome. By making its plans public the government was seeking to guide expectations and in this way to influence economic behaviour. The conquest of inflation would be swifter and less painful if all concerned, particularly perhaps those involved in wage bargaining, believed that the government would and could play its part. It was a change of 'regime' in the sense that we have used that word in the introduction to this study (page 8 above).

The centrepiece of the MTFS was a four-year path for the growth of the money supply, defined as £M3. A firm commitment was made to 'a progressive deceleration over the period' although the deceleration actually shown in the accompanying table was a very gradual one. The aim was to achieve this by a progressive reduction in the scale of public sector borrowing, not by maintaining a very high level of interest rates. A distinction was drawn, however, between the 'projection' of the PSBR, which was not intended as a target, and the deceleration in monetary growth on which a deliberately firm pledge was made.

To maintain a progressive reduction in monetary growth in these circumstances it may be necessary to change policy in ways not reflected in the above projections. The Government would face a number of options for policy changes to achieve this aim, including changes in interest rates, taxes and public expenditure. But there would be no question of departing from the money supply policy, which is essential to the success of any anti-inflationary strategy.

This last sentence did not quite say that money supply growth would decelerate year-by-year, come what may, over the next few years, although it came very close indeed. Within a matter of months the Chancellor had cause to be grateful for the slight ambiguity which could be read into this apparently inflexible declaration of intent.

The incipient recession was inevitably raising public sector borrowing, by reducing revenue and by increasing spending especially on benefits for the unemployed. Nevertheless the Chancellor was able to forecast a small reduction in the PSBR for 1980–81, compared with 1979–80. The budget measures themselves were estimated to cut the PSBR directly by £0.8 billion. There was another tax switch, raising specific duties and cutting income tax, but on a much smaller scale than that of the previous year. The lower rate of income tax at 25 per cent was abolished. Some further cuts in public spending were announced.

The White Paper on public spending was published at the same time as the budget, and completed the survey of expenditure undertaken by the government in its first year of office. The main aim was clearly stated: 'The government intend to reduce public expenditure progressively in volume terms over the next four years.' The scale of the reduction was to be about 4 per cent, comparing 1983–4 with 1979–80. As compared with the last White Paper of the Labour government the level of spending proposed for 1982–3 was down by 11½ per cent. There were to be increases in spending on defence, law and order, health and social security; the programmes to be cut back most were those concerned with industry, energy, trade and employment, housing, education and support for the nationalised industries. The costs of EEC membership were still being negotiated at the time when the White Paper was published. An agreement was reached at the end of May, under which Britain was given favourable treatment, because of our exceptionally heavy net contributions to the Common Agricultural Policy.

At the time of the budget, the Chancellor also announced that the SSD scheme for controlling the liabilities of the banking system would not be extended beyond mid-June. He had presented a Green Paper to Parliament a few days earlier on the subject of monetary control. This began from the premise that the SSD scheme had 'come virtually to the end of its useful life' and sought to find a better alternative. The paper, written jointly by the Treasury and the Bank of England, illustrates well the problems with which the authorities were wrestling as they sought to devise an operational means of achieving the objectives of monetary control to which the government attached such overriding importance.

The government declared itself satisfied with fiscal policy and interest rates as instruments for controlling the money supply in the medium term. This confidence, which in the event proved altogether misplaced, limited the scope of the consultation to tactics rather than grand strategy. The government further circumscribed the agenda by declaring its intention of retaining £M3 as the sole aggregate for which a target range would be set. The question posed was what means should be adopted for keeping that aggregate close to a predetermined path and keeping its 'short-term fluctuations' in moderate bounds.

The disagreements amongst the monetarists, and between the monetarists and the Bank of England, which lay behind the Green Paper are discussed in Part 2 below. For present purposes it is enough to say that the Green Paper signalled the success of the Bank in averting radical changes to the banking system, such as would have been required if an attempt was made to operate a system of monetary base control. Such a system would, according to its advocates, have made much more direct and reliable control of the money supply possible. It would, on the other hand, have meant such profound changes during a period of transition that the stability of the relationships between the monetary aggregates and the rest of the economy (such as it was) would have been upset to an unknown extent for an unknown period into the future. Having abandoned the SSD scheme, and having failed to replace it with any other direct control, the authorities were left with little influence over the growth of £M3. The situation was reminiscent of that following the publication of 'Competition and Credit Control' in 1971, so reminiscent that it is perhaps surprising that the same conditions were allowed to recur.

The SSD 'corset' was removed in June. In the following month £M3 (seasonally adjusted) rose by nearly £3 billion, or nearly 5 per cent. This was a far greater rise than had been expected, and there seemed no way in which it could possibly be accommodated within the target range announced at budget time. The next month there was another large increase and, after a pause in September, the spate continued unchecked. In retrospect we can see that the removal of the corset had a far greater effect on monetary growth than was expected at the time. It made possible a sustained and rapid increase in banks' balance sheets for many years to come.

This was the end of the brief phase of macroeconomic policy when it could be said that 'only money matters'. It is not easy to say what steps the authorities might have taken to stem, or reverse, the excess of monetary growth over the target. Some monetarist diehards wanted a massive auction of gilt-edged securities, but events were taking the decisions out of their hands. In fact the decision was taken in July (after the corset had been removed, but before its full implications were known) to cut minimum lending rate from 17 to 16 per cent, thus signalling that the authorities had other concerns in mind as well as their monetary target when setting the level of domestic interest rates. The retreat from monetarism had begun.

The rise in interest rates at the end of 1979 had made little perceptible difference to the growth of £M3, but it had stopped altogether the growth of the narrower aggregate M1. Apart from the bulge in July, when the 'corset' was removed, M1 was lower in the summer of 1980 than it had been the previous autumn. (In real terms it was more than 20 per cent down.)

Another indicator suggesting monetary tightness was the exchange rate, which was rising throughout 1980. By the fourth quarter the exchange rate index was 13 per cent up on a year earlier; over two years the appreciation was 24 per cent. This was at a time when inflation in Britain was running at about 20 per cent, some 5 per cent a year faster than the OECD average. The IMF index of relative unit labour costs for the United Kingdom was about 25 per cent higher in the fourth quarter of 1980 than a year earlier, nearly 50 per cent higher than two years earlier (and actually 70 per cent above its low point in the fourth quarter of 1976.) In terms of relative export prices the loss of competitiveness was, as might be expected, rather less, but the loss of profitability on exports was damaging to industry as well as the loss of markets.

The reasons for the buoyancy of sterling were much debated at the time, and it was not easy to sort out the effects of such factors as the price of oil, relative interest rates and market confidence following publication of the medium-term financial strategy. Britain at this time was roughly self-sufficient in oil, so the doubling of oil prices during 1979 and 1980 had little net effect on our balance of payments. The same was not true of our main competitors, especially Germany and Japan. Thus the markets tended to mark sterling up relative to other currencies every time oil prices rose, during the turbulent course of events leading up to the war between Iran and Iraq. Some commentators argued that this was inevitable, and that a consequential fall in manufacturing output was a necessary adjustment of the economy to its oil wealth.

Another factor helping to raise sterling must have been the high level of interest rates maintained in the United Kingdom for most of the year. Dollar interest rates by contrast were extraordinarily volatile, rising to a peak of virtually 20 per cent (on 3-month Eurodollar deposits in London) in March, but falling to below 10 per cent two months later. After staying below sterling rates for most of the summer, dollar rates shot back up to over 18 per cent in the autumn, by which time British rates were well down.

The strength of sterling, and perhaps also the fall in output, were beginning to have an effect on inflation. The measure most often quoted, the 12-month rise in the retail prices index, peaked at 21.9 per cent in May. It then moved down quite gradually, but further falls could be confidently predicted from the month-to-month changes. The old wage rate index in the third quarter showed a rise of about 19 per cent on a year earlier; the settlements being made in the latter part of the year resulted in a rise over the twelve months ahead from the third quarter of 1980 of just 9½ per cent. Possibly these signs of moderation in the rate of inflation contributed to the more moderate macroeconomic policies pursued by the government from about this time.

The November measures included some public spending increases, as well as further cuts. External finance for the nationalised industries, for example, was raised to cushion the blow of the recession. The main relaxation was a cut in the minimum lending rate from 16 to 14 per cent, and the budget monetary target for the year was in effect abandoned. Some relatively small changes were announced to the operating methods of the Bank of England, but the proposal to move to monetary base control was postponed indefinitely.

The next day it was announced that unemployment was over 2 millions and still rising fast. At this stage 'the new beginning' introduced by the Conservative government seemed an almost unmitigated failure.

THE RECESSION PROLONGED,
JANUARY – DECEMBER 1981

On 24 February, 1981 the Treasury and Civil Service Committee (TCSC) of the House of Commons published the report of an enquiry into the government's monetary policy and the basis of the MTFS. This had become a major exercise, occupying the committee for most of the preceding year. Evidence, written and oral, had been taken from the Treasury and the Bank of England, from foreign central banks, from the CBI and the TUC and from a wide range of academic economists and other interested parties. Some of the views expressed to the Committee will be featured in the discussion of the history of ideas in Part 2 below. For present purposes it is enough to outline the Committee's conclusions, which were of some importance to the subsequent course of policy. The Committee had a Conservative majority and a Conservative chairman, but it was nevertheless highly critical of the way in which monetary policy had been conducted over the eighteen months since the election.

The report concluded that 'the Medium-Term Financial Strategy was not soundly based'. It found no evidence of a direct link between the growth of the money supply and price inflation of the kind presupposed by a monetarist strategy. It was unhappy with the exclusive reliance on £M3 and argued that the exchange rate should also be taken into account when setting interest rates. It wanted more use made of econometric evidence, and it wanted less dogmatism. There should be more scope to modify the tactics of policy in the light of developments in the economy. As we have seen in the previous section, this was the direction in which events were already pushing monetary policy by the time the report came out.

This did not mean, however, that the government was about to make a U-turn and adopt Keynesian policies of reflation – far from it. It might be necessary to modify the exclusive emphasis on the money supply, but the aim of reducing public sector borrowing remained as important as ever to the Chancellor and the Prime Minister. In fact it may have been thought even more important to achieve that aim, given the failure to control the money supply. Something had to be done to demonstrate that the counter-inflation strategy had not been abandoned, or even seriously compromised. There was also a need to demonstrate to some members of the Cabinet that excessive public spending would result, not in extra borrowing, but in politically painful increases in taxation. The report of the TCSC had argued that public sector borrowing might need to rise in a recession and that the 'automatic stabilisers' of lower tax revenue and higher social security spending should not be overridden. The Chancellor did not take this advice in preparing his 1981 budget. He presented a deflationary budget in the depths of the recession.

The direct effect of the budget proposals was to raise revenue by £3.6 billion in 1981–2 or £2.7 billion in a full year. Measured relative to the effects of 'revalorising' both direct and indirect taxes in line with inflation, the budget proposals raised revenue in 1981–2 by £4.3 billion. Personal income tax allowances were not raised at all and excise duties were raised more than in line with inflation. Both these decisions had the effect of reducing real personal disposable incomes, and hence presumably consumer spending. These measures were, on any conventional calculation, directly deflationary. The economic effects of the other major tax increases were, and still are, difficult to judge. A supplementary duty was raised from oil producers, whose profits had exceeded their original expectations since the second oil price shock of 1979–80. A special tax on bank deposits was also introduced for one year only, on the grounds that high interest rates produced a windfall gain for the banks, which the exchequer ought to share. It is arguable that the effects of both these latter taxes on economic activity would be small, or even negligible.

The budget measures as a whole were a good deal tougher than expected. They were accompanied by a restatement of the MTFS in words which made only the minimum concessions unavoidable in the light of experience over the previous twelve months. It was stated more than once that something described as the 'thrust' of the strategy would be 'maintained'. It was recognised that £M3 had been giving a misleading signal and that the conduct of monetary policy required attention to a variety of indicators, including M1 as well as £M3, not forgetting the exchange rate and interest rates. Even house prices got a mention as a possible guide to financial conditions. Nevertheless a three-year path for the growth of £M3 was again given prominence, and its virtues as a medium-term guide to policy were again catalogued.

The target range set for £M3 in 1981/2 was the same, 6–10 per cent, as that shown in the Financial Statement of the previous year. Since, however, growth over the preceding twelve months was 20 per cent, well outside the range of 7 – 11 per cent set for 1980/81, the starting point was now far in excess of that originally intended. The MTFS, therefore, in all seriousness, discussed the possibility of clawing-back the excess growth already conceded. This too was very tough talking.

Talking apart, the main monetary policy measure at the time of the 1981 budget was a *reduction* of 2 per cent in the minimum lending rate. At 12 per cent, this was now 5 percentage points lower than it had been at the peak in November 1979, and lower than it had been at any time since the Autumn of 1978. Monetary policy (thus measured) had now become relatively easy. The MTFS reiterated the wish to use tight fiscal policy, rather than high interest rates, as the means of slowing down the growth of the money supply and hence inflation. The tax increases and the MLR cut in the budget were an attempt to change the 'mix' of policy in that direction. Events later in the year were to show how difficult it could be to make such a change in an open economy like that of the United Kingdom.

The hope was expressed in the MTFS that public spending would be cut back (it would be given 'the most serious attention') so that the tax burden in later years could be reduced. That also was a difficult wish to fulfil, as events later in the year were to prove. In the budget speech itself the Chancellor had to announce a few minor *additions* to spending plans for the forthcoming year.

About the time of the 1981 budget (coincidentally, one must assume), the fall in output came to an end. The lower turning point of the cycle is put at January 1981. The rise in output was, for some time, barely perceptible, in contrast with the brisk recovery from recession in 1972 and 1975. The output measure for GDP rose about 1½ per cent between the fourth quarters of 1980 and 1981. Employment continued to fall throughout the year and unemployment rose from 2 to 2½ million. Unfilled vacancies, however, showed a slight rise, from a very low base at the end of 1980.

Consumer spending rose in the first quarter of the year, but fell back a little thereafter as real incomes were cut by the budget. The savings ratio, which had been exceptionally high in 1980, was lower in 1981, as it usually is when real income growth slows down. The slight rise in total real expenditure during 1981 is accounted for by a slower rate of de-stocking – stockbuilding remained negative throughout the year, but to a decreasing extent. This is a typical pattern at the lower turning point of the cycle, reinforced on this occasion, as indeed on others, by a fall in interest rates.

The reduction in interest rates may also have contributed to the weakening of the exchange rate. The long period of sterling appreciation, almost uninterrupted from early 1977 to early 1981, was over. The trend changed even though the United Kingdon was now in exceptionally large current account surplus on the balance of payments. From now on the general trend was down, although the slide was intermittent and not very fast. Between the fourth quarters of 1980 and 1981 the effective exchange rate index fell by about 9½ per cent.

Inflation in the United Kingdom at this time was broadly similar to average inflation in the industrial world. Thus an exchange depreciation of 9½ per cent translated into roughly the same size of improvement in relative cost competitiveness. This began to reverse the unprecedented, and traumatic, loss of competitiveness which had taken place whilst the exchange rate was appreciating. As always, exchange rate depreciation brought its cost as well as its benefit. The rate of inflation, which had been brought down sharply during 1980, levelled off. The twelve month change in the RPI which was 13 per cent in January 1981, was still 12 per cent in January 1982. This pause in the process of disinflation was unexpected and unwelcome. It must have owed something to the rise in excise duties in the budget and to a sharp increase in local authority rates about the same time, but the path of the exchange rate was another major contributory factor.

In the course of the year it was felt necessary to tighten monetary policy again, that is to raise interest rates, reversing the budget-day cut. The disappointment over inflation would probably be thought of as an underlying reason for this change, although, at this time, official pronouncements would not have made a direct connection of that kind. The high level of interest rates in the world at large may have been another unacknowledged cause. Certainly MLR at 12 per cent was well out of line with eurodollar deposits yielding 17 per cent in April. The United States under President Reagan was embarking on a programme of fiscal expansion and monetary tightness which effectively set the going rate for real interest rates world wide. The United Kingdom, in trying to combine a tightening of fiscal policy with a cut in interest rates, was moving in a diametrically opposite direction. As a result we had, for a few years, *both* a tight fiscal stance *and* historically high real interest rates.

Another reason for the rise in United Kingdom interest rates in the latter half of 1981 was the failure, again, to control £M3. The trouble, as in the preceding year, arose from the rapid growth of bank lending to the private sector. The authorities had no effective means of controlling this, since it did not respond in any predictable way to the level of short-term interest rates. They could, in principle, have offset the growth of private sector bank lending by reducing the other counterparts to the growth of £M3, that is bank lending to the public sector. They did cut the PSBR as far as seemed prudent in a recession (or indeed further than seemed prudent). They might have reinforced that by selling more debt outside the banking system, although it was not proving easy to guarantee as large sales of debt as might be required. To safeguard, and perhaps expand, opportunities for funding government debt, the Chancellor announced, when presenting the 1981 budget, the first issue of index-linked gilt-edged securities. At the time this was a bold step, which was thought to have far-reaching implications. In the event the fall in inflation in later years, and the good yeild to be had on conventional gilts, limited the market for index-linked debt. When it was first issued the authorities were worried that it would be *too* attractive, for example to overseas buyers, and it was therefore restricted to the United Kingdom pension funds. In subsequent years these restrictions were lifted, but no great demand was forthcoming.

It might seem that the authorities could always meet their monetary targets by selling a sufficiently large quantity of debt, sufficiently cheap, outside the banking sector. In practice the authorities were at this period very reluctant to force the pace of funding, for example by substituting auctions for the traditional tap system as a method of selling debt. Long-term debt sells, at least in part, by offering the prospect of capital gain, so it was thought that a fall in price could actually be counterproductive in some circumstances since the market would be worried that the fall would continue. The alternative of selling large quantities of short-dated debt outside the banking system was also unattractive, as the debt instruments would be almost indistinguishable from some of the bank liabilities that were included in the definition of £M3. Control by that means might be dismissed as merely cosmetic.

The search for an effective means of controlling £M3 continued through 1981, the alternative of monetary base control having been by this time effectively excluded. Some procedural changes were announced in August. Publication of minimum lending rate was to stop. This did not mean, however, that the authorities had really abandoned responsibility for the level of short-term interest rates. The Bank of England's operations day by day in the short-term money markets would set a rate somewhere in a band agreed from time to time with government. That band would not be disclosed, but market operators would obviously know roughly what it was. The guiding hand of the Bank would be less visible, but not necessarily less effective. One advantage of being less visible might be that increases in interest rates attracted less public criticism, and the authorities were subject to less political pressure to keep them low.

The reserve asset ratio requirement, which meant that banks had to hold a minimum proportion of their total balance sheet in a liquid form was abolished. This had not been an effective brake on the expansion of banking business and was inequitable as between banks and other deposit-taking institutions. Another requirement to be abolished was that applied to the clearing banks under which they had to place non-interest-bearing deposits at the Bank of England. The main purpose of this requirement was to provide an independent income for the Bank. Under the new arrangements a smaller percentage contribution was required from all banks or licensed deposit-takers. Most of these changes had been foreshadowed in the November statement of the preceding year. None of them made it any easier to control £M3.

A new monetary aggregate, M2, had now been added to the menu. It consisted only of the retail deposits of the banking system and was thought likely, for that reason, to be a better measure of money as a transactions medium. Potentially it was a rival to £M3, but it woud be some years before its behaviour, for example its seasonal pattern, was sufficiently well understood for it to be considered as a target aggregate. In the event, enthusiasm for *any* monetary aggregate ebbed away before M2 had had a chance to prove itself. Even at this stage the argument was gaining ground within government that the logical next step was full membership of the European monetary system. It was many years, however, before that idea was allowed to emerge in public.

The design of monetary policy in the early years of the Conservative government owed much to the then Financial Secretary to the Treasury, Nigel Lawson. He was rewarded by appointment as Secretary of State for Energy in a September reshuffle. This also translated Sir Keith Joseph from Industry to Education and put Norman Tebbit in charge of Employment.

Labour-market issues were now quite as important to economic policy as questions of monetary control. A package of measures was announced in July to support employment in the face of a continuing fall in the demand for labour. In contrast to earlier special employment measures under the Labour government one condition applied to the new employment subsidies was a limit on the earnings of the workers in respect of whom they were paid. In December a more ambitious programme, costing £1 billion a year, was launched to improve training opportunities, especially for the young unemployed. The new Youth Training Scheme (YTS) began as a

one-year scheme for school-leavers combining work experience with some
further education. The spur for this reform may have been the high level
of unemployment amongst the young, but it was not just a way of reducing
the embarrasingly high unemployment numbers. From the start it was
intended also to meet a real worry that industry was neglecting training,
because of financial difficulties and doubts about the future viability of
many firms. Should demand pick up again, it was feared that shortages of
skilled labour could hold back production. There was growing concern that
standards of vocational training in the United Kingdom were much lower
than those of her industrial competitors.

Another reason often given for the relatively poor performance of
British industry was poor industrial relations. The effect of the recession
was to reduce the frequency of strikes and other disputes because workers
feared the loss of their jobs. This was reinforced by legislation proposed in
a November White Paper. Broadly, the effect was to limit the industrial
action that was immune from the civil law, rather than to use the criminal
law as had been attempted in the past.

At the end of the year the problems of implementing the government's
economic strategy was still more evident than its successes. Nevertheless
what the Chancellor had called its 'thrust' had been 'maintained'. Financial
confidence had survived the disarray over monetary control, and the
exchange rate had fallen in an orderly fashion from its unnatural height at
the beginning of the year. Inflation *was* coming down, if only slowly. The
recession had been prolonged, but in fact the prospect for output growth
was better than anyone knew at the time. The worst was over.

INFLATION SUBDUED,
JANUARY 1982 – JUNE 1983

The next eighteen months take the story up to the General Election of June
1983, won by the Conservatives with an increased majority. That election
result is sometimes attributed to the afterglow of the Falklands campaign,
sometimes to the divisions amongst and within the Opposition parties. It
was also helped by an improved performance of the economy, with
inflation at last subdued and with a stronger recovery of activity at last
in sight.

In the restatement of the MTFS at the time of the 1982 budget the aim of
economic policy was clearly stated and even, very roughly, quantified.
'Government policies are directed at achieving a rate of inflation that is well
into single figures.' At that time the increase in the RPI over the preceding
twelve months was still just over 10 per cent. The Treasury forecast showed
a rise over the next twelve months (from the second quarter of 1982 to the
second quarter of 1983) of 7½ per cent. This proved far too pessimistic.
When the election came in the second quarter of 1983 the rate of inflation
was not 7½ per cent but under 4 per cent.

The statement of policy made by the Chancellor in March 1982 differed little from that of the previous year. Fiscal policy was not tightened further, but on the other hand little was conceded to those who argued for a large stimulus to help the economy climb out of the recession. The National Insurance surcharge was cut, but only by a cautious 1 per cent, with an extra ½ per cent reduction from August 1982 to the following April. Income tax allowances were raised, just a little more than revalorisation for inflation dictated, but indirect taxes were also raised beyond that benchmark. Compared with an indexed base the budget measures reduced taxation by about £1½ billion in 1982–3 or about £2½ billion in a full year.

The text of the Financial Statement contained another long explanation of why the money supply targets were important but, alas, difficult to hit. This year the attitude was considerably more relaxed. Both the ability and the need to propound monetarism in the strict sense had decreased over the past twelve months. Much was said about institutional changes in the financial system which clouded the picture of monetary growth. The target range for the coming year was raised for the first time since the MTFS began. The old figures of 5 – 9 per cent for 1982/3 became 8 – 12 per cent. This range was applied not just to £M3 but also to the narrow aggregate M1 and to a wider liquidity total called PSL2, which included the deposits of building societies as well as banks.

The exchange rate was also mentioned, not as a target or an instrument of policy, but as an indicator. This allowed the form of monetarism to be retained, whilst making clear that a fall in the exchange rate would be regarded as a signal for an increase in interest rates. Mention was also made of money GDP, which sounded rather like a monetary aggregate but was in fact the value of total output at current prices. The forecast values of this variable, which had previously been implicit in the tables of figures describing the MTFS, were for the first time made explicit. This was not a variable which the authorities could control with any precision, and no such claim was made. Nevertheless, the forecasts of money GDP published on this and other occasions proved in the event to be quite accurate.

The Chancellor could no longer announce a budget-day cut in bank rate or in minimum lending rate as these had been abolished. He did, however, persuade the building societies to cut their recommended mortgage rate by 1½ per cent a few days after he had made his budget speech. This was one step in a continuing process of reduction in the level of short-term interest rates during much of 1982. The clearing banks' lending rates fell from 14 per cent at the beginning of the year to 9 per cent in November. This fall roughly matched the pace of the reduction in the rate of inflation, if measured over the preceding twelve months, thus keeping real interest rates on this definition broadly constant at around 3 per cent. United States interest rates were also coming down roughly in parallel, so the international pressures on the United Kingdom to keep interest rates high were also abating.

In July 1982 all remaining restrictions on hire purchase credit were abolished. The growth of personal loans that did not involve hire purchase agreements had largely circumvented the control, which now appeared as nothing but an unnecessary interference with the way in which finance houses and their customers chose to do business. Thus was abandoned what had once been one of the most powerful and reliable instruments in the hands of the authorities to manage aggregate demand. It happened that this period saw the beginning of a sustained growth of consumer spending and consumer borrowing which was to go on for many years. No doubt liberalisation of the financial system (including the abolition of hire purchase control and also the restriction on banks), facilitated this growth: it may even have been a necessary condition for it, although not a sufficient one. Views differed, and still do, as to the extent to which HP controls mattered by the time they were abolished.

Another development which may have contributed to the growth of consumption in the mid–1980s also dates from this period. As interest rates came down and the economy showed some signs of resilience, the stock market began to climb more rapidly. Having fallen, even in nominal terms, in 1980, the index was 11½ per cent up in 1981, but that still implied a real fall. In 1982, however, year-on-year its growth exceeded that of retail prices, and during that year it gathered pace. By June 1983, the time of the election, the stock market was more than 25 per cent up on a year earlier. This rise made the personal sector richer and may therefore have made it more ready to borrow and to spend.

The recovery in the United Kingdom during 1982 would have been stronger if the rest of the world economy had been in better shape. The United Kingdom recession had come earlier than most, and it was at the recovery stage that it felt the impact of recession abroad. Output for the total of OECD countries was unchanged in 1982, with the United States down by 2½ per cent, Germany down by 1 per cent and Canada down by more than 3 per cent. The United Kingdom with growth of nearly 2 per cent year-on-year was one of the better performing economies. Nevertheless, exports from this country were badly hit and the manufacturing sector in particular remained depressed.

The recovery which did take place was initiated by domestic demand, benefiting the construction industry rather than manufacturing, and especially benefiting private sector services. It was helped along by an upturn in private housing, probably caused by relatively cheap and abundant mortgage finance. The major source of demand was consumer spending, where as we have seen both increasing wealth and easier credit may have helped. Another reason for the fall in the savings ratio may have been the lower rate of inflation. Real wage growth also benefited from unexpectedly low prices; firms were passing on to their customers some of the improvement in industrial productivity which was already attracting favourable comment.

As might be expected when productivity growth leads output growth, employment for some time continued to fall. It was not until 1983 that the first quarterly rise in total employment since the recession was recorded. The rise in employment when it did come was concentrated in services and consisted, more than proportionately, of part-time jobs. This did relatively little to improve the outlook for unemployment. Although vacancies were now well up from their recessionary minimum, unemployment was still climbing and, as the election approached, this was the main blot on the government's economic record.

In the second paragraph of the MTFS in March 1982, after declaring the government's aim for inflation, the Chancellor went on to spell out the lesson that the growth of the real economy would depend on the behaviour of labour costs. 'In particular, pay increases which are excessive relative to productivity would put the recovery in jeopardy and intensify unemployment.' This could mean two things: excessive pay increases would cause price inflation and require the authorities to restrict demand; alternatively, excessive real pay increases would make labour too expensive to employ. In fact, it probably meant both. For one reason or another the government was interested in pay again, although it had no intention of reverting to the old framework of voluntary or statutory incomes policies.

It did, however, have to negotiate or set pay in the public sector and here its motives were rather different. It clearly wanted to set some kind of example to the private sector, showing that it heeded its own message about the need for pay moderation. But it had the additional aim of reducing public sector pay relative to the private sector. It wanted to reverse the movement in the opposite direction that took place just before and after the election of 1979. It wanted to save taxpayers money and it wanted to signal to the labour market that the main growth of employment opportunities was now to be found outside the public sector. The pay target for the public sector announced in October 1982 was just 3½ per cent, below the rate of inflation and well below the rate of settlements in the private sector.

Pay restraint was not so evident in the private sector, where the government could only rely on exhortation. The whole economy earnings index had risen between July 1981 and July 1982 by nearly 11 per cent. With inflation over that period at 8.7 per cent, real earnings were up by over 2 percentage points. The margin of pay over prices during the next twelve months was even more substantial. Between July 1982 and 1983 earnings rose 7.7 per cent and prices only 4.2 per cent, implying a real increase in earnings of about 3½ per cent. This was not quite the moderation which the government had hoped to encourage. Neither was it what most economists would have predicted, given the very high level of unemployment.

The fall in the rate of inflation at this period was *not* primarily the product of wage moderation. It did not come about, as many economists would have expected, in the main through the working of the labour market. On the contrary, the rate of inflation was typically lower in the event than employers and employees expected when settlements were made. The relatively low level of demand was subduing inflation in other ways, by forcing rationalisations of production that raised productivity for example, and by cutting the prices of raw materials.

This last development should be seen as part of a worldwide phenomenon. Between 1981 and 1983 inflation in Britain fell from about 12 per cent to about 4½ per cent. Over the same period in the United States inflation fell from 10½ per cent to little more than 3 per cent. One factor common to both was the movement of world commodity prices which fell significantly (in terms of the dollar or of the SDR) in both 1981 and 1982. With some delay these reductions helped the slowdown of world inflation.

The improvement in productivity was more marked in Britain than elsewhere. It began as a shake-out of labour during the recession, but continued during the upturn. It was most marked in the manufacturing sector, but was widespread throughout the private sector. It extended even, one supposes, to the public sector, where it is not measured in the statistics. It resulted in part from rationalisation and the closure of uneconomic plant, correcting longstanding inefficiencies and imitating the methods of more productive economies overseas. It benefited the whole of the economy in a variety of ways, leading to higher wages for those who kept their jobs, to lower prices for all and ultimately – although this is to anticipate later developments – to a relatively long period of sustained economic growth. In the meantime, however, it kept unemployment high.

Opposition to the government's economic policies concentrated on the issue of jobs. The Shadow Chancellor, Peter Shore, blamed the government's monetary policy for allowing the exchange rate to rise far out of line with domestic costs, making it impossible for industry to compete. This was the explanation of the recession and of the rise in unemployment. His proposed cure involved both fiscal expansion and a much lower exchange rate. It did not prove an easy argument to present, and it was not well received.

It is possible that the foreign exchange markets were upset by public discussion of the need for a large depreciation of sterling. Perhaps they were just made uneasy by the approach of a general election, which could well lead to a change of government. For whatever reason, sterling fell quite sharply at the end of 1982 and in the early months of 1983. This was one of the more abrupt slides in the long-drawn-out descent of sterling from the heights scaled in 1981. Between the fourth quarter of 1982 and the first of 1983 the sterling exchange rate index fell by 10 per cent; but half of that fall was quickly recouped in the second quarter of the year.

As sterling weakened, the fall in interest rates came to an end. The London clearing banks' base rate, having fallen to 9 per cent at the beginning of November 1982, was raised to 10 or 10½ per cent at the end of the month, and to 11 per cent in January 1983. This was not a very sharp tightening of policy in response to the fall in the exchange rate. Perhaps the authorities felt that some depreciation was desirable, or at least unavoidable. Perhaps they did not want to do too much to delay the upturn in the economy. Relative to the overall strategic aim of subduing inflation, it was a tactical retreat, but a retreat conducted in good order. If it contributed to the rise in inflation later in 1983, it did so to a quite modest extent – and by then the election was over.

By the early summer of 1983 it was evident that output growth was accelerating. A year earlier the Treasury forecast had shown growth of 2 per cent between the first halves of 1982 and 1983, and other forecasters had been a good deal more gloomy. The outturn for that period is now put at $2\frac{3}{4}$ per cent.

In his 1983 budget, the Chancellor did a little to stimulate demand, or to win favour with the electorate. He again cut taxes, on much the same scale as in the previous year. Compared with an indexed base the reductions were estimated at £1.7 billion in 1983–4 and £2.2 billion in a full year. Thus, taking these next two budgets together, the fiscal contraction of 1981 had been substantially reversed. This is especially true if one takes account of the growth of public spending above the Chancellor's intentions over this period, and the relatively low impact on demand of some of the taxes raised when fiscal policy was tightened.

It remained to restate the MTFS, and on this occasion nothing much was said that was new. The aim was still to reduce inflation, an aim which was from now on to prove very elusive. Indeed the tendency for several years thereafter was for inflation to rise slightly. Interest rates were also supposed to come down further, but that also proved a vain hope for many years to come.

For the first time, however, the growth of the monetary aggregates did fall within the target range set a year earlier. It looked as if monetary control had been re-established. The targets for 1983–4 and 1984–5 could be left unchanged. Despite this happy result, there was no move back to hard-line monetarism. The eclectic approach to the setting of interest rates was restated, with the exchange rate and a host of other variables being recognised as useful indicators of financial conditions.

In 1983, unlike the earlier election years of 1974 and 1979, the government had reason to be moderately pleased with the way the economy was developing. The 'new beginning' of 1979 had not gone at all as they had intended and the intial results seemed catastrophic, but by the time of the next election things were looking up and they had important improvements for which they could take credit. Unemployment, admittedly, was over 3 million and still rising. But the political cost of high unemployment was not nearly as great as had been expected. There had not been much rioting in the streets. In some parts of the country at least, the government was increasingly popular. There was popular sympathy for the unemployed, no doubt, but not enough to require a change of strategy, to one which gave exclusive attention to their plight. In any case the government and their supporters believed that persistence with the same strategy would soon halt the rise in unemployment. For the time being at least that was probably the limit of their ambitions.

5

CONSERVATIVE GOVERNMENT CONTINUED
1983–7

A NEW CAST, BUT THE SAME SCRIPT,
JUNE 1983 – JANUARY 1985

Having won the general election of 9 June with a majority of 144 seats, the Prime Minister, Margaret Thatcher, reallocated the top economic positions in the Cabinet. Sir Geoffrey Howe was transferred from the Treasury to the Foreign Office, to be replaced by Nigel Lawson. The result was a change of style and presentation of economic policy, rather than its substance. The new Chancellor was more self-confident, although less diplomatic, than his predecessor and he was generally believed to have a wider knowledge of economics and the concerns of professional economists. He already had experience as a Treasury minister and had personally played a large part in the design of monetary policy after the Conservative election victory in 1979. His views on the way in which economic policy should be conducted seem to have been very close to those of his predecessor. The continuity of policy between the first and second Thatcher governments owes more to this coincidence of approach than to the dominance of macroeconomic policy by the Prime Minister herself. Mrs Thatcher was not at her best in discussions of fiscal or monetary policy, and lost some of the arguments within government.

Just before the election in April, Sir Douglas Wass, Permanent Secretary to the Treasury, retired, having played an unenviable role since 1979 as the loyal servant out of sympathy with his masters' enthusiasms. He was replaced by Peter Middleton, jumping a rank in the civil service hierarchy. As a Deputy Secretary, he had taken a leading part in economic policymaking for some years, so here too the change of personnel at the top did not result in a change of course.

Just after the election, in July, Gordon Richardson retired as Governor of the Bank of England, to be replaced by Robin Leigh-Pemberton, Chairman of the National Westminster Bank. This third change served also to confirm the direction which policy had taken since 1979, rather than to divert it. Relations between the Treasury and the Bank were becoming easier, mainly because ministers had retreated from the radical monetarist positions adopted in 1979. For a few years after 1979 there had been in Britain the unusual situation of a central bank giving *less* weight to reducing inflation than did the ministers responsible for economic policy, and *more* to reducing unemployment. After 1983, a more conventional relationship was reestablished.

From the late 1960s until 1983 the British economy had been subjected to a wide variety of different treatments, none very successful. The period after 1983 was one of respite, so far as macroeconomic policymaking was concerned. Nigel Lawson frequently took credit for this in his speeches, and justifiably so. He was able to keep to broadly the same policies year after year, because the course that the economy was following was broadly acceptable to most commentators, and because opposition was relatively weak and divided. Attention tended to shift, as the government hoped it would, to structural reform, to microeconomic policies rather than macroeconomic.

The historian of macroeconomic policy during this period might be content to chronicle in detail the small-scale variations year-by-year in growth rates, inflation rates and the wording of budget statements. But it would seem narrow-minded to omit all reference to the wide-ranging reforms made between 1983 and 1987 in British economic and social affairs. They may not have been macroeconomic policy measures in the sense defined in the introduction, but they doubtless had macroeconomic effects.

One such measure was the Trade Union Bill published in October 1983. Its central theme was the expansion of union democracy: it gave members the right to elect their leaders directly, to vote on industrial action and to vote for or against their union's political funds. The motive for these changes was to break the power of union leaders, who were suspected of acting, for political reasons, in a way that conflicted with their members' interests and wishes. The development of British industry had been held back in the past, it was believed, by a wilful lack of cooperation between union leaders and management. Whether these views were justified is obviously a matter of controversy which cannot be settled here. It is worth remarking, however, that trade union members may on occasion be more militant than their leadership. Certainly the requirement for a ballot before a strike has on occasion strengthened the resolve of the union side in a dispute, rather than weakened it. The power of trade unions was weakening in the 1980s, but it is not clear to what extent this was the result of legislation.

The most impressive demonstration of union weakness and lack of solidarity was the failure of the miners' strike of 1984. There was, in this case, no doubt of the political hostility with which Arthur Scargill and the National Union of Miners (NUM) leadership faced the government of Margaret Thatcher. The main issue in the dispute was the speed with which coal production was to be reduced and old pits closed. The market philosophy followed by government, with wide public support, saw no reason to make the coal industry a special case. As the months went by, and the bitterness increased, the wish to humiliate the other side also became important to government as well as union leaders.

The miners lost the struggle chiefly because coal stocks were high, making them dependent on support from other workers, on the railways, at the docks or in steelworks – support which was not forthcoming on a sufficient scale. The mining communities themselves were not unanimously behind the strike and a breakaway union was formed to oppose the NUM leadership. Had the miners been united under a more moderate leadership with limited objectives and better tactical judgement the outcome might have been different. As it was, the result was heralded as another personal victory for the Prime Minister, reinforcing her intransigent style of government. It also reinforced the decline in public support for trade unions as such, particularly unions who sought to protect jobs rather than to raise pay.

The miners' strike had the incidental effect of distorting quite badly many economic indicators for the year 1984. The loss of coal output amounted to about 1 per cent of GDP. The effect on other industries was small and temporary, and the total effect on GDP was estimated at 1¼ per cent. Much of the lost output of coal was made good by importing oil (or exporting less from the North Sea). The resulting cost to the balance of payments was estimated at about £2 billion in the year 1984. The cost to the public sector borrowing requirement was probably about the same size. Account must be taken of these distortions in judging the record of economic growth at this time. The strike had the effect of making the path of output year by year smoother than it otherwise would have been. Thus the output estimate of GDP shows a rise of 2.8 per cent in 1984 and 3.5 per cent in 1985. Corrected for the strike, these figures would have been 4 per cent and 2.3 per cent.

The corrected figures suggest a mild cyclical peak in output relative to trend in the latter part of 1984. This is consistent with the pattern shown by several of the cyclical indicators used by the CSO. The CBI survey questions relating to stockbuilding and capacity utilisation can be interpreted in that sense, as well as some of the lagging indicators such as employment and investment in manufacturing industry. If there was a cyclical peak in 1984 it would fit well with the 4–6 year cyclical chronology evident over the preceding generation or more. But it would be a far weaker peak than its predecessors in 1973 and 1979, little more than a slight aberration from a trend in the growth of the economy which had apparently accelerated significantly in the 1980s as compared with the 1970s.

The 1984 budget was neutral in the short run, but its full-year effect was to cut taxation by £1.7 billion (compared with an indexed base). The first year effect was small because the budget included a proposal to accelerate the payment of VAT on imported goods, novelties of this kind being typical of the Lawson budgets. The main cost of this budget came from the over-indexation of income tax allowances and thresholds. The PSBR, which had risen slightly in 1983–4, was expected to fall back quite significantly in 1984–5.

The presentation of the medium-term financial strategy which accompanied the 1984 budget did not differ greatly from its predecessors. Pride of place amongst the government's objectives was still given to the reduction of inflation. The ultimate objective was stable prices but the actual projections showed the growth of the GDP deflator declining almost imperceptibly from 5½ per cent in 1983–4 to 3 per cent five years later.

Credit could be taken for the fact that £M3 was within the target range set a year earlier, but there was now some anxiety that the narrow aggregate, M1, was misbehaving. The growing practice of paying interest on sight deposits was making them more attractive. The authorities took a warning from the problems experienced in America with M1 as a target aggregate. They substitute M0, sometimes called the monetary base. This aggregate, which consisted mainly of notes and coin circulating with the public, had the unique advantage of being distorted downward rather than upward in terms of its annual rate of growth. The growing popularity of credit cards, and the practice of paying staff by cheque rather than in cash, ensured that M0 grew slowest of all the aggregates ever discussed. It was, for quite different reasons, rather a favourite of the academic monetarists. This combination proved irresistible, and it appeared on the MTFS menu each year after 1984.

The importance of the 1984 budget lies not in any adjustments made to the overall stance of fiscal and monetary policy, but in the reform of corporate taxation. Stock relief was abolished. It had been introduced when the inflation rate was high to excuse companies from paying tax on the stock appreciation element in their profits. By 1984 the rate of inflation had fallen to the point where the taxation of stock appreciation no longer seemed likely to threaten the solvency or liquidity of many companies. Whatever the justification for seeking to exempt stock appreciation from tax it had proved impossible to devise a fair and efficient way of doing so. In the years following the abolition of stock relief the ratio of stocks to output in British industry tended to fall, despite the recovery of output. This may be attributable in part to the change of tax treatment, but better financial or production management techniques, as well as high real interest rates, may have been important too.

The 1984 reforms also included the phasing out of investment allowances. On plant and machinery these had been as high as 75 per cent, 50 per cent on industrial buildings, they were reduced to zero over a two-year period. As a consequence it was possible to reduce the main rate of corporation tax from 50 per cent to 35 per cent. These changes undoubtedly made a difference to the timing of industrial investment spending. To what extent they influenced investment in the longer run is uncertain. The volume of private sector investment, excluding housing, rose by 14½ per cent in 1984 and by 13½ per cent in 1985, but actually fell in 1986.

Simultaneously with the budget the Treasury published a Green Paper with the title 'The next ten years: public expenditure and taxation into the

1990s'. It had been the aim since 1979 to reduce public spending and taxation in real terms, that is after adjusting for inflation of the general price level. In the event this aim had not been achieved. The first chart in the Green Paper showed general government expenditure in real terms rising almost continuously, and well above the previous peak under the Labour government. The burden of the Green Paper was that this trend should be halted. In the past, it maintained, total real spending had been carried on upwards by political or economic pressures operating on each particular spending programme; taxation or borrowing had been treated as the residual. The Treasury now sought to reverse this procedure. The first question should be what the nation could afford to spend in the public sector in total; then that total should be allocated across programmes according to their relative priority.

The Green Paper did not contain much information about spending plans or priorities for the next ten years. It was indeed a disappointingly slim document from that point of view: defence, for example, was covered in just six lines of text. The discussion of taxation was also quite brief, turning mainly on the prospects for the development of the North Sea. Two possibilities were considered for the long-term growth rate of GDP, 1½ per cent and 2 per cent a year. The implication was that public spending must be kept under strict control if a crisis was to be avoided. In the years immediately following, GDP growth accelerated well beyond expectation, and the growth of revenue responded more than in proportion. The Green Paper soon seemed excessively pessimistic, and the Treasury found it impossible to resist an expansion of public spending which the nation was well able to afford.

This, however, is to run ahead of events. In 1984 public sector borrowing still presented a problem. That problem was being reduced, or perhaps just disguised, by an increase in the rate at which public sector assets were being sold. Privatisation, or denationalisation, was a priority of Conservative governments for broader political and economic reasons. Its consequences for public sector borrowing were a useful side effect, rather than its main purpose. This contribution rose sharply in 1984–5. The first significant receipts of privatisation proceeds had been in 1981–2 when they amounted to nearly £½ billion from the sale of miscellaneous small blocks of shares. A similar total was achieved in 1982–3 mainly from the sale of shares in Britoil. Next year the total passed £1 billion as a large block of BP shares changed hands. In November 1984 British Telecommunications made the largest-ever share issue. So popular was it that the shares were over-subscribed four times. The market for such issues remained very good until the stock market setback in the latter part of 1987.

Despite the predominance of encouraging economic news during 1984, the exchange rate was persistently weak. The effective exchange rate index was down by nearly 9 per cent between the fourth quarters of 1983 and 1984. The fall against the dollar, which was still the focus of most news coverage, was even more marked. By the end of the year the rate was below $1.2 and the possibility of parity with the dollar was being discussed . This was a sobering prospect, given that the rate had been $2 as recently as 1981.

It is not easy to suggest any logical explanation for the pattern of exchange rate movements in 1984. The strength of the dollar at this time is often quoted as an example of the irrationality of markets, and it was soon to be reversed. The weakness of sterling is not much easier to justify. It is true that the balance of payments on current account was in deficit for part of the year, but this was easily explained as a temporary consequence of the miners' strike. After correcting for the strike there was little deterioration in the underlying balance that year. For want of a better explanation commentators at the time associated the weakness of sterling with doubts about the future of oil prices. As yet the prospect of a fall was rather remote, but it is possible that markets at the time treated sterling as a petro-currency before all else.

Interest rates in the latter half of 1984 were actually falling, with United Kingdom rates moving quite closely in line with those on eurodollar deposits. This suggests that the monetary authorities at that stage were prepared to see a depreciation of sterling and did not interpret it as a sign of financial laxity. They were to wake up with a jolt in the New Year.

EMPLOYMENT – THE CHALLENGE TO THE NATION,
JANUARY 1985 – JANUARY 1986

When interest rates fall in Britain they usually fall slowly, often inching their way down a half-percentage-point at a time; when they rise they more often rise abruptly by a percentage point or two in one go. A good example of this asymmetry is to be found in 1985. When the year opened the short-term lending rates of London clearing banks were 9½ or 9¾ per cent, having fallen in almost imperceptible stages from 12 per cent the preceding July. But the rise in January 1985 was on a quite different time-scale. They were up to 10½ per cent on the 11th of the month, 12 per cent on the 14th and 14 per cent on the 28th, a rise of over 4 percentage points within three weeks. They then spent the whole of the next six months drifting gradually down to 11½ per cent where they stayed until the end of the year.

If monetary policy had become 'permissive' during 1984 it changed significantly in the following year, prompted it seems by concern at the level of the exchange rate urgently expressed by the Prime Minister herself. The exchange rate promptly recovered by more than 10 per cent in effective rate terms, making good in six months the loss of the previous twelve. Against the dollar the change was greater, since that currency at last weakened from March 1985 onwards. The nightmare of dollar–pound parity was soon forgotten.

The 1985 budget was not a very memorable one. There were further modest cuts in income tax, partly offset by increases in indirect taxation. The effect on the budget balance, compared with an indexed base, was under £1 billion in the first year, a little more in a full year. The description of monetary policy and the medium-term financial strategy was, except to the most expert readers, unchanged. The key sentence, which read, 'significant changes in the exchange rate are also important', did not take the debate over the conduct of monetary policy much further forward. The overshooting of the PSBR forecasts in the previous financial year was adequately explained by the effects of the miners' strike. The PSBR forecast for 1985–6 showed a reduction of £3½ billion, on one interpretation a considerable tightening of the fiscal stance.

1985 as a whole was a year of relatively slow growth in GDP, if an adjustment is made for the effect of the miners' strike in the preceding year. Between the second quarters of 1985 and 1986 manufacturing output fell: the construction industry also paused in its recovery for about twelve months; it was left to services to keep the overall growth rate edging up. Exports of goods and services peaked in the second quarter of the year and did not regain that level until well into 1986; but this was largely offset in its effect on GDP by a slow growth in imports as well. Public spending was being cut back and investment, after the 'hump' of expenditure produced by the 1984 budget, was also subdued.

During this hesitant period total employment continued to edge up, but very slowly, with employment in manufacturing still falling. Unemployment (seasonally adjusted and excluding school-leavers) was still rising. Following the increase in interest rates and the exchange rate in 1985 the outlook was for growth to slow down further and the rise in unemployment to speed up again.

Criticism of the government's policies, and especially their effects on unemployment, was again becoming vocal. A cross-party group called the Charter for Jobs was set up to campaign to restore the priority once given by policymakers to the objective of full employment. It attracted support, as one might expect, from all the opposition parties and from the trade unions, but it also found favour with some businessmen and Tory backbenchers. It was against this background that the Department of Employment published its White Paper, 'Employment – the Challenge to the Nation', in March 1985.

It is perhaps significant that the paper was not presented by the Treasury. Employment was viewed as a microeconomic problem, not a macroeconomic one. 'Boosting demand without the necessary improvements to the performance of the economy would only generate higher inflation.' 'Government cannot do what the nation will not. It cannot on its own create jobs.' The watchword was 'flexibility', meaning restraint on pay, fewer strikes and less disruption, but also earlier retirement and job-sharing. There was an annex listing everything that the government had done since 1979, directly or indirectly, to promote employment. Some of the measures quoted had little obvious connection with the unemployment problem, like the derugulation of buses and taxis or the sale of publicly-owned shares in private companies. Others were much more directly relevant, especially the employment and training measures operated by the Department of Employment itself.

Special employment measures dated back to the 1970s, but as unemployment had risen their importance had grown. In 1984–5 they cost over £2 billion and 'assisted' some 700,000 people. Their effect on unemployment may not have been as great as that, but no doubt it was significant. (More detailed discussion is reserved for Part 5 below.)

The largest of the training programmes was the Youth Training Scheme (YTS) which started in 1983 mainly as a response to rising youth unemployment, but also in the hope of avoiding skill shortages as the economy recovered. It was initially a one-year scheme designed to make good some of the failures of secondary education and provide a basis on which vocational training could be built. In his budget speech in 1985 the Chancellor announced its extension to a two-year course, with a view to giving more advanced and job-related training in the second year. Of the other schemes detailed in the White Paper, one of the most important was the Community Programme, which provided part-time work for a year for the long-term unemployed, often in the public sector. The Enterprise Allowance Scheme was an attempt to set the unemployed up as independent business proprietors, a role which, unfortunately, relatively few of them were well-fitted to play.

The White Paper made no mention of the effects on unemployment of the social security system and its administration, which was the responsibility of the DHSS, not the Department of Employment. There was probably some reluctance to admit that the priority given to reducing the numbers of civil servants administering the benefit system might have made it easier for claimants on the margins of eligibility to join the ranks of the unemployed.

The approach to the unemployment problem typified by the 1985 White Paper was not the one which eventually brought about the long-awaited improvement. Repeated exhortation never achieved the hoped-for moderation in the growth of real wages and the multiplication of special employment schemes led to increasing problems of administration. A downturn in unemployment came only when economic growth accelerated and, at the same time, the administration of the benefit system was made considerably tougher in 1986.

OPTIMISM REBORN,
JANUARY 1986 – MAY 1987

In January 1986, almost unnoticed in this country, the Single European Act came into effect. This committed Britain and European countries to an ambitious programme of the elimination of barriers to trade by 1992. It also committed all members of the EEC to progress towards economic and monetary union. At the time this revolutionary proposal caused hardly a stir. It was only in 1989 when the Delors Report set out practical proposals to implement this commitment that the British took the idea at all seriously. As an issue it does not really belong in this book at all.

The narrative of economic events from the early 1970s to the mid-1980s in Britain has been, in the main, a story of problems, difficulties, setbacks and policy failures. It is a relief, therefore, to be able to end this part of the study by describing a year or two when the economy seemed to be performing really well. The recovery in output, which appeared at one time to be faltering, instead gathered pace; unemployment at last turned down and fell very rapidly; inflation remained low. For once the British economy was admired and applauded by commentators worldwide. Even at home there was more than a hint of euphoria in the air. It did not last; but let us at least remember that it was good at the time!

When the world price of oil halved between the first and second quarters of 1986 the initial reaction was that Britain, unlike other advanced industrial countries, could expect little net gain. The balance of payments surplus would be reduced and the public sector would have to borrow more. The direct and favourable effect on the price level would be offset by a downward tendency of the exchange rate. On balance, however, this third oil price shock probably contributed to the relatively good performance of the economy over the following year. By cutting the costs of industry, for example, it raised profits and by increasing the real value of wages it contributed to the buoyancy of consumption.

The exchange rate certainly weakened in the early months of the year, falling 6 per cent in effective rate terms between December and February. This must indeed be seen as part of the market's reaction to the fall in the oil price, although it is possible that some of the weakness in oil prices had already been discounted, and such expectations, 'rational' in the event, had contributed to the weakness of sterling as much as a year earlier. For whatever reason, sterling showed little further movement until the Autumn of 1986, when it went through another period of weakness.

The response of interest rates to the fall in sterling at the beginning of 1986 was similar in character to the response twelve months earlier, but on a lesser scale. Short-term rates were immediately raised by about a percentage point in January, but thereafter they soon fell back to under 10 per cent. The authorities may have concluded that such a sharp fall in oil prices made exchange depreciation inevitable, or even desirable. The pressure on them to prop up the pound was also less this time in that the dollar rate was not nearly as low as it had been in January 1985.

By 1986 the link between interest rates and the monetary aggregates was clearly broken. As earlier sections of this narrative have shown, the connection had become tenuous even in the early 1980s. The rather slower growth of £M3 in 1983 and 1984 allowed some ambiguity to remain. After

that, however, the obstinate aggregate accelerated again; at the time of the
1986 budget the growth over the preceding twelve months was about 15
per cent, compared with a target range of 5–9 per cent. The slower growth
of Mo provided a sufficient excuse for ignoring the aberration of £M3
when setting interest rates. That aberration did nevertheless point to a new
development which may have been of more real importance than the rate
of increase in £M3 as such. The bulge was caused by an increase in bank
lending to persons, an increase which contributed greatly to the gathering
speed of the growth in domestic demand.

As the public sector's deficit became smaller and the banks lent more to
the private sector, the sale of public sector debt outside the banking
system was becoming less convenient as a way of influencing the size of
the banks' balance sheets as a whole. The practice of 'over-funding' – that
is of selling more than enough public sector debt to cover the deficit
outside the banking system – might have provided a means of controlling
the wider monetary aggregates. It required the Bank of England to
purchase a large and increasing stock of commercial bills, which proved
something of an embarrassment to them. The 1986 Budget Statement
confirmed an announcement made in the preceding October, that the
practice of overfunding had been abandoned. The Budget Statement
thus gave up any pretence that the broad monetary aggregates, or wider
liquidity, or bank lending could be controlled. Instead attention was
directed to the growth rate of money GDP and to the exchange rate.
Nevertheless, for the sake of form, a target range was still set for £M3 (as
well as for Mo).

The main tax change in this budget was a cut of 1p in the basic rate of
income tax, with a cost of about £1 billion to the exchequer. It had long
been the ambition of Conservative Chancellors to reduce marginal as well
as average tax rates on incomes at all levels. The motive was, no doubt,
partly political, but it was also widely believed that marginal taxation had a
powerful effect on the incentive to work, or to work harder, even if
empirical support for these propositions was hard to find. Until 1986
priority had been given to raising the threshold at which income tax was
paid, partly so as to remove the bulk of households from the poverty trap
caused by the interaction of taxes with the withdrawal of means-tested
benefits. After 1986 the main tax concessions took the form of cuts in
marginal rates higher up the income distribution.

The months following the 1986 budget were the low point for the
recorded rate of inflation. The twelve-month rise in the retail prices index
was below 2½ per cent in July and August. The prices of materials and fuel
purchased by manufacturing fell by about 15 per cent between the peak at
the beginning of 1985 and the trough in the third quarter of 1986. Over
the same period the unit value index for all imports fell by nearly 10 per
cent. It is probably fair to say of this period that Britain imported more
price stability than was produced at home. Wages certainly continued to

increase rapidly, although that was matched by a very healthy rate of increase in output per head.

Analysis of the better performance of the economy from the mid-1980s and the reasons for it must be deferred until Part 5 of this study. Nevertheless no account of the events of this period can pass over the improvement in complete silence. The continued rise in productivity is most worthy of note. The figures quarter-by quarter, or even year-by-year, are erratic and probably inaccurate, but the general trend is more important. Output per hour in manufacturing industry grew on average by 5 per cent a year from 1982 to 1987. This compares well with the growth rate of the 1960s and is much faster than the rather miserable performance from 1973 to 1979. Productivity in other sectors of the economy is more difficult to measure, but the acceleration may have been more general.

With higher productivity and cheaper inputs came higher profits. The share of profits in the value of manufactured output (both excluding stock appreciation) had fallen to 19 per cent in 1981. It recovered to 25 per cent by 1984, already well above its pre-recession level, and went on to rise to 27 per cent in 1985 and 29 per cent in 1986. It is little wonder that businessmen were feeling optimistic again, or that the stock market was booming.

Another sign of improvement was the performance of British exports. Their share in the volume of world exports of manufactures was the same in 1987 as in 1980. This contrasts with a clear downward trend in that share for the rest of the postwar period. Movements in export volumes from year to year seem to follow changes in relative price or cost competitiveness, and the improved productivity growth rate must have influenced volume shares by this route. What is less easy to know is what part other, non-price improvements, such as reliability, continuity of production or marketing may have played. The performance of British manufacturers in the home market was less remarkable and imports of manufactured goods continued to rise very fast.

Government spokesmen naturally claimed that the better economic performance was the result of their policies. They also claimed that their policies had been consistent ever since 1979, which was much harder to accept. A case could be made out that, on the contrary, the policies were now successful precisely because they *had* been changed.

Not all the comment on the British economy in 1986 was optimistic. One worry was that the long recovery of output would soon run into constraints on physical capacity. The CBI surveys showed that much industrial plant and machinery had been scrapped during the recession. The relatively low level of fixed investment thereafter suggested that bottlenecks and over-heating could bring expansion to a premature halt.

Another worry was the balance of payments. The fall in the world price of oil was one obvious new factor that would reduce the current account surplus. After 1986 the production of oil in the North Sea was expected to decline gradually. Despite the good record of exports of manufactures, the non-oil trade balance also showed a persistent tendency towards wider deficits. Admittedly the invisible balance was in excellent shape, but its trend was less clear and its measurement was very uncertain. In August 1986 the National Institute forecast that the current account in the following year would be in deficit to the extent of over £5 billions.

For the moment these gloomy predictions proved mistaken, or exaggerated. Growth accelerated sharply in 1987 without running into bottlenecks; exports did exceptionally well. The balance of payments problem was delayed until after the period covered by this study, and after the 1987 general election. The best news of all in 1986 was the downturn in unemployment. The seasonally adjusted total peaked in July at just over 3.2 millions or 11½ per cent of the working population. Perception of the figures was clouded by a number of confusing, and probably unnecessary, changes, made in their calculation and presentation. But once the turning point was passed the fact of a marked fall was not in doubt. By the 1987 election the total had almost, but not quite, passed below the milestone of 3 millions, and the rate of fall was still accelerating.

This abrupt change took most observers, including those in government, by surprise. Its interpretation is still uncertain. The change in the employment trend is far less marked. The Labour Force Survey suggests that the number of people describing themselves as unemployed did not fall nearly as fast as the official figures for the numbers claiming benefits. It may therefore be significant that the downturn in the number of claimants roughly coincided with several new schemes designed to remove from the figures some borderline cases like the chronically sick and the early retired. Special counselling initiatives were taken about this time to interview the long-term unemployed and where possible enrol them on training courses or other programmes. The test of availability for work was also being applied more strictly from this time to those who claimed benefit. The quantitative importance of all these administrative changes was, unfortunately, not documented at the time.

By the end of 1986 what had been a well-sustained recovery was turning into a boom. The main impetus behind the growth of consumer spending had been higher earnings based on higher output per head; it was now reinforced by a fall in the savings ratio and by the extension of bank and building society credit to the personal sector. Of the many factors which may have contributed to the boom two are worth particular mention: the equity market and the housing market.

The rise in share prices was not a new phenomenon. Year-on-year the *Financial Times* ordinary share index rose 23 per cent in 1984 and another 18 per cent in the following year. A rather faster rise occurred in 1986, 28 per cent year on year, with a further acceleration in 1987 up to the date of the election. Much of this increase could well be justified by the buoyancy of profits and the prospects for their further growth in the future. But the sudden correction to prices in the latter half of 1987 suggests that the markets may have allowed euphoria to carry prices rather too high. The stock price index at the end of the year was little changed from twelve months earlier.

The increased activity of the equity market, the publicity surrounding the 'Big Bang' when the stock exchange went electronic in October 1986, and the wide public interest in privatisation stocks all contributed to a subtle change in the way economic policymaking and the performance of the economy were discussed in the mid-1980s. Increasingly economic commentary became concerned to inform the investing public, rather than to contribute to a policy debate. Interest rates and exchange rates remained very important, but equity prices became almost as much so. More and more of the serious analysis of trends first appeared in brokers' circulars. Young macroeconomists by the dozen left more traditional employment to seek, and find, their fortunes in the City. Businessmen were more aware than hitherto of the market judgement of their business prospects. The threat of takeover was a more potent spur than it had been for many years to management efficiency and cost-saving.

These developments were no doubt of pervasive influence on growth of the economy. So far as consumer spending is concerned the rise of house prices was probably more important than the increased value of equities. Households held far more wealth in the form of housing than any other, and were better informed of its market value. The average price of new houses began rising strongly in 1983 and accelerated in 1986 and 1987, on a profile rather similar to that of the equity market although not at quite so rapid a pace. The total rise from 1982 to 1987 was about 80 per cent or 12 per cent a year. It was much faster than this in the south-east, much slower in regions where employment prospects were poor.

Mortgage loans, by banks and building societies, rose rapidly in response to higher house prices and helped to sustain them. Households were able, by extending their mortgage commitments, to borrow funds that were available to finance a higher level of consumption. For first-time buyers, 100 per cent mortgages became the norm, and it became common practice to increase the size of an existing mortgage borrowing as the value of a house rose.

In such prosperous conditions it was difficult for the opposition parties to launch an effective attack on the government's economic policies as the 1987 election approached. In 1983 the Labour Party had campaigned on the need for reflation, especially higher public spending. This time the economy was growing fast, with some danger of growing *too* fast. Labour policies were again addressed to reducing unemployment, but the emphasis was now on more special measures, changes in the structure of taxation, and spending increases concentrated in particular areas where the employment effect was high and the import content of spending was low. The appeal of this approach was undermined every month by the announce-

ment of yet another fall in unemployment achieved under the policies of
the existing government.

Nigel Lawson's reputation amongst Conservative supporters rose as the
economic news became better and better. He was widely thought to have
engineered, in some very subtle way, a pre-election boom without paying
any costs in terms of inflation or exchange rate crisis. This was probably to
do him more than justice, or (one should rather say) less. Taken at their
face value his principles did not allow him to manage demand, skilfully or
otherwise. It was his good luck that the economy was booming in 1987.

There may have been an element of political calculation in the concessions made by the cabinet as a whole on public spending in the 1987 White
Paper. Nevertheless a good economic case could be made for allowing
public services like health and education a share in the general improvement of living standards. It was also possible, without a hint of fiscal
irresponsibility, to cut the basic rate of income tax by a further 2p in the
pound in the 1987 budget proposals. There was no reversal of fiscal policy
after the election.

A cynic would claim that monetary policy was more relaxed in the latter
part of 1986 and in early 1987 than a totally apolitical judgement would
have recommended. The blind-eye turned to the expansion of credit no
doubt helped to keep the consumer boom going. If the control of domestic
demand, and the final conquest of inflation, really had been the goal of
monetary policy, then perhaps a higher level of interest rates would have
been appropriate. As it was, the authorities were now more concerned with
the exchange rate than with any domestic monetary indicator. This attitude
was to be maintained for most of the next twelve months.

As the election approached, and a Conservative victory looked more
certain, sterling strengthened in the foreign exchange markets. From a low
point in October 1986 it recovered 8 per cent on the effective exchange
rate index by May of the following year. It seems that, by this time, the
Chancellor was fully converted to the cause of exchange rate stability,
although the Prime Minister remained opposed to full membership for
Britain in the European Monetary System. The pound was held for some
months, by market intervention as well as interest rate changes, in a narrow
band around a fixed parity with the Deutschmark. This was never officially
stated as government policy, but the Chancellor gave a broad hint of the
approach in April when he addressed a meeting of the National Economic
Development Council. About the same time, he finally laid an old ghost to
rest by announcing that the government no longer had any formal target at
all for £M3, or any other broad measure of the money supply.

THE SEQUEL

Every year that passes changes the interpretation of the years that have
gone before. Three years after the election of May 1987, looking back on

the optimism reborn about that time, one can only say it was greatly exaggerated.

The boom, which had served in its early stage to restore company profits and to halt the long rise in unemployment, got out of hand. Consumer spending continued to rise strongly, helped along by further tax cuts. Fixed investment reinforced the growth of demand. Both continued to rise strongly despite the stock market crash of October 1987, confounding the output pessimists. Capacity utilisation broke all records, and unemployment went on falling very fast.

The growth of personal sector credit, following its deregulation, was at first maintained and encouraged by the authorities. Any suggestion that it should, or could, be controlled in the old-fashioned way was quickly dismissed. The growth of spending was reinforced by tax cuts, particularly in the 1988 budget. The personal sector went into net financial deficit and the savings ratio fell to the lowest level since the 1950s.

The result in 1988 was a deficit on the current account of the balance of payments amounting to over 3 per cent of GDP. Interest rates were reduced following the stock market crash, but then raised from 8 per cent in April 1988 to 13 per cent in November of the same year. The exchange rate held up, but that did not prevent domestic costs rising. Inflation accelerated, reaching 8 per cent in April 1989.

In 1989 the boom came to an end, but inflation stayed high and the balance of payments deficit stayed very large. The uneasy peace between the now very different approaches of the Chancellor and the Prime Minister to monetary policy lasted whilst the going was good, but gave way to open warfare in times of trouble. Before the year was out, Nigel Lawson, the 'brilliant' Chancellor, had resigned.

These events properly belong to another history book to be written many years hence, but they are relevant here as well, because they were the result in part of the policies which had been followed in the years up to 1987. The boom showed up the limitations of the strategy followed by the government from the mid-1980s. In the May 1989 number of the *National Institute Economic Review* we wrote:

The behaviour of the UK economy, faced with a surge in domestic demand is all too consistent with past experience. Less has changed since the 1970s than might have been hoped. Despite a decade of reform of the 'supply side' of the economy, the sustainable level of unemployment has apparently risen. As full capacity is approached, wages still accelerate, imports still gain market share . . . Over the last ten years major steps have been taken towards the liberalisation of markets, and economic agents of all kinds have been encouraged to pursue their private interests with a minimum of regulation, interference or guidance. Such a system will work only if the authorities have some reliable means of controlling inflation, and are prepared to use it to the extent required, whatever the costs. Recent events call into question whether those minimum conditions are now satisfied in the UK.

In a history book written shortly after the event it is particularly difficult to stand back and judge the significance of the closing sections of narrative. Immediately after the 1987 general election it seemed as if the policies pursued by the Conservatives since 1979 (or at least since 1983) had been endorsed, not just by the electorate, but by events as well. That was the predominant view at the time. In Part 5 of this study we shall try to assess to what extent it was justified.

PART 2

HISTORY OF IDEAS

6

THE SEVENTIES, DEVELOPMENTS OF KEYNESIANISM

THE CONVENTIONAL WISDOM

Keynesian economics held a dominant position in Britain from the war until the late 1960s. No doubt it did in the postwar period develop in ways that Keynes himself would not have expected, nor approved, but it retained the presuppositions which distinguished his ideas from those of neo-classical economists. The central one was that the government should, by using fiscal and monetary policy instruments, try to regulate the level of aggregate demand, and hence output and employment. The operation of market forces was too slow or otherwise unreliable to maintain a constant pressure of demand with full utilisation of resources, but no overheating. Hence the government had a responsibility to manage the economy, intervening continuously to stabilise demand, subject only to the limitations of measurement and forecasting, and to the delay before policy action took full effect.

This was the framework within which macroeconomic policy was normally discussed up to end of the 1960s. It was used in the Treasury under Sir Alec Cairncross, Sir Donald MacDougall and Bryan Hopkin. It was used at the National Institute where David Worswick was Director, and at the Department of Applied Economics in Cambridge under Brian Reddaway. It was used by historians of economic policy including Christopher Dow and Robin Matthews. It was accepted by most politicians of all parties and by nearly all economic journalists.

In the universities Keynesianism was also dominant, but it was presented in a rather different way, with much attention given to the ideas of Hicks and Samuelson, or those of Harrod, or Kaldor, or Joan Robinson. New interpretations of Keynesian theory were also influential including those Leijonhufvud and Clower, and later that of Barro and Grossman.

In the universities there was also room for non-Keynesian approaches to economics, including the writings of postwar American monetarists, especially those of Milton Friedman. At the LSE, for example, in the late 1960s students of Harry Johnson were given an even-handed choice between Keynesian and neoclassical economics; they were expected to understand the strengths and weaknesses of both schools of thought.

Keynesianism in practice could not be concerned only with the stabilisation of output growth or the maintenance of full employment. The problems that worried economic policymakers in Britain in the 1960s were a relatively slow growth rate, recurrent balance of payments deficits and an accelerating rate of inflation. The *General Theory* had little to say about any of these preoccupations. Keynesians were divided over the usefulness of indicative planning, incomes policies, industrial policies, trade restrictions and other such detailed intervention by government in the working of the economy. By the late 1960s, however, it was clear that demand management on its own was not enough. Something, at the very least, had to be done to secure 'external' balance as well. By the 1960s the exchange rate was being discussed as if it were a policy instrument. The ideas of Mundell on the use of two instruments to meet two objectives were readily absorbed into the conventional wisdom, encouraged by the experience of the 1967 devaluation. Dealing with inflation within a Keynesian framework proved particularly difficult. It was widely, if not universally, accepted that inflation of wages, and hence prices, could be a symptom of overheating. Some, but not all, Keynesians accepted the empirical relationship of the Phillips curve. Its relation to Keynesian theory was never clarified and relatively little discussed.

In the late 1960s, as inflation accelerated, unemployment also rose, confounding the notion of a stable relationship between these two variables. This was the point from which the monetarist challenge to Keynesianism was launched, as the next section will describe. Within the conventional wisdom the reaction was different. The more cautious Keynesians concluded that lower levels of unemployment were now unobtainable, at least by standard macroeconomic policies. The less cautious, who at first were the stronger party, concluded that inflation had little or nothing to do with unemployment or the pressure of demand; inflation was caused by the 'pushfulness' of trade unionists and the only way to contain it was to negotiate an explicit policy for both wages and prices. It was argued, indeed, by Frank Blackaby amongst others, that a faster growth of output would make inflation *easier* to control as it would provide the resources to reconcile all aspirations for increases in real incomes.

This, as described in Part 1 of this study, was the basis for the reflationary policies adopted by the Heath government in its later years. Alan Budd has described these policies as, 'the apotheosis of crude Keynesianism' and said, 'it was tested to the point of destruction; and was destroyed'. Undoubtedly many economists were persuaded at this time to leave the Keynesian camp, but many, probably the majority, were not. The failure of the Heath reflation could easily be blamed on the miners and on OPEC; indeed its success in reducing unemployment, while it lasted, could be used as evidence that Keynesian policies did work at least in the short term. The Keynesian school in Britain was to show remarkable resilience right through the 1970s and beyond, maintaining its following more successfully than its counterpart in America and continuing to respond positively to the intellectual challenge of events.

In the 1970s both the Treasury and the Bank of England formed academic panels. The former had a remit limited to research and development of the Treasury's macroeconomic model; the latter was allowed to range more widely and to discuss policy. Although both bodies included economists of different persuasions, even monetarists, the influence of Keynesianism remained very important in their deliberations even in the 1980s.

MACROECONOMIC MODELBUILDING
AND CONTROL THEORY

One of the strengths of Keynesianism in Britain turned out to be its association with empirical modelling of time-series relationships. Most of the main macroeconomic models, including those used by the Treasury and the Bank, retained the traditional income–expenditure framework because it worked, even when Keynesian ideas were at their most unfashionable. The dependence of consumer spending on personal disposable income, the lag of employment behind output, the response of imports to domestic demand, the 'accelerator' response of investment and stockbuilding to output growth – all these traditional elements used and quantified by forecasters and modelbuilders since the 1950s remained in use throughout the controversies of the 1970s and 1980s.

It was not obvious at the beginning of the 1970s that this would be the case. Forecasting was then, as always, a partly informal or judgemental exercise, and many of its practitioners regarded econometrics and modelbuilding with deep suspicion. Neither the Treasury nor the Bank were especially quick to adopt large-scale computer-based models as the technology became available. There was some ambivalence about modelbuilding at the National Institute as well, and it was the team at the London Business School, under Jim Ball, who led the way, especially in the development of computer software.

The example of the big American models was also important to developments in Britain. In 1975 the Treasury, for example, when it wanted to ensure that its own model was in line with best practice, sent the present author and a colleague on a tour which involved interviews with Lawrence Klein, Albert Ando, Franco Modigliani, Otto Eckstein and users of the models at the Federal Reserve Bank and the Bank of Canada. At that time the American models seemed to be well ahead of those used in Britain, especially in their treatment of monetary policy and its effects on aggregate demand.

It proved difficult to reproduce the relationships used by the American modellers on British data. Traditional Keynesianism in this country, unlike America, was mainly concerned with the use of fiscal policy. For much of the postwar period consumer credit had been subject to direct controls, so the effect of interest rate changes on their own was quite largely obscured. The situation was little different in the 1970s when the corset was in place more often than not. What effect monetary policy might have in unrestricted financial markets was necessarily unquantifiable. The American models, following the work of Jorgensen, at this time attributed a large effect on fixed investment to changes in real interest rates. As the 1970s progressed, real interest rates became negative, both here and in America, but there was no sign of an investment boom in consequence. The caution of most British modellers in following the Jorgensen approach was justified.

The difficulty of modelling investment, and particularly its response to financial variables, meant that the debate over crowding-out remained undecided throughout the 1970s. The proposition in its strong form was that fiscal reflation was totally ineffective even in raising demand, since higher public sector borrowing necessarily meant higher interest rates and hence a cut in private sector demand, especially fixed investment. If fiscal reflation failed to raise aggregate demand, *a fortiori* it would not raise output or employment. Econometric studies in this country never found effects from interest rates on domestic demand sufficiently powerful to support the proposition in its strong form, but the issue was partly a semantic one since the effect of reflation on interest rates must depend largely on the monetary rule which the authorities are following. In the United Kingdom the crowding out proposition had an important variant in which interest rates crowded out exports rather than fixed investment because they resulted in a higher real exchange rate. Against this, some argued that the experience of most reflationary episodes, 1972 for example, was that they weakened the exchange rate rather than strengthened it, reinforcing rather than offsetting the stimulus to domestic economic activity.

The events of the 1970s also made it virtually impossible to estimate the relationship between unemployment and wage inflation. Incomes policies were in place continuously from 1972 to 1979, although of various kinds and with widely differing degrees of effectiveness. This did not mean necessarily that unemployment had no effect on wages, as it might well influence the degree of success that incomes policies achieved, but it meant that no estimated relationship could be used confidently as a guide to the behaviour of wages under free collective bargaining. The Treasury adopted an equation for earnings which was not the product of econometrics so much as the distillation of wisdom by the hierarchical procedures of the Civil Service. The National Institute solution was to have two versions of its model, one including an equation of the Phillips curve kind, and the other without.

Another limitation of modelbuilding concerned the treatment of the exchange rate. Until 1972 this could reasonably be treated as fixed. or as a policy instrument under the control of the monetary authorities. For most of the 1970s, however, the exchange rate was floating with more or less market intervention. The likely behaviour of the exchange rate was crucial to forecasting over anything but the very short term and to the analysis of policy options. Yet the data series used for empirical estimation could not begin before 1972. As the years went by the data set increased but the behaviour of the exchange rate did not become more predictable, or even become easier to understand after the event. The market seemed to be dominated by different concerns at different periods; now it was the balance of payments, now it was money supply growth, later it became the price of crude oil.

These problems limited the confidence with which models could be used to predict inflation except in the very short term. Indeed, there was no secure basis for an empirical understanding of the process of inflation within the framework used by the modelbuilders. It was argued against the modelbuilders at this time that the monetarists *did* have such an empirical basis; the rise and fall of the predictive power of M3 will be discussed below.

An incomplete understanding of inflation necessarily implied an incomplete understanding of the determination of output in the longer run. In the course of the 1970s it became generally accepted that higher inflation ultimately reduced output, principally by raising the personal sector savings ratio. Moreover, in the long run, if growth in the economy above say 3 per cent a year would result in accelerating inflation, then in the long run growth would have to be restricted to 3 per cent a year by one means or another. The empirical success of Keynesianism in understanding the short-term behaviour of output was encouraging, but it did not necessarily mean that the approach was useful as a guide to longer-term developments. It also left open the possibility that Keynesianism would be a disastrous basis for policy design, forever encouraging governments to reflate for the sake of the short-term advantage to employment, and forever adding to the rate of inflation in the vain attempt to hold unemployment below the sustainable level. Everything turned on the nature of the equations used for wages and for the exchange rate – and these were the areas in which good empirical results were hardest to secure.

Despite these persistent problems of estimation, the models were used for more and more elaborate exercises in policy analysis. Following the tradition of Tinbergen, policy design was seen as the allocation of a set of instruments to the achievement of a set of objectives. The use of control theory developed by engineers made it possible to select the time path of policy instruments which produced the optimum time path for the target variables. The underlying ideas had been taken up by economists, including Phillips in the United Kingdom and Chow in America, some years before. The development of relatively large computer-based models in the United Kingdom in the 1970s made it possible to put these ideas into practice.

They met, not suprisingly, with resistance from those with experience of policymaking in practice. They seemed totally mechanical in the way they were calculated, and wholly dependent on the quite uncertain properties of the models to which they were applied. Could the objectives of economic policy ever be specified properly as a 'quadratic loss function'? Ministers would not know what words like that meant, and if they did they would never risk exposing their true aims to opposition in such a crude and explicit way.

Despite this reaction, ideas derived from control theory became increasingly influential in the 1970s and beyond. One landmark was the publication of the Report of the Ball Committee on Policy Optimisation. The Committee was set up thanks to the efforts of one backbench Labour MP, Jeremy Bray, at a time when the Labour government lacked an overall majority in the House. The report suggested a rather modest role for formal optimisation methods based on control theory in the formulation of policy, but it gave extensive publicity to the approach. That approach was later to be adopted by modelbuilders with enthusiasm, partly because of its intrinsic intellectual fascination, partly because it cast empirical economics in such a star role, and partly because it provided a firm basis for the critique of simpler approaches to policymaking, in particular of monetarism. These further developments belong mainly to the 1980s rather than the 1970s and are discussed below.

NEW CAMBRIDGE POLICY ANALYSIS

The vitality of Keynesianism in Britain in the 1970s can be demonstrated in no way better than by its ability to grow divergent lines. The new approach adopted by Wynne Godley and his team at the Department of Applied Economics (DAE) in Cambridge from the mid-1970s was a direct and considered response to the events of the decade. For many years it was very influential, not least in the Treasury. It presented the cautious Keynesians, and the supporters of the conventional wisdom, with a challenge from the opposite wing to the main attack by the monetarists. With many years of hindsight it may appear that New Cambridge was a digression, but at the time it gave more orthodox supporters of demand management the comfortable feeling that they were in the midstream of macroeconomics in Britain.

The New Cambridge approach was a response to the difficulty of expanding the British economy without running into a balance of payments constraint. This had been the recurrent experience of the 1960s, and in the 1970s it remained as a potential threat never far from the minds of those most eager to restore full employment. New Cambridge had much less to say about inflation.

The more orthodox Keynesians, typified by the macroeconomic modellers of the Treasury or the National Institute, paid relatively little attention to the pattern of sector financial surpluses and deficits. Yet two variables of obvious policy concern, the current account of the balance of payments and public sector borrowing, were linked by the accounting identity that the sum of financial balances of all sectors must be zero. Moreover, the financial balance of the domestic private sector, persons and companies alike, seemed to be relatively stable and predictable. Thus improvements in the current balance were often, if not invariably, matched by reductions in public sector borrowing. The period after the 1967 devaluation was a case in point.

The company sector in particular, it was argued by New Cambridge economists, could not in practice finance a large deficit for a long period (and would not choose to maintain a large surplus either). Thus in late 1974 companies had to cut back their spending in response to financial pressure; failing to understand this imperative led to underprediction of the severity of the ensuing recession. This idea was to prove a fruitful one. It changed the way company taxation was regarded by most macroeconomists. It influenced the design of macroeconomic models for many years to come. Actually demonstrating the stability of corporate sector demand for financial assets proved to be difficult, however, and the special adjustments made to the Treasury model to take account of financial pressure on companies were notoriously *ad hoc*.

The policy conclusion drawn from this analysis by New Cambridge economists was that fiscal policy should be used to secure balance of payments equilibrium, not to maintain full employment. This was not as revolutionary an idea as it sounds, since they always assumed that another instrument was available, so the objective of full employment was not in fact abandoned. If there are two instruments and two objectives, the way that the assignment rule is described, linking each instrument with one objective, may not be very important. In general one would expect some adjustment of both instruments to new information about either of the objectives.

A more important question was the choice of the second instrument. The orthodox answer at this time was the exchange rate, but New Cambridge preferred import controls. These formed the main element of the 'alternative strategy' supported by a number of cabinet ministers, and vigorously promoted within the Treasury by Nicki Kaldor. Whatever the merits of that alternative, the criticism they mounted of depreciation was both pertinent and influential. The problem with depreciation, as was increasingly recognised in the 1970s, was that the resulting rise in import prices would stimulate demands for wage increases. Many saw this as a situation where a compromise was unavoidable, the cost of improving trade performance and strengthening the balance of payments was a period of faster inflation. New Cambridge economists, amongst others, went further and said that no lasting improvement in competitiveness at all could be gained by exchange rate depreciation. Wage earners had fixed aspirations for the level and growth of their real living standards. A *real* depreciation was impossible, if *real* wages were rigid. The experience of the 1970s, including the fate of successive phases of incomes policy, seemed all too consistent with this pessimistic view.

New Cambridge economics was felt by some to be too informal and eclectic in its search for empirical evidence to support its new ideas. The main reasons for the relative decline in its influence in the 1980s, however, are not of that kind. After the change of government the political importance of the approach was reduced, as it had relatively few supporters in the Conservative Party. The central focus on the balance of payments as the constraint on growth became inappropriate as North Sea oil was developed, especially when its value was increased by the second oil price shock in 1979. Moreover the idea that a balance of payments deficit is necessarily the counterpart of a deficit in the public sector was clearly inapplicable to the United Kingdom economy in the late 1980s.

7

THE SEVENTIES, THE MONETARIST CHALLENGE

MONETARISM AND NEOCLASSICAL ECONOMICS

Neoclassical economics never died out in Britain, even in the 1950s and early 1960s when it was very much a minority view. The revival of this school in the late 1960s and subsequently, however, was mainly inspired by the ideas of American economists, especially those of Chicago economists, above all Milton Friedman. Keynesianism had never won the dominant position in America that it had in Britain. Broadly speaking the Keynesians held most of the high ground along the east coast, whilst the neoclassicals retained vast tracts of the mid-west. Keynesianism was in retreat in America from the mid-1960s and it was a vigorous and successful neoclassicism that reinvaded Britain and occupied key positions here in the course of the 1970s.

The neoclassical theory of macroeconomics is based on the application of classical ideas of market behaviour to the economy as a whole. Thus the aggregate levels of savings and investment are equalised by movements in the real rate of interest, aggregate employment depends on the real wage and so on. If these markets do not function perfectly, the proper role of government is to make them work better, not to override them.

So much for the real economy; the price level, and hence the rate of inflation, is determined quite separately by the supply and demand for money. This separation is based on the fundamental axiom that nothing in the real economy depends on the units in which prices are measured. The neoclassical tradition goes further than that and says that price level changes, or changes in the rate of inflation, do not influence the behaviour of the real economy except in special cases or over relatively short periods. Unemployment, for example, will revert to its 'natural' rate within a few years whatever happens to inflation or the growth of the money supply.

Within this framework the main responsibility of government, and especially of central banks, is to keep the money supply under control. If they do that they will also keep inflation under control, and save society from the inconveniences, inefficiencies and inequities that rapid rates of inflation entail.

These ideas sounded quite novel even to some professional economists in

Britian in the 1960s but they are part of a tradition going back much further than that of the Keynesians, back to the eighteenth century, if not earlier. Within this longer and wider tradition the conventional wisdom of the British economics establishment could be seen as a short-lived and rather insular heresy, relevant (at best) only to the special conditions of the interwar depression. The revival of neoclassical economics both in America and in Britain, owed something to the eloquence and persuasiveness of its supporters, especially Milton Friedman, but it was the circumstances of the time that made the audience receptive. Inflation was becoming the problem of most pressing concern, and the conventional wisdom had little to say about it. Moreover what little it did have to say was being proved wrong by events.

The Phillips curve, although it was not a product of Keynesian theory, was widely used by Keynesian economists. It was explicitly in conflict with neoclassical theory in that it supposed a stable relationship to exist between a real variable, the rate of unemployment, and a nominal variable, the rate of inflation. As inflation accelerated in the late 1960s the relationship broke down, as any neoclassical economist would have predicted. This was a very good starting point for the neoclassical revival.

One response to the shift in the old-fashioned Phillips curve was to devise a new curve in which the acceleration of inflation, rather than the rate of inflation itself, depended on unemployment. Associated with that was the conclusion that the old-fashioned Phillips curve was vertical at a point called the non-accelerating inflation rate of unemployment (NAIRU). Strictly in neoclassical theory, however, there is no reason to expect the acceleration of inflation to be any more stably related to unemployment than is the rate of inflation itself. Friedman's 'natural' rate of unemployment was a simpler and more persuasive notion.

Neoclassical theory is a coherent and intellectually appealing whole, but it is convenient to divide its challenge to the Keynesian conventional wisdom into two distinct parts. The first concerned the working of the real economy and the understanding of macroeconomics by analogy with market behaviour. This challenged the conventional wisdom about the causes of unemployment. In contrast to the Keynesians, the neoclassical view is that unemployment, in the long run at least, is the result of the behaviour of the real economy, independent of the way the monetary authorities behave and of the resulting course of inflation. Unemployment will persist if real wages are held above the market-clearing level by the monopoly power of trade unions, or if social security benefits are set so high, relative to wages, that the unemployed have insufficient incentive to find work. This area was, and still is, one in which debate between neoclassical and Keynesian economists can become highly emotional, since the neoclassical view seems to reinforce the popular image of the unemployed as work-shy, as parasites on society, not as its unhappy victims. But this is to caricature the neoclassical view of unemployment.

The challenge of neoclassicism was also about the relative importance of aggregate supply and aggregate demand in the determination of output. The conventional wisdom was that actual output was determined by aggregate demand and moved in cycles about a trend dependent on productive potential. Some Keynesians treated productive potential as independent of demand, its growth resulting mainly from demography and the advance of technology; others would say that investment, and even technical progress or labour force participation, varied in response to the use made of existing resources, so that in the long run demand could create its own supply. Hence demand management could easily be converted into a recipe for non-stop expansion. These, to a neoclassical mind, were heretical and mischievous ideas.

The first challenge then of neoclassical economics was to the way that postwar economists in Britain had played down the role of markets and played up the role of governments. This wider neoclassical challenge should be distinguished from monetarism in the strict sense of the word.

Monetarism was the second challenge. It was asserted that government could, and should, control inflation. To do this all that was required was to identify a proper measure of the money supply and keep its growth under control, preferably to stop it growing significantly at all. This prescription rested on the propositions of neoclassical economics, in that it assumed that the effects of money supply control on the real economy, for example any reduction in output or employment, would be relatively slight and short-lived. It also rested on the special assumption that the money supply was both measurable and controllable. This again challenged the conventional wisdom in Britain, which in this case was embodied in the Radcliffe Report of 1959. The view of most British economists at the time was that bank deposits were part of a spectrum of assets similar in characteristics and readily substituted for each other. What mattered was not the quantity of bank deposits but the amount of liquidity more widely, and imprecisely, defined. Monetary policy was seen as the control of credit, rather than the control of liquid assets; it was related to the assets of the banking system not to its liabilities. There was a specifically monetarist challenge to this way of describing and conducting monetary policy which might be distinguished from the wider issues raised by neoclassical thinking about the workings of the economy as a whole. As we have seen in Part 1, this specifically monetarist challenge ultimately came to grief amidst the fluidity of British financial institutions and of the statistics relating to them. The revival of neoclassical economics and belief in the efficacy of markets continues into the 1990s.

THE EVIDENCE FOR MONETARISM

Ideas in economics do not gain wide acceptance merely by being elegant or theroetically consistent; they also need empirical evidence in their favour.

The empirical refutation of the Phillips curve was an excellent starting point for the monetarists, but they needed evidence that their propositions were correct, not just that the conventional wisdom was false. In particular they needed to demonstrate to a sceptical audience that the money supply was a useful focus for monetary policy and that control of the money supply would give control of inflation.

The first requirement, as an empirical basis for monetarism, is a stable and predictable demand for money. If the Radcliffean view was correct and bank deposits were just one of many almost indistinguishable liquid assets, then the demand for them would be unpredictable, and very responsive to small changes in the yield or availability of alternatives. At the beginning of the 1970s several recent studies gave support to the monetarists against the Radcliffeans. Using mainly quarterly data for the 1950s and 1960s Charles Goodhart, David Laidler and others had published estimates which showed the demand for money as a stable function of a few variables, notably the price level.

The waters were then muddied by the reform of monetary control in 1972. This resulted in a very rapid, and unintended, growth of the money supply – almost an experiment of nature. The result was a break in the previously stable relationship between the quantity of money and the key variables believed to determine demand. It was later shown, however, by Michael Artis and others, that a reformulation of the equation, such that interest rates were influenced by money supply growth rather than *vice versa*, showed greater consistency through the period following 'Competition and Credit Control'. The implications of that finding for monetarism were uncertain, since it had yet to be demonstrated that raising interest rates was an effective way to reduce inflation.

Published studies of the demand for money in the United Kingdom were relatively few and far between in the late 1970s. One by David Smith in 1978 finds that M3, by then the target aggregate adopted by the government, was the least stable of those he investigated, a problem he put down to the inclusion of wholesale deposits which were particularly volatile and sensitive to small changes in relative interest rates. At the end of the decade Joe Grice at the Treasury was estimating a more complicated relationship in which the demand for money depended not just on prices, incomes and rates of interest, but also on the financial wealth of the private sector, a variable peculiarly difficult to define or to measure.

It cannot be said that the monetarist position found much support in these studies of the demand for money. If anything they were an embarrassment. There was, however, another kind of empirical evidence which could be used more directly to suggest that control of the money supply implied control of inflation. Milton Friedman had made his considerable reputation as an applied economist by studying the relationship in America between variations in the growth of the money supply and subsequent variations in inflation. He found that bursts of monetary excess were always followed by bursts of inflation with a lag which was 'long and variable' but on average about two years. One could look for a similar pattern in the United Kingdom.

It was not difficult to find. The most dramatic episode was very fresh in everyone's memory. Under the Heath government, following Competition and Credit Control and as part of a deliberate expansion of demand, the money supply growth rate reached 25 per cent on average for a year. About two years later inflation had accelerated to around 20 per cent (or rather faster in terms of wholesale prices). This vivid confirmation of the central tenet of monetarism was widely quoted, for example by Brian Griffiths in his 1976 study of inflation.

More systematic published studies of this relationship were oddly scarce. Kent Matthews and Paul Ormerod at the National Institute found, to their surprise, that movements in money were more important than changes in fiscal policy in explaining subsequent growth in nominal GDP. Michael Beenstock and others at the LBS found that wholesale prices responded in proportion to monetary growth after a lag of three to four years, but their results changed if they included other variables in the equation as well. Simon Wren-Lewis, then at the Treasury, concluded from his study of data up to 1978 that the monetarist results obtained when money was treated as the only determinant of prices were misleading, since adding overseas prices or rates of indirect taxation changed them quite profoundly. He also noted that the growth of the money supply failed to explain the rise in inflation in 1979, after the end of his sample period. Subsequent events in the early 1980s were to confirm that the explanatory power of M3 for inflation had been greatly exaggerated by the particular circumstances of the early 1970s. At the time, nevertheless, it was most impressive and contributed to the support gained for monetarism during the latter half of the decade.

Even when the evidence for the causal link between money supply growth and price inflation was at its most impressive, questions were being asked about the 'transmission mechanism'. It would be much more impressive if a model could be estimated with more than one equation, showing how an excess supply of money was translated into excess demand for goods and hence to an acceleration of inflation. It was the objective of a group of empirical monetarists at Manchester led by David Laidler and Michael Parkin in the early 1970s to estimate small models of this kind, not just for the United Kingdom but for the world economy as a whole. David Laidler in 1978 published a small model of the United Kingdom based on annual data from 1954-70 which he used for interpreting history and for policy analysis.

As with the demand for money studies already mentioned it was more difficult to incorporate the post-1972 data into a structural model of the economy with monetarist properties. The modelbuilders, especially those at the LBS and the Treasury, had every incentive to do so in the late 1970s when the LBS was advocating a regime of monetary targets and the Treasury was trying to implement one. Nevertheless the role of the money supply in both those models remained problematic, not for want of an acceptable theory, but for want of good empirical results to use.

The main transmission mechanism in those models linking monetary policy with inflation was through the exchange rate. The determination of exchange rates was, as has been already mentioned, an unsolved empirical problem. In the absence of good estimated equations the determination of the exchange rate was largely 'imposed', that is settled without reference to the data. It was assumed, both by the LBS and by the Treasury in the late 1970s, that the exchange rate was powerfully influenced by the growth of M3. This then provided a powerful transmission mechanism from money to prices; but it was an untested assumption and subsequent events showed it to be unreliable.

INTERNATIONAL MONETARISM AND THE LONDON BUSINESS SCHOOL

An original and influential contribution to applied macroeconomics in the United Kingdom during the 1970s was made at the London Business School by the team led first by Jim Ball, then by Terry Burns and Alan Budd. They started, like most British economists, from a Keynesian point of view at the beginning of the decade, but responded to the monetarist or neoclassical revival earlier and more positively than many of their contemporaries. They were particularly interested in the monetary theory of the balance of payments, as expounded for example by Harry Johnson, and as put into practice by the staff of the IMF.

The balance of payments is never far from the consciousness of macroeconomists in this country. The experience of 1969 showed how strict control of domestic credit expansion (DCE), at the behest of the IMF, could lead to a satisfactory surplus, which devaluation alone had failed to achieve, at least in the time available. This lesson was to be repeated in 1977. It was readily explained by the monetary theory of the balance of payments. The growth in the money supply is roughly equal to DCE minus the balance of payments deficit. Suppose that the demand for money is unchanged, then a reduction in DCE must necessarily be matched by an improvement in the balance of payments. The idea is simple and appealing, and has been familiar to classical economists for several hundred years. It came nevertheless as an unfamiliar insight to many British economists in the late 1960s.

The theory necessarily has to change when the exchange rate is no longer fixed. The distinctive contribution of the LBS economists was to apply a monetarist view of exchange rate determination to the United Kingdom predicament in the 1970s whilst retaining many of the familiar features of the Keynesian income–expenditure approach to the domestic economy. The resulting model of the transmission mechanism was very different from those of the American monetarists or of David Laidler and his associates at Manchester.

They did not, until the end of the 1970s, include in their model of the economy any kind of Phillips curve. Higher output and employment did not therefore add to inflation by bidding up wages. They did, however, in common with the New Cambridge school amongst others, insist that the level of real wages could not for long be reduced merely by raising prices or by depreciating the exchange rate. This being the case, the price level, in the long run, depended not on domestic costs but on the prices of foreign goods either as imported inputs to production or as competing goods in both world and domestic markets. Under a fixed exchange rate, world inflation determined domestic inflation; under floating rates domestic inflation depended also on the exchange rate. They assumed that, in the long run, exchange rates would move in proportion to relative money supply growth at home and abroad (after making allowance for differences in the sustainable growth rates of output).

It was important to their argument that the domestic rate of inflation was not merely tied to the growth rate of foreign prices and the exchange rate in the very long run, the association was thought to be quite close even in the short run. They appealed to the Scandinavian inflation model, based on the ideas of Lundberg and others. In this model the prices of all tradeable goods, commonly interpreted as including most manufactured goods, always moved in proportion to world prices expressed in local currency. In other words changes in relative price competitiveness were always small and transitory. This proposition was not necessary to their general conclusion that all domestic prices were linked to world prices converted into sterling in the long run, but it encouraged them to believe that the effects of exchange rate movements on domestic costs and prices were quick, whilst their effects on the volume of trade, and hence on output and employment, were relatively slight and shortlived. Not surprisingly therefore they regarded the struggle to hold down the value of sterling in 1977 as misconceived; it sacrificed a fall in the inflation rate (which would itself incidentally have stimulated demand by cutting the savings ratio) and it gained little from delaying the inevitable loss of relative cost and price competitiveness.

The LBS economists supported the monetarist policy prescription of targets for the growth of the money suppply that were reduced progressively year on year until inflation subsided. They recognised that the process of disinflation would involve some temporary loss of output and employment, in their model mainly arising from the appreciation of the exchange rate and the delay in the adjustment of labour costs.

That cost would be minimised if the announcement of a monetary target regime persuaded everyone, including all those involved in wage bargaining, that the rate of inflation was indeed going to come down. If everyone believed that, then labour costs never need get much out of line at all, and the process of disinflation would involve little or no sacrifice of output. Towards the end of the decade, the LBS economists, in common with many others, were attracted by the hypothesis of rational expectations, introduced by a new wave of monetarist ideas coming from America, sometimes called 'new classical' economics to distinguish them from the established position of the neoclassicists.

NEW CLASSICAL ECONOMICS

Having come to terms with Friedman, Cagan, Brunner and Meltzer, Andersen and Jordan and a host of other American monetarists from the 1960s, British macroeconomists had next to absorb the even more strange and unfamiliar ideas put forward in the 1970s by such writers as Lucas, Sargent, Barro, and Kydland and Prescott. Their direct influence on policymaking in Britain may not have been great, but they contributed much to the climate of opinion and they provided the main intellectual stimulus for fresh thinking about the way fiscal and monetary policy might be conducted.

Neoclassical or monetarist economic theory was understood by most economists in the 1960s, including most of those who accepted it, as describing the behaviour of the economy in the long run; it was about the equilibrium towards which inflation, unemployment, output and so on would return, not about their movements from month to month or year to year. The macroeconomy was understood as a market, but not as a market in which excess supply or demand was continuously eliminated by price adjustments. The new classical school were not satisfied with this approach. They started from the presumption that markets worked efficiently, although they obviously had to concede that there were exceptions, often caused by government interference.

One reason for the sluggishness of market adjustment might be that expectations of future levels of price responded slowly to the experience of actual price changes. Buyers and sellers would then trade on the basis of mistaken views about future prices and it would take time for the new equilibrium to be established. New classical economists pointed out that it was in the interests of traders to find out as much as they could about the determination of equilibrium prices and that there was no reason to suppose they would make systematic mistakes. Their expectations, in other words, were rational, not merely adaptive.

From this starting point they launched a powerful attack on much of the existing body of economic theory, and especially on applied macroeconomics. From their point of view stabilisation policy was no better than a confidence trick, which could be effective only to the extent that producers or consumers were misled. If reflation did add to output even in the short run, it did so only because producers mistook general inflation resulting from faster monetary growth for a real increase in the value of the product they made. Such tricks could not be expected to work effectively if they were often repeated. Policy changes could only be effective if they were random and unpredictable. Since, however, even the short-run behaviour of markets was optimal, there was no reason at all for governments to pursue stabilisation policies. They would only make matters worse.

In a similar vein, the new classical economists argued that the relationships estimated by econometricians were not like unchanging laws of nature; they reflected the expectations of the agents whose behaviour they described. In particular, they reflected expectations about the way that governments and central banks would behave. If that behaviour changed, for example when the government adopted a monetarist rule or when floating exchange rates replaced the Bretton Woods system, then behaviour would change and the estimated equations were all obsolete. Quantitative prediction in these circumstances was simply impossible. This point is central to the Lucas critique of policymaking based on estimated models.

The new classical discussion of fiscal policy was potentially devastating to Keynesianism for yet another reason. The need to balance the finances of the public sector in the long run means that tax cuts this year imply tax increases at some unspecified period in the future. This is said to be obvious to taxpayers. They do not therefore feel any richer as a result of tax cuts and their propensity to spend will not be increased. Strictly the idea, derived from Ricardo, requires taxpayers to be immortal, but in a somewhat modified form it might have practical significance.

For a variety of reasons it was argued that the government should make clear and credible statements about its own future policy plans. It was pointed out that, having made such announcements, the authorities might then have a strong incentive to break their word. Sequences of policy actions which seemed optimal before the event might not be optimal to carry out when the time came. But rational observers would realise this, so the policy announcements would not be believed in the first place. The best way of resolving this dilemma was for the authorities to bind their own hands in some way so that their future actions were effectively precommitted; only then would their statements be credible. In the United States arguments of this kind were used in support of the move to amend the constitution and remove discretionary elements from the conduct of fiscal policy. In Britain there was a move to remove the conduct of monetary policy from the control of government, by setting up an independent commission. The Medium Term Financial Strategy perhaps made rather firmer precommitments than it otherwise would have done, because the authors were influenced by ideas derived from the new classical school.

The response of British economists to new classical economics belongs mainly to the 1980s rather than to the 1970s. There was, however, one development that was under way before the end of the decade. Patrick

Minford at the University of Liverpool was building a macroeconomic model based on new classical theory. This was a paradoxical thing to do, as he recognised, since new classical economists in America had been particularly scathing in their criticism of the American macroeconomic models. However, the Liverpool model was, in some respects at least, different in kind. It embodied the hypothesis of rational expectations. In the model all economic behaviour was governed by expectations which were in line with the predictions of the model itself. It also ensured, by assumption, that the long-run properties of the economy conformed to neoclassical theory.

Patrick Minford was thus putting new classical ideas to an empirical test. To the extent that they were correct (in the form he used them) he would be able to forecast events using his model better than more traditional forecasters could using their more conventional models. New Classical ideas had not been tested in quite this way in America. The Liverpool model was ready to start this test by the end of the 1970s, just when the Conservative government had taken office determined to follow policies on the lines that the monetarists had proposed.

Gradually the uncompromising message of the new classical school has been qualified. During the 1980s it became immensely influential amongst academic economists in Britain as well as in America, but it was taken up and used to argue for a variety of different policy prescriptions, not all of them hostile to intervention. Indeed it was used to spell out more rigorously than had been attempted before exactly why intervention was necessary. It was argued for example that the monetary authorities had an information advantage over the private sector (and that the private sector would not respond immediately or in full if the information was communicated to it). It was also argued that inertia in nominal wages and prices had a useful social function; for that reason it was both possible and desirable for the authorities to conduct a countercyclical policy. But this is to take the argument ahead in the 1980s at least as far as most British economists are concerned.

THE TRIUMPH OF MONETARISM

By the end of the 1970s the neoclassical or monetarist challenge had effectively won from Keynesianism its dominant position in Britain. Professional economists remained very divided and Keynesians were still probably in the majority in university departments, in the government service and in business and finance, but they had lost the initiative and they had lost control of policymaking. It is of central concern to the historian of macroeconomic policy in this period to ask why that happened.

The triumph of monetarism can be seen as part of a much more general move to the right in political philosophy and practice, not confined to Britain or to economic policy. It is not within the terms of reference of this study, however, to range over the wide area of social change which that observation opens up. On the contrary it is more appropriate here to narrow the focus of attention to two much more specific questions. By what means did monetarism and its adherents arrive at a dominant position? And what were the most effective arguments they could deploy?

Monetarism gained ascendancy, as new ideas must, through the conversation of influential people. It is questionable whether any of the political leaders of the Labour Party were ever intellectually convinced by neoclassical economics or monetarism as its proponents understood them. It is true that James Callaghan as Prime Minister made some speeches that sounded like monetarism. It is also true that Denis Healey in his last years as Chancellor seemed to pay as much attention to the LBS economists as he did to his official, and non-monetarist, advisers. Both were probably disillusioned with much of the conventional wisdom of Keynesianism, but it is difficult to see them as converts to neoclassicism. If they were, they must have been quickly reconverted on leaving office. The fact that they presided over somewhat monetarist policies for a time in the late 1970s may reflect the views of other influential people rather than their own.

There were, however, many genuine conversions amongst the leaders of the Conservative Party. The most prominent of all was the leader, Margaret Thatcher, but the most fervent and persuasive was Sir Keith Joseph. The centres for the refinement and dissemination of the new ideas within the Conservative Party and beyond were the Institute of Economic Affairs and the newly-founded Centre for Policy Studies (CPS).

Equally important were the converts in the Press and the City. *The Times* leading articles, when William Rees Mogg was editor, were outspoken in their condemnation of government economic policy and enthusiastic in their presentation of the monetarist alternative. Peter Jay wrote persuasively in the same paper and was also very influential. *The Financial Times* was more even-handed in its editorial comments, but Samuel Brittan who wrote for it was another convert. His *Second Thoughts on Full Employment Policy* was the first publication of the CPS, appearing in 1975. It was an outstanding example of popularisation, presenting monetarism in an attractive way so that it was accessible and appealing to many whose knowledge of economics was not nearly as profound as his. It was particularly influential because it was not written from a party political point of view.

The importance of the City monetarists hardly needs underlining, and has already been emphasised in the account of the course of events in the later 1970s given in Part 1 of this study. The commentaries produced by Gordon Pepper at Greenwells deserve special mention in this context. Alan Walters, one of the few leading British academic economists who had been a monetarist even in the 1960s, also wrote stockbrokers' circulars.

So much for the channels through which the high tide of monetarism flowed. The other question posed here concerns the arguments that carried conviction. It has been argued above that empirical evidence was in fact lacking for the most distinctive propositions of monetarism. It was, for example, impossible by the late 1970s to point to studies which demonstrated the stability of the demand for money in the United Kingdom, or the predictability of its velocity of circulation. The sequence of money supply growth, followed by inflation, in the early 1970s was quite impressive, especially as some monetarists had actually forecast the inflation before it happened. But one successful prediction should not be enough to build a reputation, or found a new school of economics. Monetarism in Britain at this stage was too new for it to have established a forecasting track record which could be compared with the mixed success enjoyed by those using more conventional methods.

More persuasive were the empirical failures of the Keynesians. They might be able to show that their policies could raise output and employment for a time, as in 1973 for example, but they could not point to any period of sustained fiscal expansion that had not led to trouble of one sort or another within a year or two. The Maudling 'dash for growth' had failed; the National Plan had been abandoned; the Barber boom was just the most recent and spectacular example of expansion which ended in tears. The idea that depreciating the exchange rate easily opened up the way to export-led growth was disproved by the events of 1968, again after the floating of sterling in 1972, and again after the sterling crisis of 1976. The 1970s also showed that incomes policies could not hold back for long the force of rising inflation and, as in 1974, might actually make inflation more difficult to control. Yet this combination of reflation, depreciation and restraint of pay was still the standard Keynesian recommendation as the 1970s came to an end, and its aim was still to restore full employment. The monetarists, and many others, by then doubted whether it was really feasible to get unemployment back down to the levels typical of the 1950s and 1960s. On this central question, however, little evidence could be deployed by either side.

One reason for the triumph of monetarism, then, was the rejection of Keynesianism. Logically the argument is not very tight: admittedly Keynesianism and monetarism cannot *both* be true, but it is quite possible to hold that both are false. Nevertheless the retreat of Keynesianism left an intellectual vacuum, and monetarism rushed in to fill it.

8

THE EIGHTIES, MONETARISM IN PRACTICE

MEASURING THE MONEY SUPPLY

At the end of the 1970s the monetarists in Britain were a group of independent-minded radical critics of the intellectual establishment; they then suddenly became the trusted advisers of government and assumed responsibility for putting their ideas into practice. No doubt this transition brought its rewards, but it also brought new and difficult choices for which their success in the theoretical debate left them ill prepared.

In theory the money supply is easy to define. It is the transactions medium of the economy, consisting of tokens that can be exchanged for goods and services of all kinds. In a primitive economy there may indeed be one, and only one, such medium, for example gold coins, and the total number of such units would be straightforward to count. A modern financial system is far more complicated, and widely different views are possible as to the appropriate definition of the money supply. As with most questions of measurement in economics, there can be no uniquely correct answer. That much would be accepted by monetarists and non-monetarists alike. The issue that divides them is whether any at all of the many possible definitions is good enough for operational purposes. At the beginning of the 1980s it seemed as if there was a superfluity of possible definitions, an *embarras de choix*. Before the decade was much older, however, it seemed that none of the definitions was serviceable after all.

The initiative in choosing £M3 as the British target aggregate came not from the small group of academic economists in this country who supported monetarism, but from the officials of the Treasury and the Bank of England. As it proved such an unfortunate choice, it is worth spelling out some of the reasons why it was made.

£M3 included notes and coin in circulation, but otherwise consisted of sterling bank deposits of all kinds, whether wholesale or retail, interest bearing or not. It included certificates of deposit issued by banks, but excluded very similar instruments issued by local authorities; it included deposit accounts at banks, but not very similar accounts at building societies. There must be something unique about banks for this to be an appropriate definition of money. Historically one of the unique features of banks in Britain was their relationship with the Bank of England.

According to monetarist theory, monetary control has everything to do with the liabilities of banks, that is with their deposits, and nothing directly to do with the assets of banks, that is with their loans. But the traditional relations between the Bank and the banks had been mainly to do with the control of credit, especially credit to the personal sector, and old ideas die hard. Because the total assets and liabilities of the banking system are necessarily the same, the Bank could go on seeking to control total credit while speaking the new language of £M3. Had a narrow aggregate been chosen which included only non-interesting-bearing bank deposits, then monetary control might have been achieved by means of interest rate movements, but the total size of the banking system would have been free to expand. Credit would have been left uncontrolled.

The Treasury has a traditional concern with the scale of public sector borrowing, which is shared by the Bank since it has the job of financing the PSBR. The merit of £M3 as a target aggregate from this point of view was that it made it advisable to limit the PSBR to the level that could be financed by debt sales outside the banking system. This had little or nothing to do with monetary control as the academic monetarists envisaged it (Milton Friedman himself was very clear on this point), but it was meat and drink to Treasury officials. The traditional concern in the Treasury and the Bank with credit and the finance of government borrowing had been reinforced in the 1970s by the officials of the International Monetary Fund on their frequent visits to London. £M3 and the medium-term financial strategy of 1980 were directly descended from discussions with the Fund Staff in the late 1960s, from DCE and the 1976 Letter of Intent.

According to the pseudo-law of monetary economics named after Charles Goodhart, any aggregate selected as a target for monetary control will quickly lose any stable relationship it may have had to the behaviour of the rest of the economy. This law was originally no more than an expression of understandable exasperation by its author when he was adviser at the Bank of England. The relationship between £M3 and prices or nominal incomes had never been good, as the preceding section has suggested. It broke down completely in the 1980s because of the liberalisation of financial markets, and because of increased competition between banks and other intermediaries. Arguably the relationship would have changed fundamentally if an attempt had been made to control £M3 directly, giving behavioural content to 'Goodhart's Law'. In fact the indirect, and ineffective, attempts to control it by raising the level of interest rates had little effect on banks' behaviour, much more on the fate of the manufacturing sector.

The story of 1979 to 1981 might have been very different if the money supply definition used had been a narrow one, such as M1 or even the later invention Mo. These *did* respond in an appropriate way to the high level of interest rates and the fall in output. They gave the right signal, whilst £M3 gave the wrong one. This became clear at an early stage to some of the academic monetarists advising the government. Alan Walters, who became an adviser to the Prime Minister in January 1981, was of this view. So was Jurg Niehans when he was specially comissioned to report on the British economy for the Centre for Policy Studies. He said it was like watching a man scalding to death in the bath, and running in hotter and hotter water, because the thermometer he was reading had the scale upside down. That thermometer was £M3.

Having invested so much in £M3 it was difficult for the government to change the definition of the target aggregate when its mistake became obvious. The academic monetarists would probably have welcomed a change to M1 or Mo at any time from the end of 1980, but the City and the Press would certainly have greeted such a move with scepticism. There were many who were genuinely concerned, even in the depths of the recession, that monetary conditions were lax, and who remained worried by the rapid growth of £M3 in the mid-1980s even though the inflation they forecast as a result seemed longer and longer delayed.

Moreover the development of interest-bearing sight deposits changed the behaviour of M1 out of all recognition. American experience with a target for M1 was not encouraging. The banking system was going through such an upheaval in the early 1980s that no aggregate could be expected to mean the same thing from one year to another. The theoretically correct solution might have been to construct a weighted average of all the available aggregates allowing the weights to reflect the transactions use of different types of deposits. In practice, as we have seen in Part 1, successive editions of the MTFS made reference to different sets of target aggregates, but gave little guidance as to their relative importance.

The problem of finding the right definition of the money supply proved to be more than a small technical matter that could safely be left to technicians. There *was* no right definition. This turned out to be the rock on which the ship foundered.

MONETARY CONTROL

Classical economics treats the money supply as directly under the control of the authorities. They mint it, or print it. In a more complex financial system it is argued that the authorities can control the monetary base, that is notes and coins together with the reserve assets of the banking system. It is further argued that control of the monetary base implies control of the size of the banks' total liabilities, and hence control of a wide monetary aggregate like £M3. This is not the way that monetary control is in fact exercised by any central bank nowadays (with the possible exception of the National Bank of Switzerland), but it is the way that most monetarists believe it could and should be exercised. The more rigorous monetarists in Britain at the end of the 1970s saw the need for a move to monetary base control as necessary if the money supply was to be the central focus of macroeconomic policy. Brian Griffiths at the City University was the most prominent advocate of the system and Alan Walters in the Prime Minister's office the most influential.

Many economists and bankers who were sympathetic to monetarism were reluctant to face the institutional changes and the uncertainty that a switch to monetary base control would require. The Bank of England would have to operate quite differently in the money markets, not setting short-term interest rates but allowing them to be determined by the balance of supply and demand. The future of the discount houses was called into question. The clearing banks would also have to behave quite differently, so that they could readily change the size of their balance sheet totals when their reserve base was under presssure. It was doubtful whether the traditional overdraft arrangements with their customers could survive. There could be much greater risks of insolvency, within the banking system and beyond, if short-term interest rates became more volatile. Exchange rates might also become unstable. It hardly bore thinking about.

The problems of defining money and of controlling it were closely connected. The theoretical model of monetary base control originally envisaged a narrow definition of the money supply, confined to non-interest bearing deposits, the transactions medium of firms and house-holds, the liabilities of retail rather than wholesale banking. It is possible that a workable system of direct control, through reserve requirements against such deposits, might have been introduced. If so, the authorities could have announced targets for a narrow definition of the money supply fully confident that the target could be hit. Whether that would have been helpful in controlling inflation or achieving other aims for the behaviour of the economy at large is a wider question. The banks might have responded by inventing new kinds of deposits, outside the chosen definition of money but sharing most of its characteristics. But at least the government would have been spared the embarrassment of failing to meet its own announced goals. And the monetarists would have had the satisfaction of seeing their ideas put to a proper test.

When £M3 growth was demonstrably far in excess of the target in the autumn of 1980, the Treasury and the Bank were in no position to bring it back under control. The only remedy the monetarists could suggest was to sell much larger quantities of public sector debt outside the banking system. The idea was right in theory but it was not realistic given the nature of long-term debt markets in London. The private sector debenture market had almost completely dried up in the 1970s when long-term interest rates became high and unpredictable. The public sector completely dominated the supply of bonds and continued to sell them especially to pension funds and insurance offices whose constitution or whose liabilities made them receptive. The prospect of capital gains was as important as the yield to the timing of sales in the the gilt-edged market.

When the money supply was rising too fast, the professionals in the gilt-edged market could clearly foresee that interest rates were likely to rise, with a corresponding fall in the price of bonds. They would therefore hold off buying until the rise in yields was complete and the prospect was again for capital gains rather than losses. This made the gilts market a totally inappropriate place for 'fine tuning' the growth of £M3.

If the target aggregate had been a narrower one, then the authorities might have been able to secure control by buying and selling short-term public sector debt outside the banking system – widening the market for Treasury bills which was now dominated by the banks, who held bills as reserve assets. That was one way in which monetary control worked in the monetarist textbooks. It presupposed a narrower aggregate than £M3. The authorities could not behave in the bond market in the way the textbooks assumed them to behave in the bill market. The monetarist model could not be applied; and no serious attempt was made to apply it.

Meanwhile evidence was accumulating that the monetarist model was not only inapplicable but also based on an incorrect interpretation of the empirical evidence. The relationship between *any* definition of the money supply and the price level seemed to have broken down. The very rapid growth of the money supply in the early 1980s was not followed, as it 'should' have been by another burst of rapid inflation about the middle of the decade. This undermined faith in the wide aggregates like £M3, and subsequently in the most popular narrow aggregate M1 as well. Only the narrowest of all, M0, seemed unaffected. Increasingly therefore M0 was used as an indicator of monetary conditions, but it was not a variable which the authorities could control directly.

In 1982 the long-awaited study of money and prices in the United Kingdom by Milton Friedman and Anna Schwartz was published. This was to have been the definitive work demonstrating rigorously the empirical grounding of the monetarist approach to economic policy. It turned out to be much less than conclusive, and in many ways dated.

It covered the period 1867 to 1975 and was therefore only indirectly relevant to the relationship between money and prices in the 1980s. It was discussed by the academic panel at the Bank of England, where it was submitted to the methodological scorn of David Hendry, Britain's most famous econometrician. The retreat from monetarism began to resemble a rout.

As early in the life of the Conservative administration as spring 1981 it was clear that the monetarists were no longer making policy. The restrictive budget of that year demonstrated that the main aim of policy was still to reduce inflation, but the means were no longer the same. What remained could be described as 'monetarism without the money supply', although that sounds like a very paradoxical approach to policymaking. It is not clear how it would differ from a kind of Keynesianism that was indifferent to the level of unemployment.

In the mid-1980s a variety of alternatives to monetarism were canvassed but none received much official endorsement from the government. Macroeconomic policy was conducted in a pragmatic, atheoretical fashion, meeting, as we have seen, with much apparent success. Neither the monetarists nor the Keynesians were happy with the situation, but Ministers were most of the time, and so was much of the general public.

9

THE EIGHTIES, ALTERNATIVES
TO MONETARISM

POLICIES TO RESTORE FULL EMPLOYMENT

In March 1981, as a response to the procyclical deflationary budget, a letter was published by 364 leading academic economists, including five who had served as chief economic advisers to previous governments. They called for an end to 'monetarist policies'. They said that there was no reason to expect that the deflation of demand would bring inflation permanently under control, or induce a spontaneous recovery in output and employment. It was a most impressive display of the strength of opposition to government policy at that time amongst professional economists in this country.

As a statement it was almost entirely negative. It asserted that there were alternative policies, which would offer a better hope of promoting economic recovery, but it did not say what they were. No doubt it would have been difficult to secure so many signatures for a positive set of proposals, since economists are a notoriously argumentative crowd. Indeed the intellectual challenge of framing alternatives to monetarism led economists to take up a wide variety of different positions. For some it was simply a matter of restating the conventional wisdom of the 1970s, but most believed that there had to be alternatives to that as well.

The rise in unemployment from one million to two, and then to three million, breathed new life into Keynesianism. It was as if the conditions which caused Keynes to write the *General Theory* were being recreated in order to restore the credibility of his followers. Demand deflation, high real interest rates and an overvalued currency were having their predictable effect on the demand for labour. Many waverers must have come back about that time to the Keynesian camp.

One special circumstance of the time made the Keynesian prescription particularly attractive. The rise in the value of North Sea oil production meant that demand could be expanded, and output could rise, without coming up against the constraint of the balance of payments which had stymied fiscal expansion for so much of the postwar period. Moreover, with the exchange rate so obviously overvalued, it seemed only common sense to cut interest rates as well and create a really strong and balanced economic recovery. If ever there was a time for a major and general reflation, this was surely it.

As the 1980s progressed the Keynesian case became less persuasive. The economy did better than the 364 economists had predicted; there was an economic recovery despite the relative weak stimulus given by fiscal and monetary policy – at first only a weak recovery, but one which gathered pace. Eventually unemployment began to fall. About the same time the balance of payments re-emerged as a policy problem. The Keynesian opportunity had been missed.

Many of those who opposed the monetarist policies of government in the early 1980s did not believe that demand stimulation on its own was a real alternative at any time. They believed that there was a relationship between unemployment and inflation. They remembered the failures of successive phases of incomes policy in the 1970s. They had proposals which they believed would work better.

The New Keynesians at Cambridge were led by James Meade, and unconnected with the New Cambridge School discussed in an earlier section. Their arguments were painstaking and always well presented. They occupied a key position in the middle ground between the monetarists and the Keynesians. The title of their programme of research, 'Stagflation', was itself an indication of its nature: it was concerned *both* with stagnation *and* with inflation; it identified two problems and was not content to prescribe a solution for the one that would risk worsening the other.

As Keynesians, James Meade and his associates still believed in demand management and indeed were more interested than anyone else in the 1980s in improving the techniques and instruments for fine-tuning the economy. They favoured small and frequent policy changes, and the use of policy rules which do not depend on detailed and accurate knowledge of the economy. But they did not believe that the aim of demand management should be to stabilise the growth rate of real output or the level of unemployment. They wanted the government to set targets for the growth of nominal GDP, and to correct divergences from them irrespective of whether they consisted of unexpectedly high inflation or real growth. The government was to behave as if it did not know, or care, about the difference. Since all governments in fact do know the difference between real growth and inflation, loving one and hating the other, this may seem a strange way to behave. However, it can be seen as a logical development either of monetarism, or of incomes policy. If the velocity of circulation is unpredictable, a monetarist might logically advocate targeting 'money GDP', and that was indeed the way the MTFS developed in the mid-1980s. But an incomes policy enthusiast might equally well target total nominal income as part of a deal with the unions by which that total was divided between profits, pay and the growth of employment. The two ends of the policy spectrum met at the middle; and there was New Keynesianism.

The essential corollary, for James Meade at least, was reform of wage bargaining to ensure that individual deals struck between firms and trade unions took account of the limited size of the national income to be divided up. That was his answer to unemployment. Without the reform of wage bargaining macroeconomic policy on its own could do nothing. Reflation on its own would just raise wages, and hence prices. The New Keynesians were not in favour of it.

Another region of the middle ground was occupied by Richard Layard, Steve Nickell and their colleagues at the Centre for Labour Economics in the LSE. Their output consisted, not of a few substantial volumes like those in the *Stagflation* series, but of innumerable small yellow-backed pamphlets, eagerly read by economists of all persuasions, and frequently reported in the serious Press. Their productivity was legendary, and their influence was considerable.

One part of that output consisted of estimating a wide variety of econometric equations linking the growth of real wages to, amongst other things, the level of unemployment. From these equations they claimed to identify the non-accelerating inflation rate of unemployment, or NAIRU, and also its main determinants. It turned out that, according to their methods of estimation, much of the rise of unemployment in the 1980s was due to a rise in the NAIRU, and only a part was due to a cyclical deficiency of demand. They too therefore were led to say that reflation on its own would not cure unemployment. They did in fact advocate fiscal expansion, but on a relatively modest scale. They were also very inventive in the design of special employment measures, involving labour subsidies of various kinds which they claimed would reduce the NAIRU and hence could lower unemployment permanently. They also, independently of their empirical work, advocated tax-based incomes policies, which they said would be more effective than the conventional incomes policies of the 1970s. This idea found some favour with middle-ground politicians, but not with either unions or employers.

New classical economists, like Patrick Minford, sometimes embarrassed Richard Layard and his CLE colleagues by claiming to agree with most of what they said. The NAIRU framework was, after all, very close kin to the natural rate of Milton Friedman. Patrick Minford was also devoted to the estimation of time-series equations to identify the long-run causes of the rise in unemployment. His equations differed from the Layard-Nickell equations in the much greater importance he attached to the effect of social security benefits on the level of unemployment. He also identified trade union membership as a key determinant of unemployment, and more generally he blamed the failure of real wages to adjust quickly and smoothly to clear the market for labour. For him, as indeed for the government in many of its official pronouncements, the problem of unemployment was essentially one of excessive real wages, and the cure was to make the labour market work better – so as to get real wages down.

About the middle of the 1980s there was a subtle change in the way unemployment was discussed. The idea of 'hysteresis' was introduced. It was suggested that unemployment might be self-perpetuating. A rise in unemployment, initially due to deficient demand, might if uncorrected become 'structural', become part of the NAIRU, become in Friedman's sense 'natural'. It was as if a spring, having been overstretched, would not when released revert to its original shape – hence the obscure name applied to the alleged phenomenon.

It began as an observation of what seemed to be happening to unemployment in Britain, and indeed elsewhere in the world. Unemployment remained very high in the mid-1980s, but there was no further deceleration in the rate of inflation; hence the NAIRU must have risen. Various explanations were then offered as to why it might have happened. Trade union bargainers were interested only in the welfare of 'insiders', and the unemployed were 'outsiders'. The long-term unemployed were becoming unemployable (or thought to be so) and no longer counted as effective members of the labour supply. The 'human capital' of the labour force, that is its skills and experience, was being depleted by the long-drawn-out recession and by changes in the structure of output.

The implications of the hysteresis hypothesis could be variously interpreted. One conclusion would be that high unemployment was now so firmly entrenched that policy should aim to mitigate its social effects, not to cure it. But another, more optimistic, conclusion was that the forces of hysteresis could be put into reverse. The spring could be distorted again, but compressed, rather than stretched. The way was open again for the advocates of reflation.

About this time, however, the tide turned and unemployment began to fall rapidly. This did not end the debate, but took away some of its urgency. It also threw a new light retrospectively on some of the debates of earlier years. If unemployment could fall so fast in 1987, for example, and inflation not (yet) be rekindled, was the level from which unemployment fell really 'natural'? What had happened to the stable relationship on which the calculation of NAIRU depended? The issue remained undecided and most economists watched the fall with bewilderment, and a suspicion that all was not quite as it seemed.

FOCUS ON THE EXCHANGE RATE

In 1983 Willem Buiter and Marcus Miller presented a paper at the Brookings Institute in Washington describing for an American audience the 'experiment' with monetarism that had recently been conducted in Britain. The theoretical model they used to interpret this episode drew on the writings of Rudiger Dornbusch, and concerned the way in which the exchange rate reacts to expectations of future inflation and the difficulties that arise when the exchange rate 'overshoots'.

The hypothesis of rational expectations, originally associated with the American new classical school, was adopted in the 1980s by economists from quite different traditions. It came to be quite generally accepted that theoretical ideas about economic behaviour are best worked out on the assumption that all economic agents understand how the economy works and make no systematic mistakes in predicting market behaviour or the conduct of economic policy. The use of the hypothesis in this way does not mean that the public is never mistaken, only that economic theory should not rest on the assumption that such mistakes will remain uncorrected. It brought about a profound change in the way macroeconomists reason, especially when discussing the consequences of change in the way that policy is conducted. The change of regime in Britain after 1979 made the new theory very topical and hastened the dissemination of the new ideas.

All kinds of economic variables are affected by expectations: levels of output, employment, quantities traded, wages, prices and stocks of assets held. But most variables are also subject to inertia, because it is costly to change them, so that they do not adjust fully in one jump when expectations change. It is arguable however that prices in financial markets are perfectly flexible and costless to change. They are therefore free from inertia, unless the monetary authorities or some other agent intervenes to smooth their path. One such price is the exchange rate. It was obvious to the most casual observer around 1980 that the behaviour of the exchange rate was crucial to an understanding of the effects on the British economy of the 'new beginning' made by the Conservative government.

The thesis of Buiter and Miller was that the announcement of a convincing counterinflation strategy changed expectations profoundly. The effect of the news was greatest on those prices which moved most flexibly. There was little effect on wages, but a considerable effect on the exchange rate. Inflation was brought under control, but relative prices were, for the time being, severely distorted. In particular the real exchange rate (the relative price of home and foreign production) was too high. This threw the burden of adjustment to the new policy regime on to the manufacturing sector, requiring it to contract to an extent that was in the longer term unnecessary and inappropriate.

The role of the exchange rate was a topic of central concern to the Treasury and Civil Service Committee of the House of Commons in their 1981 enquiry into a monetary policy, referred to in Part 1 of this study. (Both Willem Buiter and Marcus Miller were amongst the advisers assisting the Committee.) The exchange rate issue was clouded by the fact that the world price of oil had risen abruptly at about the same time as the new government took office. It was impossible therefore to distinguish conclusively how large the effects of the new policy regime on the real exchange rate had been.

It is clear nevertheless that the extent of the real appreciation went beyond what advocates of the new regime expected or intended. As mentioned above, both the Treasury and the London Business School models had exchange rate equations that depended on the growth rate of

£M3. The argument, which had no empirical basis, was that the exchange rate depended on expected relative prices at home and abroad, and expected prices depended on the growth of the money supply. The models had to be rebuilt when £M3 broke through the target bounds and the exchange rate nevertheless rose to the sky.

From 1981 onwards economists in this country became more sympathetic to the idea of exchange rate targets. The old Bretton Woods system, and the conduct of policy prior to the 1967 devaluation, was reassessed. It no longer seemed as it had in the 1970s, like the policy of the Dark Ages. Some assurance of exchange rate stability would help industry to plan ahead. Never again would the rate be allowed to rise in the face of all logic, as it did in 1979. An intellectual coalition was being formed in favour of exchange rate targets, but it included an odd assortment of allies, whose views as to the way exchange rate targets should be used were not at all in harmony.

There were monetarists, or ex-monetarists, including Samuel Brittan of *The Financial Times*, who transferred their allegiance from the money supply to the exchange rate after the fiasco with £M3. They wanted, above all, to have a 'nominal anchor' to the system, so that the monetary authorities were obliged to combat inflation. A money supply target should have provided this. When it failed to do so, they opted for the exchange rate instead. An extra advantage was that the link between the exchange rate and inflation was easily comprehensible, unlike the link between money and prices. Moreover, in the mainstream macroeconomic models of the United Kingdom, tight monetary policy, that is raising interest rates, worked to reduce inflation mainly through its effect on the exchange rate. The most appropriate measure of the tightness of policy might well therefore be the exchange rate itself.

These 'hardline' advocates of exchange stability were joined by Keynesian or ex-Keynesian economists whose main concern was to preserve the competitiveness of British industry. What they wanted was assurance that exchange rate appreciation would never again get out of hand. They suspected the government, especially the Prime Minister under the influence of Alan Walters, of unreconstructed monetarism even in the late 1980s and of an inclination to let free markets do their worst. This was the way the representatives of industry tended to argue. It was also the position adopted from 1985 by the *National Institute Economic Review*.

An exchange rate target pursued by one country in isolation seemed unlikely to be a very firm commitment. There was no longer a world monetary system for Britain to rejoin; but there was the European Monetary System (EMS) of which Britain already was strictly speaking a member, although a member who had been excused from keeping the rules of the club. The link with Europe was an added political attraction for some exchange rate enthusiasts, for example those associated with the Social Democratic Party (SDP). For others it was the stern traditions of the

Bundesbank and the way it dominated the EMS which made an exchange rate regime particularly attractive.

Others found the prospect of a link with Europe distinctly offputting. One reason for this was the continuing importance of exchange controls in defending the pattern of exchange rates within Europe. It was feared that the EMS would prove unstable if another large country was added to it and that the long-run cost of British membership would be a return to controls on capital flows or even on domestic credit. This was the line of argument which seems to have convinced the Prime Minister. Her opposition was the main reason why Britain remained on the fringes of the EMS in the period covered by this study. The divisions within government on the issue ensured that the conduct of monetary policy remained for much of the 1980s in a state of confusion and indecision, but they were papered over quite successfully until after the 1987 election.

POLICYMAKING WITH MACROECONOMIC MODELS

At the end of 1987 the National Institute organised a conference to which the principal modelbuilding teams presented papers illustrating the use of models to analyse policy issues. It was an occasion for some stocktaking of developments in theory and practice over the ten years since the report of the Ball Committee and since the publication of the *Demand Management* volume edited by Michael Posner.

Modelbuilding continued to flourish in Britain during the 1980s, although it was somewhat in eclipse in North America. One reason was the pioneering work on time-series econometrics carried out in this country, by David Hendry and others, and the resulting academic interest in empirical macroeconomics. This was reinforced by the encouragement, and financial support, given by the Social Science Research Council (SSRC) especially when Michael Posner was its chairman. A bureau was set up at Warwick University to monitor and disseminate the work of the teams in receipt of SSRC funds. The continuing relevance of models to policy design was recognised by the Treasury and the Bank, who continued to maintain their own models, and to use them for forecasting and policy analysis. There was a brief period in 1979 when it seemed possible that quantitative work of this kind was so out of keeping with the new monetarist philosophy that it would be abandoned by the Treasury. The arrival of Terry Burns from the London Business School as Chief Economic Adviser ensured that its position was secure. In fact the Treasury forecasters under Huw Evans gained an enviable reputation for accuracy and the research work done by Treasury modelbuilders was still well-regarded by their academic colleagues.

Well before 1987 most of the macroeconomic models had been adapted so that they could embody the hypothesis of rational, or consistent, expectations. This was not only true of the new classical models built by Patrick Minford and Michael Beenstock, but also of non-classical models including those of the National Institute and the Treasury. Traditional calculations like expenditure mutlipliers could now be made on the assumption that firms' output expectations, which guided their investment or their employment decisions, were consistent with the forecasts of output made by the model itself. The main conclusion drawn from the work was that the rational expectations hypothesis applied to the Keynesian features of a model would serve only to reinforce its Keynesian characteristics. There was, in other words, nothing uniquely 'rational' or 'consistent' about classical economics.

As in the 1970s the determination of the exchange rate was the greatest headache for empirical modellers. They now had more years of relevant data to investigate, and the spectacular appreciation of 1979-80 in the data set to explain. Even so it was difficult to identify stable behaviour. The rational expectations hypothesis was particularly radical in its implications for exchange rate modelling. In fact the main determinant of the exchange rate at one point in time seems to be the expectation of its future movements. These expectations must, in a consistent model solution, be the same as the movements which actually take place. But any model solution must be over a finite period of time, so the expectations held at the end of that period must be determined in some other way. This problem of the 'terminal conditions' continued to bedevil modelbuilders and most of the solutions adopted were based on *a priori* reasoning rather than empirical observation. Partly for that reason model simulations were sometimes conducted on the assumption that the exchange rate was fixed by monetary policy and unaffected by changes in other variables.

The financial sectors of the models more generally proved difficult to estimate, partly because of the institutional changes following the abolition of exchange control, the removal of the 'corset' and later the 'Big Bang.' The London Business School model had the most sophisticated treatment of financial flows, but it was partly 'imposed' rather than estimated. No model could offer a stable set of estimated relationships describing the determination of £M3 or the way that aggregate interacted with the rest of the economy.

It was the aim of all the macroeconomic modelbuilders in the 1980s to augment their models by including a more comprehensive treatment of the 'supply side' of the economy. The framework used in most cases was similar to that developed by Layard and Nickell at the LSE. The models could be reinterpreted in terms of their NAIRUs. Relative price terms appeared in the equations for such variables as employment, investment and the supply of labour. Thus the models, or most of them, seemed to be evolving towards an eclectic position in which more market-related mechanisms of adjustment were recognised, as well as the 'disequilibrium' responses which typify income–expenditure models in the Keynesian tradition. It would be an exaggeration to suggest that there was in effect a single consensus model acceptable to all applied macroeconomists in the mid-1980s in Britain, but we were closer to one than the readers of newspaper articles and political speeches might imagine.

A convergence of views was also evident in the way macroeconomic policy was being discussed by most academic economists around 1987. The issue of 'rules versus discretion' had been resolved into one of alternative ways of specifying policy reactions. No-one seemed in favour of inflexible targets which the authorities were committed to hitting in all circumstances; but no-one seemed inclined to leave the authorities free to respond judgementally to events with no precommitment at all. The experience of the early 1980s had shown the folly of over-commitment, but it had also shown that a reputation for toughness and consistency was an asset. The experience of the 1970s had shown what damage could be done by a reputation for weakness and vacillation.

So the search was on for an optimum set of 'feedback' rules, indicating how policy instruments like interest rates and the fiscal balance should respond to developments in the economy. Debate about these 'feedback' rules was marked by technical sophistication and the display of intellectual virtuosity rather than the clash of economic or political doctrines. There was a willingness to recognise that the best rules would be robust ones, that is rules which would work well in the other models, not just the model for which they were originally designed. Something like intellectual humility was to be found in the policy recommendations of most applied macroeconomists. Few, if any, of them had lived through the preceding decade without making confident predictions that they now regretted.

PART 3

BRITAIN AND THE WORLD ECONOMY

10

THE WORLD ECONOMY

Both the narrative of events and the history of ideas have shown how open the British economy is to influences from abroad. That alone would justify, in a history of macroeconomic policy in Britain, a brief account of developments in the world economy during the 1970s and 1980s. But the behaviour of the British economy parallels that of other countries, even in aspects like the rise of unemployment, where it is unlikely that the relationship is a simple one of cause and effect. International comparisons may throw light on the reasons why the British economy behaved as it did. Broadly we shall be concerned with the first kind of issue, the effect of world events on Britain, in this section and with the second kind of issue in the remaining sections of Part 3. Three developments in particular had profound effects on Britain: the management of international economic relations under a system of floating exchange rates, the consequence of the cartelisation of oil production, and the slower growth of output and productivity, in almost all industrialised countries during the 1970s.

INTERNATIONAL ECONOMIC RELATIONS

In the opening years of the 1970s, just before the beginning of the period covered by this study, the Bretton Woods system of fixed exchange rates against the dollar, established at the end of the second world war, broke up. The first major sign of weakness had been the devaluation of sterling in 1967, but it was the decision of the United States to devalue the dollar (in the sense that its value was reduced both in terms of gold and foreign currencies) which removed the keystone of the arch. New parities were set under the Smithsonian agreement in December 1971, but it proved impossible to rebuild a 'fixed-rate' system once it was known that the position of even the dollar was not impregnable. In February 1973 the dollar was again devalued, this time without the need for an international conference to lend dignity to the occasion. Almost immediately thereafter the attempt to maintain any pretence of exchange rate stability was abandoned, and the international monetary system became *de facto* one of floating exchange rates, although periodic intervention by central banks went on. Sterling itself had been floating since June 1972.

The move to floating rates was not the result of decisions deliberately taken by central banks, individually or collectively. It was the result of failure, followed by abdication. There were therefore no new rules to be followed. It seemed at first as if each country could go its own way, adopting without consultation whatever policies suited its domestic circumstances. Thus it seemed possible for some countries to press for full employment by expanding demand, allowing their exchange rates to fall and doing the best they could to suppress any resulting inflation. Their more conservative neighbours would have no reason to object. Their aim of maintaining price stability would be assisted by exchange rate appreciation. That might be the theory of a floating rate system, but the practice turned out to be quite different.

Efforts to coordinate policies between the major industrial countries became more, not less, active. The regular meetings of the IMF and the OECD continued, with the benefit of the increasingly sophisticated analysis provided by the Fund staff in Washington and by the Secretariat in Paris. Indeed the level at which international economic relations were discussed was raised by the annual summit meetings between presidents and prime ministers. It is possible to doubt the real influence of all these international meetings on subsequent policy action by the governments represented at them. Nevertheless, the effort was made to consult regularly, and in the process a kind of international public opinion developed which probably did influence events quite profoundly. In the forming of that opinion, it seems, Anglo-Saxon and especially British economists played a disproportionate part, perhaps because they were more vocal than most, more self-confident and argumentative. Yet in the end it was often the more pragmatic conservative views expressed by little-known economists or officials from Germany, France or Japan that actually carried the day.

Under the old Bretton Woods system countries with balance of payments deficits often needed to borrow from the IMF so that they could intervene in support of their currencies. The IMF would impose conditions when such loans were made, which the staff and other member states believed would ensure that the borrower restored his economy to balance, so that the loan could be repaid. Despite the change to a floating rate system such lending and borrowing continued. Britain was again a major borrower in 1976, as described in Part 1.

More generally international policy coordination was still required, because the system did not produce a pattern of current account balances which seemed appropriate or sustainable. This was especially true at the beginning of the period after the 1974 rise in oil prices; and it was again true at the end of the period as the fall of the dollar in 1986 failed to correct the very large deficit on the current account of the United States. Continuously throughout the period countries in deficit were being urged to restrain domestic demand, whilst countries in surplus were being urged to expand. Generally the deficit countries felt the pressure more acutely than those in surplus. That too was a tradition carried over from Bretton Woods.

It was not just issues of relative adjustment, like exchange rates and payments equilibrium, which made up the agenda of international meetings. There was at least as much need for discussion of the stance of macroeconomic policy to be adopted by the major countries considered as a group. Much of this was veiled in the politeness and platitudes of diplomacy, but real exchanges of view took place nevertheless. Some governments pressed for a cautious policy with strict control of the money supply and a watchful eye on fiscal deficits. They urged this discipline on their neighbours as well as practising it themselves. The United States in particular received advice of this kind in abundance. Other voices urged a more expansionary policy, encouraging Germany and Japan in particular to take more risks. Small countries, as a rule, wanted the large ones to expand fast, since they were dependent on them as a market for their produce. Increasingly through our period the more cautious voices became predominant.

If exchange rate flexibility failed to eliminate the need for policy coordination, it was not for lack of active markets. The volume of business in foreign exchange expanded very rapidly in the 1970s and 1980s and exchange control measures were progressively relaxed. The dollar remained the chief unit of account and the currency in which most central banks held their reserves. The importance of sterling diminished, but the existence of a free and very active market in London gave it a role greater than the share of Britain in international trade on its own would justify. Increasingly the markets paid attention to the value of the yen. The deutschmark took on a new role, described below, as the hub of the European Monetary System (EMS).

Exchange markets were extremely active, and much economic expertise was devoted to advising participants, yet the resulting behaviour of exchange rates did not always seem to accord with economic fundamentals, that is with the underlying pattern of relative inflation rates or the need for balance of payments adjustment. The example of the sterling appreciation in 1980 has been discussed already. The appreciation of the dollar from 1980 right up to 1985 was even more difficult to justify in terms of fundamentals. It was followed by a sharp fall or market correction. These episodes convinced many economists and policymakers that the floating rate system could produce sustained misalignments and suggested to some that central banks should intervene on a larger scale and take the initiative by declaring their exchange rate objectives. The problem facing all monetary authorities, which remained unsolved throughout the period covered by this study, was that market forces were too strong for them to overcome. Confidence in the ability of central banks to dominate the market could not be restored after the breakdown in the early 1970s. At the end of our period, in the mid-1980s, opinion was swinging back towards greater exchange rate stability and large-scale intervention was resumed, following the Plaza agreement of 1985. But it was not very successful. The precise objectives set then and also by the Louvre agreement of February 1987 were never made public, but it is clear that they were not fully achieved. All this uncertainty, confusion, experiment and failure in the management of world financial markets had a profound effect on the conduct of monetary policy in individual countries, not least the United Kingdom. However wise, however consistent, domestic policy might be, it was always at risk of being blown off course by turbulence from overseas. The future of the international monetary system was as unresolved in 1987 as in 1974.

By contrast, real, if very slow, progress was made towards reestablishing exchange rate stability within Europe. Initially, when the Bretton Woods system broke down, the European countries decided to operate narrower bands of exchange rate flexibility around their common rate against the dollar. This was referred to as 'the snake within the tunnel'. In the turbulent years of the earlier 1970s this arrangement came unstuck many times. The French and Italian inflation rates were much faster than that of Germany and, despite strict exchange controls, it was impossible to preserve any set of cross-rates for more than a short period. In 1979, however, the European Monetary System was introduced after an initial bilateral agreement had been reached between France and Germany. It proved far more durable than any other attempt at reforming international monetary arrangements in this period. The reasons for Britain's failure to join the exchange rate mechanism, which is the main function of the EMS, have been discussed already. For those who did join, it worked in practice rather like a small-scale Bretton Woods system, with the mark playing the role of the dollar and with a looser discipline on the other currencies involved, because realignments were much more frequent. By the mid-1980s there was less underlying difference between Germany on the one hand and France and Italy on the other over the priorities of macroeconomic policy and their rates of inflation were tending to converge. In these circumstances it became possible again to talk of the ultimate goal of monetary union.

Such talk raised in acute form for Britain the old dilemma which had vexed international economic relations ever since the war. Was Britain a world economic power in her own right, with an independent role to play in world affairs, a worthy member of the top nations' club, the G5? Or was Britain an integral part of Europe, benefiting from closer association with Germany, France and the rest and coordinating priorities and policies with theirs? The choice was too difficult to make; decisions were simply put off, again and again.

WORLD INFLATION AND THE PRICE OF OIL

The course of world inflation can be described using the average rate of increase of consumer prices in the seven major industrial countries. This had been persistently positive throughout the 1950s and 1960s, but apart from a brief episode at the time of the Korean War, it was contained below 5 per cent a year. After 1974 it varied considerably from year to year, but averaged about 9 per cent. In the mid-1980s it dropped back down again to between 2 and 5 per cent, a rate similar to that of the 1960s.

In describing world inflation, and seeking to interpret its course from one decade to another, it is tempting to imagine the world as a single closed system, a global market place in which all prices are bid up or down by the balance of world demand and world supply. This approach is much more appropriate however for some prices than for others. There is clearly not a world market for labour, nor is there a world market for the many goods and services which must in their nature be locally produced. Even for some manufactured goods that are extensively traded, it seems that their prices reflect costs in the producing area as much as the prices of the goods with which they compete. For many primary commodities on the other hand there is indeed a single world market, in which prices change continuously in response to bids and offers.

The early years of the 1970s saw one of the price booms to which commodity markets are prone. The export prices of primary producers in dollars rose by about 50 per cent in 1973 and by a further 30 per cent in 1974. One element in this was compensation for the fall in the value of the dollar subsequent to the Smithsonian agreement mentioned above. Another was the special demand for some commodities that had been created by the war in Vietnam. There was also pressure on grain prices from increased demand by the Soviet Union. These special factors apart, the price boom was attributable to the buoyancy of world industrial output as most of the major economies were expanding simultaneously. The initial rise was magnified by speculative purchases. It was an example of the inflationary consequence of overheating at the world level, and the dangers of a repetition were seldom far from the minds of policymakers for at least a decade thereafter.

This potentially explosive force in the event lay dormant for the whole of the period covered by this study. Non-oil commodity prices did indeed continue to rise during the 1970s, but not, on average, faster than the prices of manufactured goods traded on world markets. The largest rise was in 1977, but it was followed by actual falls in the dollar–price index for commodities in the two following years. During the 1980s falls in commodity prices became larger and more general. Between 1984 and 1986, for example, the real value of non-oil commodities, that is their purchasing power in terms of manufactured goods, fell by as much as 25 per cent. This fall helped to slow down the rate of world inflation and raised real incomes in the industrial countries, including Britain. Thus non-oil primary commodities were important both in initiating and in ending the inflationary experience of the 1970s, and in both cases price movements were, in part at least, a reflection of the pressure of demand in global markets. But the most important commodity price of all, the price of crude oil, was subject to influences of a quite different kind, following the cartelisation of production by the Organisation of Petroleum Exporting Countries (OPEC).

The price of crude oil must be given special attention in any account of world inflation since the 1970s. The economist, in describing its behaviour, may talk about supply and demand in the world oil market, but the historian must concentrate his attention on three special events, each in its way unique and linked to the political circumstances of the time. These events are the quadrupling of oil prices in 1974, their doubling in 1979 and their halving in 1986.

The market for oil never was a truly competitive one like those for some other traded commodities. Until the 1960s prices were set by a group of oil companies at a low level which reflected production costs rather than the scarcity value of finite oil reserves. The formation of OPEC shifted the balance of power from the oil companies to the governments of producer countries, especially those in the Middle East. The dramatic way in which that power was first used was the result of the war between Israel and the Arabs. There is no way of knowing what action OPEC might have taken without that pretext; perhaps the cohesion of the cartel at that stage depended more on the common loyalty of its most powerful members to the Arab cause than on a common interest in exploiting their mineral wealth. Once the power of the cartel had been demonstrated, on the other hand, it was economic interest rather than political sympathy that held it together.

The world economy was inflation-prone before 1974. This was demonstrated, not just by the rise in other commodity prices already discussed above, but also by the increasing rate of wage increases in most countries from the latter half of the 1960s onwards. Moreover the fourfold rise in oil prices came just after the break-up of the international monetary system. The monetary authorities in the United States and the major countries were in a sense 'caught off-guard'. There were no clear rules to be followed in these new circumstances. They did not know how to react.

The average rate of inflation for the major seven industrial countries rose to 13.5 per cent in 1974 and fell back slowly to about 11 per cent in the following year. Meanwhile the average change in real output in these same countries, which had risen very strongly in the early 1970s, was close to zero in 1974 and minus 0.5 per cent in 1975. As a group they also had a deficit on their balance of payments with the rest of the world averaging about 0.3 per cent of GDP in 1974, which was restored to a small surplus by the next year. The average rate of unemployment (on standardised OECD definitions) rose from 3.4 per cent in 1973 to 3.7 per cent in 1974 and 5.4 per cent in 1975.

The United Kingdom government argued, more consistently than any other, that the appropriate response to the rise in oil prices was fiscal expansion to maintain demand and output, until such time as the oil exporting countries could spend their new-found wealth. This view was the intellectual basis for IMF initiatives to increase official lending facilities, but it was regarded with some suspicion, especially in Germany.

If outcomes are taken to reveal the preferences of policymakers world-wide, then it seems that they were prepared to tolerate high rates of inflation in the mid-1970s, because the alternative as they saw it was deeper recession and a steeper rise in unemployment. At the time, however, the situation was far from clear and decisions were taken on a view of the forecast which was, in many respects, too optimistic. The recession in 1974 was much deeper than generally expected and inflation rather faster. On the other hand there was deep concern about the financing of the collective balance of payments position, which may have been exaggerated. The immediate problem of placing the vast surplus of funds that accrued to the oil producers was solved by private sector banks more effectively than the monetary authorities had reason to expect. But the long-term conse-quences of this 'solution' for third-world debt remained to haunt the 1980s.

The second oil price shock of 1979 was again a by-product of war, this time the conflict following the revolution in Iran. As a percentage increase the price rise was much smaller this time, but the addition it made to costs and prices in the oil-importing countries was of similar magnitude. The rate of inflation for the major seven industrial countries was 7 per cent in 1978 and rose in 1980 to 12.3 per cent. Thus at the time of the second oil price shock the underlying rate of world inflation was still much higher than it had been before the first shock. Yet the rate of world inflation at the second peak was never quite as high as it had been at the first. The immediate effect of the second shock on output growth also appears rather less marked than the first. The average growth of output fell to 1.1 per cent in 1980, but recovered to 2 per cent in 1981 and only became negative in 1982. It would seem strange to attribute this 1982 world recession to the *direct* effects of the second oil price shock on real incomes in the oil-importing countries.

In reacting to the second shock, policymakers had the experience of the first to draw on. The lesson they learnt was the need for caution and the need to maintain discipline to prevent a sustained rise in inflation. Between the mid-1970s and the early 1980s the philosophy of policymaking had changed everywhere, although not anywhere perhaps as dramatically as it had in Britain. The goal of maintaining full employment was more readily sacrificed on this occasion to the goal of price stability. The 1982 recession was mainly it seems the consequence of tight monetary policy, especially in the United States. This could be interpreted as an indirect and delayed consequence of the second oil price shock. In retrospect it is clear that OPEC had overplayed its hand.

The third oil price shock was the fall in 1986. Unlike the earlier shocks it was not set off by political developments in the producer countries. In order to sustain in the mid-1980s the level of the oil price set by the OPEC cartel after 1979, it was necessary to hold back production. The producers failed to reach agreement over production sharing, and were obliged to let the price fall back sharply.

The effect on world inflation of a fall in the oil price is not, it seems, symmetrical with the effect of a similar price rise. With world inflation in 1985 already below 4 per cent, there was relatively little room for a further reduction unless prices, and indeed wages, in some countries were actually to fall.

Moreover the policy response to the third oil price shock was by no means symmetrical with the first and second. When oil prices rose, importing countries cut back the level of domestic demand to limit the scale of their balance of payments deficits. They did not feel the same need to add to demand to compensate for a move into surplus when oil prices fell. The real income transfers between consuming and producing countries would in principle be symmetrical, but their effects on world demand and output may not have been the same. In 1974, and to a lesser extent in 1979, the oil producing countries were simply unable to spend their new wealth as fast as it accrued. By 1986 however their economies were more fully developed and they were in many cases importing up to the limit of their financial resources. When their real incomes were cut that did constrain them to import, and consume or invest, less.

By the end of the 1980s world inflation was very low indeed. In some countries it was actually negative. But it would be misleading to suppose that the experience of high inflation in the 1970s and early 1980s had left no scars. Two real changes had come about in the course of the 'battle against inflation' as it was commonly called, which were not quickly reversed when the battle was won.

The first was the rise in interest rates. When inflation was at its highest, world real interest rates, on any measure, were for many years negative – that is, investors well knew that the real value of their financial capital was being eroded. As inflation came down, however, nominal interest rates fell less, opening up a positive real return, which was high by historical standards. The persistence of this relatively high real yield can be explained in many ways. It may have had something to do with the increase in government borrowing in the United States. But it almost certainly owed a lot to the fear of renewed inflation in the minds of central bankers. Such fears are not easily set to rest.

The other legacy of the 1970s and 1980s was an average level of unemployment much higher than it had been in earlier postwar decades. That increase, however, was unevenly distributed across countries, being marked in Europe, much less so in America. It cannot be explained without discussion of the circumstances of individual countries, which is delayed until Chapter 11 below.

The average growth rate of output in the member countries of OECD from 1964–73 was 5 per cent a year; from 1974–87 it was 2½ per cent. The corresponding figures for the growth of labour productivity were about 4 per cent and about 1½ per cent. (In the case of the United Kingdom and one or two other countries there was some reacceleration of productivity growth in the 1980s, but this was not the general experience.) If we knew the reasons for this change of trend it might well provide clues to the understanding of the equally marked slowdown in the growth of the British economy – one of the problems that perplexed policymakers in the 1970s. Britain's experience was just one example of a worldwide phenomenon.

If one takes a sufficiently long view, and accepts that estimated growth rates are comparable between periods many decades apart, then it appears that the 1950s and 1960s were a period of unusually rapid growth, and that the 1970s saw a reversion to a more normal pace. This way of looking at the postwar period suggests that the cause of the slowdown in the 1970s should be sought in the exhaustion of some special factors that operated for the two preceding decades.

From 1950–73 the growth of labour productivity was very fast in Europe, and even faster in Japan. In these countries the rate of growth was much more rapid in those years than it had been in any measured prewar period. This contrasts with the situation in the United States where the growth of labour productivity was not very different after 1950 to what it had been since 1913. It may be significant that the *level* of labour productivity was much higher in America. This has led to the suggestion that the fast growth in Europe and Japan was part of the process of catching up with American practice in technology or industrial organisation.

To this must be added, in explanation of the fast growth everywhere between 1950 and 1973, a progressive movement towards greater liberalisation of trade and payments. This did not only involve dismantling the apparatus of special wartime controls. It went far beyond that in reversing the moves to protectionism and regulation of the interwar years. This resulted in a progressively better allocation of resources both within countries and between countries. It is also plausibly argued that the maintenance of full employment in the postwar period may itself have helped to accelerate the growth of productive potential.

This 'golden age' ended in the early 1970s, to be followed by an age of disappointment and confusion. Problems recurred which had been thought to have been overcome; the achievements of a whole generation were lost almost overnight.

Slower growth was by no means the only problem that hit the world economy around the beginning of the 1970s. As we have seen it was at about this time that inflation accelerated, the world monetary system broke down, oil prices quadrupled, and unemployment in many countries began to rise substantially. Parsimony calls for explanations which cover more than one of these roughly contemporaneous turns for the worse.

A Keynesian explanation would cover the rise in unemployment as well as the slow growth of output, and it would still find supporters in this country. Aggregate demand, if it is, on its own, to explain persistently slow growth, must have fallen further and further below the supply potential of the world economy. This would be consistent with the appearance of a trend rise in unemployment. It is difficult however to reconcile the hypothesis of growing demand deficiency with the experience of world inflation which was rapid throughout the 1970s, and at times accelerating.

Demand-side explanations need to be supplemented by postulating an exogenous increase in inflation, caused by OPEC or trade union militancy or the breakdown of the Bretton Woods system. The actual course of output year-to-year and even decade-by-decade then depends mainly on the choices made by policymakers as between accepting higher inflation, or trying to put downward pressure on it by deflating demand. Despite any protests they might make to the contrary, governments were, according to this hypothesis, managing demand and thus determining the levels both of employment and of output. It may still be true, however, that they had little real choice in the matter, since it was only by slowing down output growth that the rate of inflation could be kept within bounds at all. If so, it was OPEC and the trade union militants who were really to blame for slow growth and for rising unemployment.

The main difficulty of this explanation has already been hinted at. It may be appealing as an explanation of rising unemployment and, to that extent, of growth below productive potential, but it does not really explain why the trend of productivity growth itself should slow down. The initial response of employers to hoard labour during a downturn, could hardly be maintained if the downturn lasted more than a decade. In the long run a lower level of output might well, because of diminishing returns to scale, be associated with *higher* labour productivity, not lower. The demand-side explanation of slower growth has, surely, to be supplemented by a supply-side change in the productivity trend originating at about the same time.

By a rather similar chain of reasoning, a *purely* supply-side explanation proves unsatisfactory. It fits with higher inflation and lower productivity, but it cannot on its own explain rising unemployment. It seems we have to accept an explanation of slower growth which includes *both* deficiency of demand, probably caused by the policy response to inflation, *and* a slower growth of productive potential beginning about the same time. How might the slower growth of supply have come about?

It is not possible to argue that innovation had lost its impetus, that mankind had run out of good new ideas in the 1970s, when the information technology industry was in its infancy. Technological advance seems to be an inherently explosive process, one which tends to increase at an increasing rate. If so what we seek is an explanation of the special factors that held the process of applying new technology back during the 1970s and 1980s. The implication is that, could those obstacles be removed, the growth rates of the earlier postwar period could be matched, or even bettered.

It has been argued that the increase in the price of oil was damaging to the supply side of the world economy (as well as adding directly to inflation and the problems of economic policymakers). Certainly some investment must have been diverted from the expansion of capacity to new technologies intended to conserve energy. But it is difficult to demonstrate that the scale of such effects is anything like adequate to account for the differences between growth rates before and after 1973.

Another possible culprit is the growth of the public sector relative to the rest of the economy. (Some recent OECD publications give prominence to this factor.) The evidence for its importance is mixed. The ratio of government receipts to GDP rose significantly between 1973 and 1984 in Japan, in Europe and in the United Kingdom; it rose by much less in the United States and in Germany. Moreover the rise in the 1970s and 1980s continued a trend which was already evident in the 1960s. Granted that the overall level of taxation could serve to moderate the growth of supply, it is nevertheless difficult to point the finger at this factor as the *main* explanation of the changes with which we are concerned.

Perhaps the least unsatisfactory explanation that can be offered is that attitudes to work changed around the end of the 1960s in most advanced countries. There was less willing cooperation between workers and management, a change which showed itself both in wage militancy and as increasing resistance to innovation. There may have been a shift in the balance of power, or of negotiating strengths, within firms. Certainly the share of profits in the value of total output tended to decline in the 1970s. The role played by trade unions varied from country to country, but the phenomenon of reduced cooperation may have been more general. It is easier to speculate about the social relations necessary to the process of production, much more difficult to formulate hypotheses that can be tested in practice. Nevertheless it is very plausible that changes in industrial relations are at least as important to the growth of productivity as are changes in technology or the availability of resources.

11

THE BRITISH ECONOMY COMPARED
WITH OTHERS

The advent of floating exchange rates, the three oil price shocks and the slower growth of output and productivity – these developments affected all of the major industrial countries in the 1970s and 1980s. The ways in which policies were adapted, and performance was impaired, reflect the special characteristics of each case. By comparing cases something may be learnt of the reasons for the relative success or failure of each. It should be possible to throw some light on the history of the British economy in particular by making comparisons with the contemporary history of a number of other, more or less similar, countries. The ones chosen are the United States, Germany, France and Sweden.

THE UNITED STATES OF AMERICA

It would be difficult to exaggerate the influence of American economists on the development of ideas in Britain; most of our leading academic economists have spent some years at an American university – not a few are permanent exiles. Many of the textbooks used in graduate studies of economics in Britain are written by Americans; some teachers even use American texts for their introductory courses. The history of ideas about macroeconomic policy in Part 2 of this study is in the main the history of British reactions to American ideas. It is important therefore to recognise how different our economy is from theirs.

The United States is four times the size of Britain in terms of population and vastly greater in terms of land area. Their level of real income is some 40 per cent higher than ours. They have a relatively small public sector. Their traditions are of private provision in health and social welfare. They are rightly proud of their great entrepreneurs, rightly less proud of their public administration.

In America international trade accounts for under 10 per cent of GNP, compared with 25 per cent in Britain. America is not only an industrial giant, but also a major producer and exporter of food and raw materials. If macroeconomics is about the determination of output and prices it is difficult to see how the same theoretical model can be applied to both. America is almost a closed economy, self-contained in its behaviour and autonomous in its policy action. Britain is near the opposite end of the spectrum, dependent on world markets and making policy in response to events or decisions taken abroad, on which it can exercise little or no influence. It is perhaps surprising, in view of this contrast, that events in the two countries in our period run parallel to the extent they do.

In Britain fiscal and monetary policy are both securely in the hands of central government. In the United States the administration is often unable to enact the fiscal policy of its choice, because of opposition in Congress, or able to do so only after long and frustrating delays. The Federal Reserve Board can go its own way, sometimes conducting a monetary policy which is deliberately at odds with the priorities of the President and his advisers. The overall stance of policy is not so much a compromise as a result of conflicting pressure which often satisfies no-one, and for which no-one is unambiguously responsible. There may be merits in the separation of powers laid down by the Constitution, but the consistent application of policy action to clearly-stated goals of economic management is not one of them.

Despite this and despite the traditional American suspicion of government management of anything, in the 1960s under Presidents Kennedy, Johnson and Nixon economic policy was conducted within the Keynesian framework. Economic growth was rapid, averaging 4½ per cent a year from 1962–9, thanks partly to the growth of military spending and the war in Vietnam. Inflation remained low until the closing years of the decade when it began to accelerate ominously. The 1970 recession, caused partly by cuts in government spending, did little to slow down inflation, although unemployment rose sharply. The response of the Nixon administration was to impose wage and price controls, initiated with a 90-day freeze in August 1971. (The parallel with incomes policies in Britain under the Heath government is an obvious one.)

The verdict of most commentators on the effect of these wage and price controls is that they had a significant effect when they were first introduced, but that this weakened over time, and was all lost in a 'bounce-back' when they were finally lifted in 1974. (A similar judgement has been passed on incomes policies in this country.) Meanwhile the inflationary situation had been greatly worsened by the worldwide rise in commodity prices, by the depreciation of the dollar and by the first oil price shock. The appropriate response of fiscal and monetary policy to supply-side shocks like these became the main macroeconomic issue for debate in America in the 1970s. To what extent should policy be 'accommodating'? Should the in-built stabilisers of the tax and social security system be allowed to operate, thus raising the fiscal deficit? Should the money supply be allowed to grow any faster?

As the decade went on it became clear that the response of the American economy to inflation was not exactly the same as that of most economies in Europe. The difference turned on the behaviour of wages. When consumer prices rose as a result of the oil price or related shocks, wages in most

European countries, not least in Britain, rose almost immediately in response. It was as if wages were indexed to prices, as indeed on occasion in many European countries they were. In America, however, the tradition of fixed long-period wage contracts remained, with very little provision for indexation. When prices rose, *real* wages in America fell. This 'rigidity' turned out to be one of the strengths of the United States labour market, keeping inflation within bounds and helping to maintain employment. The record of employment in America during the 1970s is indeed impressive. The average rise from 1970–79 was nearly 2½ per cent a year, compared with only ½ per cent a year in the rest of the OECD area. The obverse of this picture was a relatively slow growth of productivity, but it had the effect of holding unemployment virtually flat in America, comparing 1979 with 1972, at a time when elsewhere it was trending upwards.

The United States economy had responded well to the depreciation of the dollar following the Smithsonian agreement, and the subsequent move to floating rates. The volume of exports rose by no less than 24 per cent in 1973 and, with the onset of recession in the following year, the volume of imports fell sharply as well. The United States current balance was in surplus in 1974, thanks to the competitiveness of manufacturing but also to domestic oil production and to growing exports of food. In 1975 the surplus was over 1 per cent of GDP, unusually large for any country in relation to trade flows. The effective exchange rate for the dollar rose in 1976, but fell back again before the end of the decade.

These external developments were not, however, the main focus of macroeconomic policy. The level of interest rates was of pervasive importance to the United States economy in a way that the exchange rate was not. Short-term rates were raised in 1973 and 1974, contributing to the depth of the recession, In 1975 they came down abruptly and the next year recovery got under way. The growth rate in 1976, 1977 and 1978 was well maintained at around 5 per cent a year, enough to produce a good cyclical fall in employment. Inflation, however, remained rather high, with some tendency to accelerate. This time there was no prices and incomes freeze. Instead there was a new and quite dramatic phase of monetary policy.

In July 1979 Paul Volcker became chairman of the Federal Reserve Board. The discount rate was then progressively raised from 9½ per cent to 12 per cent by the end of the year. In October changes were announced in the way that monetary policy would be implemented. It is worth dwelling for a moment on the nature of these changes, and of their consequences for interest rates and economic activity.

Monetarism in America proved as difficult to implement as monetarism in Britain. The fundamental difficulty was the same in both cases: much increased reliance was placed on the measurement of monetary aggregrates at a time when banks and related financial institutions were changing the nature of their business in ways that made consistent statistical series impossible to maintain. In the United States the interpretation of the narrow aggregates, especially M1, was the issue of most pressing concern; but, as in Britain, the course of all aggregates, large or small, must be regarded with great suspicion as an indicator of anything at all at any time from the mid-1970s to the late 1980s.

The measurement problem in America was the fundamental one, although the control problem was also serious. Because the main focus was on narrow aggregates, the Federal Reserve Board (FRB) could be reasonably confident of hitting its monetary targets at least over a run of years, provided it was not inhibited by the need to keep interest rates stable or low. It never faced the impossible task of corralling a runaway £M3 which so vexed the Bank of England. The question in America was rather whether the Federal Reserve Board could, or should, try to control the money supply on a short-term basis, month-to-month, or quarter-to-quarter.

The new operating procedures introduced in October 1979 were designed to facilitate closer control of M1, by keeping a close watch on bank reserves and allowing greater volatility to interest rates. They did not amount to monetary base control of the kind advocated at the time in Britain as well as in America, but they were a significant step in that direction. The banks' reserves could not be controlled precisely by the FRB, but it could rely on influencing the banks by varying the price at which they could borrow.

Technically the new procedures cannot be described as altogether successful. They did achieve for a period at least a deceleration of monetary growth, accompanied by a rise in the general level of interest rates. The degree of interest-rate volatility that accompanied the tightening of monetary policy proved to be a problem in its own right. The money markets developed an obsession with monthly or even weekly, money supply data which encouraged short-term speculation on an unwelcome scale. The short-term volatility of bank reserves and the monetary aggregates themselves seem to have increased, rather than diminished.

All this seemed profoundly important at the time. In retrospect perhaps the most significant outcome was the increase in interest rates. The Federal funds rate rose from about 11 per cent, on average in 1979, to 16½ per cent in 1981; the prime rate on short-term business loans from 12½ per cent to about 19 per cent. These rates were well in excess of previous records. They had a pervasive effect, not just in America, but on the world economy as a whole.

Monetarism was effectively in command in America even before Ronald Reagan was elected President in October 1980. The economic policies of his administration obviously invite comparison with those of the Thatcher government in Britain. The underlying aims were so similar that the contrast between the outcomes in the two countries merits study. Perhaps the most intriguing contrast of all is that between the tight fiscal policy in Britain with the persistent federal deficit in the United States.

The Reagan administration did not intend to preside over fiscal extravagance. At the end of the 1970s the Republicans were in favour of balancing the budget; indeed many of them wanted to reform the United States Constitution so as to make deficits illegal. Nevertheless the financial balance of general government in the United States, having been in surplus in 1979, was in deficit to the extent of about 1 per cent of GNP in 1980 and 1981, rising to 3½ per cent in 1982 and 1983. The federal deficit as commonly discussed in the United States was larger than this, but the surplus of state and local government provided something of an offset. These general government deficits, moreover, seemingly moderate by international standards, have to be set alongside the exceptionally low household savings ratio in America; even a small public deficit might be difficult to finance at home.

The Reagan administration failed to balance its books because Congress would not respond to the tax cuts by cutting public expenditure in non-defence areas to the extent required. British Chancellors of the Exchequer always have difficulty in persuading their colleagues to cut spending, and this was true of the Thatcher government as of others, but once Cabinet has made up its collective mind, Parliament is not often an insurmountable obstacle. That is one familiar contrast between the conduct of economic policy in the two countries. More surprising perhaps was the decision of the Reagan administration to go ahead with tax cuts, despite the failure to cut spending. This was a very different response from that of Sir Geoffrey Howe in 1981. For completeness one should add that the revenue from oil taxes was benefiting the United Kingdom to a disproportionate extent, but the difference of fiscal stance is very striking nevertheless.

Keynesians, in Britain as well as in America, welcomed the fiscal expansion in America as the right policy, even if it came about for the wrong reason. On the most optimistic view, the tax cuts would encourage the growth of real output, whilst the high level of interest rates would reduce inflation. The course of events in the early to mid-1980s gave some support to this interpretation.

The United States experienced an unusual 'double-bottomed' recession; a small fall in output in 1980 being followed by a weak recovery in 1981, and a much sharper fall in 1982. Inflation rose higher, and stayed high longer, than it had in 1974. It was in double figures in 1979, 1980 and 1981. Thereafter the performance of the economy began to improve rapidly. The American economy recovered strongly in 1983 and 1984, with growth of 3½ per cent followed by over 6½ per cent. This compared with about 2 per cent followed by 3½ per cent in the rest of the OECD area. At the same time the rate of inflation fell to about 3–4 per cent. Unemployment, lagging a year behind, fell from 9½ per cent of the labour force in 1983 to 7 per cent in 1985. In the rest of the OECD area the employment rate was constant, or slightly rising, at an average of 8½–9 per cent. It was no wonder then that President Reagan could fight the 1984 election on the record of his economic polices, and win again.

The resilience of the American economy owed much to fixed investment. Housing, which is a very volatile component of expenditure in the United States increased in 1983 by no less than 42 per cent, with a further, smaller rise in the next year. Business investment was also very strong, rising by 17½ per cent in 1984, stimulated by cuts in corporate taxation. The savings ratio fell in 1983, contributing to a good rise in consumer spending. Overall real domestic demand rose by 5 per cent in 1983 and by no less than 8½ per cent in 1984, making the recovery significantly stronger than that of 1976 and 1977 at the corresponding phase of the previous cycle.

It is difficult to judge to what extent this recovery was policy induced. Monetary policy became more 'flexible' and 'pragmatic' after 1982 (in the United States as well as in Britain) and many indicators besides the monetary aggregates guided the actions of the FRB. Short-term interest rates did fall back from the high level of 1981, but they remained high relative to the rate of inflation. If investment or consumption responds to real, rather than nominal, interest rates then the strength of the recovery is very difficult to explain.

Certainly the fall in inflation itself was impressive. From about 10½ per cent in 1981, the annual rate of increase of consumer prices came down to little over 3 per cent in 1983, before rising back a little in the following year. One reason for this success of 'Reagonomics' at this stage was the concurrent strength of the dollar in foreign exchange markets. Between 1980 and 1985 the dollar effective rate rose by 33 per cent.

This is an interesting point of similarity between the consequences of monetarism in America and Britain. In both the exchange rate was allowed to float freely, a policy sometimes called 'benign neglect'. In both, interest rates were raised sharply, and held at a high level, avowedly for domestic reasons. In both the exchange rate rose, adding to real incomes, whilst reducing inflation. As Britain is by far the more open economy the exchange rate is much more important to prices and to real incomes; but the appreciation of the dollar was more substantial, and continued for about five years. (This parallel supports the view that the strength of sterling at the beginning of the 1980s was due to the announcement of a tight monetary regime rather than due to the increased value of oil production in the North Sea.)

The strength of the rise in domestic demand in America, together with the appreciation of the dollar, resulted in a rapid growth of imports, 24 per cent in 1984 alone. Exports were far from keeping pace, and the current account of the balance of payments deteriorated. By 1984 the deficit was over $100 billion, or 2.8 per cent of GNP. For a country as self-sufficient as America this is a remarkably large balance; imports exceeded exports in the ratio 5 to 3. Perhaps the most extraordinary aspect of the situation was the continuing strength of the dollar. This seemed to most economists at the time to defy explanation and to be irreconcilable with any objective assessment of the longer-term prospects for the currency. Yet it persisted. The faith of many commentators and policymakers in the wisdom embodied in financial markets was sorely tried.

The character of the recovery in America in the early 1980s differed in several respects from that in Britain, beginning about the same time and gathering pace a few years later. Productivity growth was not strong, partly because labour was being transferred from productive uses in manufacturing, made unprofitable by the high exchange rates, to less productive uses in services, ex-steelmakers serving 'fast food' being an example often quoted. There was employment growth in some very 'low-tech' activities as well as in the latest computer software for the Star Wars defence programme. A popular view in Britain at the time was that this American flexibility provided an enviable alternative to unemployment.

Another contrast with British experience was the slow growth of real wages in the American recovery. This may have been partly due to the migration of firms and workers to areas, mainly in the south and west, where unionisation was weak. It may also have been a realistic response by labour leaders in manufacturing to the threat of foreign competition while the dollar was so high. Ministers in Britain exhorted employers and unions to follow the American example; but they spoke in vain.

The dollar peaked in early March 1985. It was by that time common ground between central banks, if not with electioneering politicians in America, that the dollar was far too high. The Plaza agreement, between the members of the Group of Five (an unofficial top-nation cabal associated with the IMF) was designed to produce an orderly decline in the value of the dollar, not to prevent adjustment taking place. In the event, the dollar went on falling throughout 1986, 1987 and beyond. It fell further and faster than it had risen, again raising some questions as to the rationality of exchange markets and provoking very large and sustained intervention. The Louvre agreement of 1987 was a vain attempt to bring the fall to an end. While the dollar continued to fall it was difficult for the current account of the balance of payments to register an improvement. As fast as export volume responded to one period of depreciation, another period of the same would raise import prices. Since the total value of imports was much larger than the total value of exports it was particularly difficult for the balance to climb out of the J-curve trap.

Any improvement in the balance of payments was further delayed by continuing growth in the United States at a rate similar to that of the rest of OECD area. Pleas to the Japanese to stimulate domestic demand met with some response. Appeals to Germany to do the same were turned down. Policy coordination was the leading topic of conversation amongst policymakers and academic macroeconomists alike in the mid to late 1980s; yet the practical results at that time seem to have been small.

The main contribution expected from the Americans in any such coordination exercise was a reduction in the fiscal deficit. This was in any case a matter of concern to many politicians in America. In 1985 Congress passed the Balanced Budget and Emergency Deficit Control Act, commonly called the Gramm-Rudman-Hollings Act. In essence this was a deterrent rather than a programme of fiscal reform. It required across-the-board and arbitrary reductions in all spending if agreement was not reached between Congress and the Administration to a sufficiently rapid path back to fiscal responsibility. The deterrent had some effect, even though the Supreme Court ruled that the Act as originally passed was unconstitutional. Progress was painfully slow and by 1987 the best that could be said was that the *growth* of the deficit was no longer out of control.

The size of the twin deficits of the Federal government and on the balance of payments was one of the main preoccupations of international meetings at this time. But America is a vast economy relatively immune to external influences, and its progress was not obviously impeded. Growth at 3 per cent a year, in 1985, in 1986 and in 1987, was broadly in line with the average of the 1970s and unemployment continued to come down. By the end of 1987 unemployment was at about the same level as it had been in 1974 when the period covered by this study begins. (Over the same period, unemployment in Britain rose from 3 per cent of the labour supply to about 10 per cent.) Inflation remained low, despite the fall in the dollar, thanks to falls in oil and commodity prices, as well as to the moderation of wage increases. The ordinary American citizen had some excuse for complacency.

THE FEDERAL REPUBLIC OF GERMANY

In the 1970s and 1980s West Germany and Britain were countries of broadly the same size, in terms of land area and of population. Germany still had a rather larger, and less productive, agricultural sector. German industry was also rather larger as a share of total employment, but it was much more productive than the corresponding sector in Britain. As a consequence the average standard of living in Germany was about 30 per cent higher than in Britain. The reasons for these differences may be sought in the economic and political histories of the two countries since the late nineteenth century, if not earlier. Our present concern is rather with their contrasting experience from the mid-1970s to the late 1980s.

The performance of the German economy for much of that period was watched with admiration and envy by most of her European neighbours. This was particularly true of the rate of inflation, which averaged only 3.8 per cent from 1974–87, compared with an average for the whole of Western Europe of 9.6 per cent. Moreover the rate of employment in Germany remained relatively low throughout the 1970s, although it did increase sharply in the early 1980s and subsequently remained very high.

Macroeconomic policy in Germany for the whole of the postwar period has been based on broadly the same principles, with some shift of emphasis but no upheavals of the kind experienced more than once in Britain. Fiscal and monetary policy have both been generally cautious and conservative with the emphasis, particularly at the Bundesbank, on the need to hold down inflation. Industrial and trade policy have been liberal, at least in comparison with other European countries. On one interpretation this policy combination has been the cause of low inflation, a strong balance of payments and a generally good rate of growth. On an alternative interpretation it is the underlying strength of the German economy that has made possible the luxury of a free trade policy and an independent central bank.

Responsibility for macroeconomic policy in Germany is diffuse as compared with the United Kingdom, although no more widely shared than it is in the United States. Within the Federal Government responsibility is divided between the Economics Ministry and the Finance Ministry, often led by ministers of different political parties within a multi-party coalition. The *Länder* and *Gemeinde* have more independence than any local authorities in Britain, and the conduct of fiscal policy is greatly complicated by the need to reconcile their interests and ambitions with national priorities. The Bundesbank is by law independent of the Federal Government in the exercise of its duty to 'safeguard the currency'. Yet exchange-rate management is in principle the responsibilty of the Federal Government, not the Bank. It is perhaps surprising that the conduct of macroeconomic policy, and the coordination of fiscal and monetary action, work as well as they do.

The conduct of policy in Germany is usually described as pragmatic, being governed by no one philosophy or doctrine, neither Keynesian nor monetarist, although in spirit rather closer to the latter than to the former. The closest Germany came to accepting Keynesianism was in the late 1960s and early 1970s under the Schiller regime. In response to the 1966–7 recession, fiscal policy was directed more to the maintenance of full employment. A demand stimulus was given to increase the growth rate, which was no longer high in comparison with the rest of Europe. An anti-cyclical fiscal reserve was set up and the Federal Government took the legal powers required for demand management under the 1967 Act to Promote Economic Stability and Growth. There was, about the same time, a move to strengthen the procedure for consultation over economic policy with employers and unions, using the framework of concerted action. The consensus thus established was for many years regarded in Britain as an example of the kind of friendly partnership into which a more formal kind of incomes policy might, with good fortune, ultimately evolve. In the event such cooperation in Germany was not without friction and its importance to the formation of policy declined, until it actually broke down in 1977.

The early 1970s saw the acceleration of inflation to a rate, 5½ per cent in 1972, which was rather lower than in France or Britain, but which caused some alarm in Germany. Part of the blame was taken by the 'pushfulness' of trade unions in Germany itself, but much of the inflation was regarded as imported from America. Capital was moving out of the dollar, seeking a safer haven and in the process the money supply of many European countries, but especially of Germany, was swollen by central bank sales of the local currency. Exchange controls on inward flows were tightened in mid-1972. These proved insufficient and the mark, which had been floated and refixed in 1971, was refloated (upwards) in 1973. At the time of the first oil price shock there was already much concern over the threat of inflation in Germany and steps had already been taken to moderate the growth of demand. Unlike other oil-importing countries, Germany did not run a balance of payments deficit in 1974. On the contrary its current account surplus rose to over $10 billion (2.7 per cent of GNP). This remarkable outturn was made possible by a tightening of monetary policy and a halt to the growth of output. Even in that dismal year German exports continued to grow well.

The tightening of monetary policy in the mid 1970s was followed by the introduction of a new system of targets for central bank money. This was defined as currency in circulation plus the reserves required by banks to back their domestic liabilities. It was not, despite its name, closely related to the monetary base. It was more like a weighted average of alternative money supply definitions, with the more liquid deposits (for which more reserves were required) given the most weight. Control depended, as in Britain, on the use of interest rates to influence the demand for bank deposits. There was no *direct* control of the reserve base of the banking system. There was therefore no guarantee that targets would in fact be hit.

In practice the targets were not always hit, partly because the Bundesbank could not determine the demand for bank deposits at all precisely. It was also partly because, in their pragmatic way, the German authorities sometimes decided that it would not be expedient to raise interest rates, or allow the exchange rate to rise as high as it turned out in the event they would have to, if central bank money was to be kept in the target range. Nevertheless the divergences from target range were not always in the same direction, and never so scandalously large as were the overshoots of £M3 targets by the British authorities in the early 1980s.

By 1974 it appeared that the tightening of policy in Germany might have gone too far. Fiscal policy became rather more expansionary, as spending plans were brought forward and taxes cut. During 1975 unemployment rose sharply to over 1 million. Short-term interest rates, which had risen as high as 12 per cent in 1973, were brought down sharply to 5 per cent or less. The growth of central bank money was allowed to exceed its target. It cannot then be said of German monetary policy in the 1970s that it was consistently directed at reducing inflation. On the contrary, it was the outcome of a compromise between objectives for inflation and for unemployment no different in kind from those reached by other countries facing the same dilemma. What *is* true, however, is that the German inflation rate was lower in 1974, and again in 1975, than the rate in any other member country of the OECD.

1976 saw a strong recovery from recession, with growth in GNP of 5½ per cent, leading to a fall in unemployment in the following year. Nevertheless, the current account of the balance of payments remained in surplus. Commentators at home, and more especially commentators abroad, felt that Germany was not using all the 'margin for manoeuvre' that this gave for expansion of domestic demand.

This was the period when the 'locomotive' theory of growth was most popular in the discussions at meetings of the OECD. The idea was that the stronger economies, especially at this time Germany and Japan, should grow faster, thus helping, or enabling, other less fortunate countries, for example the United States and the United Kingdom, to speed up their growth as well. Many economists, traditional conservatives as well as fashionable monetarists, poured scorn on the idea, but the German government felt obliged to take it seriously.

In 1978 the annual summit meeting of heads of state and government happened to meet in Bonn, giving the hosts a political interest in the demonstrable success of policy coordination on that occasion. Partly for that reason the German government agreed to take measures that would expand domestic demand. The sequel to that decision was to have a lasting effect on the perception of economic policy in Germany and the subsequent attitude of the German authorities both to policy coordination as such and to fiscal expansion of any kind.

In 1979 the growth rate in Germany accelerated from 3 or 3½ per cent to 4 per cent and unemployment came down from 3.7 per cent of the working population to 3.3 per cent. To that extent, Germany itself benefited from the 'locomotive' approach. But in other respects the outcome was less favourable. The second oil price shock came, by an unfortunate coincidence, just at the time when the modest extra stimulus given to domestic demand in Germany was taking effect. The consequence was an abrupt swing into current account deficit for the first time since 1965. The rate of inflation also accelerated, from under 3 per cent to a little over 4 per cent, a modest acceleration compared with the OECD average, but worrying nevertheless.

The much publicised fiscal expansion of 1978 was followed, in 1979, by a sharp tightening of monetary policy. Short-term interest rates averaged 3.7 per cent in 1978, but 6.7 per cent in 1979, and rose even higher subsequently. This helped to keep the DM appreciating (in terms of its 'effective' index) despite the deterioration of the current account.

Throughout the 1970s, the German economy maintained, largely unqualified, its reputation as the 'strong man of Europe'. As with all other industrialised countries its performance was very disappointing compared with that of preceding decades, but it still excelled in comparison with its peers. In the 1980s, however, its record was to be less enviable, and its policy pronouncements less confident. The belief got around, spread in the main by pessimists in Germany itself, that the great days were over, that the economy was becoming less dynamic and less flexible, showing signs of senescence if not actual decay.

Discussions of fiscal policy became increasingly preoccupied with the growth of public sector debt. Anglo-Saxons, especially those brought up in the Keynesian tradition, tended to regard this as a neurotic symptom, perhaps even as an excuse for inaction for which the true motive was different. Nevertheless it was true that the ratio of debt to income was rising, and on some projections seemed set to rise continuously for many years. Britain might have faced a similar problem, but for the good fortune of North Sea oil. Given the diffuse responsibility for taxes and public spending in Germany it would have been more difficult to reform the *structure* of the budget, so as to reconcile the same impact in demand with a better fiscal balance. The problem seemed especially intractable if the rise in unemployment, from 3.3 per cent in 1980 to 8.2 per cent in 1983, was understood as structural and irreversible, rather than merely cyclical.

Throughout the 1970s, and for most of the 1980s as well, the level of unemployment in Germany compared favourably with that of the average in all OECD countries, and very favourably with that in Britain. By the late 1980s, however, it is possible to question, for the first time time, whether the labour market actually did work better in Germany than elsewhere. By then unemployment had been falling for some years in the United States, and for a shorter period also in Britain, whilst in Germany it showed little variation. The fall in the demand for labour in the 1970s in Germany was absorbed to a considerable extent by adjustment in the size of the labour force. Even though the population of working age rose considerably faster in Germany than in Britain from 1970 to 1984, the rise in the labour force was considerably slower. Full-time education expanded more rapidly and there was a gradual trend towards earlier retirement for men. Female participation rates in Germany also rose relatively slowly. Moreover the inflow of 'guest workers', especially from Turkey, which had been considerable in the 1960s, slowed down and was even, to a limited extent, reversed.

The German government, despite its avowed devotion to a free-market philosophy, did not refrain from intervention designed to prevent the loss of jobs. As in Britain and elsewhere in Europe official action was taken to delay or prevent redundancy. The need for 'special employment measures' was less in Germany because youth unemployment in particular remained low. That could be attributed to the comprehensive system of vocational training for school-leavers already in place, and much admired elsewhere, not least in Britain.

The initial rise of unemployment in the early 1980s, if not its obstinately high level thereafter, was a consequence of a low level of aggregate demand. In 1981 output was constant year-on-year, followed by a 1 per cent fall in 1982. This was not nearly as deep a recession as that in Britain at about the same time, but neither was it followed by so brisk a recovery in the mid-1980s. From 1983 to 1987 growth in Germany averaged 2½ per cent, compared with 3½ per cent in Britain.

The success of the German economy for most of the postwar period was built on export-led growth which ensured a continuing surplus on the balance of payments, and contributed to an appreciating exchange rate. That, in turn, helped to keep down inflation. In the 1980s all this was called into question. Export growth was strong in 1984 and 1985, but in 1983 and again in 1986 the volume of exports actually fell. The deficit on the current account, which first emerged in 1979, was not eliminated until 1982. The effective exchange rate for the DM fell in 1981 and again (marginally) in 1984. Fixed investment fell by 10 per cent between 1980 and 1982 and grew at a disappointingly slow pace thereafter. Against this not much could be set except the achievement of a very low rate of inflation, actually a negative rate in 1986.

An article written by the present author and others in 1985 comparing macroeconomic policy in Britain and Germany ended with the following conclusion. 'To sum up, German experience does offer us one example of the way in which economic policy can be conducted and shows that it works well in the right circumstances. The underlying problems of the British economy are more severe. It may be that more intervention of a micro-economic kind as well as more conscious management of aggregate demand is appropriate to an economy like ours. A rather Germanic policy is now being pursued in this country so it may be easier to judge whether that is so after another year or two have passed.'

In the event the performance of the British economy over the next year or two surpassed all expectations, although this owed something to exchange-rate depreciation and public spending increases that were not at all Germanic in character. It is also true that, over these same two years, the strength of the German economy itself was being seriously questioned. But looking back from the beginning of the 1990s the judgement passed in 1985 again looks the right one.

FRANCE

There was a time when France, rather than Germany, was the continental neighbour that Britain was most often urged to emulate. The French economy grew very rapidly from the mid-1950s to the late 1960s, outstripping most OECD countries, and this was widely attributed to the French system of indicative planning. The National Plan of 1964, in this country, was an unsuccessful attempt at imitation. In the 1970s and early 1980s, however, French achievements were less impressive and her experience was held up as a warning more often than it was cited as an example to be followed.

The French economy is, of all those considered in this study, the one most similar to the British. The size, in terms of population, of the two countries is very close. The standard of living in France is higher, but only by about 20 per cent in the early 1980s. Agriculture accounts for a larger proportion of output in France, but the employment shares of industry in the two countries are much the same. Openness, as measured by the share of imports in GDP, is 25 per cent in both cases.

The problems experienced by the two economies in the period of this study may be traced to rather similar underlying weaknesses. Both were handicapped by an outdated industrial structure, continuing to specialise in producing goods with too low a skill content for an advanced industrial economy, lagging behind Japan, America and Germany in industries based on new technology. In both it was said that markets were inflexible, prices and wages were being set by convention rather than by the balance of supply and demand. In both there was deep political division, not least over the conduct of economic policy.

Despite these similarities French experience contrasts in several significant ways with Britain. The annual growth rate of output in France was positive in all but one year right through the 1970s and 1980s. The average growth rate was good, quite good even in the 1970s, and the amplitude of cyclical variation was unusually low.

Variation in the rate of inflation in France was also mild. The highest annual rates of increase in consumer prices recorded were in 1974, 1980 and 1981, all about 13½ per cent, far lower than the peak rates in Britain (or even in Japan). With the exception of these years French inflation was in the range of 9–12 per cent continuously from the mid-1970s to the mid-1980s. Unemployment also showed relatively little variation about its rising trend. In no year after 1973 did the average annual unemployment percentage in France fall. If stability, in the sense of year-to-year predictability, were the secret of success, the French performance would have been enviable. However, although there were few dramatic 'stops' and 'goes', the high average level of inflation and the trend rise in unemployment in France were both indications of failure to respond successfully to the problems that beset all advanced economies after the mid-1970s.

Indicative planning was just one part of the wide-ranging apparatus of government intervention in the running of the French economy. Equally, or more, important was the direct control of credit, by means similar to those followed in Britain during the 1960s. The controls influenced not just the quantity of credit extended by the banking system but also its direction. Foreign exchange transactions were also comprehensively controlled. Thus the French monetary authorities could, to a much greater extent than those of Britain or Germany, isolate domestic financial markets from overseas influences. Interest rates could be used to defend the franc without necessarily damaging the prospects for fixed investment at home. These controls remained in place longer in France than in Britain, but were largely dismantled in the latter part of the 1980s as part of a move to liberalisation and as a step towards a more unified European financial system.

Direct intervention in price setting was also the practice for much of the period with which we are concerned. Incomes policies of the British kind proved unnegotiable in France, thanks to the political composition of the trade union movement. The French government had instead to rely on its influence on wages through the setting of public sector pay and the national minimum wage, together with controls on prices. When price control was lifted in 1978 the immediate effect on inflation was almost imperceptible, calling into question how real a restraint the controls had been beforehand. Perhaps the controls did little more than codify the sort of conventional 'cost–plus' formula for pricing which firms would in any case have followed.

When inflation rose to about 10 per cent a year, and settled at that rate for a decade, indexation of wages became largely mechanical and uncontested. The economy appeared to be adjusting to an inflationary steady state, and some questioned the real advantage of a vigorous counter-inflationary policy. Nevertheless when, from the mid-1980s, the problem was tackled consistently for several years, inflation was in fact reduced as effectively in France as elsewhere.

The relative stability of growth and of inflation in France, at least as compared with Britain, was not the result of consistently applied medium-term policy rules. On the contrary, the course of policy from the mid-1970s to the mid-1980s followed a series of alternating expansionary and contractionary phases.

The events of 1968 antedate the period with which we are most concerned, but they are a necessary starting point for an account of economic policy in France in the 1970s. A series of strikes forced a humiliating agreement on the government including an increase of 35 per cent in the national minimum wage. It is tempting to draw a parallel with the miners' strikes in Britain in 1972 and 1974. In both cases a failure of economic policy threatened to undermine political stability. As in Britain, economic policymakers lived for many years in fear of militant trade unionism, reluctant to do anything that would disturb a fragile peace. This may be seen as one reason why, in both countries, inflation was relatively high.

From 1969 to 1972 consumer price inflation in France was around 5–6 per cent and the economy grew very fast. In each year from 1969–73 the growth rate exceeded 5 per cent and unemployment was steady at about 2½ per cent of the labour force. But this was the end of the golden age of the French economy.

Unlike Germany, France continued to grow quite fast in 1974 despite the first oil price shock. French interest rates were also increased, but they lagged a bit behind. Perhaps for that reason the French current account, unlike the German, moved into deficit. This was corrected the following year when growth slowed down. Growth, indeed, came to a standstill in 1975 and the Chirac administration embarked on a programme of expansionary measures estimated to add about 2 per cent to GDP. The central bank discount rate was cut from 13 per cent to 8 per cent and this was reinforced by fiscal policy. The economy grew strongly through 1976, suggesting that the expansionary programme was working well. It was accompanied, however, by an exceptionally rapid rise in import volume, about 17 per cent year-on-year. The current account of the balance of payments swung back into deficit.

There followed a balance of payments crisis of the kind so familiar to both France and Britain for much of the postwar period. In March 1976 the franc was obliged to leave the 'snake', the arrangement by which the European currencies were then tied together, and the effective exchange rate index fell by about 8 per cent between 1975 and 1977. France had, it seems, expanded to the limit of the 'external constraint'. This relatively painless depreciation of the franc can be contrasted with the agonising sterling crisis which began about the same time. The French economy was less exposed to international capital flows and public opinion in France itself was less wedded to the new monetarist philosophy. Perhaps for this reason the French experience was altogether less traumatic. Nevertheless the outcome was similar, 1976 was a turning point for macroecomonic policy in both countries.

The next phase of French policy was contractionary, under the aegis of the *Plan Barre*. The rhetoric of the new regime sounds rather like a prototype for the monetarist 'experiment' in Britain. The conquest of inflation was the prerequisite for achieving all other goals of economic policy. A target was set for the growth of the money supply – although few French economists have ever claimed that there is any demonstrable relationship between money and prices in France. Public spending plans were cut and taxes were raised, with a view to restoring a better fiscal balance. The idea of a target for full employment was abandoned.

This combination of fiscal austerity with the devaluation that had already taken place would be enough to explain the sizeable balance of payments surplus earned in 1978 and 1979. The franc was now stable. Yet the rate of inflation remained constant at around 10 per cent. It seems that, at this period at least, French inflation was not very sensitive to the pressure of demand. Moreover the immediate effect of higher indirect taxation was, of course, to *raise* prices, not to lower them.

This was the situation at the time of the second oil price shock, bringing in France as elsewhere higher inflation and a loss of output. In Germany the consequences of the Iranian revolution tarnished the reputation of fiscal expansion and international policy coordination. In France the same events soured the last years of the Barre regime and helped to bring Mitterrand to power. Thus can the reputations of economic statesmen, and the economic doctrines they espouse, be made or broken by events over which they have exercised no influence at all.

The victory of the Left in France in June 1981 was remarkable for an event which did not happen. As it became clear which way the election was likely to go, and as the policy proposals of the socialist party were spelt out the exchange rate did not, as one would expect, fall sharply. Thus the new administration became committed to the defence of a value for the franc inconsistent with the expansion of domestic demand on which it was bent.

There now began an episode which convinced many policymakers, not only in France, that fiscal expansion was no longer an effective option and doomed to disappointment. The Mitterand expansion was in fact quite modest in scale, estimated to add between 1 and 2 per cent to GDP, not as much as was added by Chirac in 1975 for example. Social security benefits were raised, and the main addition to domestic demand took the form of higher consumer spending. This came at a time when world demand generally was very slack and producers all over the world had abundant spare capacity. The result was a rise in import volume, not nearly as large as that of 1976, but worrying nevertheless. At the same time exports fell, and the balance of payments in 1982 was in larger deficit than ever before. Most disappointing of all was the lack of response from output, and hence unemployment, French firms were slow to meet the growth of consumer demand and were at the same time cutting back on fixed investment, perhaps because of the uncertainty created by the new government's plan for nationalisation.

By mid-1982 the reflationary strategy had been scrapped to be replaced by a new contractionary phase following a new devaluation. The course of political economy in France seemed set to continue its familiar pattern. But in fact the pattern changed around the middle of the 1980s. The rate of inflation which, as we have seen, had been high but relatively constant for a decade, started to fall. It was 7½ per cent in 1984, under 6 per cent in 1985, and then in 1986, thanks to the third oil price shock, it fell abruptly to under 3 per cent, lower than at any time since 1967. Thus France achieved the same 'victory' over inflation as was achieved in Britain, without a deep recession and without the monetarist framework of our medium-term financial strategy.

After the expansionary policies of 1982 were abandoned, one of the main themes of French economic policy has been the closer integration of Europe. It is as if the lesson drawn from the failure of national policy was the need to surrender independence altogether. This involved the emulation of other member states of the European community, especially Germany. That was one reason for the move to dismantle direct controls on financial markets. It was also one reason among many for the greater emphasis on exchange rate stability. The EMS had become one of the main determinants of monetary policy in France. The wish to delay and to minimise realignments put continuous downward pressure on inflation, but required the maintenance of relatively high interest rates which may have held back the rate of growth. French experience within the EMS during the late 1980s is now, at the beginning of the 1990s, being quoted in Britain as an example of the way in which the exchange rate mechanism can be used successfully to change inflationary expectations.

Like Germany, and unlike Britain, France grew slowly in the 1980s, slowly even by the standards of the good years in the 1970s. Unemployment stabilised at around 10 per cent of the labour force and, as in Germany, there was no suggestion of a downturn even at the end of the period covered by this study. There was something of the same gloom in France in the latter part of the 1980s as there was in Germany, complaints that the economy was too inflexible, too old-fashioned to compete with Japan or the newly industrialised economies. This contrasted with the self-confident mood at that time of the born-again businessmen of Britain.

Having stressed at the outset the similarities between France and Britain, it is right to conclude by recalling some of the differences. The contrasting experience of unemployment is particularly interesting. In Britain much of the increase took place in, or soon after, the recession years. There was a 'shake-out' of workers from manufacturing, construction and the nationalised industries, most of them men. Thus unemployment in Britain looks like a cyclical problem. In France, however, there is a more trend-like rise, and the problem of youth unemployment was particularly acute. Jobs for girls were especially scarce. In France, moreover, the rise in unemployment probably owed little or nothing to the generosity of social security provision, as is often alleged in other countries, notably in Britain.

The experience of inflation in the two countries was also very different. The irregular and unpredictable path in Britain may have been far more damaging than the steady, if rather brisk, pace in France. Finally it is perhaps significant that the traditions of French economics, and economic policy, are different from those of Britain or America. The history of ideas that influenced policymaking in Britain set out in Part 2 of this study contains little or no reference to developments on the continent of Europe.

SWEDEN

Sweden was one of the few advanced Western economies to maintain full, or almost full, employment throughout the 1970s and 1980s. As such it had a particular fascination for economic commentators in Britain. The economic policies of successive governments in Sweden had, moreover, much in common with those followed by the Heath and Wilson governments in Britain; national income policies, labour subsidies, high taxation and government spending, together with a willingness to use exchange depreciation as a means of maintaining international competitiveness. The results in Sweden were not unambiguously beneficial, but they were good enough to keep alive in Britain the belief that the Swedish model was the one to imitate. It is for that reason that Sweden merits a brief mention in this section of the present study.

Sweden is a small economy, very open to foreign trade, more so even than Britain. The average standard of living is amongst the highest in the world, higher than in America. Its industrial strength once rested on steel and shipbuilding, but high-technology engineering has also expanded rapidly and offers a better basis for future prosperity.

From 1960 to 1973 the annual growth rate of the Swedish economy was 4.1 per cent, a little below the European average of 4.7 per cent. During the 1970s growth in Sweden slowed down abruptly, but no more than in line with experience elsewhere. The average annual rate of growth in Sweden was 1.4 per cent from 1974–82, compared with 1.9 per cent for Europe as a whole. The unemployment rate in Sweden rose between 1972 and 1982 from 2.2 per cent to 2.6 per cent whilst on average in Europe it rose from 3.1 per cent to 9.2 per cent.

Nevertheless by the early 1980s there was talk of a Swedish economic crisis, discontent with economic policy in Sweden itself as well as criticism from observers abroad. The rate of inflation from 1974–82 averaged 10.3 per cent a year, similar to the European average. Productivity growth had been very slow, well below the European average. The general government financial balance, which had been in surplus up to 1977 was, by 1982, in deficit to the extent of 6½ per cent of GDP. The current account of the balance of payments had been in deficit since 1974 with a record figure of 3.7 per cent of GDP in 1982 itself. It was easy to blame these developments on the extravagance of government spending, especially spending on industrial support, income transfers, training programmes and public sector employment.

The Social Democrats returned to power in 1982 after six years of government by a coalition of centre and right-wing parties. The economic policies adopted in response to the problems inherited by the new government did not amount to a radical break with the past. The maintenance of full employment remained an overriding concern, whilst both fiscal and incomes policies were still used to equalise the distribution of incomes. The main concern was to correct the external deficit by devaluation coupled with fiscal contraction to curb domestic demand and bring the government deficit under control. The closest parallel in Britain would be the policies of Roy Jenkins when he was Chancellor of the Exchequer in 1968. The mix was also similar to that recommended to Britain by the IMF at the end of 1976. In Sweden at least it worked rather well.

The fall in the effective exchange rate of the krona was 20 per cent between 1981 and 1983. Thereafter it remained broadly constant until the late 1980s. As inflation in Sweden remained relatively high for a few years, whilst it was slowing down quite sharply in most other industrial countries, the effect of the devaluation on relative price competitiveness was somewhat eroded. This was a slow process however, despite the extreme openness of the Swedish economy, thanks to the brake provided by incomes policies.

The effect of the devaluation on output and trade was encouraging. Export volume rose by more than 10 per cent in 1983, a year when total world trade was almost static. The growth of the volume of imports was also held back. GDP was up by 2½ per cent that year, and the recovery was reasonably well maintained thereafter. Unemployment, which had peaked at the relatively modest rate of 3½ per cent in 1983, fell back by 1987 to 2 per cent. By 1984 the current account deficit on the balance of payments was eliminated; the general government deficit was also much reduced.

By the mid-1980s Sweden was also sharing in the general reduction in inflation. The rise in the consumer price index was little over 4 per cent in both 1986 and 1987, a trifle faster than the OECD average, but little different from the rate in Britain.

In 1986 the American Brookings Institute undertook a thorough study of the Swedish performance. It found much to criticise. In Sweden in the 1970s, it was said, 'the hard choices were postponed, and the postponement created still more serious dilemmas for the future'. Sweden had been 'living beyond its means'. Major efforts had been made to put this right in the 1980s, but the improvements were seen as possibly just a 'temporary respite from more fundamental deterioration'.

Yet there is also some, rather reluctant, admiration in the report of the study. The Swedish labour market seemed to work surprisingly well, despite all the interventions of government. Swedish industry continued to innovate despite the dead hand of bureaucratic subsidisation. The relative austerity of the 1980s was a step in the right direction.

The maintenance of full employment was applauded, but the relatively high rate of inflation was seen as its cost. 'The Swedish experience does not support the view that training, public employment, and other labour market policies can make it possible to enjoy both full employment and stable prices. In Sweden as elsewhere, public commitments to maintain full employment add upward pressure on wage costs and hence to inflation. The Swedish experience in labour markets and other areas yields no magic solutions that make economic choices easier.'

Compared with British experience it is not so easy to dismiss the suspicion that the Swedes employed some kind of magic as part of their economic strategy. How else could they reconcile in 1987 an inflation rate of 4 per cent with an unemployment rate of under 2 per cent? If magic it was, it would appear that the same spells and incantations were not efficacious on our side of the North Sea. The experiment had been tried in Britain in the 1970s with the results that have been recorded in Part 1 of this study.

BRITAIN AND THE WORLD ECONOMY

The purpose of this review of economic developments abroad has been to throw an indirect light on the history of the British economy. Our problems were not unique; neither were the solutions which were tried out in this country. It may now be helpful to summarise some of the similarities and differences.

It can scarcely be emphasised too strongly that Britain is part of a world economy. The history of output growth year-by-year in the major OECD countries for example shows broadly the same pattern. The coincidences of timing seem to be too close to be explained merely by the fact that one OECD country's exports may be another OECD country's imports, and all were obliged to absorb some common 'shocks'. In the same way the variation in rates of inflation over time is strikingly similar, more similar than could be explained by mutual trade. Moreover, as we shall see in Part 5 of this study the best correlation is between United Kingdom and world inflation in terms of 'own currency' prices, not after correcting (as import or export prices would) for changes in exchange rates.

Table 11.1 compares economic performance in the United Kingdom with the other members of the so-called Group of Seven (G7) and with the whole of the membership of OECD. The periods of comparison were chosen by the statisticians at OECD, as beginning and ending with years when output was generally high relative to the underlying trend.

Growth was slower in the periods covered by this study than in the preceding two periods in all the countries shown in the table. There was nothing exceptional about United Kingdom experience in this respect. Indeed the slowing down was *less* in this country than on average elsewhere. In 1960–68 we lagged behind the seven-country average by 1.9 per cent a year, in 1968–73 by 1.1 percent, in 1973–9 by 1.2 per cent, and in 1979–87 by only 0.8 per cent. We were at the tail end of this growth league in the first three periods, but came fifth in the final period.

The table also shows that inflation was on average faster in the major countries after 1973. There are some exceptions however: in Japan inflation was much lower in the 1980s than it had been in the 1960s, and there was not much difference between the two periods in Germany. As the world average rate of inflation rose, so did the variation across countries. Britain was top of the inflation league for G7 countries in 1968–73 and second only to Italy in 1973–9; in 1979–87 it was also below France. Over the period as a whole our relative performance in respect of inflation was always bad, although not outstandingly so.

The figures for unemployment are less comparable across countries than the figures for growth or inflation. It is potentially misleading to compare levels at one point in time, although changes over time may be more informative. The upward trend in unemployment was a worldwide phenomenon, but it was far steeper in some countries than in others. The

Table 11.1 *Economic performance in the seven major economies 1960–87*

	US	Japan	Germany	France	UK	Italy	Canada	Total	Total OECD
Growth rate of GDP (per cent per annum)									
1960–68	4.5	10.2	4.1	5.4	3.1	5.7	5.5	5.0	5.0
1968–73	3.2	8.7	4.9	5.5	3.3	4.5	5.4	4.4	4.5
1973–79	2.4	3.6	2.3	2.8	1.5	3.7	4.2	2.7	2.7
1979–87	2.6	3.8	1.4	1.7	1.8	2.2	2.9	2.6	2.5
Rate of inflation (consumer price indices)									
1960–68	2.0	5.7	2.7	3.6	3.6	4.0	2.4	2.7	2.9
1968–73	5.0	7.0	4.6	6.1	7.5	5.8	4.6	5.5	5.7
1973–79	8.5	10.0	4.7	10.7	15.6	16.1	9.2	9.4	9.9
1979–87	5.8	2.7	3.1	8.4	7.6	12.5	7.0	5.8	6.5
Unemployment (as a percentage of total labour force) (average level)									
1960–67	5.0	1.3	0.8	1.5	1.5	4.9	4.8	3.0	3.1
1968–73	4.6	1.2	0.8	..	2.4	5.7	5.4	3.2	3.4
1974–79	6.7	1.9	3.5	4.5	4.2	6.6	7.2	4.9	5.2
1980–87	7.6	2.5	6.9	8.9	10.1	9.5	9.7	7.1	7.8

Source: OECD Historical Statistics, 1960–87.

rise was a relatively gentle one in America and Japan (as also in the Scandinavian countries, in Austria and in Switzerland). It was severe in Germany and France (as well as in Belgium, the Netherlands and in Spain). Britain was amongst the countries which suffered most.

The circumstances in which macroeconomic policy was made in Britain were broadly the same as those to be found in other countries of the same kind. We had to respond to the same world events. The breakdown of the fixed exchange rate system may indeed have affected Britain more than most other countries, because London remained one of the centres of currency dealing, and sterling one of the main currencies traded world-wide. The other great upheaval of the early 1970s, the first OPEC oil shock, affected Britain in much the same way as it did other industrial countries. What was special was our position at the time of the second oil shock, when the United Kingdom was a major oil producer itself.

The intellectual climate in which policy was made was also international. The ideas that had dominated macroeconomics in Britain in the 1950s and 1960s, and which had formed the 'postwar consensus' were largely home-made. Demand management was an export from Britain to the rest of the world, as also were some features of incomes policy. But in the 1970s we imported monetarism from America. A rather special kind of monetarism was put into practice here, which differed significantly from the American variety, but the policies of the Conservative government after 1979 were part of a worldwide swing to the right in economic policy, from which few if any OECD member countries were excluded.

Although Britain had joined the European Economic Community in 1973 its effect on macroeconomic policy was slight. France and Italy were regarded more as warnings of policies to be avoided, than as examples to be followed. The influence of Germany on policy in Britain was also weak, perhaps surprisingly so. Right at the end of the period attitudes were changing again, and the prospect of closer association with Europe was seen to have advantages. The experience of both France and Italy within the European Monetary System was viewed with special interest, and the idea that monetary policy could be set for all Europe by the Bundesbank was not without its attractions.

Policymaking in Britain is centralised in the Treasury and the Bank of England, and these two institutions are bound by their constitutional position to work closely together. Parliament, even with a minority government, is in no position to seize the initiative. Other government departments seldom interfere; and local government has no macroeconomic role to play. In contrast to America or Germany, macroeconomic policy can be decided in one room; one might think for that reason it would be more intellectually coherent.

The influence of professional economists on macroeconomic policy was stronger, during this period, in Britain than elsewhere. The economists in the Treasury and the Bank of England had a tradition of closer policy involvement than their counterparts in America or Germany. Many economists outside government also saw their role as influencing policy, rather than simply learning how the economy works. This was a period of profound disagreement amongst economists in Britain, more so even than in America, far more so than in Continental Europe. Politicians in Britain were thus exposed to a superfluity of strongly-worded and contradictory professional advice.

The identification of political parties with rival schools of economics at this time, although never complete, was closer in Britain than elsewhere. At the same time the strife between the parties was embittered by the circumstances in which the Conservatives lost office in 1974. Both these special circumstances tended to produce more extreme versions in Britain of macroeconomic policy designs which were common in milder form elsewhere. Certainly the presentation of policy was exceptionaly dogmatic on occasion, even if its actual execution was not always so rigorous or consistent.

British policy may have been, or at least may have sounded, extreme, but it was clearly based on ideas which were the common property of policymakers throughout the world. It was, indeed, becoming more difficult during this period for individual governments to stand out against the trend. They risked finding an unsympathetic response from their counterparts overseas when they asked for help, as the Labour government found in 1976. They also risked alienating market opinion, as the French found in 1982. The foreign exchange markets played an increasing part in the determination of policy in most countries, and the views on which market verdicts were based might be called the lowest common denominator of views all over the world. They responded vigorously when New York, Frankfurt, Tokyo and London were all of one mind; they gave little weight to national peculiarities of judgement.

There were still, nevertheless, some smaller countries, which followed policies suited presumably to the wishes of the electorates, and well out of the mainstream of international opinion. Two such countries of relevance to this study are Sweden and Switzerland. A short section has been devoted to Sweden above because it seems like an 'experiment of nature', a country which put into practice the policies favoured here by many economists of the centre-left. The results, as we have seen, were moderately favourable. Unemployment in particular was kept very low.

Switzerland had a similar attraction for some on the right in Britain. (It was the place Mrs Thatcher chose for her summer holiday.) It came as close as any country to operating a monetary-base control system. Economic policy was kept to the minimum. The growth rate of output was low, lower even than in Britain; but the rate of inflation was also exceptionally low, just a little higher than in Germany. Moreover the rate of unemployment in Switzerland was lower than in any other country of the OECD, under 1 per cent even in the 1980s.

It might have been better if policy in Britain had sought the middle ground, neither Sweden nor Switzerland, but something between the two. Instead it shifted first in one direction and then the other. The continual uncertainty as to what policy was going to be may have reduced its effectiveness. There was not enough time for one set of policies to build up their credibility. Much of the period was characterised by crises and reforms of a quite fundamental kind. At any time a change of government would have brought about the undoing of much that had been done before. The possibility of such a change was never far away.

In Part 4 we shall be looking in more detail at the conduct of policy in this country, and in Part 5 at the performance of the economy. It is too soon to draw conclusions as to how the two were related. International comparisons suggest that our experience of output growth in this period was not remarkable, but was becoming rather less bad than it had been. It is arguable, however, that macroeconomic policy can do little to influence the growth rate except in the short-term. What was more remarkable was our poor ranking on both inflation and unemployment, the two evils which macroeconomic policy is traditionally intended to attack. It is possible that the adversarial nature of the debate about macroeconomic policy, more striking here than elsewhere, contributed to our poor performance.

PART 4

THE CONDUCT OF POLICY

12

INTRODUCTORY NOTE ON METHODS
OF ANALYSIS

There is a difference between the approach of Parts 1–3 of this study and that of Parts 4 and 5. We shall now try to stand back from the events and ideas of this period of the recent past, and treat them, almost clinically, as so much data for investigation. Parts 4 and 5 will include reports of a variety of statistical estimates and tests applied to time-series observations of economic variables over the period covered by this study, or parts of it. If there is a story to tell about the conduct of macroeconomic policy during these years, the aim now is to get the numbers to tell that story, rather than rely on the accounts given by policymakers or observers at the time, or on the memories that remain.

Such an approach requires a careful use of words, especially the ambiguous words used in the discussion of macroeconomic policy, such as 'conduct' and 'stance'. A definition has already been given in the introduction for the word 'macroeconomic'. That limits the concern of this study to policies of government designed to achieve macroeconomic aims, for example those of full employment and price stability. This part of the study is concerned exclusively with the use of monetary and fiscal policy to those ends.

The questions to be addressed can be put in simple words. What did the Treasury and the Bank of England actually *do* in these years? How did they behave? Was their behaviour the same all the time? If not, how did it change? The idea is to investigate that behaviour in much the same way as the behaviour of other economic agents, by looking for relationships between policy acts and the circumstances in which they took place. Such relationships would then describe how policy was 'conducted'. But this definition uses the notion of a 'policy act' which itself needs to be defined.

The taking of decisions about macroeconomic policy is a complicated business involving many layers of responsibility. The results of those decisions are policy actions. These actions, or policy 'measures' as they are often called, are best described by their immediate consequence for things which the decision-takers can directly control. Thus the result of a budgetary decision may be a cut in the basic rate of income tax; that is a policy action. The consequence for public sector borrowing in the subsequent year may or may not be as intended. It must depend on the behaviour of the economy at large, not just on the conduct of the policy.

In much the same way, the monetary authorities can act to raise the level of short-term interest rates, but they cannot be sure what effect, if any, that will have on the exchange rate or on the growth of the money supply.

Thus the conduct of policy can be defined by reference to the movements over time in a number of economic variables directly controlled by policymakers, including tax rates and interest rates as well as others. When these variables change, that is a policy measure, and when they do *not* change that too is the result of a deliberate policy choice. Policymakers see part of their job as being to decide the appropriate settings for those policy instruments. Some of these, notably the level of interest rates, are kept under continuous review. Others, like rates of taxation, are reconsidered according to a well-established procedure once a year or more frequently if circumstances dictate.

One method of analysis used below will be the estimation of policy reaction functions. These are descriptions, in the form of mathematical equations, of the way in which the behaviour of policy instruments has been related to that of other economic variables. They show, for example, how short-term interest rates in this country have reacted to movements in similar interest rates overseas or to forecasts of the rate of price inflation. The methods of estimation used are the same as those applied by macroeconomic modelbuilders to the explanation of behaviour in the rest of the economy. This method works well for interest rates, but for most aspects of fiscal policy we shall have to use a less formal approach.

In the introduction to this study we touched briefly on the idea that macroeconomic policy might follow a rule or 'regime'. We said that the policy debate nowadays was less about particular acts of policy, more about the choice between alternative rules for reacting to events. The reaction functions to be estimated in this study can be seen as defining a regime, although the term is also applicable to less formal ways of describing the conduct of policy.

At the end of Part 2 we also took up the theme of policy rules, and imagined their being devised explicitly by a mathematical optimisation procedure. What we shall try to do in Part 4 is to estimate what rules, on average, over the period, seem to have been followed in practice. Whether they were optimal or even whether they were deliberately chosen at all, we cannot say, but of course we shall be looking for rules which a sensible government or central bank might conceivably have chosen.

In Part 3 we criticised the conduct of macroeconomic policy in Britain as being inconsistent and unpredictable, shifting first in one direction and then in another. If this is a valid criticism we might expect to find that estimated reaction functions are unstable from one period to the next. The theory of economic policy now puts great emphasis on predictability and the way in which the conduct of policy influences expectations. It is worthwhile therefore considering briefly what the implications might be for the economy when there is a change in the way that policy is conducted, a change in the reaction function of the authorities.

The first point to note is that any knowledge of the economy that has been built up under the old rule is made partly obsolete by the introduction of a new one. Suppose for example that the change was from a rule which kept real interest rates constant to one which kept the real exchange rate constant. Knowledge built up under the old regime would have little or nothing to say about the effect of real interest changes on investment. This would make all forecasts of output or activity less reliable and expensive mistakes could be made as a result.

This first point should be distinguished from the Lucas critique already described in Chapter 7 above. The two arguments reinforce one another in support of continuity in the conduct of policy. The point of the Lucas critique is that the behaviour of the economy under the new regime will actually be different from the behaviour under the old regime, since expectations about the conduct of policy have a pervasive effect on private sector decisions. The old models will not just be irrelevant in the new situation; they will actually be incorrect.

As we shall see it is very important when we come to assessing the effects of policy to be clear whether the rules that describe the conduct of policy are known to the public or not. We shall be estimating policy reaction functions using the data for the whole period available to us now. But the knowledge which could be acquired by estimation of this kind during the period itself was obviously much more limited.

Reaction functions cannot, of course, be applied to policy measures which are, of their very nature, one-off events. Statistical analysis tells us nothing about the reasons for the abolition of exchange control in 1979 for example, still less for the decision not to join the exchange rate mechanism. Even so, this method of analysis provides a useful fresh look at the way some important decisions regularly taken over a crucial period in the development of the British economy. It provides a rigorous definition of the term 'conduct' in relation to macroeconomic policy.

The common use of the expression 'policy stance' raises a rather different set of issues. It seems to offer something more than a description of the way policy instruments are currently set, but it is by no means clear what the extra information content may be. A possible interpretation is that it refers to policy intentions: the monetary authorities 'stand ready' to combat inflation for example. More commonly, however, it means something about the effect that policy is having on the economy. The 'weighted cyclically-adjusted budget deficit', for example, has been called an index of fiscal policy stance, in the belief that it measures the contribution made by public spending and taxation to aggregate demand. For similar reasons the stance of monetary policy is variously identified with the level of real interest rates, or the real value of the money supply.

These measures all depend for their validity on some theory of the way the economy works. The use of the budget deficit, for example, when it is weighted and cyclically-adjusted, as an index of the stance of fiscal policy, belongs with a Keynesian account of what determines total expenditure and output; it makes little sense outside that context. Similarly there is little merit in using real interest rates as an index of monetary policy unless they are believed to have a predictable effect on investment or savings behaviour. Misunderstandings amongst economists often arise when the behavioural assumptions underlying a chosen approach to the measurement of policy are not spelt out.

We shall adopt an approach which has, at least, the merit of clarity in its behavioural assumptions. We shall use the National Institite's econometric model of the United Kingdom economy as our representation of the way the world works (providing first a brief account of its main features). Within that framework we can provide quantified estimates of the effects on the economy of any well-specified act of policy. Indeed simulations provide a single-valued index of the effect on the economy of a whole package of measures, whatever its composition may be. The effect on total output is amongst the many economic effects such a policy simulation can estimate. That effect could be described as a change in the stance of policy associated with the policy act or acts, but the word stance is so ambiguous that it is probably better not to use it in this context at all.

The use of a macroeconomic model to estimate effects requires that changes in policy be very carefully defined. This may seem tedious, but it is a necessary discipline if one is to talk about policy with any precision. The effects of the policies actually adopted must be compared with a counterfactual case, a case in which a different set of policies was in place. It is not a matter of finding the *correct* alternative, but of defining one or more interesting points of comparison.

To sum up, there are two ways of describing policy. One is to say how the various instruments, directly under the control of the authorities, were set. The other is to say what effect it had on the economy that these instrument settings, rather than some other possible instrument settings, were chosen. There is no third description, no way of characterising the stance, the thrust, the tightness or looseness of policy which does not already prejudge the way the economy responds.

ESTIMATING THE EFFECTS OF
MACROECONOMIC POLICY

A macroeconomic model is a set of mathematical equations which describe the behaviour of the economy. Each equation embodies a piece of economic theory. The numbers in the equations, the parameter values, are estimated from observation of the movements in the variables concerned over some period of the past. In the case of the Institute's model used here, the data for most of the equation estimates are quarterly observations from the late 1960s (or early 1970s) to 1987 or thereabouts. Thus the estimates refer broadly to the period with which this study itself is concerned. This is fortunate, and it contrasts with the more usual situation where one is using a model estimated over the data of the past to make predictions about the behaviour of the economy in the future.

In constructing a model there is a necessary, and generally healthy, tension between the need for theoretical rigour and the need to be true to empirical observation. Models differ partly because different modelbuilders strike a different balance between these conflicting claims. Moreover, the same evidence is notoriously open to many explanations. The discipline of constructing a quantified model does eliminate some theoretically attractive hypotheses; quite often a programme of research will show that some expected interaction is very weak, even if it cannot be proved not to exist at all. But some relationships, for example those that determine the behaviour of the exchange rate, will always be subject to profound uncertainty, about their form as well as about the numbers involved. Some of the progress that was made in modelbuilding during the period of the study has already been described in Part 2 above. We spoke there of a tendency for views about the workings of the economy to converge towards the end of the 1980s, as both monetarists and Keynesians abandoned their most extreme positions. Even when economists agree, however, the uncertainty surrounding their pronouncements is not necessarily any the less.

Before reporting any estimates of the effects of economic policy, the broad characteristics of the model will be briefly described. (The version used is Model 11 as described in the manual dated December 1988, with some minor modifications resulting from changes following the release of new data by the Central Statistical Office early in 1989.)

Spending by consumers, according to the model, depends, in the traditional way, on their real disposable incomes, but also on interest rates, the cost of borrowing and the availability of credit, as well as the real value of financial assets held by the personal sector. Spending by firms on fixed investment and on stockbuilding depends on actual and expected changes in the level of output, on interest rates, on capacity utilisation, on company sector finance and on relative prices. Exports of goods and services depend on the level of activity in the world economy and on the relative competitiveness of United Kingdom production. These, together with the exogenous level of public spending, add up to give total final expenditure. The distribution of that between domestic output and imports depends on capacity utilisation, relative prices and on the growth rate of total demand.

In the short term output movements are determined by fluctuations in demand, but the level of capacity utilisation and of unemployment cannot rise or fall without setting corrective mechanisms into action. As the pressure of demand rises both wages and prices are bid up, accelerating inflation, so that the real value of income and wealth is reduced and, as a consequence, consumption is reduced as well. Moreover, excess demand raises imports relative to domestic output, and a worse balance of payments means a fall in the exchange rate, resulting again in faster inflation. Thus an addition to total demand, for example higher public spending on goods and services, raises total output in the short run, but not necessarily for more than a few years. The long-run effects differ in kind from those experienced initially, being supply-side effects resulting from changes in the capacity of the economy to produce, changes in the determinants of the NAIRU, or else compositional effects due to differing levels of productivity, import requirements and so on in different sectors of the economy.

By holding the exchange rate fixed we can use part of the model to calculate an *ex ante* effect. It is not an estimate of what the effect of policy changes actually would be, but it is nevertheless useful as an index of the scale on which policy was operating at a particular time (as compared with a convenient counterfactual alternative policy). When the model as a whole is used to calculate what the effects of policy changes actually are, the exchange rate equation plays a crucial role. This is especially true when we solve the model on the assumption of consistent or rational expectations. This means that the path of the exchange rate in the future as it is calculated by the model is assumed to be the same as the path that the market, at any time, expects. When news hits the market, even if it is news about changes in the economy expected in the distant future, the exchange rate jumps up or down so that its current value is consistent with a new long-term equilibrium on the balance of payments. (The way forward-looking models of this kind work has already been outlined in Chapter 9 above.) This means that policy changes first influence the economy when they are announced, or otherwise come to be expected, which may be long before they are put into effect. An alternative version of the model works on the assumption that expectations are adaptive rather than rational – in other words expectations are influenced only by the actual observation of changes in the economy.

13

THE CONDUCT OF MONETARY POLICY

The approach to the analysis of policy described above fits monetary policy rather well. There is plenty of scope for estimating statistical relationships between interest rates and the indicators to which the monetary authorities may be reacting. Examples of such relationships are given below. It is also relatively straightforward to estimate, using a macroeconomic model, what would have been the effect of a counterfactual policy – in this case a policy of keeping interest rates constant. The model can be put to further use: one of the estimated reaction functions can be implanted in it to see what difference that makes to the workings of the economy as the model would portray them.

It may be objected, fairly enough, that this analysis leaves out much of monetary policy as the Bank of England and the Treasury saw it during the 1970s and 1980s. A study of this kind has, unfortunately, to be selective, but this section will touch briefly on the topics which might have been developed had time and space allowed.

One of the major themes of this book is the fundamental difference made to macroeconomic policy by the floating of the exchange rate. Exchange-rate movements are described in Part 5 as consequences of policy and not as policy acts. However, exchange-market intervention by the Bank of England would properly be described as a policy act and it would be good to know what its consequences were. The view commonly taken is that the funds available to the authorities are modest, and that they are unable to influence exchange rates greatly just by virtue of buying or selling currencies. The fact of their intervention may neverthe-less have some effect as a signal, although the magnitude of such signalling effects is difficult to estimate. What we *do* attempt to quantify below is the effect of changes in official foreign exchange reserves on interest rates. When the authorities are intervening a loss of reserves will suggest the need for higher interest rates, whilst an increase will allow interest rates to fall.

Monetary policy also involves the market for public sector debt of all kinds, from short-term Treasury bills or National Savings deposits, to long-term National Savings certificates or gilt-edged securities. The authorities were selling new debt all the time as well as trying to manage the stock of debt outstanding. These activities must have had some consequences for the objectives of macroeconomic policy, but we have no way of quantifying them.

The supplementary special deposits scheme, popularly called the 'corset', was in place for much of the time in the earlier years of our period. It has been described briefly in the course of Part 1 above. Its abolition in 1980 marked the end of an era because it was done in a way that virtually precluded its reintroduction. At about the same time exchange controls were lifted and regulation of hire-purchase terms was ended. The authorities were positively encouraging banks and the financial institutions to go out and compete with one another to expand their business.

These are not changes that are susceptible to the kind of quantified analysis to be attempted in this part of the study. They will feature only as possible explanations of the higher level of interest rates (other things being equal) in the 1980s as compared with the 1970s. This is not to underplay their importance. As we have seen in Part 1, the liberalisation of credit played a big part in the recovery of consumer demand from the mid-1980s, and the boom which followed.

Control of the money supply, although it was central to the presentation of policy in our period, does not feature much in the analysis of monetary policy offered here. The question of whether the money supply determines inflation is deferred to Part 5 below. We shall see that the statistics for the broad monetary aggregate, £M3, seem to have had systematic effects both on interest rates and on fiscal policy measures. In no real sense, however, was the money supply under control. It was not directly determined by the policy actions of the authorities and rhetoric which implied that it was can only be called misleading.

Some of that rhetoric treated fiscal policy, that is the scale of public sector borrowing, as if it were an instrument of monetary control. We shall be discussing fiscal policy at some length in later sections of Part 4. In the last section of that part of the study, we shall consider briefly how fiscal and monetary policy were related to one another, either as complements or as substitutes.

SETTING SHORT-TERM INTEREST RATES

Strictly speaking the authorities do not set the short-term interest rates most often quoted, for example the yield on 3-month Treasury Bills. Nevertheless their control, operated by rather different means at different times during the period of this study, was always close.

In setting interest rates the authorities take account of the state of sentiment in financial markets. That sentiment in turn must be based in part on hints the authorities themselves may drop about their own future actions. At times the strength of feeling, in gilt-edged markets as well as in short-term money markets, may have been such that the hand of the authorities has, in effect, been forced. Is the resulting change in interest rates then a policy act, or the outcome of a market process? Unfortunately there is no way the two can be disentangled by analysis of the data. Perhaps they were too closely compounded to separate even in the minds of those whose behaviour we seek to study.

In a historical study of monetary policy, the aim is to find a way of describing policy actions which corresponds as closely as possible to the way in which decisions were in fact taken. This suggests that a close study is needed of the way in which interest rate changes were justified. The difficulty with this approach is that the authorities are always able to cite a range of indicators which they claim to take into account, but they give little or no guidance as to the relative weights they attach to each. Using our relatively short series of monthly or quarterly data the aim is rather to identify simple relationships which may hold over a run of years, possibly surviving almost unchanged across periods when the *description* of policy action has changed many times.

The success or failure of monetary policy is judged by the contemporary and subsequent behaviour of a small set of macroeconomic variables. It is reasonable to suppose therefore that policymakers will always be influenced by the movements of these variables, whether or not they say so, and whether or not they make use of other indicators or intermediate targets as well. The rate of inflation must take pride of place as the criterion above all others by which policy achievement in this field is assessed – the 'judge and jury' as Nigel Lawson himself decribed it. As we have seen, for much of the period we are concerned with, the money supply was treated as an intermediate target because it was thought to be the main determinant of future rates of inflation. We shall try therefore to estimate how much weight was given in practice to £M3 when setting interest rates. Another traditional aim of macroeconomic policy is to limit fluctuations in the pressure of demand, measured by unemployment, capacity utilisation or the deviation of output from the trend of capacity. It is obviously interesting to find out whether any trace of countercyclical action can be found in monetary policy even in the 1970s and 1980s.

In an open economy it is inevitable that actual and expected movements in the exchange rate will influence monetary policy. This is not just a matter of concern about the effect of depreciation on the domestic rate of inflation. Exchange stability is seen by many of those involved in industry and finance as worth pursuing for its own sake. The monetary authorities are under constant pressure to resist exchange-rate movements. This concern influences their reactions to changes in interest rates overseas. For similar reasons changes in the foreign exchange reserves could trigger an interest rate response.

The way policymakers behave reflects both their priorities and their view of the way the economy works. They may, for example, not use interest rates to cut unemployment, even though they give cutting unemployment high priority. That might well be appropriate if there was some other instrument (say fiscal policy) which could achieve the same result at lower cost. It is seldom possible to distinguish value judgements from judgements of fact by examining behaviour which results from both in combination.

ESTIMATION RESULTS USING QUARTERLY DATA

For this section the data to be explained are quarterly observations of short-term interest rates, more specifically the 3-month Treasury Bill yield. The series is plotted on Chart 13.1.

The range is wide, from a low point of 5.7 per cent at the end of 1977 to a high of 16.7 per cent in the first quarter of 1980. The main features to be explained include the decline through the late 1970s (interrupted by a sharp peak at the end of 1976), the climb from the trough of 1978 to the twin peaks of 1980 and 1982, and finally the slow and irregular descent which continued to the end of the period shown.

In examining the quarterly data we shall be looking for simple relationships to describe behaviour on average over the whole period. We shall also, for reasons which will become clear at a later stage, confine our attention to variables which are consistent with the National Institute's macroeconomic model.

Chart 13.2 shows the profile of *world* interest rates, calculated as a weighted average of representative short-term rates for the United States, Japan, Germany and France. On average United Kingdom rates were well above world rates as defined for the study. There is some similarity in the timing of peaks and troughs, but also some striking differences. Thus the world peaks of 1974 and 1981 may help to explain the United Kingdom peaks in the same years, but the events of 1976 and 1980 need some other explanation.

Chart 13.1   *UK interest rates (Treasury bill yield)*

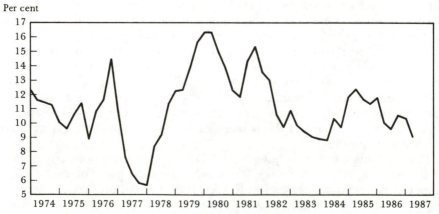

Per cent

Chart 13.2   *World interest rate*[a]

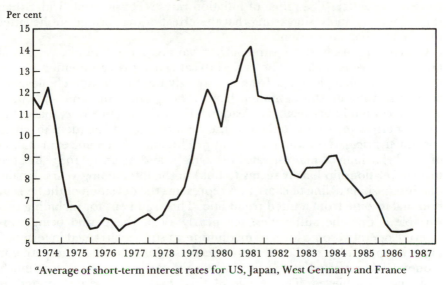

Per cent

[a]Average of short-term interest rates for US, Japan, West Germany and France

Chart 13.3   *UK inflation rate*[a]

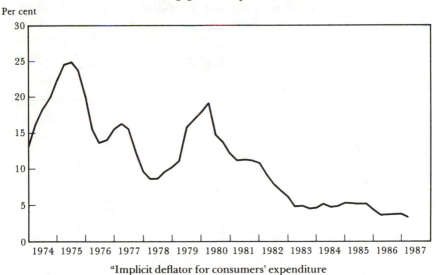

Per cent

[a]Implicit deflator for consumers' expenditure

Chart 13.3 shows the rate of inflation in the United Kingdom, that is the annual percentage change in the consumer price index calculated over the four quarters ending with the one plotted. There were two formidable peaks in 1975 and 1980, with a subsidiary peak between them in 1977 as well as a good trough in 1978. Having fallen to a quite moderate rate by

1983, inflation showed relatively little variation on this measure from year to year thereafter. The range of inflation rates is considerably wider than that of interest rates, suggesting that the effect of the former on the latter may be less than one-for-one.

Charts 13.4–13.6 show three other variables used in the statistical analysis described below. The cycle in real activity is represented by the deviation of unemployment from its strongly upward trend. The level of activity is rising on this definition from 1976–9 and from 1982–7, with a sharp recession in between. The path of the real exchange rate, that is the sterling effective rate multiplied by the ratio of United Kingdom to world consumer prices, is shown on Chart 13.5. This may offer some explanation of the behaviour of interest rates in 1976–7, and again in 1985, but the inverse relationship hardly seems to hold in the intervening years. Finally the 'hump-shaped' line of chart 13.6 represents the deviation of the level of nominal income from a fitted trend line. The argument for including this variable is that the authorities, for nearly all of the period being considered, operated some form of medium-term strategy, framed in terms of money supply targets. These targets were seldom met, but the path for money GDP expected at the time when the targets were set, was much more nearly achieved. The profile of this chart could be interpreted as saying that the pressure to hold back the growth of nominal incomes increased all the way from 1974–80, but thereafter fell back as the threat of inflation abated.

Chart 13.4   *Unemployment – deviation from trend*

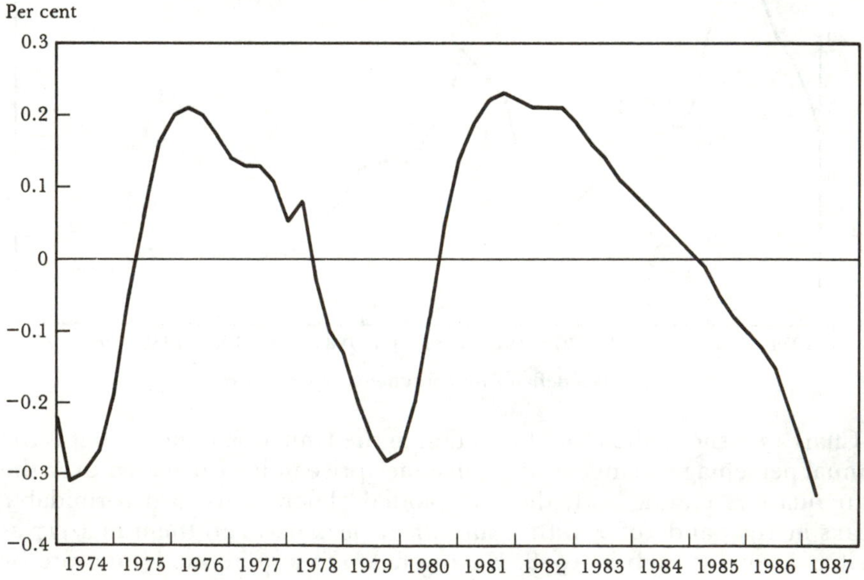

Per cent

Chart 13.5 *Real exchange rate*[a]

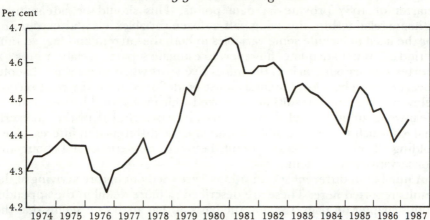

[a]Effective exchange rate index corrected for relative consumer price inflation at home and abroad (natural logarithm)

Chart 13.6 *Nominal GDP – deviation from trend*[a]

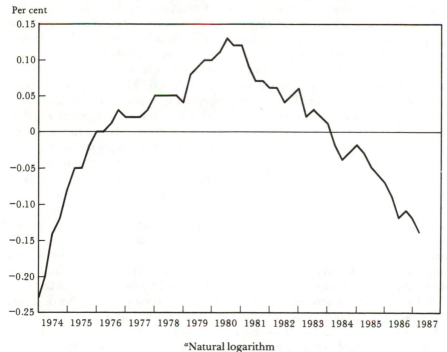

[a]Natural logarithm

Quarterly observations from the first quarter of 1974 to the second quarter of 1987 provide 54 data points. This should be adequate to estimate relationships involving half-a-dozen variables, even after allowing for the need to include some variables in both the current and lagged time periods. It is not adequate, however, to estimate separate relationships for shorter sub-periods, such as the initial five years when there was a Labour government. That closer analysis must be deferred until the next section below in which some results are reported which use monthly observations. Meanwhile an additional dummy variable was included in the quarterly analysis which made it possible to estimate the difference in interest rates, holding all other variables constant, between the periods of Labour and Conservative government.

A number of different specifications were tried out before arriving at the results reported here. These are described in more detail in the appendix to this chapter on page 187. On the basis of that analysis it seems that the quarterly equation which best represents the determination of interest rates from 1974–87 is as shown in the box below.

The most consistent and robust finding was that interest rates in this country respond to interest rates in world financial markets, immediately, but not fully in proportion. The natural interpretation to put on this is that the monetary authorities have been concerned that rates in this country should keep pace with rates abroad, because they have not wanted to see large capital movements into or out of sterling, or because they have preferred when possible to keep the exchange rate broadly stable. The level of the real exchange rate itself seems in addition to have a direct influence on interest rates. When sterling is weak (as in late 1976 and in early 1985 for example) interest rates are raised; when sterling is strong (as in 1977 or later in 1985) interest rates are reduced. The effect of inflation on interest rates is small, perhaps surprisingly so. An increase of a percentage point in the rate of inflation results after some time in a rise of at most a quarter of a percentage point in interest rates. This could be because the rate of inflation expected in the future is more relevant to interest rates than the rate of inflation in the past, and expectations do not adjust one-for-one to experience of outturns. If, however, the forecasts of inflation actually published each quarter by the National Institute are added to the analysis they do nothing to improve the explanation. Reducing inflation was the principal declared aim of monetary policy thoughout this period, yet the data suggest that the actual behaviour of interest rates in response to changes in the rate of inflation was weak and sluggish. This worked in both directions: up to 1980 real interest rates were often negative, sometimes markedly so (nominal rates well below the rate of inflation); after 1980, as inflation came down, they were always positive. Nominal rates did not come down to match the fall in inflation.

Using interest rates to offset the cyclical movements in real activity was hardly a fashionable idea at any time between 1974 and 1987 (although it

Box 1 *Results using quarterly data, 1974–87*

The equation was first estimated as a static relationship to investigate the long-run response of the level of interest rates to its determinants. The preferred equation was:

$$r = -15.3 + 0.67 \ rf + 0.24 \ Inf - 2.9 \ Unp + 11.9 \ Ngdp$$
$$(0.18) \qquad (0.09) \qquad (1.5) \qquad (4.1)$$

$$-17.0 \ Lreff - 3.2 \ Dum - 0.18 \ time$$
$$(5.8) \qquad (1.7)$$

R^2 = 0.62   54 observations from 1974 (Q1) to 1987 (Q2)
DW = 0.71   (figures in parentheses are coefficient standard errors)
DF (Dickey-Fuller test statistic) = −3.5
where r is the yield on UK Treasury Bills
　　　rf is an index of world interest rates
　　　Inf is the annual percentage rate of inflation
　　　Unp is the logarithm of unemployment
　　　$Ngdp$ is the logarithm of nominal GDP
　　　$Lreff$ is the logarithm of the sterling effective exchange rate index multiplied by the ratio of UK to world prices.
　　　Dum has the value unity up to 1979(Q2) and zero thereafter. Time is a quarterly time trend.

To estimate the speed of adjustment of interest rates towards this long-run relationship a dynamic equation was estimated as follows:

$$\Delta r = 0.05 + 0.44 \ \Delta r_{-1} + 0.21 \ \Delta r_{-2} + 0.53 \ \Delta rf - 16.9 \ \Delta Lreff - 0.47 \ Res_{-1}$$
$$(0.17) \qquad (0.14) \qquad (0.29) \qquad (17.0) \qquad (0.11)$$
R^2 = 0.58   52 observations from 1974 (Q3) to 1987 (Q2)
DW = 1.9   Instrumental Variables Estimation
　　where Δx means the change in the variable x
　　x_{-1} means the value of x in the preceding period
　　Res is the residual from the 'static' equation reported above

A rather similar result was obtained by estimating the dynamic and static responses in one unrestricted equation:

$$\Delta r = 0.46 \ \Delta r_{-1} + 0.18 \ \Delta r_{-2} + 0.36 \ \Delta rf - 15.3 \ \Delta Lreff - 0.48 r_{-1}$$
$$(0.14) \qquad (0.13) \qquad (0.52) \qquad (17.6) \qquad (0.15)$$
$$-11.9 + 0.19 \ rf_{-1} + 0.05 \ Inf_{-1} - 2.4 \ Unp_{-1} + 5.0 \ Ngdp_{-1}$$
$$(0.19) \qquad (0.08) \qquad (2.0) \qquad (7.1)$$
$$- 3.4 \ Lreff_{-1} - 1.4 \ Dum_{-1} - 0.07 \ time$$
$$(8.4) \qquad (1.6)$$
R^2 = 0.61   52 observations from 1974 (Q3) to 1987 (Q2)
DW = 2.1   Instrumental variables estimation

has arguably become fashionable again a year or so later). Yet analysis of the figures suggests that deviations of unemployment from its upward trend *did* influence the authorities in setting short-term interest rates. The effect was, admittedly, not really commensurate with the scale of cyclical variation, especially in the 1980s recession. The rise in unemployment between the end of 1979 and the beginning of 1981 would on these estimates have been enough, other things being equal (which they were not), to reduce interest rates by just 1.5 percentage points.

In addition to both inflation and unemployment, it seems possible to identify a rather weak effect from the level of nominal GDP. This is intriguing, because it suggests that the authorities were not entirely unconcerned by the phenomenon of 'base drift'. They did not, in other words, regard each year's inflation rate as a completely new battle to be fought afresh. It was part of a campaign, with longer-term objectives. The zeal with which they resisted inflation in one year depended to some extent on how successful they had been up to that point. After a particularly bad year they would try harder; when good progress had been made they tended to rest on their laurels.

Finally the dummy variable for the change of government in 1979 makes it clear that the level of interest rates was higher under the Conservatives, all other things being equal, by a significant margin, about 3 percentage points. It may be that the whole pattern of responses shifted as well, but we do not have enough data points to investigate that possibility. For the present we can only report that this shift in the whole level of interest rates seems quite a robust finding. It may represent a different set of priorities between the two political parties, or else it may result from a changed view of the way that monetary policy works. It could be regarded as a necessary consequence of the deregulation of the financial system. The abolition of exchange control, of the supplementary special deposits scheme and of hire purchase controls, for example, all increased the need to rely on interest rates as the main weapon in the armoury of counterinflation policy.

The results of those estimates using quarterly data are encouraging in that the interest rate responses to economic indicators all seem to go in the right direction, and to be on a plausible scale. Despite the many changes in the way monetary policy was described between 1974 and 1987 some sensible interpretation can be made of average behaviour over the period as a whole. The next section describes some further estimates using monthly data. In that context we shall estimate the effects of some further variables, notably the growth of the money supply and the level of foreign-exchange reserves; and we shall look again at the stability of the reaction functions estimated over sub-periods of the data.

ESTIMATION RESULTS USING MONTHLY DATA

The main advantage of using monthly data is that the much larger number of observations makes it possible to look separately at the determination of interest rates under the Labour government, 1974–9, and under the Conservatives, 1979–87. In the course of the investigation, it soon became clear that the average behaviour in the two sub-periods was different, and that the difference was not just a matter of the average level of interest rates as the estimates based on quarterly data had assumed.

It was indeed impossible to estimate any plausible relationship for interest-rate movements in the Labour government period using only the variables included in the quarterly data set. The results for that sub-period on its own were improved quite dramatically when we added as an additional variable the level of the foreign exchange reserves at the beginning of the month. This should come as no surprise, since foreign exchange intervention was on a large scale during this sub-period, to support the pound in 1976 and to hold it down in 1977. In those circumstances clearly the movement in the exchange rate itself was not the only signal from the exchange market to which the authorities would respond.

There were no official targets for the money supply in the early years of the Labour government, but even then there was a great deal of public comment on the rate of monetary growth and sentiment in the markets was affected. For much of the period prior to 1979 the 'corset' was in place as a means of controlling the banks' balance sheets directly, but interest rates may have been used as a back-up. The growth rate of £M3 was therefore included in the specification of the monthly reaction functions.

The second box shows the estimation results for the period up to the 1979 election. The static equation fits the data rather well ($R^2 = 0.89$) and the test statistic indicating the existence of a well-defined static relationship between these variables is also relatively satisfactory (DF = -5.5). The interpretation of monetary policy under the Labour government given by this equation is plausible enough. The most urgent signals were those which came from the foreign exchange markets, including reserve movements as well as rate movements. The response to £M3 was weak, but not insignificant. There was also a response to the unemployment figures, which was large relative to that estimated for the period as a whole on the quarterly data described above. On the other hand the response to the rate of inflation was so weak as to be almost non-existent.

The dynamic equation also reported in the box confirms these results. It implies a long-run solution for the level of interest rates similar to the static equation when estimated directly. There is no significant long-run response to inflation at all. The short-term responses were most vigorous, as one might expect, to the signals coming from the exchange market.

The third box shows corresponding estimates for the (rather longer) period of Conservative government. These estimates also seemed to benefit from including the value of the reserves, although here the contribution of that variable to the explanation is less than it was in the first sub-period. We also included the value of industrial production multiplied by the index of wholesale prices as a monthly analogue to the quarterly series for GDP at current prices.

Box 2   *Results using monthly data, 1974–9*

The best of the static equations for this sub-period was:

$$r = 130 + 0.46\ rf + 0.09\ Inf - 6.3\quad Unp - 8.9\ Lreff + 0.09\ Mon$$
$$\quad\ (0.25)\quad (0.05)\quad (1.91)\qquad (4.1)\qquad\quad (0.04)$$
$$- 6.2\ Fcres + 0.25\ time$$
$$\ \ (0.4)$$

$R^2\ = 0.89$ 62 observations from 1974(M4) to 1979(M5)
$DW = 1.3$
$DF\ = -5.5$ (figures in parentheses are coefficient standard errors)

The variables are as defined in Box 1 above except that *Fcres* is the (logarithm of the) SDR value of the foreign exchange reserves, and *Mon* is the growth rate of the broad monetary aggregate £M3.

The best of the dynamic equations was:

$$\Delta r = 59 + 0.28\ \Delta r_{-1} - 20.1\ \Delta Lreff - 2.48\ \Delta Fcres - 0.42 r_{-1}$$
$$\qquad\quad (0.10)\qquad\ (9.9)\qquad\ (1.15)\qquad\quad (0.13)$$
$$+\ 0.09\ rf_{-1} - 2.7\ Fcres_{-1} - 3.69\ Unp_{-1} - 2.7\ Lreff_{-1} + 0.02\ Mon_{-1}$$
$$\quad (0.24)\qquad (0.9)\qquad\ (1.72)\qquad (3.0)\qquad\ (0.03)$$

$$+\ 0.11\ time$$

$R^2\ = 0.62$ 61 observations from 1974(M5) to 1979(M5)
$DW = 2.0$ Instrumental variables

The growth of the money supply is still only a weak influence on interest rates. To understand this one should recall that the period from 1979–87 included not only the strict monetarist regime immediately after the election, but also the more pragmatic approach of the mid-1980s when £M3 was no longer a target aggregate, and its signals were deliberately ignored.

The contrast between the static equations for the two sub-periods is an interesting one, and supports the view that the use of monetary policy changed in some respects, but not in others. Under the Conservatives interest rates *did* respond to indicators of inflation, although the coefficient is still rather low. When inflation went up by 1 per cent, the average response was to raise interest rates (all else held constant) by just ½ per cent. Unemployment no longer features in the relationship at all. The size of the response to foreign interest rates under the Conservatives was the same as it had been under Labour, both coefficients being smaller than that estimated from data for the period as a whole. Movements in the exchange rate still mattered as much as under Labour, but the effect of change in the reserves had diminished. The fit of the static equation in the second sub-period is almost as good as in the first, and the test statistic for the existence of a well-defined long-run relationship is also similar.

There are several further differences between the dynamic results for

---

Box 3 *Results using monthly data, 1979–87*

The best of the static equations for this sub-period was:

$$r = -7.2 + 0.48\ rf + 0.51\ Inf - 8.8\ Lreff - 3.4\ Fcres + 19.0\ Nip$$
$$(0.10)(0.07)(2.1)(1.0)(6.4)$$
$$+\ 0.19\ Mon - 0.09\ time$$
$$(0.05)$$

$R^2 = 0.85$ 97 observations from 1979(M6) to 1987(M6)

$DW = 0.91$

$DF = -5.6$ (figures in parentheses are coefficient standard errors)

The variables are as defined above except that Nip is the (logarithm of the) index of industrial production multiplied by the wholesale price index.

The best of the dynamic equations was:

$$\Delta r = -10.2 - 0.17\ \Delta r_{-1} + 0.25\ \Delta rf - 18.6\ \Delta Lreff - 0.20\ r_{-1} + 0.26 rf_{-1}$$
$$(0.12)\phantom{\Delta r_{-1}}(0.62)(7.4)(0.07)\phantom{r_{-1}}(0.11)$$
$$-\ 8.9\ Lreff_{-1} + 12.9\ Nip_{-1} + 0.04\ Mon_{-1} - 0.10\ time$$
$$(2.1)\phantom{Lreff_{-1}}(5.0)\phantom{Nip_{-1}}(0.02)$$

$R^2 = 0.44$ 97 observations from 1979(M6) to 1987(M6)

$DW = 1.97$ Instrumental variables

---

the two sub-periods, but it would be quite wrong to place emphasis on the detail of what must be a most uncertain statistical exercise.

It is worth mentioning briefly one other test that was carried out (see appendix below). The monthly observations for the whole period 1974–87 were divided into two sub-sets, one in which the relationship we had estimated pointed to a need for interest rates to rise, the other in which a fall was indicated. We then reestimated relationships separately for those two sub-sets of data. The idea was to test for asymmetries of response, and the results confirm that such effects possibly did exist. Thus, interest rates in general rose abruptly when the exchange rate was falling, but fell more slowly when the exchange rate was rising, it also seemed that interest rates were quicker to fall in response to a rise in unemployment than they were to rise if unemployment fell.

The results of the reaction function estimates, quarterly as well as monthly, might be summarised in this way. Throughout the period covered by this study, United Kingdom interest rates were set very much with an eye to external markets. They moved when world rates moved, although not one-for-one in terms of percentage points. Reserve changes or exchange rate movements were signals which the authorities could never ignore. The growth of the money supply (£M3) and the level of nominal GDP also had some effect. The difference between the Labour and Conservative governments can be summarised in either of two ways. One could simply say that interest rates were higher in the later sub-period (other things being equal), or one could say that their use as instruments of domestic economic policy shifted. Unemployment had an effect on interest rates in the early years, whilst inflation had little or no effect. After the change of government the opposite was the case. This contrast between the two sub-periods should not be made in isolation from the rest of economic policy. Under Labour the main instrument used to reduce inflation was not monetary policy but incomes policy. Under the Conservatives the main instruments used to contain the rise in unemployment were special labour market measures and youth training.

HISTORY REWRITTEN WITH THE INTEREST RATE CONSTANT

Having been at some pains to discover why monetary policy was as it was year-by-year, we turn now to a new problem. What difference did it make? Macroeconomic models are designed to answer questions of this kind.

A natural starting point is a counterfactual simulation showing history as it might have been if interest rates had been held constant every quarter from 1974–87. If it is right to describe the routine of monetary policy as the setting of short-term interest rates, then the limiting cases of policy inactivity would be to keep interest rates unchanged all the time. (Until the 1950s it was normal for interest rates to remain unchanged for several years at a time.)

A counterfactual simulation is not really an alternative view of history; it is simply a construct of the model. No model provides a full explanation of the past; in constructing a counterfactual one we assume that the bits of the past that the model cannot explain, the residuals in the equations, would have stayed the same. That is just an act of faith. Moreover there are special conceptual problems with counterfactual simulations using a model with consistent expectations. We have to assume in effect that forecasters would have made the same errors in the counterfactual case as they did in the real world. That is a particularly heroic assumption to make, and not one we would wish to defend.

It is convenient to assume the average level of interest rates unchanged over the period as a whole, so in the simulation the Treasury Bill Rate is set at 11.2 per cent throughout. Thus the main differences from actual history (see table 13.1 below) are that the interest rate stays high in 1977 and 1978 instead of falling sharply; that it does not rise abruptly as it did in 1979–80; and that it tends to stay a little higher in the mid-1980s than it was in real life.

The differences between the base run and the simulation, especially the differences in the exchange rate, depend on the extent to which it is assumed that interest rate changes were anticipated. In the case shown here all interest rate changes are anticipated, and their consequences for

Table 13.1 *The economy with a constant interest rate*

	Interest rate		Exchange rate		Rate of Growth[a]		Rate of Inflation[b]		Consumer Spending[c]		Fixed investment[c]	
	Actual	Variant	Actual	Variant	Actual	Variant	Actual	Variant	Actual	Variant	Actual	Variant
1975	10.4	11.2	−7.8	−7.8	−1.9	−2.0	24.3	23.8	−0.5	−0.4	−2.0	−2.5
1976	11.4	11.2	−14.2	−14.8	2.0	2.1	16.5	15.8	0.3	0.3	1.7	1.5
1977	8.1	11.2	−5.2	−5.2	2.8	2.9	15.9	16.4	−0.5	−0.4	−1.8	−2.0
1978	8.5	11.2	0.3	−3.4	3.5	3.5	8.3	10.0	5.6	5.5	3.0	1.9
1979	13.4	11.2	7.2	6.4	3.0	3.2	13.4	13.2	4.2	4.0	2.8	4.8
1980	15.7	11.2	10.1	13.9	−2.9	−2.7	18.0	17.0	0.0	0.3	−5.4	−2.7
1981	13.5	11.2	−1.2	1.8	−1.4	−1.8	11.9	11.5	0.0	0.3	−9.6	−10.0
1982	12.0	11.2	−4.7	−2.1	2.2	1.6	8.6	7.4	0.9	0.8	5.4	4.1
1983	9.8	11.2	−8.0	−7.9	3.4	3.1	4.6	3.4	4.5	4.2	5.0	2.8
1984	9.5	11.2	−5.5	−6.8	2.8	3.0	5.0	3.8	1.8	1.4	8.6	7.5
1985	11.9	11.2	−0.7	−1.1	3.5	4.0	6.0	4.6	3.7	3.8	3.8	4.8
1986	10.6	11.2	−8.2	−7.7	2.9	3.3	3.5	3.3	5.7	6.0	1.7	2.4
1987	9.6	11.2	−1.6	−2.1	4.7	4.8	4.1	4.7	5.4	5.4	8.3	8.4

[a] Percentage change in GDP at constant prices, year-on-year.
[b] Percentage change in the retail price index, year-on-year.
[c] Growth rate per annum.

output and inflation are fully understood. This is the extreme, but analytically useful, case of rational expectations.

The differences from the base run (that is from what actually happened) are small, perhaps surprisingly so. Interest rate effects on domestic demand were small in the 1970s because consumer spending was determined mainly by personal sector income, which was raised when interest rates went up. In the 1980s consumers were more heavily in debt and interest rates gained more leverage. There are some significant effects on investment particularly in the 1980s. The effects on inflation mainly arise from the inclusion of the cost of mortgage interest in the retail price index. The effects on other measures of inflation are very small.

The effects on exchange rates shown in table 13.1 are small and may, at first sight, appear perverse. Thus in 1979 holding interest rates flat at 11.2 per cent would apparently have resulted in even more of an appreciation than occurred in fact. The paradox is explained by the assumption of perfect foresight. In such a world exchange rate movements must compensate for differences in interest rates so as to equalise the return on assets in domestic and foreign currency. If, as in the case described below, interest rates had been unanticipated, the exchange rate would have jumped up when the news reached the market and then depreciated more slowly down again equalising the return on assets *after* the jump. With perfect foresight however there are no jumps, because there is never any 'news'.

The main conclusion to draw from this simulation is that the scale of the changes to the domestic economy resulting directly from variation on the rate of interest over this period was quite small, especially in the early years. Obviously this result reflects the properties of the model used to obtain it, but those properties are not out of line with those of other United Kingdom models. It appears that the magnitude of the effects increased in the 1980s. The effect of interest rate 'surprises' on the exchange rate is discussed further in the next section.

THE INTERACTION BETWEEN
MONETARY POLICY AND THE ECONOMY

The conduct of monetary policy can be described by a time path for short-term interest rates. In that case it is natural to compare, as we have just done, the actual path of interest rates with an alternative path, for example with a path that was totally flat. But another, and perhaps more illuminating way of describing the conduct of monetary policy is to use an estimated reaction function. This then tells us how monetary policy and the economy interacted to produce the actual path of interest rates. We can also ask how interest rates and the economy would have been different if either policy or the environment had been different.

The method used to explore these interactions involves writing an estimated reaction function as an additional equation in the macroeconomic model. But naturally any results obtained by this method depend on the characteristics of the particular macroeconomic model used (in this case the model estimated by the National Institute in the latter part of 1988). Before presenting any numerical results therefore it may be worth making a few more general points.

The reaction function estimated from quarterly data described above shows how interest rates responded to foreign interest rates, inflation, unemployment, nominal incomes and the real exchange rate. But all these variables are themselves influenced by interest rates, directly or indirectly. Thus the outcome for interest rates depends on an interaction of policy with the economy. This is true even though interest rates are directly under the control of the monetary authorities, who use them as a policy instrument.

The effect that interest rates have on the economy depends on their relation to the yield on alternative assets. In a closed economy the most important comparison may be with the yield on real assets (represented for example by equity capital); in an open economy like that of the United Kingdom, the most important comparison is probably with interest rates abroad. If these alternative assets are regarded as very close substitutes for the assets whose yield is set by the authorities, then in practice the difference in expected real returns between them will never be very great. The reaction function will in practice never tell the authorities to move interest rates in such a way as to open up a wide gap. Thus one could say *both* that real yields depend mainly on 'productivity and thrift', as classical economics requires, or on real yields abroad, as capital mobility suggests, and *also* that interest rates are set by the monetary authorities so as to achieve their policy objectives. The two statements sound incompatible but they are not so in fact.

A given model of the recovery may exhibit quite different kinds of behaviour when different reaction functions are embedded in it. For example a model which is dynamically stable under one policy regime may be unstable under another; some combinations of models with policy regimes will produce trade cycles in the economy with more or less amplitude and regularity. It is arguable that a reaction function would never produce instability or violent oscillations in the economy when combined with a model representing the economy, as the authorities at the time believed. (If it did then the authorities would have foreseen the unstable consequence of their behaviour.) Instability would suggest rather that the authorities based their reactions on a mistaken view of economics – or at least a view different from the one represented by the model now being used. In fact when we marry up our estimated reaction function with the National Institute model, the two seem to work happily enough together.

We referred above to the possibility that the nature of the reaction function governing monetary policy is public knowledge. That is the assumption we made when we entered it in the Institute's model. All changes in interest rates are correctly anticipated by the market. On the other hand the reaction function of the authorities is *not* forward-looking. It is important to bear these assumptions in mind when interpreting the results reported below. With this preamble we now turn to the numerical results themselves.

The reaction function used was the one set out in the box on page ooo. The first experiment consisted of adding a constant £400 million a quarter (at 1985 prices) to public authorities' consumption, assuming that the change is unanticipated. The results are summarised in table 13.2. (These are *not* counterfactual simulations like those in table 13.1; their purpose is simply to demonstrate the properties of the model with the reaction function embedded in it.)

If interest rates are held constant the exchange rate jumps down by 3½ per cent and stays there. The initial drop in the exchange rate, and the higher level of economic activity adds to inflation for the first couple of years. With the interest rate responding according to the estimated reaction function, the picture is quite different. The initial drop in the exchange rate is little more than ½ per cent, but it subsequently increases, until after ten years it is almost 3½ per cent, as in the fixed interest rate case. The rise in interest rates is not instantaneous, but spread over the first five quarters, and it amounts to less than ½ percentage point. The effect on inflation is slight, and spread over a long period.

The effects of a shock to private sector demand, not reported here in detail, are broadly similar. Again the main consequence of the interest rate reaction is to delay the exchange depreciation, and hence to spread out the

Table 13.2 *Effects of an addition to public authorities' consumption*

per cent

Quarter	Output		Exchange rate		Price level		Interest rate
	Fixed interest rate	Interest rate reacts	Fixed interest rate	Interest rate reacts	Fixed interest rate	Interest rate reacts	
1	0.5	0.4	−3.6	−0.7	0.4	0.1	0.1
2	0.6	0.4	−3.7	−0.7	0.7	0.2	0.2
3	0.7	0.5	−3.7	−0.7	1.1	0.3	0.2
4	0.8	0.5	−3.8	−0.8	1.4	0.4	0.3
8	0.8	0.4	−3.8	−1.0	2.7	0.8	0.4
12	0.4	0.3	−3.8	−1.3	3.7	1.3	0.4
16	0.2	0.3	−3.7	−1.6	4.3	1.6	0.4
20	0.0	0.2	−3.6	−1.8	4.2	1.8	0.4
40	0.0	0.1	−3.5	−3.2	3.7	3.1	0.5

consequences for inflation over a longer period. In no case was there any suggestion of instability. With, or without, an interest rate response, output growth was little changed over the longer term as a result of the addition to demand. Neither was there any suggestion of the kind of response to demand shocks that would explain a trade cycle of regular period.

Table 13.3 shows the results of a second experiment in which the rate of interest on overseas assets was raised by 2 percentage points. The direct effect on domestic interest rates, as shown by the coefficient on foreign interest rates in the estimated reaction function is less than 1 per cent. But there are also indirect effects particularly because the United Kingdom exchange rate falls. During the first year the increase in United Kingdom interest rates comes close to 2 per cent, but in later years it falls away. Eventually it falls even below the direct effect predicted by the reaction function. This is because unemployment is rising, because inflation has fallen (after its initial rise), and because the real exchange rate has been increased.

One possible reason for a rise in interest rates overseas could be a faster rate of world inflation. This is the case illustrated in table 13.4. Initially the exchange rate hardly changes at all, and United Kingdom interest rates are increased by about 1 percentage point. In the longer term, world inflation is only offset in part by exchange rate appreciation, and as a result United Kingdom inflation rises, although not by as much as 2 per cent a year. Over time United Kingdom interest rates rise, although very slowly, in response to the rising level of nominal incomes.

It has been stressed that these results depend on the assumption that future interest rate changes are correctly anticipated by the market. The

Table 13.3 *Effects of 2 per cent higher interest rates overseas*

per cent

Quarter	Output	Exchange rate	Price level	Interest rate
1	0.1	−4.6	0.5	1.4
2	−0.1	−4.5	0.9	1.8
3	0.0	−4.6	1.2	1.9
4	0.0	−4.6	1.5	1.7
8	0.0	−4.2	2.7	1.0
12	−0.3	−3.6	3.4	1.2
16	−0.6	−3.0	3.5	1.0
20	−0.7	−2.3	3.1	0.8
40	−0.7	1.3	0.2	0.4

Table 13.4 *Effects of 2 per cent higher interest rates and inflation overseas*

per cent

Quarter	Output	Exchange rate	Price level	Interest rate
1	0.0	0.1	0.1	0.8
2	−0.1	0.3	0.1	1.2
3	−0.1	0.5	0.2	1.4
4	−0.2	0.7	0.3	1.3
8	−0.2	1.5	1.1	0.8
12	−0.3	2.5	1.9	1.1
16	−0.3	3.3	3.0	1.1
20	−0.5	4.1	4.1	1.2
40	−1.2	7.1	8.4	1.4

way the simulation is set up precludes the authorities from surprising the market. There is an asymmetry in our assumptions: the authorities only react to events after they have happened, whilst the behaviour that determines the exchange rate is forward looking. For our final illustration we make a different assumption. We look at the shift in monetary policy in 1979 represented by the dummy variable in the estimated reaction function, and ask what effect that had on the economy, assuming that it was *not* anticipated by the market. For this purpose the simulation starts in 1979 and the differences between model runs with and without the dummy variable include a jump in the exchange rate in the first quarter. The results are shown in table 13.5.

The direct effect of the regime change in 1979, according to the reaction function, was to raise interest rates, all other things being equal, by 2.9

Table 13.5 *Effects of the 1979 shift in monetary policy*

	Output	Exchange rate	Price level	Interest rate
1979	−0.6	+12.5	−2.6	
1980	−1.8	+16.4	−8.6	+1.4
1981	−1.0	+15.9	−13.7	+0.3
1982	—	+15.8	−17.1	+0.8
1983	+0.5	+15.3	−18.0	+1.1
1984	+0.5	+14.7	−17.4	+1.3
1985	+0.5	+14.0	−16.7	+1.5
1986	+0.6	+13.4	−16.0	+1.6
1987	+0.6	+12.7	−15.3	+1.7

percentage points. As the table suggests, however, what actually happened was that the exchange rate jumped up substantially and the rise in interest rates, taking account of indirect as well as direct effects, was around 1½ percentage points or even less.

The size of the exchange rate jump, about 16 per cent beginning in the second quarter of 1979, is of course only a very rough estimate, heavily dependent on the precise way in which the simulation has been carried out. It is interesting, nevertheless, to set it alongside the scale of exchange rate appreciation which actually took place about this time. In fact the effective exchange rate index rose by 7.2 per cent in 1979 and a further 10.1 per cent in 1980 (year-on-year). The estimates reported here suggest that *all* of that appreciation could be explained by the unexpected shift in the behaviour of the monetary authorities. (This contrasts with the view popular at the time that the rise in the exchange rate was mainly due to a change in the real price of oil.)

In the simulation the exchange rate overshoots its long-run value, depreciating relative to the base run from 1980 onwards. It is likely that overshooting did occur in the real world, since the exchange rate depreciated year-on-year from 1981–7 inclusive. This would be consistent with the view that the shift in the reaction function was unexpected when it first took place in 1979, but that the subsequent behaviour of interest rates was more generally in line with market expectations. Relatively high interest rates which are anticipated by the market imply, as suggested above, a *downward* trend in the exchange rate. That observation would seem to characterise the experience of the 1980s in the United Kingdom rather well.

We have tried in this section to throw some light on the effects of monetary policy on the economy, particularly effects working through the exchange rate. It has not proved as straightforward an exercise as it sounds. The size, even the direction of the effects depends on whether we believe them to have been anticipated or unanticipated. This should serve to underline the problems which beset the authorities when they attempt to influence aggregate demand or inflation in a predictable way under flexible exchange rates. The nature of the game is quite different from that played by the authorities in the era of Bretton Woods.

APPENDIX TO CHAPTER 13

THE ESTIMATION OF INTEREST RATE
REACTION FUNCTIONS

The study used both quarterly and monthly data, for the period 1974(Q1) or (M4) to 1987(Q2) or (M6). When using quarterly data the aim was to find a simple and robust relationship to describe the average behaviour of interest rates over the period as a whole using variables which are themselves explained in the National Institute's macroeconomic model. When using monthly data several further explanatory variables were added and the date were split into sub-periods. The aim was to get closer to the indicators to which the authorities actually responded, and to distinguish between average behaviour under Labour and Conservative governments. The main results, and the conclusions drawn from them, are set out above. This appendix documents the research in rather more detail.

The method of approach adopted with both quarterly and monthly data was as follows. Static equations were first estimated by ordinary least squares. On this basis a preliminary view was taken of the variables to be included in the preferred dynamic equations. The residuals from these static equations were then included, alongside other variables, in equations to explain the *change* in interest rates in each period. Finally unrestricted dynamic equations were estimated and their long-run properties compared with those of the corresponding static equations.

Quarterly data
The variables used are defined as follows:

r Yield on UK Treasury Bills. (Based on monthly series in *Economic Trends* by averaging 4 end-month figures)

rf Overseas short-term interest rates. (For US, Germany, France and Japan with weights 0.392, 0.224. 0.166 and 0.218 respectively)

Inf   4-quarter rate of change of the consumers' expenditure deflator

Unp   The logarithm of unemployment, seasonally adjusted (from *Department of Employment Gazette* table 2.1)

Ngdp   The logarithm of gross domestic product at current prices, seasonally adjusted

Reff   The logarithm of the 'real' sterling effective exchange rate index (i.e. the index multiplied by the UK consumers' expenditure deflator and divided by an index of world consumer prices)

Dum   A dummy variable = 1 1974(Q1) to 1979(Q1)
                            = 0 1979(Q2) to 1987(Q2)

Pfrc   The National Institute forecast of price inflation over the year ahead

Winf   World inflation (the 4-quarter percentage change in an index of world consumer prices)

Mon   The 4-quarter percentage growth rate of £M3 (now called M3) (from *Economic Trends* Annual Supplement 1989, table 33)

Some of the more interesting results are reported in table 13.A1

Equation (1) which is reported in the box on page 175 implies: that a rise in foreign rates of 1 percentage point raises United Kingdom rates by 0.67 percentage points; that the response to inflation is only about one to four; that a fall in unemployment of about 200,000 will lead to a fall of 0.3 percentage points in interest rates; that a 1 per cent appreciation of the United Kingdom real exchange rate reduces interest rates by 0.17 percentage points; and that a rise of 1 per cent in the level of nominal GDP adds 0.12 percentage points to interest rates. All these effects were judged to be

Table 13.A1 *Static equations using quarterly data (dependent variable is r)*

	(1)	(2)	(3)	(4)	(5)	(6)[a]	(7)[b]
Independent variables							
Constant	−15.3	−21.5	−12.3	−14.4	−48.9		
Time trend	−0.18	−0.26	−0.17	−0.19	−0.11		
rf	0.67	0.59	0.47	0.73	0.81	0.40	0.55
Inf	0.24	0.31	0.20	0.27	0.28	0.10	0.13
Unp	−2.94	−1.16	−1.37	−3.53	−3.62	−4.96	−6.77
Ngdp	11.9	12.8	10.9	12.8	13.5	10.3	17.6
Reff	−17.0	−19.8	−17.9	−18.1	−13.7	−7.02	−18.1
Dum	−3.2	−3.8	−3.4	−3.2		−2.9	−4.2
Pfrc				−0.09			
Winf			0.30				
Mon		0.14					
R^2	0.62	0.65	0.63	0.63	0.60		
DW	0.71	0.76	0.71	0.75	0.64		
DF	−3.50	−3.50	−3.46	−3.54	−3.37		

[a] Coefficients implied by long-run solution of unrestricted dynamic equation (instrumental variables).
[b] As note (a) (OLS).

plausible orders of magnitude for average reactions over the period as a whole.

Equation (2) shows that the inclusion of the money supply as an extra variable hardly changes any of the other coefficients.

Equation (3) shows the world rate of inflation with a positive coefficient. We would be expecting to find a negative coefficient if the policymakers reacted to *real* interest rates overseas.

Equation (4) shows that the National Institute inflation forecast is not significant if included alongside the actual rate of inflation over the past year.

Equation (5) shows the effect of omitting the dummy variable, which is to raise the coefficient on foreign interest rates and reduce that on the real exchange rate, but otherwise to leave the coefficients broadly unchanged.

About 60 per cent of the variation in interest rates can be explained by these static regressions, but all show evidence of dynamic misspecification. The Dickey-Fuller statistic (DF) tests the stationarity of the residuals, and hence the possibility that no long-run relationship of this kind exists at all. In no case can the possibility of non-stationarity be rejected.

Dynamic equations using specifications based on Equation (1) are reported in the box on page 175. The restricted equation identifies short-term responses to foreign interest rates, and to the real exchange rate, but not to other variables. The coefficient on the residual from the static equation is significant at conventional levels, implying that the existence of a long-run solution cannot be rejected.

The long-run solutions implied by the unrestricted dynamic equation (estimated by instrumental variables and by OLS) are shown in the final column of table 13.A1. (The instruments used included world inflation and lagged values of variables already in the regression.)

Monthly data
The variables are defined as follows:
r, rf, Unp, Reff and *DUM* – all as above for the quarterly data.

Inf	the 12-month change in the retail price index excluding rent (because the mortgage interest rate is used as a measure of the imputed rent on owner-occupied housing)
Nip	(the logarithm of) a monthly proxy for nominal GDP, formed by multiplying the index of industrial production by the wholesale price index (seasonally adjusted)
Mon	the 12-month change in £M3. After 1982 end-calendar-month data (break-adjusted) were supplied by the Bank of England. Prior to 1982 mid-month data are interpolated and then adjusted so that the sum of annual data is consistent with the quarterly data in *Economic Trends*
Stres	(the logarithm of) the sterling value of UK foreign exchange reserves excluding gold

Fcres   (the logarithm of) the SDR value of UK foreign exchange reserves excluding gold

A static equation estimated over the whole sample period gave the following result:

$$r = 3.5 + 0.71 \; rf + 0.19 \; Inf - 2.3 \; Reff - 4.0 \; Fcres - 5.2 \; Unp + 20 \; Nip$$
$$\quad\quad (0.09) \quad\; (0.04) \quad\;\; (2.5) \quad\quad (0.5) \quad\quad (0.7) \quad\quad\;\; (2)$$

$$- 0.06 \; time$$

$$R^2 = 0.71 \quad\quad DF = -4.37 \quad\quad DW = 0.42$$

(note the absence of a dummy for the change of government in 1979). The coefficients are correctly signed, and broadly similar to those in the quarterly regressions, but the addition of a small negative coefficient on the level of the reserves reduces the significance of the real exchange rate. The *DF* statistic is higher but the issue of stationarity is still not conclusively resolved.

An unrestricted dynamic equation, estimated by OLS over the whole sample period, gave the following result:

$$\Delta r = 18.04 + 0.23 \; \Delta rf - 17.1 \; \Delta Reff - 5.2 \; \Delta Reff_{-1} - 2.11 \; \Delta Stres$$
$$\quad\quad\quad (0.13) \quad\quad (3.2) \quad\quad (3.1) \quad\quad\quad (0.66)$$

$$-1.86 \; \Delta Stres_{-1} - 1.70 \; \Delta Stres_{-2} - 0.14 \; r_{-1} + 0.12 \; rf_{-1}$$
$$(0.68) \quad\quad\quad (0.67) \quad\quad\quad (0.05) \quad\quad (0.06)$$

$$+ 0.02 \; Inf_{-1} - 3.26 \; Reff_{-1} - 0.48 \; Stres_{-1} - 1.21 \; Unp_{-1}$$
$$(0.02) \quad\quad (1.38) \quad\quad (0.35) \quad\quad\quad (0.46)$$

$$+ 4.72 \; Nip_{-1} + 0.009 \; time$$
$$(1.35)$$

$$R^2 = 0.41 \quad\quad DW = 2.14 \quad\quad LM(12) = 15.9$$

The long run solution is:

$$r = a + b \; time + 0.86 rf + 0.14 \; Inf - 23 \; Reff - 3.4 \; Stres - 8.6 \; Unp + 34 \; Nip$$

The whole data period was used to investigate the hypothesis that the behaviour of the authorities was asymmetric as between circumstances in which interest rates were raised, and circumstances in which they were reduced. Interest rates tend to rise fast, and fall slowly. Moreover some situations possibly call for more urgent action than others: the need to adjust interest rates is more pressing when the exchange rate is falling than it is when it is rising; conversely, upwards movements in unemployment may be more likely to trigger a quick response.

The method used was as follows. A dynamic equation was estimated over the whole data period in restricted form, that is using the residuals from the static equation described above to define the long-run equilibrium. The

Table 13.A2 *Asymmetric estimates*

	Upward pressure	Downward pressure
Constant	0.0	0.2
Δrf	-0.03	0.54
Δrf_{-2}	0.10	0.26
$\Delta Reff$	-17.6	-11.9
$\Delta Reff_{-1}$	-6.8	-5.5
$\Delta Stres$	-2.3	-2.7
$\Delta Stres_{-1}$	-2.4	-2.0
$\Delta Stres_{-2}$	-2.8	-1.3
ΔUnp_{-1}	-4.1	-8.0
Res_{-1}	-0.1	-0.3

Note: Res is the residual from the static regression.

Table 13.A3 *Dynamic equations for sub-periods (dependent variable is Δr)*

	1974(M4)–1979(M5)		1979(M6)–1987(M6)	
	IV	OLS	IV	OLS
Constant	59	48	-10	-10
Δr_{-1}	0.28	0.35	-0.17	-0.17
Δrf	—	—	0.25	0.27
$\Delta Reff$	-20.1	-6.4	-18.6	-19.4
$\Delta Fcres$	-2.5	-2.9	—	—
r_{-1}	-0.42	-0.53	-0.20	-0.20
rf_{-1}	0.09	0.28	0.26	0.26
$Fcres_{-1}$	-2.7	-3.5	—	—
Unp_{-1}	-3.7	-2.6	—	—
$Reff_{-1}$	-2.7	-0.5	-8.9	-9.0
Nip_{-1}	—	—	12.9	13.0
Mon_{-1}	0.02	0.04	0.04	0.04
time	0.11	0.12	-0.10	-0.10
R^2	0.62	0.67	0.44	0.44
DW	2.0	2.0	2.0	2.0
Sargan's Chi-Squared test	4.0	—	6.1	—

data set was then divided into two sub-sets according to whether the interest rate move indicated by that dynamic equation in each period was up or down. (It would be wrong to use the direction of *actual* movements in interest rates to divide the data into sub-sets, because this could produce a spurious asymmetry in the estimates.) Table 13.A2 shows the results for the two sub-samples.

The results are consistent with the expectation that the authorities respond more rapidly to the exchange rate when it is signalling the need for an interest rate rise, than when it permits an interest rate fall. They also confirm that the response to rising unemployment could be more urgent than to falling unemployment. The different short-run coefficients on foreign interest rates are not so easy to interpret. For the rest of the investigation symmetry was assumed.

Monthly data for sub-periods

A stability test for a static equation estimated over the whole sample period with monthly data indicated that most of the coefficients changed between the pre- and post-1979 sub-periods. Static equations for the two sub-periods are shown in the boxes on pages 178 and 179. The R^2 statistics are high in both sub-periods and the DF statistics are now on the borderline for rejection of non-stationarity.

Finally, unrestricted dynamic equations were estimated for both sub-periods, using OLS and also Instrumental Variables (IV) methods. The preferred results are shown in the boxes. Table 13.A3 also shows OLS results. It proved difficult to find satisfactory instruments, especially for the exchange rate. (This is related presumably to the well-known difficulty of estimating satisfactory equations of any sort to explain exchange rate movements.) None of the IV results quite passed the Sargan Chi-Squared test for the validity of the instrument set.

14

THE CONDUCT OF FISCAL POLICY

Fiscal policy does not lend itself very easily to the kind of quantified statistical analysis that has been applied to interest rate setting. Acts of fiscal policy take many different forms: changes in tax rates, in the coverage of taxes, and in the method of assessment; changes in rates of benefit, in rates of subsidy, in plans for current or capital spending by government departments or local authorities; and a multitude of small administrative decisions which together add up to major policy reviews. The first thing to do in a study of this sort is to chronicle the main changes in public spending and in taxation, and that is done in the next two sections.

The scope for statistical analysis is also limited by the infrequency of fiscal policy measures. In normal times there is just one public spending White Paper and one budget a year. In the third section of this chapter the annual budgets are reviewed and a simple, not to say naive, example of an annual reaction function is presented. The fourth section deals with the subject matter of annual budget speeches and medium-term financial strategies, and discusses what effect they may have had on the economy, over and above the effects of the budget measures themselves. The fifth section looks at the effects of fiscal policy on the finances of the public sector itself.

Many attempts have been made in the past to summarise fiscal policy with a single indicator of fiscal stance. The concept of a stance as we have seen is an elusive one; we shall try to be precise. In the sixth section of this chapter we bring up to date earlier estimates of the public sector's financial deficit, weighted and cyclically adjusted. The uses and limitations of such a measure will be made clear. In the seventh section a different approach is adopted, using the macroeconomic model to derive a counterfactual history in which fiscal policy is held constant (in a way that will be defined). The two interpretations of the course of actual policy from year to year are not vastly different. Finally, in the eighth section, the reaction function approach is applied to the explanation of the adjusted fiscal deficit. Because of the inherent limitations of that indicator the analysis is again kept relatively simple.

Taxes and public spending are, of course, matters of microeconomic policy as much as macroeconomic, but those aspects will not be covered in this book. Our interest here is in fiscal policy as a means of influencing inflation, unemployment or aggregate demand. It has been argued, for two quite different reasons, that it is useless for this purpose.

The first argument is that only measures which influence the growth of the money supply will influence the rate of inflation (or even in some versions influence aggregate demand). In other words the rise in interest rates necessary to neutralise the effect of a fiscal expansion on monetary growth will also offset its effect on demand. The approach adopted here is rather to look at fiscal policy changes in isolation, assuming that interest rates are unchanged. The question of the coordination between fiscal and monetary policy is put off until the final section of this chapter.

The second argument is more sweeping in its conclusions. We have referred to it already in Part 2 above. It is said that fiscal policy has no macroeconomic effects, because of the intertemporal budget constraint. In other words a tax cut now necessarily entails higher taxes in the future to service the increment to the national debt. Taxpayers looking ahead will know this and not be misled into thinking they have more disposable income to spend. It may be a weakness of the analysis that no account at all is taken of this elegant idea. When we speak of the effects of fiscal policy we mean only the direct effects. We have no way of knowing whether taxpayers actually thought that budget changes in taxation were permanent or temporary, and how such expectations would have affected their immediate spending decisions. What we are concerned with here is the effects that work by changing the current level of income which consumers have at their disposal. We can ask only what direct contribution fiscal policy makes to the attainment of short-term macroeconomic objectives, and what role governments assigned to them in that respect.

PUBLIC SPENDING AND MACROECONOMIC POLICY

The control of public expenditure is one of the chief functions of the Treasury, which is also responsible for the conduct of macroeconomic policy. It would, however, be misleading to describe public spending as an instrument of macroeconomic policy. It has, on a few occasions, been necessary to use the ability of the Treasury to influence the level of public spending as a means of influencing the level of aggregate demand or inflationary pressure in the economy, but that is the exception not the rule. The coverage of public spending in this book will be correspondingly sparse.

The Chief Secretary to the Treasury has ministerial responsibility, under the Chancellor, for the control of public spending and is himself a member of the Cabinet. It is he, rather than the Chancellor, who conducts the negotiations with other ministers that decide departmental spending programmes and the relative priorities within and between them. There is a second permanent secretary with overall responsibility for the public spending side of the official hierarchy within the Treasury. Although he is subordinate to the Permanent Secretary of the Treasury, he enjoys a considerable independence and his concerns are very different from those of his colleagues in the finance and taxation divisions. He is advised by the Deputy Chief Economic Adviser and a team of microeconomists, who specialise in public sector issues.

The annual round of public spending decisions has been well described elsewhere. Its main aim, from a Treasury point of view, is to ensure that government collectively keeps the spending ambitions of individual departments within bounds. To that end plans are made up to five (latterly only three) years ahead. These are revised each summer and form the basis for the Autumn Statement and the White Paper usually issued early in the following year. The focus is the allocation of spending to programmes, (defence, social security and so on) rather than on its composition by economic category (consumption, investment, transfers, subsidies and so on). The implicit question is, 'how will all this be paid for?' rather than 'how will it affect the economy?'

Yet, inevitably, public spending does have a very considerable effect on the economy, planned or unplanned. Public authorities' consumption, that is their spending on goods and services, accounts for some 20 per cent of gross national product; transfers from government account for some 20 per cent of personal disposable income. In this section we shall describe briefly how the main economic categories of public spending have changed over the years covered by this study.

Table 14.1 gives annual figures for public authorities' consumption at 1985 prices. It has increased in every year except 1977 and 1985 and the variation in its growth rate from year to year has been less than that of gross domestic product. Comparing the periods of Labour and Conservative government there was some change of trend. The average growth of public consumption was slower under the Conservatives, although the growth of the economy as a whole was faster.

The figures for the recession years are particularly interesting. In the mid-1970s recession, the growth of public consumption was speeded up in a way which tended to maintain the level of total output and employment. In the recession at the beginning of the 1980s on the other hand, the growth of public consumption slowed down, although it did not actually fall. This contrast may owe something to the different attitudes of successive governments, or their advisers, to the use of public spending as a counter-cyclical instrument. But a purely political explanation is also possible. In 1975 a Labour government had just been elected on a programme which included many commitments to additional spending on social services; and in 1981 a Conservative government had recently been elected with commitments to reduce the size of the public sector.

Perhaps the most clearcut case of public consumption being used to further macroeconomic ends is the fall in 1977. This followed the succes-

Table 14.1 *Public expenditure on goods and services*

	Public authorities' consumption at 1985 prices (£bn)	Growth rate (%)	Growth rate of GDP at 1985 prices	General government fixed investment at 1985 prices[a] (£bn)
1974	63.7	1.9	−1.6	(9.8)[b]
1975	67.2	5.6	−0.8	(9.1)[b]
1976	68.1	1.2	2.7	(9.2)[b]
1977	66.9	−1.7	2.6	8.2
1978	68.5	2.3	3.0	7.9
1979	69.9	2.2	2.7	7.7
1980	71.1	1.6	−2.2	7.2
1981	71.3	0.3	−1.1	6.1
1982	71.8	0.8	1.8	7.2
1983	73.3	2.0	3.7	7.9
1984	74.0	0.9	1.7	8.4
1985	74.0	—	3.8	8.4
1986	75.4	1.9	3.0	8.7
1987	76.0	0.9	4.2	8.7
Av. 1974−79		1.9	1.4	
Av. 1980−87		1.1	1.9	

Source: 1988 *Blue book.*
[a] Excluding purchases less sales of land and existing buildings.
[b] Calculated from 1980 prices and adjusted to 1985 prices.

sive packages of measures in 1976 including the final package that won the seal of IMF approval for British economic policy at the end of the preceding year. It was, in the memorable words used at the time, the 'blood on the carpet', which proved that government was willing to sacrifice its social aims to restore financial stability. It was also a victory for the spending side of the Treasury over departments, the point at which effective control was restored after several years when it had been lost.

Table 14.1 also shows the volume of fixed investment by central and local government. This is a much smaller total than that of public consumption but a much more volatile one. Public investment was very heavy in the early 1970s, a period for example of extensive road building. In the late 1970s and early 1980s it was cut very sharply back, first by the Labour government in their period of retrenchment, then by the Conservatives in their period of austerity. When public spending has to be cut it is much easier, administratively and politically, to cut or delay capital spending than it is to cut current spending that involves direct employment or entitlement to benefit. From 1981−7 the level of public investment gradually recovered, although it never again reached the heights of the early 1970s.

In the mid-1980s it was argued − by the construction industry, by the Labour opposition, but also by disinterested non-political commentators − that the level of public investment was much too low. The case was twofold,

Table 14.2 *Transfers and Subsidies*

	Current grants to personal sector (£bn at 1985 prices)[a]	Percentage increase	Subsidies (£bn at 1985 prices)[a]
1974	26.2	5.2	10.4
1975	27.7	5.6	10.2
1976	29.6	7.0	8.3
1977	30.4	2.6	6.9
1978	33.2[b]	9.0	7.0
1979	34.2	3.1	7.6
1980	35.8	4.9	8.0
1981	39.4	10.0	8.0
1982	42.4	7.6	6.7
1983	44.1	3.9	6.9
1984	45.3	2.8	7.9
1985	46.8	3.2	7.2
1986	48.6	3.9	5.9
1987	48.4	−0.4	5.3

Source: 1988 *Blue Book.*
[a] Deflated by consumer price index.
[b] Family allowances were replaced by child benefits from April 1977, and tax allowances were reduced.

macroeconomic and microeconomic. It was linked to the high level of unemployment and also to the physical deterioration of the infrastructure: the stocks of housing, hospitals, schools and drainage systems. Not all microeconomists were impressed by the case for more spending. They said that too many roads had been built in the early 1970s. The more traditional arguments for public works went largely unheeded. The path of public investment proved to be markedly pro-cyclical in the 1980s. The constraint on spending was relaxed as central and local governments both benefited from the buoyancy of their revenues in the long recovery period.

Table 14.2 shows the time path of current grants to the personal sector, that is national insurance benefits, supplementary benefits and various other transfers paid by central or local government. Over the whole period the total of grants paid has almost doubled in real terms, whilst national income only rose by a quarter. The size of the real increase is largely explained by the growing numbers of beneficiaries, both retired and unemployed.

Spending on social security benefits cannot be controlled in the same way as other kinds of public spending. It has never been cash-limited, because it depends on entitlement. This does not mean however that government was totally passive in the face of rising numbers of beneficiaries. There were several reforms of social security during the period, new benefits were invented and old ones abolished. Moreover, the scale of uprating each year included an element of discretion. In the earlier years benefits were uprated in line with wages or prices, whichever rose the faster; later they were uprated in line with prices only. Although the number of beneficiaries must depend mainly on demography and the condition of the labour market, the way in which benefits are administered influences take-up. The fall in real benefits shown for 1987, the last year in table 14.2, is partly explained by a shift to more rigorous testing of the availability for work of the unemployed.

The path of current grants tends to be anti-cyclical, simply because unemployment (and, more generally, poverty) rises during recessions. This is evident in the 10 per cent rise in the real value of benefits paid in 1981 and, to a lesser extent, in the rather smaller increases in 1975 and 1976. This response is one of the automatic stabilisers built into the tax and benefit system. These stabilisers cannot easily be overridden by cutting entitlement to benefits, even if the government wished to.

Table 14.2 also shows public spending on subsidies (as defined in the national accounts). One large element in this is the notional subsidy to housing constituted by the deficit on the revenue account of local authorities, which is (rather artificially) affected by interest charges as well as rents. The broad picture is unaffected by this convention. Subsidies were raised sharply in 1974 in an attempt to hold down the cost of living, and to a lesser extent to maintain consumer demand. As inflation abated the subsidies were progressively reduced. This was another important battle won by the Treasury at the time of the 1976 sterling crisis or soon after. The increase in 1980 is largely due to higher interest rates and hence higher notional subsidies to local authority rents. It can hardly be thought of as a deliberate countercyclical or counterinflationary intervention.

No simple pattern of behaviour in the response of public spending to the level of economic activity or inflation can fit the whole period. The use made of subsidies and public works in the mid-1970s has no parallel in the recession and inflation of the early 1980s. The contrast in public consumption is not so great, as it followed a relatively constant growth pattern in good times and in bad. The most markedly anti-cyclical element of spending was current grants, but that was for structural reasons, not the result of deliberate policy acts.

At the beginning of our period the two sides of the Treasury had to come together each time a package of measures was introduced or contemplated. The economic effects of even quite trivial or esoteric changes in the size or structure of public spending were given detailed attention. It was believed that the multiplicity of instruments at the disposal of the government made management of the economy easier. By the end of our period attitudes were totally different. The main concern was the size and efficiency of the public sector itself. The expenditure side of the Treasury was becoming more like a Bureau of the Budget, less like a Ministry of Economics.

The result was a more businesslike attitude to the management of the public sector, but there was loss as well as gain in the change of emphasis.

The zeal of the Conservative government in the 1980s to limit the size of the public sector resulted in widespread dissatisfaction with relatively poor provision of health care and education. The growth of national output was in some degree lopsided. It may also have meant that the total number of jobs created during the expansion of the 1980s and the speed of the fall in unemployment were less than they could have been, had public spending been higher and taxes higher as well. Such considerations seem to have carried little, if any, weight in public spending decisions after 1979.

TAXATION

There was a progressive shift of attention during our period from macroeconomics to microeconomics in the discussion of taxation as a policy instrument, just as there was in the case of public spending. The annual budget in the spring continued to be the high point of the year so far as economic policy was concerned, but the content of the budget speech, and of informed comment on it, changed. In the 1970s the main issues discussed were the state of the economy, in terms of output, employment and inflation and what the budget might do to improve it. In the 1980s attention shifted to tax reform and to the effect on incentives of the structure of taxation for both the personal and corporate sectors. Nevertheless, the budget occasion, with the publication of the official economic forecasts and the medium-term financial strategy, was still a major macroeconomic event. It was still a big day for the macroeconomists of the National Institute and the London Business School as well as for the taxation specialists at the Institute for Fiscal Studies. In this book we shall, naturally, concentrate on the macroeconomics of taxation.

Table 14.3 shows the total revenue collected by central government under various heads identified in the national income and expenditure accounts. In table 14.4 the same figures are presented in real terms, that is after deflation by the consumer price index. These sets of figures do not correspond exactly to acts of policy because the revenue collected in any year depends on the buoyancy of the tax base as well as on the parameters of the tax system that the Chancellor sets at budget time. Forecasting revenues for the coming year is a difficult task, at which neither official nor independent forecasters have proved very successful. It would therefore be mistaken to interpret the detailed paths of taxation as direct results of government decisions. The evolution over a period of several years may nevertheless fairly be set down to the government's credit or blame.

The evolution of personal income tax as shown in table 14.4 is, perhaps rather surprisingly, somewhat different from the public perception of the changing severity of income taxation. Leaving 1974 aside, the real revenue raised *fell* consistently under the Labour government and *rose* (or at best hardly changed) throughout the period of Conservative government. This is partly explained by the more rapid rise in real personal incomes under

Table 14.3 *Taxation at current prices* £ *billion*

	Taxes on income		National insurance contributions			Central government's other taxes on expenditure
	Persons	Companies	Employees	Employers	NIS	
1974	9.8	2.5	2.0	2.8	—	8.3
1975	14.4	1.9	2.6	4.1	—	10.1
1976	16.7	1.8	3.1	5.1	—	11.8
1977	17.2	2.9	3.5	5.7	1.0	13.8
1978	18.5	3.5	3.7	6.1	1.7	15.3
1979	20.2	3.9	4.4	6.9	3.0	20.1
1980	24.3	5.2	5.4	8.2	3.5	24.7
1981	27.6	5.6	6.7	8.8	3.7	28.5
1982	29.8	6.5	8.3	9.3	2.8	31.9
1983	31.4	7.0	9.7	10.5	1.9	35.3
1984	32.6	7.9	10.4	11.3	1.1	38.8
1985	35.1	9.3	11.2	12.2	—	43.0
1986	38.0	9.2	11.9	13.4	—	47.5
1987	40.4	11.2	13.0	14.7	—	51.3

Sources: 1988 and 1985 *Blue Books.*

the Conservatives but that is not the only influence. The share of income tax in personal income fell from 15 per cent in 1975 to 12 per cent in 1979. A deliberate attempt was being made to bargain income tax cuts in exchange for wage moderation (see Part 1 above). As between 1979 and 1987 the share of tax in personal income was little changed.

Since income tax changes were one ingredient of almost every budget over the period of this study it is particularly interesting to see how the path of tax revenue relates to the condition of the economy year by year. Does that give any clue as to the way in which discretionary changes in fiscal policy were in fact being used?

The falls in real revenue in 1977 and in 1979 are procyclical in the sense that they added to demand at a time when economic activity was already recovering. Similarly the rise in real revenue in 1980 and 1981 would tend to reinforce the recession and the fall in real revenue in 1982 and 1984 to reinforce the recovery. It is hard to believe that income tax was being used as a means of stabilising output growth at any time during this period at all.

There was some tendency for tax revenue to rise faster than incomes when inflation accelerated. This was particularly marked in 1974 and 1975, but on a smaller scale the same thing happened in 1980 and 1981. It is relatively easy to use income tax in this way so long as the value of tax allowances is set each year in nominal terms. After 1977 the Rooker-Wise amendment required that tax allowances should rise in line with inflation in the absence of legislation, and fiscal drag could no longer operate as a

Table 14.4 *Taxation at 1985 prices*   *£ billion*

	Taxes on income		National insurance contributions			Central government's other taxes on expenditure
	Persons	Companies	Employees	Employers	NIS	
1974	32.8	8.2	6.7	9.3	—	27.6
1975	38.7	5.1	7.0	11.0	—	27.1
1976	38.7	4.3	7.2	11.8	—	27.4
1977	34.8	5.9	7.1	11.5	2.0	27.9
1978	34.3	6.5	6.9	11.3	3.2	28.4
1979	33.0	6.4	7.2	11.3	4.9	32.8
1980	34.1	7.3	7.6	11.5	4.9	34.7
1981	34.8	7.1	8.5	11.1	4.7	36.0
1982	34.6	7.5	9.6	10.8	3.2	37.0
1983	34.7	7.7	10.7	11.6	2.1	39.0
1984	34.3	8.3	10.9	11.9	1.2	40.8
1985	35.1	9.3	11.2	12.2	—	43.0
1986	36.4	8.8	11.4	12.8	—	45.5
1987	37.3	10.3	12.0	13.6	—	47.3

Sources: 1988 and 1985 *Blue Books.*

concealed form of tax increase. Even so, a tendency for average income tax rates to move up and down with inflation persisted.

The figures for company taxation include petroleum revenue tax and corporation tax paid by oil companies operating in the North Sea (but not royalties). That accounts for their higher level in real terms in the 1980s. That apart, the revenue from corporate taxation follows non-oil company profits with a year's lag. (The timing of revenue receipts in the mid-1980s is distorted by the impact effect of tax reforms in the 1984 budget.)

The macroeconomic effects of company taxation are little understood and, perhaps for that reason, it has seldom been used to stimulate demand or to curb inflation. The one occasion within this period when company tax clearly was used as an instrument of macroeconomic policy was 1974, when it was cut in an attempt to avert a deeper recession and widespread corporate bankruptcy.

The third and fourth columns of table 14.3 show national insurance contributions paid by employees and employers. (Strictly speaking these are not taxes at all, but their economic impact is believed to be very similar to that of direct and indirect taxes respectively.) If the rates of contribution are left unchanged, and the floor and ceiling levels are indexed to wages, then both kinds of contribution will rise in proportion to the national wage and salary bill. In fact the share of contributions rose from 10½ per cent in 1974 to about 12½ per cent in 1976, then levelled off and even fell slightly. There was another steep rise from under 12 per cent in 1980 to over 14 per cent in 1983, followed by stability for the remainder of the period.

The increases were considerably steeper for employees than for employers, especially in the 1980s. But, this should be set alongside the fifth column in table 14.3 which shows the national insurance surcharge, an explicit payroll tax. If this is included with employers' national insurance contributions, then the rise from 1974–80 is about 75 per cent in real terms. The fall between 1980 and 1987 is 17 per cent in real terms – a significant cut in the tax on jobs.

One reason for raising national insurance contributions was the continuing belief that they should finance national insurance benefits, despite an open-ended exchequer contribution. As we have seen, benefits rose strongly for most of the period of this study because of the age structure of the population, because of rising unemployment and because take-up improved. Grants from central government covered some 14 per cent of spending by the social security funds in 1977. The share rose to a peak of 16 per cent in 1979 and then fell even in the recession years of 1980 and 1981. By 1987 that share was down to just 7 per cent thanks to the buoyancy of contributions, in line with earnings. Economic arguments probably played a relatively small part in deciding the level of national insurance contributions, or in the rise and fall of the surcharge. It was, admittedly, a commonly held view in the 1980s that payroll taxation, explicit or implicit, was quite inappropriate at a time of high unemployment. All the main macroeconomic models at the time showed a reduction in employers' contributions as an effective way of shifting the NAIRU. That may well have been one reason why the surcharge was abolished and why employees' contributions rose disproportionately. Another commonly held view was that employers' contributions added to cost inflation. That did not stop the Labour government from raising them, or imposing the surcharge, in the latter half of the 1970s, although in the process they must have made the incomes policies of the period more difficult to sustain.

Consideration of their impact on prices clearly *did* influence the use of other expenditure taxes in the incomes policy era. From 1974–8 revenue hardly rose in real terms, even though the volume of consumer spending was up by nearly 5 per cent. The very different attitude of the new government is shown by the figures for subsequent years, shown in the final column of table 14.3. The share of expenditure taxes (thus defined) rose from 13½ per cent in 1978 to nearly 17 per cent in 1982, and contined to rise slowly thereafter.

As with income tax, part of the explanation may be purely administrative or presentational. It is rather inconvenient, and risks unpopularity, to raise the rates of specific duties on drink and tobacco every year in line with inflation, especially when inflation is high. By the 1980s it was taken for granted that this had to be done, and in any case inflation was much lower. Another explanation would be political. Expenditure taxes fall disproportionately on the less well-off, so to raise them could be egalitarian. That argument would weigh more with a Labour than with a Conservative government.

We have now described most of the main categories of spending and taxation which might be thought to play a major part in the use of fiscal policy for macroeconomic ends. The major items of the general government accounts left out are local authority rent and rates, trading surpluses, debt interest payments and receipts, grants paid abroad, and taxes on capital.

There are two kinds of questions about fiscal policy which deserve further consideration. The first concerns its motivation. This is best described by looking at the measures announced year-by-year in the budget alongside the economic forecasts made at the time. The other kind of question concerns the effects which fiscal policy changes had on the economy. To answer that kind of question we need a model of the way the economy works. Estimates using the National Institute's model will be presented below.

BUDGET JUDGEMENTS

Each year at budget time, usually in March, the Chancellor of the Exchequer makes his budget judgement. He then proposes a set of budget measures and the Treasury publishes a Financial Statement and Budget Report (FSBR). This section, and the next, are based very largely on analysis of fourteen such documents issued in the years 1974–87 inclusive. (A supplementary FSBR was published in November 1974. There were also packages of fiscal measures in several years of the 1970s announced at times other than the budget, with more or less documentation. After 1976 an Autumn Statement was published each year. For present purposes, however, it will suffice to concentrate attention on one budget per annum.) The framework of the budget judgement at the beginning of our period was demand management in the Keynesian tradition. The Treasury prepared a report on the state of the economy, together with a forecast of the growth of real expenditure and output. The judgement to be made was how much to add to real expenditure or to subtract from it. The effect on the financing of the public sector itself was a secondary matter, although not one which was ever ignored altogether.

Even by the late 1970s the emphasis had shifted. The Treasury was less confident of its ability to manage demand, more concerned about the financial and monetary implications of public sector borrowing. After 1980 the centrepiece of the FSBR became the medium-term financial strategy (MTFS) which will be the subject of the next section. This confirmed the shift of emphasis to public sector borrowing and for some years talk of demand management seemed very old-fashioned or heretical. In the mid-1980s, however, the role of monetary targets was reduced and the scale of the PSBR no longer caused anxiety. The focus of attention shifted

Table 14.5 *Official economic forecasts and outturns 1975–87*

	Growth rate of GDP to first half of following year		Increase in retail price index to 4th quarter of current year	
	Forecast	Outturn	Forecast	Outturn
1975	1.5	1.5	n.a.	25.3
1976	4.0	2.9	n.a.	15.0
1977	1.0	2.6	13.0	13.0
1978	3.0	3.0	7.0	8.1
1979	−1.0	−0.3	16.0[a]	16.0[a]
1980	−1.5	−3.1	16.5	15.3
1981	1.0	2.0	10.0	11.9
1982	2.0	3.2	9.0	6.2
1983	2.5	2.2	6.0	5.0
1984	2.5	3.8	4.5	4.8
1985	2.5	2.9	5.0	5.5
1986	2.5	3.6	3.5	3.4
1987	2.5	4.3	4.0	4.1

Sources: Forecasts from FSBR tables. Outturns from 1988 *Blue Book* and *Economic Trends.*
[a] From third quarter of 1978 to third quarter of 1979.

back to expenditure and output, but to expenditure and output at current prices, not in real terms. One could talk again without inhibition about the need for government to manage demand, although the roles of monetary and fiscal policy in that management remained controversial.

The apparatus of short-term economic forecasting at the Treasury survived through these vicissitudes. Indeed the coverage of the published forecasts increased considerably after the passing of the Bray amendment to the 1976 Industry Act. Thereafter forecasts were published for inflation and the balance of payments as well as for real output growth (but not for employment or unemployment). The Conservative Chancellors continued to publish these forecasts, even though they complained about having to do so, and even though the forecasts seemed at times almost completely irrelevant to the way in which the budget judgement was presented. The forecasts are prepared by the Treasury economists, but published on the authority of the Chancellor. This implies that the Chancellor can have the last word in deciding what the forecasts should be.

Forecasts of growth and of inflation are shown in table 14.5, together with the latest estimates of the corresponding outturn. As the table suggests, the record of offical forecasts over this period was generally good. Up to 1978 the growth rate was on average correctly predicted, with the year-to-year errors within the margin of measurement accuracy. The 1980 recession was deeper than forecast and the recovery was faster. From 1983–7 the official forecasts always showed 2½ per cent growth, whilst the outturns were consistently higher after 1983. The official forecasters could take comfort from knowing that others, for example the National Institute, were underpredicting by a wider margin.

The official predictions of inflation were also reasonably accurate (bearing in mind that the twelve-month periods covered by the figures shown in table 14.5 were partly elapsed when the forecasts were made). The most significant error was in 1982 when the abruptness of the slowing down in inflation was not foreseen.

The inherent unpredictability of the economy is one of the reasons why demand management never has been, and never could be, precise. Judging by the figures in table 14.5 the growth rate of the economy would in fact have varied from year to year by about a percentage point or so even if the Treasury had been able and willing to take fiscal action on the scale required to produce exactly the same post-budget forecast of growth every year. The post-budget forecast of growth was *indeed* identical for five years from 1983–7, yet the actual growth rate had a standard deviation of ¾ per cent. But the *main* reason, of course, why the growth rate was not constant over the period as a whole was that the Treasury was not trying to make it so.

Table 14.6 shows the budget measures as costed in the FSBR each year from 1974–87. This is as close as we can get to measuring the policy acts contained in the budget proposals. Unfortunately the definition cannot be identical for the period as a whole, since the method of presentation in the FSBR changed several times. Up to 1981 figures were given for public sector borrowing before and after budget changes in the financial year just beginning. Thereafter we have to use instead the figures provided for the direct effects of the budget on 'public sector transactions'. Some change of definition is implied. making the figures before and after 1982 not entirely consistent. More seriously, the choice of measures on the expenditure side to include in 'the budget measures' varied from year to year and was made in part for presentational reasons. In most years the main measures were on the tax side, and unambiguously in the budget, but the problem is not a trivial one. With that warning we can examine the first column of table 14.6 to see whether there may have been some consistent principles guiding budget judgements over the period as a whole.

It is clear at a glance that budgetary policy was not designed to stabilise the growth of real output. The five contractionary budgets, in 1974 and 1975 and in 1979–81, fell in the recession years. The most expansionary budget (at current prices) was in 1987, the year when output growth was most rapid. It would be easier to believe that budgetary policy was aimed mainly at moderating the rate of inflation. A technical point must be made in this context. The figures used in table 14.6 for the cost or yield of budget measures are calculated from a non-indexed base. In other words it is assumed that tax allowances would have stayed the same in nominal terms without the budget measures. There are alternative estimates (available for later years only) which estimate budget effects relative to an indexed base,

Table 14.6 *Budget measures 1974–87* £ bn at current prices

| | Total cost/yield of budget measures[a] | Public sector borrowing requirement | | |
		Outturn for previous financial year	Forecast for current year before budget changes[b]	Forecast for current year after budget change
1974	−0.72	4.28	3.45	2.73
1975	−1.20	7.60	10.26	9.06
1976	0.67	10.77	11.29	11.96
1977	1.06	8.82	7.41	8.47
1978	1.96	5.71	6.58	8.54
1979	−2.98	9.23	11.29	8.31
1980	−0.81	9.12	9.35	8.54
1981	−3.29	13.46	13.86	10.57
1982	2.34	10.6	7.2	9.5
1983	1.94	7.5	6.3	8.2
1984	0.30	10.0	6.9	7.2
1985	1.02	10.5	6.1	7.1
1986	1.55	6.8	5.5	7.1
1987	2.90	4.1	1.0	3.9

Sources: FSBR for each year, various tables.
[a] 1974–9 calculated from columns 3 and 4. 1980 and 1981 direct effects of the budget on PSBR as stated in FSBR. 1982 to 1987 direct effects of the budget on public sector transactions (change from non-indexed base in current financial year).
[b] 1974–9 forecasts 'before budget changes' taken from FSBR tables 1980–87 calculated from columns 1 and 4.

that is one in which tax allowances rise in line with inflation. These alternative estimates show all budgets as less expansionary, but especially the budgets in years of high inflation. Even if this adjustment is *not* made the table suggests that contractionary budgets are correlated with high inflation.

One of the striking features of table 14.6 is the near constancy of the post-budget forecasts of the PSBR shown in the final column. The figures stood at £8½ billion for four successive years in the late 1970s and then at £7 billion for three successive years in the mid-1980s. This does not seem to have been accidental. The outcome often differed substantially from the forecast, but then measures were taken in the next budget to bring it back on track. The process could work in both directions, as can be seen by comparing 1977 and 1978 with 1979 and 1980.

The level of the PSBR forecast does rise a little in the recession years, and it falls in the boom year of 1987. To that extent the built-in stabilisers of the fiscal system were not altogether overridden by budget measures. As we have seen the main countercyclical influences came from the cost of social security payments. The budget measures themselves were procyclical but not sufficiently so to remove any effect of the cycle on public sector borrowing.

The generally downward trend of the PSBR, more pronounced in real than in nominal terms, can be accounted for in a variety of ways. The growth of revenue from North Sea oil taxation meant that a given PSBR had a less contractionary effect on domestic demand. Since it was by its nature a temporary addition to revenue, a case could be made out that the government should save it rather than spend it as it accrued.

As the rate of inflation was lower by the mid-1980s the cost of debt interest payments was falling. In other words an inflation tax took the place of higher revenue in the 1970s. In fact the official balance sheet statistics show the real net worth of the public sector *rising* in the 1970s because the real value of the outstanding national debt was being eroded by inflation. In the early to mid-1980s, although the scale of borrowing was reduced, the real net worth of the public sector fell.

In tables 14.5 and 14.6 we have only thirteen annual observations, not many on which to base a statistical analysis of fiscal policy. But the results of multiple regression are not always obvious to the naked eye, even with such a short time-series as this one. We shall therefore present the results of a very simple and primitive form of reaction function.

The variable to be explained (F) is the real fiscal adjustment, that is the total cost or yield of budget measures, as in the first column of table 14.6, deflated to 1985 prices. The variables to which policy may respond are the level of unemployment (U) and the growth rate of £M3 ($DM3$), both in relation to a trend (t) to be estimated. Also in the regression equation is the pre-budget forecast for public sector borrowing at 1985 prices (B). (It proved difficult to find a consistent relationship with inflation over this period.) The estimated equation is:

$$F = 10.9 + 0.0023U - 0.31DM3 - 0.36B - 0.81t$$
$$\quad\quad (0.0021) \quad (0.11) \quad\quad (0.13) \quad (0.48)$$

$$R^2 = 0.70 \quad\quad DW = 1.7$$

Other things being equal, an increase in unemployment of one million is estimated to call forth a fiscal expansion of £2.3 billion at 1985 prices, although the standard error on the coefficient means we cannot reject the hypothesis that there would be no response at all. If the growth of the money supply were 10 percentage points a year higher, the fiscal response would be more contractionary by £3.1 billion. If the *pre*-budget forecast of the PSBR is increased by £1 billion, other things being equal, the fiscal adjustment will offset £0.36 billion of that increase.

As with the more complicated relationships for monetary policy described in Chapter 13 above, it must be emphasised that this equation describes average behaviour over the period as a whole, giving the same weight to each annual observation. Thus the general finding of some positive association between high unemployment and fiscal expansion does not alter the fact that in 1981 for example the Chancellor clearly gave little weight to unemployment, then rising sharply, when deciding on a contractionary budget. That particular event aroused a lot of controversy and may, for that reason, play a disproportionate part in memories of the period.

PLANS, PROMISES AND PRECOMMITMENT

Some of the most fascinating developments in the theory of macroeconomic policy since the 1970s have been concerned with the benefits of precommitment. By saying in advance what it is going to do, and promising to stick to that decision, a government may be able to achieve a better outcome for the economy than it would by keeping its options open. The medium-term financial strategy, adopted in Britain in 1980, was, amongst other things, an attempt to exploit this theoretical possibility.

It is not unusual for governments to provide some indication of their policy intentions, or of their priorities as between different objectives. This is the stuff of which budget statements have always been made. It is a useful sharing of information, helping all those concerned to make rather better economic forecasts. Typically, however, such statements are not regarded as firm commitments. In economic policy, as in most other kinds of policymaking, governments are expected to change their minds. A precommitment is much more than a sharing of information. If it is believed, it will influence the behaviour of the economy more profoundly than would a mere statement of current policy plans.

To take a not unrealistic example, suppose that the government is concerned both to reduce inflation and to maintain full employment. If it is concerned only about the current situation it may well compromise between these aims and allow a moderate rate of inflation to go uncorrected. But the rate of inflation today depends on what rate of inflation is expected tomorrow. If it is thought that the government in the future will take a tough stand against inflation, letting future levels of unemployment rise, then inflation will begin to fall straight away – at no immediate cost in terms of current unemployment at all. But this expectation of a tough stand in the future will only be created if the government enters into a binding commitment. The statement that its current intention is to be tough in the future is not enough, because when the time comes to be tough it may well seem better to delay the measures again. Only by making a binding promise can the problem of time inconsistency be overcome. (For a further discussion see Chapter 7 above.)

The disadvantage of precommitment is that it may be based on false or incomplete information. Thus a promise to bring down inflation by specified fiscal or monetary measures may turn out to be based on a misunderstanding of the way the economy works. The purpose of precommitment is to get round the problem of time inconsistency, but worse difficulties could arise if the promise is framed in the wrong way. The ideal solution would be to make a conditional precommitment, which specified exactly how the government would fulfil its promise in all conceivable states of the world, or of knowledge. Unfortunately such conditional precommitments are not easy to draw up.

The idea of a medium-term strategy using fiscal and monetary policy to reduce inflation did not begin with the MTFS of 1980. On 6 April, 1976 Denis Healey said: 'This budget must also grapple with the problem of the medium term. It must lay the foundation for a strategy which will enable Britain to enter the 1980s with full employment, stable prices and an economy in balance both at home and abroad' (*Hansard* Col. 238).

Later that year, having secured a loan from the IMF, he announced economic measures which were part of 'a medium-term programme for national recovery'. The difference was that on this occasion he entered into a binding precommitment to the IMF in respect of public sector borrowing and the growth of domestic credit expansion. That commitment was very precise: DCE would be kept to £9 billion in the twelve months ending 20 April, 1977, to £7.7 billion in the following year and so on; similarly precise statements were made about the PSBR. The government was reluctant to enter into such commitments and found them humiliating, but the IMF team said that without such promises there would be no loan. The agreement with the IMF was a firmer precommitment than the British government could make in any other form, and it was believed. The result was a dramatic recovery of confidence in the foreign exchange market. The numbers in the Letter of Intent had been chosen so that the promise would be easy to fulfil; in the event it was over-fulfilled. This episode is probably the best example in the period covered by this study of the effect of a policy precommitment on the behaviour of the economy.

The medium-term financial strategy of 1980 was like a Letter of Intent written by government of its own free will. There was no need to seek funds from foreign agencies as sterling was strong and the balance of payments in surplus. But public sector borrowing was felt to be excessive, causing difficulties in the market for public sector debt. The inflation rate was high and the money supply was growing fast. The MTFS was designed as a stabilisation policy, a gradual path back towards price stability and sound finance. The wording of Part II of the FSBR 1980–81 was designed to carry conviction, without creating too many hostages to fortune.

The most firm commitment was to control of the money supply. 'To reduce inflation [the goverment] will progressively reduce the growth of the money supply', (para 2), 'The government has announced its firm commitment to a progressive reduction in money supply growth' (para 3). This was explicitly described as a means of influencing expectations about inflation. A distinction was drawn between 'projections' for public sector finance on the one hand and the 'money supply policy' on the other. The projections were conditional on events at home and abroad; the money supply policy was not. The only hesitation was over the actual numbers for the money supply. The reduction in the growth of £M3 was to be 'broadly along the lines of' the path so prominently shown in a table, and a footnote said that the definition of the money supply might have to be changed. In the light of events, such hesitation was well justified. Thus the commitment, firm as it sounded, was not quite watertight. And in the event it was not kept, either in the letter or in the spirit. The course of subsequent events is desribed in Part 1 above.

The form of precommitment turned out to be unfortunate in several respects. It was excessively firm in relation to particular policy measures, that is, to control of the money supply. An element of conditionality was introduced, by the cautious footnote, but it was not drafted in such a way as to keep the element of commitment intact when new information, about the role of £M3 in the economy, became available, No explicit commitment was made to a path for inflation, the ultimate purpose of the strategy. Since inflation did in fact fall, it seems with hindsight (and as some argued at the time) that a firm commitment to an inflation target might have been a better mast to which the government's flag might have been nailed.

The purpose of precommitment is to influence expectations. To test its effectiveness we could look at the forecasts made at the time. The figures in table 14.7 are taken from the February issues of the *National Institute Economic Review* each year from 1974–88. They show the latest recorded outturns and the forecasts for inflation as measured by the consumer price index.

In the late 1970s, forecasters usually expected that the rate of inflation would slow down. This was, of course, partly because they perceived it doing so in the recent past, but also because they believed that incomes policy would be increasingly effective. The actual rate of inflation was faster than they expected every year from 1974–8. In the 1980s, however, inflation was almost always *lower* than expected. For three years in a row, from 1983–5, inflation was expected to accelerate whilst in fact it slowed down. There is no suggestion then that the commitment to fight inflation using tough fiscal and monetary policies expressed in successive versions of the MTFS affected expectations as intended. The Treasury itself overforecast inflation in 1982 and 1983.

Neither is there evidence that the element of precommitment in the MTFS improved sentiment in the foreign exchange market. The Letter of Intent of December 1976 had an immediate effect on confidence in sterling. When the first MTFS was drawn up, however, confidence in sterling was already strong and the effective exchange rate index had already risen by 18 per cent over the preceding two years. The rate rose for a few more quarters but peaked early in 1981. From that point the trend was generally downwards.

In economic policy, as in any other branch of politics, it is difficult for

Table 14.7 *Inflation forecasts from the National Institute Economic Review*[a]

Percentage rate of inflation

	Preceding year estimated outturn	Current year forecast
1974	10.1	13.8
1975	16.6	18.9
1976	24.1	10.3
1977	13.7	12.2
1978	12.9	8.0
1979	7.7	9.9
1980	15.4	15.4
1981	12.9	9.6
1982	10.9	9.6
1983	6.5	7.9
1984	5.2	6.5
1985	4.6	6.6
1986	4.8	4.2
1987	3.9	4.7
1988	3.3	5.0

[a] Change in the consumer price index between fourth quarters as estimated and forecast in the February issues of the *National Institute Economic Review*.

governments to precommit themselves effectively even if they sincerely wish to do so. The MTFS was an interesting example of the contortions involved in trying to tie one's own hands behind one's back. As the 1980s advanced there was increasing interest in the alternative of an external commitment, more particularly a commitment to full membership of the EMS. That would indeed have restricted the freedom of manoeuvre of macroeconomic policy in Britain – an argument in its favour as well as an argument against.

THE PUBLIC SECTOR BALANCE SHEET

The borrowing of an individual household or firm is necessarily judged in relation to its balance sheet position. The prudent scale of borrowing in any one period obviously depends on the debt already outstanding; and (just as obviously) depends on the assets held, their value and their liquidity. The underlying concern which could in some circumstances limit the prudent scale of public sector borrowing is similar in kind. It is also sometimes argued that the intertemporal balance sheet constraint, which prevents governments from borrowing for *ever*, determines the way markets or individuals respond to tax changes. It is therefore remarkable that the annual budget statement and Public Expenditure White Papers make little or no reference to either public sector assets or liabilities, and that estimates of the balance sheet position of the public sector were, until 1987, only very infrequently made.

Valuing public sector assets is often difficult, if not arbitrary. Many of the problems are similar in kind to those that beset anyone drawing up a balance sheet for an individual or a firm. Moreover, there are very important influences on the future income or expenditure of the state which cannot be capitalised. Thus the balance sheet position is not a complete guide to the financial strength or weakness of the public sector. The same is, of course, true of the balance sheet of a firm or a household, whose credit will always depend in large part on subjective assessments of future earnings. With all these necessary caveats it is nevertheless interesting to know how the balance sheet position of the public sector changed over the period of this study.

The figures in table 14.8 are taken from the *National Income Blue Book* for 1988, with the subsectors within the public sector consolidated. The total net wealth of the sector is deflated to 1985 prices using the index of home costs per unit of output.

The valuation of tangible assets is beset with difficulties. The CSO figures for plant and machinery for example, are compiled from investment data assuming a fixed life for all real assets. The value of the public sector's capital stock is based on current replacement cost. Thus the value of the industries in public ownership is based on the volume of their physical assets, not on the present value of their future trading surpluses, or on the prices for which the industries could be sold if they were privatised.

The valuation of tangible assets is inherently difficult because for most of them there is no market in which a price might be set. However keen a government might be on privatisation it is unlikely that it could sell the existing road system. Another limitation of the estimates in this respect is that maintenance expenditure is not capitalised, so a failure to keep the roads in adequate repair does not damage the public sector balance sheet. The local authorities' housing stock accounts for a high proportion of the public sector's tangible assets and is valued on the basis of its market price with sitting tenants.

The net financial liabilities of the public sector are valued at market prices. The largest component is central government fixed interest securities, many long-dated. When current period interest rates rise in the market the value of these gilt-edge securities falls, reducing the indebtedness of the public sector. (No such adjustment is made to the value of public sector assets.) That phenomenon accounts for a great deal of the short-term variation in the net wealth of the sector. Very few of the liabilities of the public sector have a value indexed to the rate of inflation. A rise in the general price level strengthens the public sector's balance sheet position because the value of its tangible assets is assumed to rise in line with replacement costs whilst its net financial liabilities are unchanged.

Table 14.8 *The public sector consolidated balance sheet*   *£ billion at end-year*

	Tangible assets	Net financial assets	Net wealth	GDP deflator	Net wealth at 1985 prices
1975[a]	123.9	−45.9	78.0	37.5	208.0
1976	142.0	−53.7	88.3	43.0	205.3
1977	160.6	−66.4	94.2	48.2	195.4
1978	186.6	−67.1	119.5	54.0	221.3
1979	228.3	−70.0	158.3	61.0	259.5
1980	271.6	−81.0	190.6	72.3	263.6
1981	286.3	−83.0	203.3	79.7	255.1
1982	298.8	−106.3	192.5	85.2	225.9
1983	318.8	−116.2	202.6	90.0	225.1
1984	320.2	−115.6	204.6	95.1	215.1
1985	342.4	−124.9	217.5	100	217.5
1986	346.4	−125.0	221.4	102.6	215.8
1987	380.7	−133.8	246.9	107.7	229.2

Source: CSO *Blue Book*, 1988.
[a] Calculated using growth rate from figures given in Bryant, C., 'National and Sector Balance Sheets', *Economic Trends*, May 1987

This effect of inflation on public sector finance explains the general direction of the figures in table 14.8. During the latter part of the 1970s the net wealth of the public sector was rising in real terms despite the widespread anxiety at the time about the scale of public sector borrowing. In contrast, in the first half of the 1980s the real net wealth of the sector was falling, despite the widespread belief that fiscal policy was exceptionally restrictive.

The Conservative government was criticised by Lord Stockton in a memorable phrase for 'selling the family silver' so as to be able to cut personal taxation. The balance sheet figures show the extent to which this was a valid claim. They take account of the privatisation of public utilities, the sale of council houses and the sharp reduction in fixed investment in the public sector. The resulting fall in real net wealth is hardly a dramatic one; the credit of the government was in no way impaired, but clearly it was a trend which could not continue indefinitely. Some indeed might argue that the years when North Sea oil revenue was at a peak should have seen a net rebuilding of taxpayers' capital rather than a rundown. In the event the public sector moved into substantial financial surplus at the end of the 1980s and the talk was soon of how quickly the national debt could be repaid. At no time did the balance sheet position of the public sector place an immediate constraint on the ability of the government to borrow. Given the uncertainties of measurement there must indeed be some doubt whether the budget position was stronger or weaker in 1987 compared with 1974. This contrasts with the situation in some other major countries,

Italy for example and perhaps the United States, where concern about the fiscal prudence of government really was justified.

Discussion of fiscal policy usually makes much of the surplus or deficit on the public accounts, variously defined. There are three quite different reasons for being interested in this balance: first, because of concern about the financial prudence of fiscal policy; second, because of concern about the monetary effects of government borrowing; third to assess the direct effects of public spending and taxation on aggregate demand. In each case, however, the deficit is a very imperfect summary of the information needed to address the questions likely to be raised.

The financial prudence of public spending and taxation can only be judged by reference to balance sheet totals, as discussed above. The monetary consequences of government borrowing depend entirely on the method of finance adopted, an issue to be discussed below. In this section we are concerned with fiscal policy as one arm of demand management. As has been suggested already, the deficit is an inadequate and confusing measure to use for this purpose as well.

Traditionally three shortcomings of the deficit are cited if it is to be used as an index of fiscal stance or impact. The deficit needs to be cyclically adjusted to remove the effect on it of variation in the level of economic activity, since higher output produces higher revenues and saves spending on social security benefits. The deficit also needs to be weighted because some kinds of taxation and spending have more effect on aggregate demand than others. Adjustments of these two kinds can quite readily be made, and some estimates are presented in table 14.9.

The third of the traditional adjustments to the PSBR takes account of inflation, treating the consequent fall in the real value of public sector debt as if it were a form of taxation. Disagreements as to the way this adjustment should be made or indeed whether it should be made at all, illustrate well the conceptual limitations of any single-valued indicator of fiscal stance. They also explain the decision not to make any inflation adjustment at all in the estimates prepared for this study.

Clearly the real value of public sector debt is central to the discussion of fiscal prudence as has been shown above. Its relevance to aggregate demand is less clear. There probably are wealth effects on private spending as well as income effects – indeed the distinction between the two may be little more than a matter of semantics if the private sector is free to borrow and lend on any scale it wishes. There is every reason to suppose therefore that inflation has an effect on aggregate demand. It is a different matter, however, whether that effect should be deducted from the impact attributed to fiscal policy.

Table 14.9 *The public sector deficit, with adjustments*

percentage of GDP

	Financial deficit unadjusted	Cyclically adjusted[a]	Weighted and cyclically adjusted[a]
1974	2.4	0.3	0.8
1975	4.0	0.6	1.3
1976	3.5	0.9	1.0
1977	1.0	−2.0	−1.0
1978	1.7	−0.8	−0.7
1979	1.1	−1.3	−1.0
1980	1.2	−2.8	−1.0
1981	−0.1	−5.4	−1.9
1982	−0.5	−6.2	−1.9
1983	0.2	−4.7	−1.4
1984	0.8	−4.2	−1.4
1985	−0.5	−4.7	−2.1
1986	−1.1	−5.0	−2.4
1987	−2.0	−5.1	−3.0

[a] Normalised so that 1973 first quarter is zero and based on trend growth in real GDP of 2 per cent a year.

The case for making an inflation adjustment in the present context is strengthened by the argument that the rise in debt interest payments which occurred in the 1970s was the consequence of higher inflation, not of expansionary fiscal policy. However, the rise in interest rates was in fact insufficient to compensate for inflation, so a full inflation adjustment would leave fiscal policy looking distinctly contractionary, and that too could be thought misleading. All one can say is that these points need to be borne in mind in interpreting the figures shown in this section. There is no such thing as a correct measure of fiscal stance.

The financial deficit of the public sector is consistent with the national accounts, where it is described as the net acquisition of financial assets (with sign reversed). It differs from the public sector borrowing requirement in that it takes no account of net lending by the public sector or of receipts from privatisation. The deficit was exceptionally large in the mid-1970s, but was cut back quite sharply in 1977, following the sterling crisis of the previous year. It was further reduced in the early 1980s by the proceeds of North Sea oil taxation, by sales of council houses and by the deliberately tight budget of 1981. As the economy recovered from the recession, increasing tax revenue, and as public spending was brought under tight control, the account moved towards surplus (interrupted in 1984 by the effects of the miners' strike).

The cyclical adjustment provides an estimate of the size of the deficit consistent with steady growth of GDP at 2 per cent a year, similar to the average growth which actually occurred. The built-in fiscal stabilisers are mimicked by adding to revenue and reducing social security payments in proportion to the excess of trend GDP over actual. The assumed elasticities of tax yield with respect to GDP are as follows: personal income tax, 1.64; non-oil company tax, 1.00; national insurance contributions, 0.85; indirect taxes and subsidies, 0.67; gross trading surpluses, 1.00. Each 1 per cent added to output is assumed to reduce unemployment by 110,000, saving £145 million a year at 1980/81 prices from spending on current grants.

The level of the adjusted series is essentially arbitrary and the first quarter of 1973 has been set equal to zero purely to maintain consistency with earlier estimates. It is *not* intended to suggest that the pressure of demand could (or should) have been sustained at that level for the next fourteen years. The trend of the series is also arbitrary, being determined by the 2 per cent growth of GDP. The interest of the calculation lies in the year-to-year movements of the series which are relatively insensitive to the way the cyclical adjustment is made.

The general shape of the second column in table 14.9 is similar to the first, implying that the major changes in the deficit were not the result of the output cycle. As one would expect, the most significant corrections are to the recession years 1974–5 and 1980–81. In the latter period, fiscal policy is now interpreted as significantly contractionary, an interpretation with which few would quarrel.

The weighting system used for the third column is intended to take account of the mix of taxes and of spending. Direct public spending on goods and services is given a large weight as it adds directly to total output; personal sector taxes and transfers are given a rather smaller weight on the grounds that their effect is blunted by offsetting changes to personal savings; other items are given little or no weight. As a result the figures in the third column differ from those in the second, particularly in years when there were large changes in such items as taxes on oil production, sales of council houses or payments to the EEC. The weighting system used was as follows: real current spending on goods and services, 1.20; relative price of public consumption, 0.59; capital spending (excluding net sales), 1.00; current grants to the personal sector, 0.65; income tax and NI contributions, 0.59; non-oil company taxes, 0.39; indirect taxes and subsidies, 0.51; gross trading surpluses, 0.33; net property income and rent, 0.20; net capital transfers, 0.20; taxes on oil companies, 0.20. Rough adjustments have also been made to the later years to offset the effects of privatisation (on the grounds that it has little immediate implication for the profits or the investment of the industries concerned) and of the miners' strike in 1984.

The third column brings out the fact that many of the tax increases and expenditure savings in the latter part of the period had a relatively small effect on demand. By contrast the measures taken in 1976 and 1977 were relatively 'demand rich'.

This third column tells a relatively simple story. Fiscal policy measured in this fashion was exceptionally expansionary (that is, the adjusted deficit was larger) in 1974, having been made progressively more expansionary since reflation began in 1970. Therefore policy became tighter. Three episodes of tightening stand out in particular.

The first was between 1976 and 1977 when both tax increases and spending cuts were used to reduce government borrowing and the growth of aggregate demand. The measures were made more severe than they otherwise would have been by the sterling crisis of 1976 and the subsequent negotiations with the IMF. According to this measure, there was no major relaxation of fiscal policy in the late 1970s even though the IMF no longer influenced policy and a general election was approaching.

The second tightening of policy came in 1981 despite the recession and the rise in unemployment. Like its predecessor in 1976, it was presented as a means of regaining monetary control, as well as making room for an expansion of the private sector. On this occasion there seems to have been something of a bounce back in 1982. The third and final tightening was in 1985–7 and it was to some extent involuntary. Receipts from taxes on income rose faster than expected, but since the economy was expanding rapidly there was only limited scope for tax-cutting budgets.

It is important to recognise the limitations of any of these series, even column 3, as a guide to the interpretation of fiscal policy. They do *not* identify policy acts, that is deliberate choices by government as distinct from the passive response of the system to events. That can only be done by the close study of budget statements, public expenditure White Papers, and the like. The references sometimes found to the cyclically-adjusted deficit as discretionary are misleading: its movements from year to year still reflect what might be called passive responses, such as the consequence of higher interest rates for debt interest, the consequences of oil prices for oil taxation and so on.

Neither do these adjustments enable fiscal policy to be judged against an appealing counterfactual. Implicitly the comparison is with an alternative case in which the weighted or cyclically-adjusted deficit was held constant. To do that exactly would in practice be very difficult, and not obviously desirable. It corresponds *very* approximately to keeping tax and benefit rates constant over the cycle, whilst keeping both revenues and spending constant as a proportion of gross domestic product in the long term. If the aim is to approximate to a counterfactual of this kind then there is much to be said for approaching the problem directly, and making use of a macroeconomic model.

A COUNTERFACTUAL SIMULATION OF FISCAL POLICY

The effects of tax changes on the economy are not instantaneous. Initially consumers, for example, change their spending less than in proportion to a change in their disposable incomes; the second round effects on investment involve a further delay. One advantage of a macroeconomic model is that it takes account of such lagged adjustments, which are ignored in calculations like those in the preceding section.

The results of any counterfactual simulation must reflect the properties of the model used. In the case of fiscal policy simulations it is useful to draw a distinction between estimates of direct effects and indirect effects. The direct effects include the addition to GDP of public spending on goods and services, and the demand effects (with multipliers and accelerators) of changes in personal and company sector taxes. These will be estimated in roughly the same way by most macroeconomic models.

The indirect effects include the consequences for wages, for interest rates and for the exchange rate, together with the implications of these consequences for output, inflation and everything else. These effects vary greatly across models, in some cases reinforcing the direct effects on output, in other cases offsetting those effects in part or in whole. The timing of these indirect effects is also very uncertain, but with some presumption that they are more important in the long term than in the short. The effects on interest rates must, in any case, depend on the policy assumptions chosen for the simulation. For present purposes it is convenient to assume that interest rates are unchanged; the way in which fiscal and monetary policy have in fact interacted is a question to be discussed in a later section.

The effects of fiscal policy on the exchange rate depend on the assumptions made about expectations. As with the interest rate simulations reported in Chapter 13 above, a permanent change in taxation or public spending would have a far greater effect on the exchange rate than one which is interpreted as transitory. Moreover the behaviour of the exchange rate must be closely linked to that of interest rates. If interest rates are expected to rise in response to a fiscal expansion, then the exchange rate may well jump up; if interest rates are unchanged the most significant effect of fiscal expansion would be to make the balance of payments worse, causing the exchange rate to jump down. The simulations reported are based on the convenient fiction that the exchange rate would not have changed at all.

The assumption made about expectations is still of some importance, because, in the model used, decisions about employment, stockbuilding, wage settlements and a few other variables are forward looking. Two simulations are reported therefore: one (Case A) in which all changes in fiscal policy are anticipated, as well as their consequences for output, and another (Case B) in which expectations are adaptive, that is to say based on past experience alone; there is no anticipation at all, either of policy changes or of their results.

The counterfactual case is designed, as far as possible, to show a neutral or no-change fiscal policy. At the same time, however, it is intended that its effect both on output and on the financial balance of the public sector should not be large on average over the period as a whole. This is to avoid the complications which would otherwise be caused by cumulating differences in flows of debt interest, and to protect the plausibility of the assumption that the exchange rate and interest rates are unaffected (the same in the base run and in the simulation).

Accordingly, it is assumed that:

(i)   public authorities' consumption grows in volume at 1.4 per cent a year;

(ii)   public investment *falls* in volume in line with its actual trend (with an adjustment for privatisation);

(iii)   the real value of current grants to the personal sector rises by 3 per cent a year plus the adjustment for unemployment included in the model;

(iv)   income tax allowances are all indexed to inflation, and the elasticity of revenue with respect to taxable income is 1.4;

(v)   the equations for company tax (including oil taxes) are used, implying that the 1986 tax reform *does* take place in the counterfactual case;

(vi)   national insurance contributions are a constant proportion of the wage and salary bill, and the NI surcharge is zero throughout;

(vii)   the yields of VAT and other customs and excise taxes rise in line with consumer spending;

(viii) local authority rates, and all subsidies rise in line with consumer prices, whilst protective duties rise in line with the value of imports.

Thus the simulation removes all the more important discretionary tax changes and smoothes out the erratic path of the most important categories of public spending. But it retains the main properties of the tax system as it responds to cyclical variation in output, as well as the response of spending on benefits to unemployment. It also, however, removes a certain amount of short-term movement in both spending and tax receipts which was unplanned before the event, and also typically unexplained after the event. Thus, even now, the distinction between deliberate acts of policy and their consequences is not quite as watertight as one would wish. The results are presented in table 14.10.

On average the growth rate of output is a little faster in the counterfactual case than it was in reality, but this result depends on features of the counterfactual case which are essentially arbitrary. (In particular, the growth rate of public spending over the period as a whole has hardly been changed, although arguably a neutral policy might have involved a much faster rate of increase.) It is more interesting to look at the variation in the growth rate from year to year. It appears that actual fiscal policy (compared with the counterfactual case) reduced growth significantly on two occa-

Table 14.10 *Counterfactual simulations of fiscal policy*

	Public sector financial deficit (% of GDP)			Gross domestic product (percentage growth rate)			Balance of payments on current account (% of GDP)			Rate of inflation (% increase in RPI)		
	Actual	Case A	Case B	Actual	Case A	Case B	Actual	Case A	Case B	Actual	Case A	Case B
1974	5.6	5.3	5.2				−3.9	−3.8	−3.9			
1975	7.1	8.1	7.9	−1.9	−2.5	−2.6	−1.4	−1.2	−1.2	24.3	24.0	24.5
1976	6.7	8.8	8.7	2.0	3.4	3.0	−0.7	−0.9	−0.7	16.5	14.1	14.6
1977	4.2	6.7	6.9	2.8	4.9	5.1	−0.1	−1.1	−0.9	15.9	13.6	13.0
1978	4.9	5.1	5.4	3.5	3.3	3.7	0.6	−0.1	−0.2	8.3	9.1	7.8
1979	4.3	4.6	4.5	3.0	2.3	2.5	−0.3	−0.7	−0.9	13.4	12.6	12.9
1980	4.5	5.2	5.1	−2.9	−2.8	−3.0	1.3	1.0	0.8	18.0	14.9	15.8
1981	3.1	5.2	5.2	−1.4	0.1	−0.3	2.7	1.8	1.9	11.9	11.2	11.5
1982	2.7	5.1	5.2	2.2	3.6	3.6	1.7	—	0.1	8.6	6.4	6.5
1983	3.4	4.8	5.0	3.4	3.2	3.4	1.3	−0.5	−0.5	4.6	5.6	4.7
1984	4.0	4.6	4.7	2.8	2.6	2.9	0.6	−1.3	−1.5	5.0	6.0	5.6
1985	2.7	3.3	3.3	3.5	3.3	3.3	0.9	−0.9	−1.0	6.0	5.8	6.1
1986	2.1	2.8	2.8	2.9	2.6	2.5	0.1	−1.7	−1.8	3.5	4.0	4.2
1987	1.2	1.7	1.7	4.7	4.7	4.5	−0.7	−2.5	−2.5	4.1	4.9	5.1

sions: in 1976 and 1977, and again in 1981 and 1982. Of these, 1977 was a year of above average growth, 1981 was a year of recession, whilst 1982 was in line with trend. Taking all thirteen years together and calculating standard deviations in annual growth rates indicates that fiscal policy (defined by reference to this simulation) hardly changed at all the amplitude of output fluctuations. It was, on balance, neither stabilising nor destabilising. The popular view that it was seriously destabilising puts too much weight on one budget in 1981 which was not typical.

The effects on inflation consist mainly of the direct consequences of changes in indirect taxation and subsidies. Indirect taxes rise more slowly and rates of subsidies do not fall in the counterfactual case, so the rate of inflation is lower until 1982. The estimated indirect effects on inflation, resulting from changes in the pressure of demand, are quite small, but their magnitude is uncertain. Undoubtedly they could well be larger in reality, especially if the assumption of a fixed exchange rate were relaxed. The estimates for the public sector deficit and for the deficit on the balance of payments are also shown for the counterfactual case, confirming that they are not so large as to be implausible.

The most striking conclusion to be drawn from the estimates in table 14.10, however, is the small scale of the policy effects relative to the variation in output and inflation. Policy changes did not cause the main features of boom and slump, inflation and disinflation; neither did policy changes do much to correct them. As with the estimates of the effects of interest rate charges presented in Chapter 13, the abiding impression is that policy was inactive relative to the size of the problems by which it was confronted.

CAN THE COURSE OF FISCAL POLICY BE EXPLAINED?

We have now constructed two alternative indices of fiscal policy, neither entirely satisfactory: the financial deficit weighted and cyclically adjusted, and the estimated output effects of policy compared with a counterfactual simulation. Happily the results of the two quite different approaches to measurement are not greatly different.

The calculations based on the financial deficit are shown in table 14.9 on page 215; the output effects shown in the simulation are implied by the figures in table 14.10. The correlation between these two estimates of the effects of fiscal policy year by year is 0.89. That close association owes something to the fact that both series show a similar trend towards tighter policy over the period as a whole. But the degree of the trend shown by both measures is largely arbitrary, reflecting assumptions made simply for convenience of calculation. The correlation between changes in the two measures, calculated for each year, is rather lower at 0.61.

The many differences in methodology or assumptions account for the differences in these two measures. One important difference is in the treatment of public sector pay: in the calculations based on the financial deficit, variations in pay relativities are treated as if they were the result of fiscal policy changes, whilst the model runs treat them as part of the economic environment. Another difference refers to changes in subsidies, which are given much more weight in the calculations based on the deficit than they are by the macroeconomic model; this helps to explain why the deficit-based calculations suggest a significant tightening of fiscal policy in the mid-1980s, which is not in evidence at all in the model-based measure.

In this section we take the estimates of the weighted and cyclically adjusted deficit and seek to explain their movements quarter by quarter in terms of a reaction function. This was the technique applied to the quarterly and monthly movements of interest rates in Chapter 13 above. Its use for the interpretation of fiscal policy is subject to more serious limitations.

Interest rates really are set by the authorities almost continuously reacting to events in financial markets or to news about the development of the economy. The changes in the quarterly and monthly data used really do result from the decisions of policymakers. Taxes and public spending decisions are usually taken just once a year. Thus the quarterly observations of the deficit, or statistics derived from it, do not represent the results of a quarterly decision process. Moreover, as we have been at pains to point out, the size of the deficit, even after adjustment, reflects many things as well as policy decisions. Thus the reaction function presented here must have a rather different interpretation. The conduct of fiscal policy was such that a relationship of this kind could be estimated between a particular index of fiscal policy and a set of economic indicators. That fact tells us something about the conduct of fiscal policy, but the estimated relationship cannot claim to be the decision rule itself.

The results are best if we treat the tightening of policy after the 1976 crisis as a special event, represented by a dummy variable having the value of one in all subsequent periods. Both the level (relative to a trend) and the rate of growth of M3 appear to influence fiscal policy. It is also possible to detect some effects from (the change in) inflation and in capacity utilisation both having the appropriate sign. The preferred equation is:

$$Def = 33.6 + 0.08 \ time - \underset{(0.50)}{1.54} \ Dummy + \underset{(0.13)}{0.17} \ Def_{-1} \underset{(6.4)}{-9.9} \ \Delta \log M3$$

$$\underset{(3.2)}{-3.4} \ \log M3_{-1} + \underset{(0.14)}{0.46} \ \Delta CUD - \underset{(0.054)}{0.046} \ \Delta Inf_{-2}$$

$$R^2 = 0.81 \qquad DW = 1.9$$

where *Dummy* is 0 up to 1976(Q4), thereafter 1; *Inf* is the annual percentage growth rate of the CPI; *CUD* is an index of capacity utilisation and M3 is the broad money supply.

Although this looks like an eminently sensible explanation of the course of fiscal policy, it is not a robust one. The finding of an appropriate response to both the output cycle and inflation was the result of trial and error. The fact that one is lagged two periods, and the other not at all, raises the suspicion that the favourable results may be accidental. The finding of a significant response to the money supply figures is rather more robust, and does confirm statements made about the motivation of budget changes during the period. In particular the 1981 deflation, which had little justification in relation to inflation and none at all in relation to output, could well be interpreted as a last attempt to bring M3 under control after the bid to use interest rates for that purpose in 1979 and 1980 had evidently failed.

No strong claims can be made for this estimated reaction function. At best it has identified some average responses, over a period when the conduct of fiscal policy was changing, and when the Treasury itself found it difficult to formulate and stick to any clear rules. If it is impossible after the event to estimate a satisfactory policy reaction function, it would have been even more difficult to predict during the period what fiscal policy was going to be in the future. Most changes in fiscal policy, therefore, must have been unexpected when they occurred, a fact which should, according to the theory of economic policy, have made them all the more potent.

THE FISCAL-MONETARY MIX

So far fiscal policy and monetary policy have been described and analysed in isolation from each other, as if they were quite unrelated. But Treasury ministers have responsibility for both, and they might be expected to operate them in harmony. The two instruments might be made to serve one grand strategy. This final section of Part 4 will be concerned with the policy mix, the way that joint decisions were taken over the setting of these two instruments.

Broadly speaking raising interest rates and raising taxes (or cutting public spending) do similar things to the economy. They both reduce domestic demand by reducing either consumer spending or private investment. A lower pressure of demand will tend to reduce inflation and improve the balance of payments, but at the same time it will reduce output and raise unemployment. In the management of demand, fiscal and monetary policy are substitutes for one another. The effects of the two instruments on the growth of the money supply were also important for policy during this period. Higher interest rates were generally believed to help sales of gilt-edged securities outside the banking system as well as reducing the demand for bank loans. By these routes they were expected to slow down the growth of the assets of the banking system, and hence the growth of the banks' deposit liabilities. Thus high interest rates were deployed as a means of controlling monetary growth, even though most of the bank deposits within the definition of the money supply were themselves interest-bearing. In fact this method of control proved unreliable, as Part 1 has described. Tax increases were also supposed to reduce monetary growth by reducing bank lending to the public sector. Thus the same monetary target might in principle be achieved with higher taxes and lower interest rates, or vice versa (at least in the short to medium-term). In this sense also fiscal and monetary policy would substitute for one another.

The two instruments could also be thought of as alternative ways of reacting to pressure on the exchange rate. An increase in interest rates (provided it was not already discounted by the market) would produce a jump up in the exchange rate. An unexpected tightening of fiscal policy (with no associated change in interest rates) might have a similar effect, because it would improve the prospect for the balance of payments and hence reduce the risk premium attached to sterling.

If the authorities had only one policy aim, whether it was demand management, or monetary control, or exchange rate stability, it would seem that one instrument would suffice. The case for using two instruments would rest on a preference for small instrument changes, or on uncertainty as to the effect of either instrument on its own.

If, as is generally the case, the authorities have several policy aims, then it would seem possible to achieve two of them by appropriate settings of two instruments. In practice, however, this is not an easy matter to achieve. For example, it would obviously be good to achieve both full employment and price stability, but during our period that combination was clearly unattainable, at least by means of macroeconomic policy alone. The difficulty in this case is that both instruments influence both objectives mainly by changing the pressure of demand – and a high enough pressure for full employment would have been too high for price stability.

There are several examples within our period of attempts to vary the fiscal–monetary policy mix and to achieve more than one objective as a result. Under the strategy agreed with the IMF in 1976, the pressure of demand was kept low by a tightening of fiscal policy, whilst the real exchange rate was held down by reducing interest rates. The aim was to achieve export-led growth and an improved balance of payments.

The 1980 medium-term financial strategy was similar, in that the aim was to put the main burden of counterinflation policy (and monetary control) on a tightening of fiscal policy. The other objective was not expressed in terms of a lower real exchange rate but of lower interest rates (whether nominal or real) to encourage private sector investment. In the event interest rates remained high despite the tightening of fiscal policy, and the strength of the real exchange rate played a considerable part in reducing inflation.

In the mid-1980s it was expressly argued by the Treasury that fiscal policy could *not* be used for demand management, because it was changed too infrequently. The burden of reducing inflation was now placed on interest rates; thus reversing the assignment set out in the original MTFS. It is arguable, however, that fiscal policy was in fact tightened (or eased less than it otherwise would have been) in the budgets of 1986 and 1987, because the authorities were concerned that interest rates, and the exchange rate, should not rise too high.

Table 14.11 below sets alongside one another the change in interest rates each year, and the change in the adjusted fiscal deficit. Over the period as a whole there is a weak negative correlation between the tightening of monetary and fiscal policy thus defined. In 1977 this is particularly true, as interest rates fell sharply and taxes were raised. The situation in 1981 was rather similar; the famous deflationary budget of that year was partly offset by the reduction (from a very high level) of nominal interest rates. Subsequently policy changes were more modest in scale and tended to reinforce one another. In 1983 for example both fiscal and monetary policy were slightly relaxed, whilst both were somewhat tightened in 1985.

The reaction functions estimated in this study are another way of summarising policy over this period. They do not directly identify the aims of policy, or the assignment of instruments to objectives, but they do contain some information about the signals to which the two arms of policy appeared to respond.

It seems that both fiscal and monetary policy were used to reduce inflation during the period. Both interest rate changes (for part of the

Table 14.11 *Fiscal and monetary policy 1974–87*

	Change in interest rates	Change in adjusted fiscal deficit
1974	+1.8	+0.8
1975	−1.2	+0.5
1976	+1.0	−0.3
1977	−3.7	−2.0
1978	+1.0	+0.3
1979	+4.5	−0.3
1980	+1.9	—
1981	−2.0	−0.9
1982	−1.6	—
1983	−1.8	+0.5
1984	−0.3	—
1985	+2.3	−0.7
1986	−1.3	−0.3
1987	−1.1	−0.6

period at least) and budgetary measures were triggered by variations in the rate of inflation itself. In neither case, however, was the response very quick or vigorous. The response of both monetary and fiscal policy to the growth rate of the money supply is explained by the belief that it was a forward indicator of inflation (as well as a target variable in its own right).

There is also some evidence that both fiscal and monetary policy responded to the level of real economic activity, to cyclical variations in unemployment or capacity utilisation. It is one thesis of this study that demand management, in that limited sense, was never altogether abandoned. The reaction function approach suggests that fiscal and monetary policy again tended to move in the same direction in response to indicators of the pressure of demand.

There were nevertheless important differences in the use made of the two instruments. Clearly the foreign exchange market was of great importance to monetary policy. Interest rates responded to foreign interest rates, to the exchange rate itself, and to the level of the reserves. There is no suggestion that fiscal policy did the same, except on one special occasion. In 1976 there was a tightening of fiscal policy agreed with the IMF as part of the solution to the sterling crisis. Otherwise fiscal policy seems to have been governed by domestic considerations, including a view of the appropriate and sustainable level for public sector borrowing itself.

If we knew precisely what the aims of the authorities were and their relative priority, we could compare estimated reaction functions with the responses which would have been optimal according to a particular macroeconomic model. As things stand such a comparison cannot be made in detail but the reference to control theory suggests three concluding comments about the use made of fiscal and monetary policy in our period.

First, the finding that both instruments were used to respond to the same or similar information, suggests that there was no unique assignment of instruments to targets. In general unique assignment is sub-optimal so this seems to be a point in favour of the rules that have in fact been followed.

Secondly, the use of interest rates to influence the exchange rate (or at least to respond to its movements) is a subject of some controversy amongst economists interested in optimal control. One problem often mentioned in this context is that the improvement in the prospect for inflation when the exchange rate rises is an improvement at the expense of inflation in other countries. If policy rules were coordinated across countries the role of the exchange rate as an intermediate target might have to be altogether different.

Finally the dynamic form of the reaction functions is not unlike the form of those prescribed by control theorists. Thus the *change* in interest rates is influenced by the *change* in the real exchange rate as well as by its level (derivative control); the level of *prices* appears in the rule as well as the rate of *inflation* (integral control). It is worth noting also that the long-run *level* of interest rates appears in the rule which determines their current period *change*. This suggests, plausibly enough, that the authorities are not indifferent as to the level of interest rates in the long term. (In technical terms, interest rates appear in the welfare function to be maximised.) Similar considerations apply to the public sector borrowing requirement in the reaction function for fiscal policy.

But a technical discussion of optimality would be the wrong note on which to end this review of the conduct of macroeconomic policy. The main impression is not one of technical brilliance; neither were the results achieved by policy at all satisfactory. On the contrary, the authorities were struggling with economic problems beyond their control, and quite uncertain what model of the economy to adopt as they tried to put things right. It is surprising that any consistency at all can be found by a statistical analysis of their behaviour.

PART 5

THE OUTCOME FOR POLICY OBJECTIVES

WHAT CONSTITUTES A POLICY ACHIEVEMENT?

Governments are very ready to take the credit when the economy is behaving well and they usually have to take the blame when it is behaving badly. In the 1970s and 1980s the central issue of political dispute was the state of the British economy. That, more than defence, law and order, constitutional reform, or foreign affairs, dominated the debates amongst the political parties. It was believed to have a deciding effect on the outcome of general elections.

The effects of what governments actually did over this period could easily be exaggerated. The estimates we have shown of the effects of both fiscal and monetary policy measures in Part 4 are rather strikingly small. If industry prospered or decayed, if the tide of employment ebbed or flowed, if the threat of hyperinflation was immediate or remote, this was the result of the world environment or of changes in social attitudes at home, rather than the determination or skill shown by ministers and their advisers. Much of the time they were feeling their way in the dark, doing what they thought public opinion required of them and hoping that all would be well.

In Part 5 we look at the aspects of economic behaviour for which policymakers, fairly or unfairly, were held responsible. The first sections deal with the balance of payments and the exchange rate; this is followed by a more detailed look at inflation and at unemployment; the final sections are concerned with the growth rate of total output and the influence on it of the macroeconomic policies covered in this study.

It is never possible to identify unambiguously what the contribution of policy to the outcome for the economy has been. Policy actions as defined in Part 4 can be treated as one influence amongst many on the course of history. Some analysis along those lines has already been attempted using the National Institute's macroeconomic model. But in another sense, the appropriate measure of policy effectiveness is the outcome itself. A totally inactive policy would in this sense be totally successful if the outcome was, by chance, precisely what the policymakers wanted to happen.

There is a natural tendency for policymakers to claim after the event, if circumstances permit, that what did happen was indeed what they intended. In the mid-1980s for example, there was a notable shift in ministerial speeches from emphasis on the elimination of inflation to the proposition that rapid economic growth was a measure of policy success. Policymakers are reluctant to state their priorities unambiguously, because that would mean admitting that some interests were being sacrificed in favour of others. There is therefore no official measure of social welfare against which the outcome can be evaluated.

There is, in practice, a reasonable consensus about the aims of macroeconomic policy. Ideally all would like to see both full employment and price stability, although some would question whether macroeconomic policy as such can do much to reconcile the two. The status of the balance of payments and of the exchange rate is less clearcut. Neither is generally regarded as defining a final objective of policy. A satisfactory external account may contribute to economic wellbeing in the long run – it may even be a necessary condition for economic growth – but it is not an end in itself. In a rather similar way a strong or stable exchange rate, although it is sometimes a source of pride, is not an objective in its own right. The final section of Part 5 is about the effect of macroeconomic policy on the growth of national output or real income. The acceleration of growth has undoubtedly been the aim of economic policy broadly defined to include industrial policy, market regulation, and so on. It is a more open question whether it should be included amongst the aims of macroeconomic policy as described in this book. This is an issue we shall take up in its proper place.

EXTERNAL BALANCE AND THE
EXCHANGE RATE

THE BALANCE OF PAYMENTS

The balance of payments was one of the main anxieties of policymakers in Britain for most of the 1950s and 1960s. It became more acutely troublesome in the early 1970s, but then with the rise in oil production, the problem went away. It returned only in 1988, just after the end of the period covered by this study. The figures for the current account are shown in table 15.1.

At the beginning of the period, in 1974, there was little doubt that a deficit on the balance of payments was a serious problem. It was still possible to think of supply and demand on the foreign exchange market as the result of trade and its finance. Even in the mid-1970s the situation was changing. The run out of the pound in 1976, and the run back into it in 1977, were not the result of changes in the trade balance. The volume of purely speculative flows could already dominate the current account, and swamp intervention by the authorities.

By the 1980s it could be argued that the current account was a matter of indifference. Exchange control had been abolished and the scale of capital flows through the banking sector particularly was vastly in excess of those generated by the need to finance trade or other current payments. The currency in which assets were held had less and less connection with the nationality of the person or company that owned them. The demand for sterling was a worldwide demand, part of the currency dealings of banks and others who took positions quite unrelated to any actual or possible wish to buy or sell goods made in Britain. If the current account, or the monthly trade figures, still mattered at all it was solely because of their effect on expectations or on confidence in the market.

It was not a stated aim of policy at any time to run a large surplus on the current account of the balance of payments, or to build up the nation's holdings of assets abroad. Such an objective would not have been well regarded if it had been announced at meetings of the IMF or the OECD, and the scale of the surplus in the early 1980s attracted some criticism abroad.

The external balance sheet of the United Kingdom economy is summarised in table 15.2. The external liabilities of the public sector exceeded its

Table 15.1 *The balance of payments on current account* £ *billion*

	Visible trade		Visible balance		Current account	
	Oil	Other goods	Total	(as % of GDP)	Total	(as % of GDP)
1974	−3.4	−2.0	−5.4	−6.4	−3.2	−3.8
1975	−3.1	−0.3	−3.3	−3.2	−1.5	−1.4
1976	−3.9	−0.0	−4.0	−3.2	−0.9	−0.8
1977	−2.8	0.5	−2.3	−1.6	−0.2	−0.1
1978	−2.0	0.4	−1.6	−1.0	1.0	0.6
1979	−0.7	−2.7	−3.4	−1.7	−0.5	−0.3
1980	0.3	1.0	1.4	0.6	3.1	1.4
1981	3.1	0.2	3.4	1.3	6.9	2.7
1982	4.6	−2.4	2.2	0.8	4.7	1.7
1983	7.0	−8.0	−1.1	−0.4	3.8	1.3
1984	6.9	−11.5	−4.6	−1.4	2.0	0.6
1985	8.1	−10.4	−2.3	−0.7	3.3	0.9
1986	4.1	−12.8	−8.7	−2.3	−0.2	−0.1
1987	4.2	−14.3	−10.2	−2.5	−2.5	−0.6

Sources: CSO *Pink Book* 1988 and 1985, *Economic Trends* 1989.

external assets in the mid-1970s, especially at the end of 1976, following the sterling crisis of that year. Having built up a small positive balance in 1977 it was kept in the black for the rest of the period. In the final year, 1987, the reserves rose particularly fast, as market intervention on a large scale was resumed to hold the pound down against the dollar.

The United Kingdom private sector built up its external assets in 1976 as British banks moved out of sterling. The large swing in the official reserves between 1976 and 1977 was offset by transactions of other United Kingdom residents. Even before the abolition of exchange control the movements in private sector net external assets were larger than those of the public sector. After 1979 the private sector built up its overseas portfolio rapidly, by acquiring assets and as result of capital gains. The external balance sheet position of the country as a whole became much stronger. The value of total net external assets rose from about 2 or 3 per cent of annual GDP in the mid-1970s to 20 or 30 per cent in the mid-1980s. From being negligible proportion of total national wealth (as measured by the Central Statistical Office in its national balance sheet estimates) they rose to about 5 or 6 per cent.

From the point of view of the owners of wealth in the nation as a whole this represented a diversification of assets which could well be judged prudent. The oil revenue from the North Sea allowed the country as a whole to run a payments surplus for six years in succession. The simultaneous abolition of exchange controls, and the suspension of exchange market intervention, meant that the bulk of the overseas assets accrued to

Table 15.2 *Levels of United Kingdom external assets and liabilities*

end-year

	Net external assets (£bn)				
	Public sector	Private sector	Total	As % of GDP	As % of national net worth
1974	−0.8	3.1	2.3	2.7	n.a.
1975	−1.4	4.0	2.6	2.5	n.a.
1976	−3.9	8.8	4.8	3.9	0.9
1977	2.0	4.4	6.4	4.4	1.1
1978	3.1	10.3	13.4	8.0	1.8
1979	5.8	6.3	12.1	6.1	1.3
1980	5.3	12.0	17.3	7.5	1.6
1981	4.3	27.5	31.8	12.5	2.8
1982	3.7	38.3	42.0	15.1	3.4
1983	3.4	51.0	54.3	17.9	4.0
1984	4.1	76.2	80.3	24.8	5.4
1985	2.3	78.1	80.3	22.7	5.0
1986	3.5	109.8	113.2	29.9	6.3
1987	9.6	79.9	89.5	21.6	4.4

Sources: CSO, *Pink Book* and *Blue Book*, 1988.

the private sector, not to the official reserves. The capital gains may have been much larger as a result, since much of the private sector investment was in equities.

THE VOLATILITY OF THE EXCHANGE RATE

The break-up of the Bretton Woods system and the transition to a multilateral system of floating exchange rates was the result of market pressure, not the intellectual conversion of finance ministers and central bankers. In the United Kingdom we held to the 1949 priority as long as we could; having been obliged to devalue the pound in 1967, we tried repeatedly to establish a new rate against the dollar, until June 1972 when the pound was allowed to float as 'a temporary measure'.

Exchange rate policy had a shadowy existence during the period covered by this study. On two occasions, 1977 and 1987, exchange rate stability was an explicit aim of policy. At the other exteme, in 1979 and 1980, it was explicitly *not* an aim of policy. For most of the period its status was ambiguous but, as we have seen in Part 4, exchange markets had a persistent and profound effect on the conduct of monetary policy. Judging by actions rather than by words, exchange rate stability was an aim of the monetary authorities in the United Kingdom for most, if not all, of the period.

Table 15.3 *Exchange rate changes*

		Percentage change in the effective exchange rate index (per quarter)							
1975	2	−3.2	1979	2	5.5	1983	2	4.7
	3	−4.1		3	5.2		3	0.7
	4	−2.7		4	−3.1		4	−2.0
1976	1	−1.2	1980	1	5.0	1984	1	−1.8
	2	−8.1		2	1.6		2	−2.4
	3	−2.4		3	2.3		3	−2.1
	4	−7.2		4	3.5		4	−3.7
1977	1	3.6	1981	1	1.7	1985	1	−4.0
	2	−0.4		2	−4.0		2	9.4
	3	0.2		3	−7.4		3	4.1
	4	2.2		4	−0.9		4	−2.7
1978	1	2.7	1982	1	1.6	1986	1	−5.9
	2	−5.8		2	−0.9		2	1.2
	3	0.9		3	1.2		3	−5.4
	4	0.0		4	−2.4		4	−5.3
1979	1	2.2	1983	1	−9.8	1987	1	2.5

average absolute change 3.35

	Percentage change on a year earlier (per annum)				
First Quarter					
1976	−10.7	1980	12.9	1984	1.5
1977	−13.8	1981	9.5	1985	−11.8
1978	4.8	1982	−10.5	1986	4.3
1979	−2.8	1983	−11.6	1987	−7.0

average absolute change 8.43

Source: *Economic Trends Annual Supplement, 1988.*

Table 15.3 shows the percentage changes in the effective exchange rate index in each quarter from 1975 (when the data series begins) to 1987. The average change was a depreciation of 0.8 per cent. The largest quarterly change was 9.8 per cent in the first quarter of 1983, the smallest was zero in the fourth quarter of 1978. The average absolute change was 3.35 per cent.

The series shows evidence of positive autocorrelation, with runs of successive pluses and minuses extending over a year or two. The second part of the table shows change over successive (non-overlapping) four–quarter periods. These vary from just 1.5 per cent in the year up to the first quarter of 1984 to 13.8 per cent in the year up to 1977. The average absolute change is 8.4 per cent. These are large figures in the calculations of businessmen and indeed of anyone who tries to forecast the behaviour of the economy.

It is more difficult to say what volatility was over periods longer than a year. If the calculation is begun in 1976 the average absolute change over

Table 15.4 *Exchange rate forecasts (or assumptions) in the National Institute Economic Review*[a]

	Forecast	Outturn	Percentage difference
1975	−4.0	−12.9	+10.2
1976	−1.8	−10.4	+9.6
1977	+1.5	+2.0	−0.5
1978	−1.2	+2.8	−3.9
1979	nil	+10.8	−9.7
1980	nil	+6.4	−6.0
1981	+5.0	−9.1	+15.5
1982	nil	−9.2	+10.1
1983	−2.0	−2.1	+0.1
1984	−6.6	−6.4	−0.2
1985	−6.4	+0.2	−6.6
1986	−0.7	−5.7	+5.3
1987	−3.6	+7.2	−10.1
Average change/error	*−1.5*	*−2.0*	*+1.1*
Average absolute change	2.5	6.5	6.8

Sources: National Institute Economic Review and *Economic Trends Annual Supplement, 1988.*
[a]Percentage change between first half of present and succeeding year, in the effective exchange rate index.

non-overlapping two-year periods is 14.5 per cent. Beginning in 1977 however the years of rising and falling rates cancel out, and the average absolute change over two years is only 7 per cent.

Variability as such imposes fewer costs if it is predictable. Notoriously, however, exchange rates are difficult, perhaps impossible, to forecast. The quarterly runs of successive rises and falls suggest that forecasting should in principle be able to reduce the uncertainty of future exchange rates. In practice, however, the behaviour of the market seems to change too often for a model to be estimated and put to profitable use.

Table 15.4 shows the exchange rate projections published in the *National Institute Economic Review* at the beginning of each year from 1975–87. Their status was not always exactly the same: some are described as assumptions, that is to say interpretations of the current intentions of policymakers; others are described as forecasts, although these too must be contingent on assumptions about interest rates and market intervention. The figures refer to the percentage change in the effective exchange rate index between the first half of the year in which the forecast is made and the first half of the succeeding year. They are thus forecasts of the rate of appreciation or depreciation rather more than a year ahead. (This particular time span was chosen because for part of the period only half-yearly figures are quoted in the *Review*.)

The forecasts or assumptions were strikingly unsuccessful, their average absolute error being larger than the average absolute change in the exchange rate. The correlation between forecast and outturn was close to zero. There is no reason to suppose that other forecasters were any more successful.

The scale of unpredicted variation in the exchange rate was such as to make macroeconomic forecasting of any kind significantly more difficult. Thus an error of 6 per cent on the exchange rate a year ahead would translate, other things being equal, into an error of about 1½ per cent on the price level and about a third of 1 per cent on the level of output (using the properties of the present National Institute model).

Exchange rate volatility was unpopular, not just with economic forecasters, but with everyone who had to take decisions on which the exchange rate had a bearing. Up to about three months ahead provision could be made to cover known receipts or payments of foreign currency in the forward market; beyond that it became more diffcult or expensive. Moreover, forward markets cannot be used so effectively to eliminate risk when the size or timing of the transactions is itself uncertain. One cost of exchange rate flexibility must have been the reluctance of some cautious producers and consumers to engage in foreign trade at all, and another cost must have been the mistaken decisions made by some of those who were not deterred.

It would be wrong to assume, however, that volatility is necessarily and always damaging. The theoretical case for floating exchange rates is that market signals tell traders about relative abundance and scarcity, helping them to increase their own prosperity and the efficiency of the economy as a whole. The volatility of the exchange rate may be an indication that it is doing its job properly, transmitting useful signals about a volatile environment.

INTERPRETATIONS OF EXCHANGE RATE BEHAVIOUR

The behaviour of exchange rates still remains deeply mysterious. The theory of how exchange rates *ought* to behave is well developed, but the many attempts that have been made to estimate econometric equations explaining the movements of the sterling exchange rate have met with little or no success. The problem is not just one of prediction; even with the benefit of hindsight little of the observed variation in the exchange rate can be explained.

This does not mean, of course, that particular episodes in the history of the pound cannot be quite convincingly explained by reference to the circumstances of that particular time. Almost every day the financial press prints some account of exchange rate appreciations and depreciations, together with the comments of dealers or market analysts which seem to account well enough for the events that are reported. But the factors cited as favourable or unfavourable to sterling vary from year to year, even from week to week.

We have emphasised in Part 4 the effects on the exchange rate of interest rates, and of expectations about the conduct of monetary policy in the future. If sterling and foreign currency assets are regarded as perfect substitutes then the difference between interest rates at home and abroad should be reflected in anticipated movements of the exchange rate. The difficulty of using this theory to explain movements in the exchange rate as they actually occur is that one cannot usually distinguish changes in interest rates or in exchange rates that are anticipated from those which are unanticipated.

We shall not attempt in this section to give a full account of the behaviour of sterling over the fifteen years covered by this book. Instead we shall draw attention to two issues sometimes neglected by commentators which may nevertheless be of some importance. First we shall emphasise that sterling was part of a world currency market and its movements had to mirror those of the other currencies taken together. Secondly we shall tabulate some of the structural influences on the demand for sterling, of which the value of North Sea Oil is one, but by no means the only one that is worth reckoning.

The most obvious alternative to sterling as an investment currency has always been the dollar, and that is the bilateral market in which the volume of transactions in sterling is greatest. Dealing in sterling against yen or Continental currencies has been much lighter because of exchange controls and a shortage of supply of market instruments. It is possible that attitudes to the dollar and expectations about United States monetary policy have had a disproportionate effect on sterling – that is an effect not justified by the importance of the United States as a trading partner with the United Kingdom, or as a competitor in third markets.

Charts 15.1 and 15.2 show effective exchange rate indices for sterling, the Deutschmark, the French franc, the dollar and the yen. Because of the way these indices are constructed it is broadly true that falls in one index will be matched by net rises in the others. Thus the rise of sterling between the beginning of 1979 and the end of 1981 is matched initially by a fall in the effective rate for the yen and subsequently by a fall in the Deutschmark. One of the most striking features of these charts is the massive rise and fall of the dollar effective rate in the course of the 1980s. One counterpart to the rise in the dollar was the fall in sterling from 1981–4.

These relationships can be summarised by calculating correlations between the changes in the effective exchange rate indices. For the changes between first quarters in successive years (thirteen non-overlapping annual observations) the correlations are as follows: Sterling/Dollar, −0.29; Sterling/Deutschmark, −0.09; Sterling/French franc, +0.29; Sterling/Yen, +0.15. Although none of these correlations is statistically significant at the 95 per cent level they are consistent with the suggestion above that the attitude of markets to the dollar may influence the effective rate for the pound disproportionately.

Chart 15.1   *Effective exchange rates for UK, Germany and France*

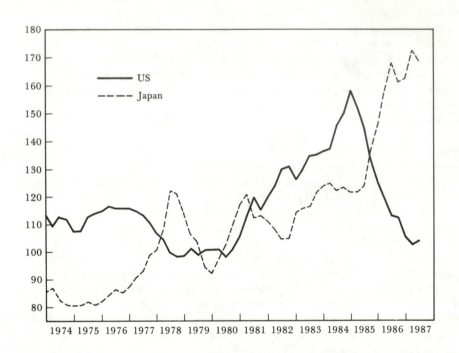

The rise of sterling, against its long-run trend, in 1979 and 1980 was explained by commentators at the time as due, at least in part, to the rise in the world price of oil, which doubled in the course of 1979. The argument was that the United Kingdom had a small surplus on trade in oil, so that the oil price shock improved the balance of trade at a given real exchange rate (and a given level of world activity); in other words it raised the equilibrium real exchange rate for sterling. The other industrial countries moreover were very dependent on imported oil, so that their real exchange rates had to fall. This explanation is supported by the depreciation of the yen effective rate in 1979 and of the Deutschmark effective rate in the next year. (It is not obvious, however, why it took the Deutschmark market a year to react to the oil shock.) If this interpretation were correct however the 1986 fall in oil prices should have produced the reverse pattern of exchange rate changes. It is true that the Deutschmark, and especially the yen, rose sharply in 1986 and 1987, but sterling was unaffected, if one takes account of its downward trend over the period as a whole.

It could be misleading to concentrate attention on the oil price to the exclusion of other identifiable influences on the equilibrium real exchange rate for sterling. The oil price was one of many factors which influenced the current account of the balance of payments over these years. If the

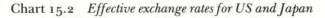

Chart 15.2   *Effective exchange rates for US and Japan*

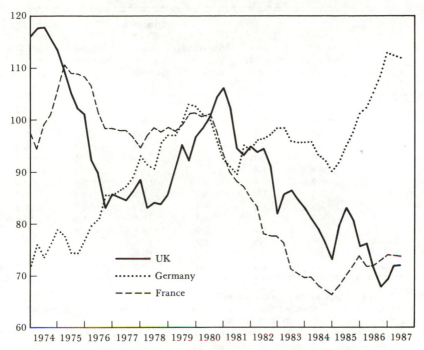

exchange rate responded to this factor, it probably responds to others as well. Table 15.5 tries to be more comprehensive. It shows estimates of the effect on the United Kingdom balance of payments (at a given exchange rate and a given level of activity at home and abroad) of five separate influences that can be identified.

The first column shows the value of North Sea oil production. This production can all be scored as a benefit to the trade balance whether it is exported or used at home, since the level of oil consumption in the United Kingdom is virtually unaffected by activity in the North Sea. The second and third columns show transfers (mainly payments by the British government to international organisations) and interest, profits and dividends. Both these items can be treated as largely invariant to the level of competitiveness and to the balance of trade; they are exogenous influences on the balance of payments to which, in equilibrium, the real exchange rate must adjust. Similarly the outflow of capital following the ending of exchange control, roughly estimated in the fourth column, which features in the capital account, requires an offsetting change in the current account, and hence in the equilibrium real exchange rate.

The fifth column contains estimates of a rather different kind. Most econometric studies of United Kingdom trade performance suggest that the real exchange rate for sterling must depreciate gradually to offset a loss

Table 15.5 *Some structural effects on the balance of payments* £ *billion*

	Value of NS oil (1)	Transfers in the balance of payments (2)	Net property income (3)	Structural capital outflow[a] (4)	Adjustment for non-price competitiveness[b] (5)	Total of columns (1) to (5) (6)	Column (6) as a % of manufactured exports (7)
1974	—	−0.4	1.5	—	—	1.1	8.2
1975	—	−0.5	0.9	—	−0.5	−0.1	−0.6
1976	0.6	−0.8	1.6	—	−1.3	+0.1	0.5
1977	2.1	−1.1	0.3	—	−2.4	−1.1	−4.3
1978	2.8	−1.8	0.8	—	−3.5	−1.7	−6.1
1979	5.7	−2.2	1.2	—	−4.9	−0.2	−0.6
1980	8.8	−2.0	−0.2	−3.0	−6.8	−3.2	−9.2
1981	12.0	−1.5	1.2	−3.3	−8.0	0.4	1.1
1982	13.9	−1.7	1.4	−3.4	−10.0	0.2	0.5
1983	16.3	−1.7	2.8	−3.8	−12.2	1.4	−3.5
1984	19.6	−1.8	4.4	−3.9	−14.2	4.1	8.8
1985	19.0	−3.1	2.8	−4.2	−15.9	−1.4	−2.7
1986	9.0	−2.2	5.1	−4.3	−16.6	−9.0	−16.5
1987	10.1	−3.5	5.5	−4.4	−18.5	−10.8	−17.8

Sources: CSO, *Blue Book* and *Pink Book*, 1988 and 1985.
[a] An allowance for the effects of exchange control abolition, based on figures for portfolio investment abroad by UK financial institutions.
[b] Equal to 3 per cent of manufactured exports in 1975 and cumulating at a further 3 per cent a year up to 1983, but a constant percentage thereafter.

of relative quality or non-price competitiveness if the manufacturing trade balance is not to deteriorate when all economies are growing in line with their productivity trends. This need for a real depreciation seems (according to estimated trade equations) to have abated from about 1983, and this is reflected in the slower growth of the adjustment shown in column five after that period. Summing across the first five columns gives the total of identified structural effects on the balance of payments, shown in the sixth column.

The positive effect of the rise in the value of oil production from 1976–84 is virtually offset by the adjustment for non-price competitiveness and the outflow of capital. It is only at the very end of the period that these calculations point to the need for a large or sustained change in the real exchange rate for sterling.

It seems that the path of the real exchange rate bore little resemblance to that implied in equilibrium by identified structural influences on the current account. The real appreciation between 1977 and 1981 seems quite unjustified, and the subsequent real depreciation from 1981–7 seems a necessary correction. It also looks as if the pound was seriously overvalued at the end of the period. The emergence of a large current account deficit in 1988 confirms that diagnosis.

The model simulations reported in Chapter 13 suggest that the change of monetary policy regime in 1979, assuming it was unanticipated, could account for the sharp appreciation in the pound at about that time. There may be other examples of changes in the exchange rate due to unanticipated changes in monetary policy, but without data on interest rate or exchange rate expectations they cannot be identified.

Throughout the period one is also confronted with movements in the exchange rate which seem arbitrary, and hence disruptive. If the exchange market was conveying useful information to the rest of the economic system, thus improving economic efficiency, it is remarkable how difficult we find it after the event to say just what that information was. Any signal there may have been seems to have been drowned in a great deal of noise. In the next section we try to assess how the United Kingdom would have fared had the exchange rate been fixed.

HISTORY REWRITTEN WITH THE EXCHANGE RATE FIXED

In this section we use one more time the technique of model simulation adopted in Part 4. The National Institute's macroeconomic model of the United Kingdom economy is used to calculate the path the economy might have followed right up to 1987 if the exchange rate had remained constant at its value in the first quarter of 1974. The difference between that path and the true history of the economy could be described as the direct effects of exchange rate flexibility.

As with the simulations reported in Part 4 above, it is necessary to make an assumption about expectations. The normal assumption in policy analysis is that expectations are consistent: the movements in the exchange rate that actually took place (together with their consequences for output and inflation) were correctly anticipated; in the counterfactual case the fixity of the exchange rate was also in line with expectations. This is the basis of simulation A, as reported in table 15.6 below. An alternative assumption is that expectations depend only on observed behaviour, being exclusively backward-looking, so that none of the changes in the exchange rate or indeed in output or inflation, are anticipated. That is the basis of simulation B. As the table shows, the main differences between the two cases are in the timing of the effects.

It would be unrealistic to assume the same path for interest rates in a fixed exchange rate context as in actuality. We have not attempted to guess what level of interest rates might have been necessary to establish the credibility of the policy in its initial stages, or to defend sterling if it came under speculative attack. Instead we assume that the fixity of the exchange rate was immediately accepted by the market, and never questioned subsequently – a very favourable assumption to make, no doubt. In that case United Kingdom interest rates would never have differed markedly

Table 15.6 *The economy with a fixed exchange rate*

	Change in the exchange rate		Short-term interest rate		Rate of inflation[a]		
	Actual	Sims A&B	Actual	Sims A&B	Actual	Sim A	Sim B
1975	−7.8	—	10.4	7.0	24.3	20.6	21.4
1976	−14.2	—	11.4	6.0	16.5	7.8	9.2
1977	−5.2	—	8.1	5.9	15.9	7.8	8.5
1978	0.3	—	8.5	6.5	8.3	3.7	2.6
1979	7.2	—	13.4	8.7	13.4	10.2	8.9
1980	10.1	—	15.7	11.6	18.0	22.5	21.8
1981	−1.2	—	13.5	13.1	11.9	18.5	19.1
1982	−4.7	—	12.0	10.7	8.6	9.8	11.4
1983	−8.0	—	9.8	8.3	4.6	1.6	2.6
1984	−5.5	—	9.5	8.8	5.0	−0.1	−0.5
1985	−0.7	—	11.9	7.5	6.0	−1.0	−3.0
1986	−8.2	—	10.6	6.0	3.5	−1.6	−2.7
1987	−1.6	—	9.6	5.8	4.1	−1.0	−0.2

	Rate of growth[b]			Balance of payments[c]		
	Actual	Sim A	Sim B	Actual	Sim A	Sim B
1975	−1.9	−2.1	−2.0	−1.4	−1.0	−1.2
1976	2.0	1.2	0.9	−0.7	−0.4	−0.3
1977	2.8	2.5	2.1	−0.1	−1.5	−1.3
1978	3.5	4.4	4.5	0.6	−1.4	−1.1
1979	3.0	4.6	4.7	−0.3	−2.6	−2.2
1980	−2.9	−1.2	−0.7	1.3	−0.9	−0.5
1981	−1.4	−1.4	−0.9	2.7	1.9	1.9
1982	1.9	0.4	0.0	1.7	1.2	1.4
1983	3.4	2.4	1.9	1.3	0.3	0.9
1984	2.8	2.9	2.8	0.6	−1.1	−0.3
1985	3.5	4.5	4.9	0.9	−2.2	−1.4
1986	2.9	4.4	5.0	0.1	−3.0	−2.5
1987	4.7	5.7	5.7	−0.7	−4.7	−4.0

[a] Percentage change in the retail price index, year-on-year.
[b] Percentage change in GDP at constant prices, year-on-year.
[c] The current account of the balance of payments as a percentage of GDP.

from the average of world interest rates, so that the expected yield on domestic and foreign assets would be the same. (We also assume that fiscal policy would have been the same had the exchange rate been fixed. We are *not* trying to show what macroeconomic policies would have been necessarily in the circumstances of the time to achieve exchange rate stability.)

A full analysis of the fixed exchange rate alternative should take account of the way in which the model itself would have changed. Presumably trade would have been encouraged, both imports and exports, because some of the uncertainty would have been eliminated. Firms engaged in trade or international competition would, presumably, have changed the basis on which prices were set both at home and abroad. The nature of wage bargaining would have been different if both firms and unions knew that the exchange rate was not going to depreciate. Unfortunately none of these effects can be quantified, so they are left out of the calculation. What we show is the consequences of a different exchange rate assumption, for inflation, for output and for the balance of payments, keeping the structure and parameters of the model unchanged.

Fixing the exchange rate at the beginning of 1974 would have been a heroic task, as the rate of inflation in 1975 was over 20 per cent. If it could have been successfully accomplished the rate of inflation would in fact have fallen very sharply according to the model, coming down to around 2–4 per cent in 1978. The cost would have been a rather slower recovery of output after the recession, and a continuing deficit on the balance of payments.

From 1978–80 the character of the simulation exercise is different, because the exchange rate in reality was appreciating. Thus the counterfactual shows a more rapid rebound in inflation, reaching well over 20 per cent in 1980 year-on-year and remaining very high in 1981 as well. This illustrates well the role of the exchange rate in curbing inflation in the initial years of Conservative government. In the fixed exchange rate run the recession of 1980–81 is milder than it was in reality, but it is not eliminated. Unemployment still rises to over two million by the latter half of 1981. The current account of the balance of payments would still have crossed over into surplus.

From 1981–8 the exchange rate fell each year. Thus the simulation involves a continuing exchange rate appreciation compared with reality. Inflation would have been completely eliminated from 1983 according to the model simulation, actually going negative. The recovery from the recession would have come a little later in 1983, but thereafter growth would have been even brisker than it was in fact. The balance of payments problem, which in reality was delayed until 1988, would have been evident from 1986 or 1987 at the latest. Holding the exchange rate up might have become very difficult by the end of the period.

On average over the thirteen years shown in table 15.6, inflation would have been 3 per cent a year less. Growth would have been just a little faster. The balance of payments would on average have been in small deficit, rather than in balance.

The range and variability of rates of inflation year-on-year would have been increased. According to the model the exchange rate has a quick and powerful effect on domestic inflation (a property which is open to question and discussed further in Chapter 17 below). The standard deviation of inflation rates in table 17.1 is 8.5 per cent for simulation B compared with 6.2 per cent in actuality. The simulation is adding to inflation in 1980 and

1981 when it was in any case high, and subtracting from inflation in 1985 and 1986 when it was in any case low.

The effect on the variability of output growth is very small. The standard deviation of growth rates is 2.5 per cent in simulation B, compared with 2.3 per cent in the real world. Over the years 1976–84 the standard deviation is lower in the simulation. Eliminating the variation in the exchange rate – one important economic variable – is likely to involve increasing the variation in some others. It is an open question whether the benefits of stability in one area exceed the costs of increased instability elsewhere. Judgement on the case for fixing the exchange rate is therefore held over until it can be considered in a wider context in Part 6 below.

16

UNEMPLOYMENT

FULL EMPLOYMENT AS A POLICY OBJECTIVE

If full employment is the aim of macroeconomic policy, then macroeconomic policy was a failure throughout the period covered by this study. It failed in comparison with the earlier postwar experience in Britain itself, and even with the contemporary history of most other industrial countries. One of the purposes of this section is to look back and ask with the benefit of hindsight whether the aim of holding down unemployment was in fact an appropriate one, a desirable outcome which might realistically have been achieved. Alternatively did the meaning of unemployment change between the 1960s and the 1970s in such a way as to change its significance for policy? Were policymakers misled by the numbers, feeling guilty when there was no need?

The expression 'full employment' has never been taken literally, to mean no unemployment at all; indeed it would be surprising if any economy could be so organised that there were no workers 'resting between jobs'. Economies must adapt to change however they are organised, and adaptation means shifting resources, including people, from one activity to another or one location to another. Within a firm, a government department or an army, there are always individuals waiting to be redeployed. They may be bored and frustrated, but they are a necessary part of the larger operation in which they are involved.

In countries where unemployment is very low, or officially non-existent, those looking for work, or waiting to be allocated work, will be employed in some other capacity. Whether they are productively employed or not will depend on circumstances. In some circumstances their last employer will in practice continue to pay them although they are producing little or nothing. If unemployment benefits are paid it is inevitable that some people will claim them who do not in fact want to find work, whilst some of those who become unemployed will inevitably stay unemployed for longer if they are in receipt of benefits not very far below the pay they could expect to receive in work. Thus the very fact of paying unemployment benefit results in a higher level of unemployment than considerations of economic efficiency on their own would dictate. Full employment must be understood to mean a level of unemployment taking account of these considerations, a level which will vary to some degree from time to time and across countries.

The case for maintaining full employment in this sense rests on three independent arguments. The first is that unemployment beyond this necessary minimum is a waste of resources, a waste of the goods and services which the unemployed might have produced. In fact the argument is a good deal broader than that, since the level of demand which leaves the economy below full employment will typically involve shorter average hours of work for those who do have jobs and also the withdrawal from the labour force of some workers who would be prepared to take a job but may not actively look for one.

The loss of output associated with a low pressure of demand can be very substantial. In 1984, for example, the actual level of output was about 10 per cent below capacity, if that is estimated by projecting the trend of GDP starting from the top of the previous cyclical peak. We shall consider later on whether a high or low pressure of demand is better for the economic performance of the country in the long run. For the present it is important to emphasise that the loss of output each year should be scored up and cumulated to assess the social cost of any subsequent improvement in the trend growth rate.

The second argument for full employment is that unemployment is unfair, because the loss of real income falls disproportionately on the unemployed and their dependents. More broadly this is an argument about the distribution of income, applying not only to the unemployed but to others such as those forced into early retirement or disability by the shortage of work. It applies most forcibly to the long-term unemployed, who seem to be less likely to find work the longer that they have been looking for it. This is an anti-poverty argument and could be satisfied in principle by a sufficiently generous provision of benefits, but in practice it influences macroeconomic policy to some extent as well.

Thirdly, and closely related, there are moral, social and political arguments about the need for all citizens to participate in economic life in order to be full members of society. It is said that young people in particular are alienated by unemployment, making it difficult for them to identify with the community and making them more likely to drift into crime. One of the surprises of the 1970s was the tolerance of society for sustained high levels of unemployment. Before the event it was widely believed that unemployment much above a million could lead to widespread riots or even to revolution. In fact unemployment over three million did not even prevent the government from being re-elected in 1983. Unemployment did cause a great deal of individual misery and resentment, and there was certainly widespread sympathy for the unemployed, but this did not have the political consequences that many politicians themselves expected. In that sense, if in no other, the significance of the unemployment numbers had indeed changed.

As we have seen in Part 1 above, the response of successive governments to the need to do something about unemployment took the form of special employment measures rather than macroeconomic reflation. The case against reflation was most explicitly argued by Nigel Lawson in his 1984 Mais Lecture: macroeconomic policy should be assigned to the control of inflation and microeconomic policy to the promotion of employment. He said, moreover, that the reverse assignment had been made by earlier governments with damaging results. This argument does not, however, dispose of the case. If there are two instruments and two objectives then the correct setting of both instruments generally depends on the desired value of both objectives – the two instruments should be set jointly, like solving two simultaneous equations in mathematics.

Moreover, it is possible that the best hope of maintaining full employment lies in the use of macroeconomic and microeconomic policy to reinforce one another. Clearly it might be damaging to the long-term health of the economy to try to sustain a perpetual boom in demand so as to put off the necessary adjustments in labour markets or the structure of industry. On the other hand it may be easier to make such adjustments when demand is reasonably strong. In the latter half of the 1980s for example the administration of unemployment benefits was tightened up considerably. This was done in the context of a strong cyclical upturn. Had the same measures been taken earlier in the decade they would have been much more unpopular, and possibly less successful. The existence of special employment measures as an additional instrument does not mean that the maintenance of full employment is not a proper aim for macroeconomic policy.

It is very important, however, in the conduct of macroeconomic policy, to judge correctly what level of unemployment is in fact sustainable. The sustainable level of unemployment is often equated with the 'natural' rate, to use the term of Milton Friedman, or the NAIRU, to use the acronym invented at the London School of Economics (see Part 2 above). These terms have almost succeeded in supplanting the term 'full employment' in the writings of economists, although not in the popular mind. So far as this section is concerned, we will stick with the notion of full employment, seeking to find out what level of unemployment that in practice would entail. We shall then ask whether full employment in that sense was in fact attainable in Britain in the 1970s and the 1980s.

MEASURING UNEMPLOYMENT

The official United Kingdom unemployment figures collected every month refer to the number of claimants, that is the number of people claiming social security benefits on the grounds that they are unemployed. By contrast, the international standard measures of unemployment used by the ILO and the OECD include all those who have been engaged in the search for work in the last month and who are available for work if they

Table 16.1 *Two definitions of unemployment* *Per cent*

	1971	1972	1973	1974	1975	1976	1977	1978	1979	1980
Searchers[a]	3.6	4.0	3.0	2.9	4.3	5.6	6.0	5.9	5.0	6.4
Claimants[b]	2.9	3.1	2.1	2.2	3.6	4.8	5.2	4.9	4.5	6.1
	1981	1982	1983	1984	1985	1986	1987			
Searchers[a]	9.8	11.3	12.4	11.7	11.2	11.2	10.3			
Claimants[b]	9.1	10.4	11.2	11.4	11.6	11.7	10.3			

[a] OECD, *Economic Outlook*, Table R17, June 1989.
[b] OECD, *Economic Outlook*, Table R18, June 1989.

succeed in finding it. Estimates of unemployment on this, or related, definitions for the United Kingdom are available from the population census every ten years, from the Labour Force Survey and from the General Household Survey annually since 1976.

Coincidentally the two measures of unemployment at the end of our period gave very much the same reading. The Labour Force Survey in Spring 1987 showed 2.87 million unemployed on the ILO/OECD definition compared with 2.95 benefit claimants. As it happened the total number of those who were claiming benefit, but not 'seeking work' on the international definition, was very similar to the number seeking work but not claiming benefit.

The census of 1971 (grossed up to the United Kingdom level) showed 1.03 million unemployed, and the census of 1981 showed 2.35 million, an increase of 1.32 millions. Over the same period the number of benefit claimants (on a constant definition) rose from 0.56 million to 1.93 million, an increase of 1.37 million. In this case two estimates of the *level* of unemployment do not match up so closely, but the two estimates of the *increase* over a ten-year period are roughly the same. Irrespective of the measure used, it seems that unemployment in 1981 was much higher than it had been a decade earlier.

For some periods the two definitions do show rather different movements from year to year. Table 16.1 above shows the annual movements from 1971–87.

The most marked divergences occur in the early 1980s. Search unemployment peaked in 1983 but claimant unemployment went on rising slightly for another three years. In 1985 and 1986 the claimant count was actually higher than the standard international definition of unemployment but, as we have seen, the two came into line again in 1987.

For some purposes one might prefer the claimant definition as a measure of unemployment. Clearly that provides the better index of unemployment as a call on public spending or as part of the 'dependency culture'. It may be that the claimant count also measures alienation from society better, but the concept is in any case a rather imprecise one. As a measure of the margin of slack in the economy, or the output wasted as a result of unemployment, the search-based numbers would be preferred.

The main message is the same form both series. Unemployment rose substantially during the 1970s, and very substantially indeed in the 1980s, standing at over 10 per cent for much of the decade. It seems as if there was excess supply of labour on a grand scale for much of that decade. Since the two series are measured independently, they reinforce one another. We turn next to other indicators of the pressure of demand in labour markets to see whether they confirm that message, or lead us to question it.

OTHER INDICES OF EXCESS SUPPLY OF LABOUR

Most indicators of economic activity follow a very similar cyclical pattern with closely corresponding peaks and troughs. It is relatively easy therefore to say of any year whether the pressure of demand was rising or falling. The cyclical pattern shown by the unemployment series is easy to confirm. Thus, in 1981 when unemployment rose so sharply, there was a fall in output and employment about the same time. In the labour market there was a sharp fall in vacancies, in overtime worked and in the proportion of firms who said that their output was limited by labour shortages.

It is much more difficult to make comparisons over a longer period of time. Yet the questions we would most like to answer are of this kind. Was the pressure of demand really so much lower in the mid-1980s than in the mid-1970s or the mid-1960s? As with unemployment itself there is always the suspicion that the meaning of any indicator series changes gradually over time. Nevertheless the evidence shown in table 16.2 is clearly relevant.

The number of vacancies at job centres was much the same in 1987 as in 1979, and not much lower than in 1974. This evidence seems to conflict fundamentally with that of the unemployment numbers. We know, however, that the proportion of total labour market turnover handled by the job centres rose during the 1970s, and presumably the ratio of vacancies in job centres to total vacancies rose as well. All one can say therefore is that the level of total vacancies at the end of the period probably indicated a considerably higher pressure of demand in the labour market than one would guess from looking at unemployment data above.

The data for overtime hours worked in manufacturing point to a similar conclusion, although again it is not a clearcut one. The rise in hours of overtime worked by manufacturing industry in the mid-1980s suggests that some kinds of labour may have been in short supply despite the high level of unemployment.

Perhaps the best evidence comes from the CBI Survey, which has the merit of distinguishing skilled labour from unskilled. Beginning in the aftermath of the 1973 cyclical peak there was widespread evidence in 1974 of excess demand for labour, even for unskilled labour. The pressure of

Table 16.2 *Indicators of United Kingdom labour market*

	Vacancies at job centres (000s)	Hours of overtime working in manufacturing industry (GB) million hrs per month	CBI Survey (Oct) % of firms limited by	
			Skilled labour	Other labour
1971	131	15.3	13	2
1972	147	16.0	13	3
1973	307	17.0	51	27
1974	298	16.4	34	15
1975	157	12.3	12	2
1976	122	14.0	15	3
1977	155	15.6	19	5
1978	210	15.5	27	5
1979	241	14.9	20	3
1980	134	<u>11.5</u>	4	1
1981	91	9.4	3	1
1982	114	9.9	3	0
1983	137	10.2	6	1
1984	150	11.4	8	1
1985	162	12.0	15	1
1986	188	11.7	12	1
1987	235	12.7	19	5

Sources: National Institute Economic Review, Economic Trends 1989. *Employment Gazette.*

demand was higher in the first year covered by this study than in any other. The peak in 1978 was far below that in 1973, and was followed by a very sharp fall during the 1980–81 recession. The recovery during the mid-1980s was slow, so that in 1987 the pressure of demand for labour was still below even the 1978 peak. (In fact the next peak came in 1988 at a level very similar to that of 1978.)

This is probably a more reliable account of the overall pressure of demand for labour than that presented by unemployment data on their own. The disadvantage of the CBI Survey lies in its limited coverage of the economy, in which manufacturing had a declining share. Its merit is that it comes very close to measuring directly the margin of slack as perceived by employers. If employers believe their output is constrained by the difficulty of recruiting or retaining labour even when unemployment is high, then unemployment cannot be a good indicator of unused labour resources.

Another point to emphasise, however, is that the pressure of demand for labour according to the CBI Survey was low for most of the period and much lower on average in the 1980s even than in the 1970s. The Survey could be taken to indicate full employment in 1973, and 1974, perhaps from 1977 to 1979 and possibly again in 1987. That still leaves nine out of the fourteen years covered by this study in which employment clearly was not full, if we take the Survey as our guide.

Table 16.3 *The growth of earnings* *Percentage increase*

	Wages and salaries per person employed	Consumer price index	Real wages and salaries per person employed
1972	12.4	6.3	5.7
1973	12.6	8.4	3.8
1974	17.8	16.7	1.0
1975	30.1	23.7	5.2
1976	13.0	15.9	−2.5
1977	10.4	14.9	−3.9
1978	13.6	9.1	4.1
1979	15.2	13.5	1.5
1980	19.4	16.3	2.6
1981	12.8	11.2	1.4
1982	8.9	8.8	0.0
1983	8.5	4.9	3.5
1984	5.8	5.1	0.7
1985	7.3	5.3	1.9
1986	8.0	4.4	3.4
1987	7.4	3.8	3.5

Sources: CSO, *Blue Book*, 1988 and 1982.

Another guide to the pressure of demand in labour markets may be the growth of earnings. Table 16.3 shows wages and salaries per person employed, the widest definition of average earnings in the economy as a whole. The third column of the table shows this series deflated by the contemporaneous value of the consumer price index to give a series for real earnings. (It is open to question whether a better deflator would be lagged prices, or possibly the price rise expected at the time the earnings increase was negotiated.) The series is slightly distorted by the loss of earnings resulting from strikes. This depresses the growth of earnings in 1974 and again in 1984, raising the growth rate in 1975 and 1985.

The very high pressure of demand for labour in the early 1970s is confirmed by the growth of real earnings from 1972–4 or 1975. The fall in real earnings in 1976 and 1977, however, must be associated with the operation of incomes policy in those years. Moreover, the catching up of real earnings in 1978 presumably owes something to the relaxation of incomes policy at that time. No doubt the severity of the successive phases of incomes policy owed something to the state of the labour market at the time when they were negotiated, but it would be perverse to give an account of wages and salaries in this period as if collective bargaining were unrestrained.

With no incomes policy in place to confuse the picture, one might expect wage movements after 1980 to be a better guide to the pressure of demand in the labour market. Remarkably, however, real wages (as measured in table 16.3) continued to rise right through the recession. This could be because price inflation was over-forecast, perhaps because the pressure of demand was even lower in product markets than it was in the market for labour. By the mid-1980s real wages were again rising above trend as had happened around previous cyclical peaks.

It is clear from table 16.3 that it is a far from straightforward matter to identify the level of unemployment at which inflation is constant, or at which the labour market is in equilibrium. No doubt the pressure of demand influences the relative bargaining strength of trade unions and employers and it may also be reflected in the wages offered by firms in industries which are not unionised. But it is unlikely that the level of unemployment is the only dimension of demand pressure that is relevant. Firms are most likely to concede large wage increases when their output is being held back by shortages of labour, a situation which could arise, as the CBI Survey suggests, even when total unemployment is high.

Estimation of the NAIRU or equilibrium level of unemployment depends on the existence of a stable relationship involving unemployment and the growth of real earnings. In practice econometric equations of this kind are not very reliable: they do not fit the data very closely and they tend to be revised rather frequently. This does not mean that NAIRU estimates are of no value, but it does mean that they are very imprecise. The underlying notion that demand pressure cannot be held above a maximum fixed by labour market structure is surely correct and salutary. But it seems that this maximum cannot be discovered for certain by any process other than trial and error. It was almost certainly exceeded in 1973, when demand pressure looked excessive on almost any measure. It may have been exceeded in 1979 or in 1987, but the evidence is far from conclusive.

SPECIAL EMPLOYMENT MEASURES

One reason for advocating special employment measures would be that they shift the natural rate of unemployment, or the NAIRU, to make a lower level of unemployment compatible with macroeconomic equilibrium. Starting in 1975, and continuing to 1987 and beyond, a remarkably large number of quite heterogeneous policy measures were introduced all designed with this end in mind. Since they were microeconomic rather than macroeconomic in character they will not be discussed in detail in this book. It is necessary nevertheless to devote a short section to them, if only because they operated on a sufficient scale to affect somewhat the interpretation of the unemployment numbers.

The need to do something about unemployment was uppermost in the minds of governments throughout the period covered by this study (even when they were doubtful whether there was much that they *could* do). They were aware of the political costs of inaction; in other words they wanted to be seen to be doing something. But there is no need to ascribe purely cynical motives to them; they were also acutely aware of the social damage that unemployment was doing. The wide variety of measures attempted, and the relatively short periods for which many of them were in operation, bear witness to the perplexity surrounding this whole area of policy. There was no coherent programme, just a series of expedients. Many of the measures were introduced hastily and some ran into problems of administration and accountability.

The underlying concern was to reduce unemployment without running into other macroeconomic constraints such as inflation, the balance of payments or the growth of public spending. The merits of the measures were actually assessed in terms of 'cost per job created', with little attention paid to the productivity of the work in question. As a result, some of the schemes came to be thought of as merely offering unemployment by another name, disguising the problem rather than solving it by creating real jobs.

The various schemes differed in their motivation and method of operation. Initially in the late 1970s the Temporary Employment Subsidy was introduced, as its name implies, as a means of keeping jobs open during what was still seen as temporary period of slack demand. Part of the idea was that subsiding labour would help some industries to compete more successfully in world markets. There was thus a protectionist element in the scheme, which led to hostility from the EEC, and eventually to its demise.

One alternative to an explicit job subsidy was to provide employment in the public sector, for example under the Community Programme and its various forerunners. The cost of unemployment benefit necessarily falls on the public sector, so the net cost to the taxpayer of putting the unemployed to work was relatively low. No doubt some useful work was done in the process, although there were persistent complaints that some of the jobs were a waste of time, like digging holes and filling them in again.

Some of the schemes were aimed specifically at unemployed young people, a group which attracted particular attention and sympathy. One reason for concentrating on them was that their years immediately after leaving school were thought likely to influence their attitude to work subsequently, that a vital opportunity might be lost for them to undertake training and gain work experience. The effective training content of schemes like the YTS, however, was widely criticised. It was even suggested that the schemes provided firms with a cheap way of employing young people in simple tasks as office juniors or errand boys, and replaced more effective training through more traditional apprenticeship schemes.

One of the most controversial issues with some of the schemes was the rate of pay. By the mid-1980s the overt purpose was to encourage employers to take on workers at lower rates of pay. Increasingly there was pressure on the unemployed to take a place on one of the schemes even if the net improvement of income relative to receiving social security benefit was very small. It was argued that pressure of this kind would help to reduce rates of pay for unskilled work of all kinds, thus creating more jobs.

In the early 1980s many on the fringes of the labour market, unable to find satisfactory employment, tried to make a living in self-employment by setting up as decorators, hairdressers and so on. This trend was encouraged by the Enterprise Allowance Scheme which supported for a year those of the unemployed who wanted to give self-employment a trial, and who could raise a minimum of capital.

Table 16.4 below gives the official figures for the total numbers in assisted employment schemes in each year. The numbers built up rapidly in the late 1970s and reached over 0.8 million by the end of 1980. They then fell back to around 0.6 million and stayed at about that level until 1986 when they again rose a little.

Before setting these figures alongside the time path of claimant unemployment, it is useful to distinguish the schemes which applied particularly to young people – since the claimant series now in use excludes all those under eighteen. The second column therefore shows the total of those covered by schemes other than the YTS and its forerunners, the Youth Employment Subsidy, the Community Industry Scheme and Training for Skills.

It is unlikely that any of the schemes actually reduced unemployment by as much as the numbers they assisted would indicate. When a job was saved by the Temporary Employment Subsidy, for example, it is quite likely that a job in a competing firm would be destroyed. A worker on the Community Programme might well, directly or indirectly, take the place of another worker in normal employment. Estimates were made at the time of these displacement effects, but there is no way of checking their accuracy.

Suppose, as a broad order of magnitude, that two-thirds of the assisted adult employment was an effective reduction in the claimant unemployed. In that case their effect at the end of 1980 was around 450,000. This would imply that, in the absence of special employment measures, unemployment would have been nearly 2.5 million instead of just over two million at that time. Subsequently the effects of special measures on *adult* unemployment decreased considerably; at the peak in 1986 when unemployment was 3.3 million, the effect of special employment measures was probably to reduce it by about 0.2 million.

Adjusting the figures to take account of these calculations would not alter greatly the shape of the unemployment series. The cyclical rise in the recession would be rather greater, and the long-term upward trend just a little more marked.

Relative to the scale of the unemployment problem, the special employment measures, taken as a group, were ineffective. Proposals to introduce similar measures on a much larger scale were rejected on the grounds of administrative infeasibility. They were cheap in terms of costs per job compared with a general cut in taxation or a general increase in spending,

Table 16.4 *Special employment measures*   *Thousands*

	Total assisted employment[a]	Excluding schemes designed for under 18-year olds[b]
end year		
1975	3	3
1976	166	159
1977	311	244
1978	255	171
1979	344	230
1980	828	670
1981	550	269
1982	643	231
1983	662	234
1984	661	249
1985	669	274
1986	735	355
1987	810	366

Source: Department of Employment Gazette.
[a] Includes Temporary Employment Subsidy, Temporary Short-time Worker Compensation Scheme, Small Firm Employment Subsidy, Training for Skills, Youth Employment Subsidy, Young Workers Scheme (later New Workers Scheme), Community Industry, Youth Training Scheme, (and its forerunners, Youth Opportunity Programme, Training Opportunities Scheme and Work Experience Programme), Community Programme (and Short-term Employment Programme, Job Creation Programme, Community Employment Programme), Employment Training (and Joint Training Scheme), Job Start Allowance, Job Release Scheme, Job Splitting Scheme, Enterprise Allowance Scheme and others.
[b] Excludes Youth Training Scheme and so on, Youth Employment Subsidy, Community Industry and Training for Skills.

but they needed imaginative planning, close supervision and the cooperation of private sector employers. To make a really major contribution to
reducing unemployment by this route would have involved intervening in
the running of individual industries or firms to an extent comparable with
that needed for a successful incomes policy. Such intervention was against
the philosophy of the Conservative governments after 1979, and might not
have been practicable under any government. Although understandable as
a response to an acute policy dilemma, the record of the special employment measures is not an encouraging one. They were no substitute for an
unconstrained use of more conventional macroeconomic policy levers.

THE TREND RISE IN UNEMPLOYMENT

It is clear from the discussion so far that the rise in unemployment from
under 3 per cent in 1974 to over 10 per cent in 1987 was not just due to a
fall in the pressure of demand for labour between the beginning and the
end of that period. It was not simply the same kind of phenomenon as the
rise in unemployment that occurs in every cyclical downturn. That does not

mean, however, that it owed nothing to macroeconomic policy, or the experience of demand pressure over the period from 1974–87 as a whole. In this section we shall look at alternative explanations of the upward trend in unemployment. In the following section we draw some conclusions about the consequences of macroeconomic policy and the sense in which unemployment was an outcome of it.

We have already mentioned the concept of the NAIRU (the non-accelerating inflation level of unemployment) and expressed some doubt as to the possibility of establishing its level at any point of time – which must make it difficult to use as a tool of historical description. If we were to adopt this approach we would have to recognise that anything which shifts either the supply or the demand for labour in relation to the real wage could also shift the sustainable level of unemployment. Thus a trend rise in unemployment might, on this reasoning, be accounted for by any number of events including some which seem rather remote causes – changes in the mix of taxation, for example, or in the relative price of imports. Some interesting historical analysis of this kind has been done using various models of the British economy. The approach adopted here, however, is more modest in its scope, concentrating on a limited number of factors which are likely to be of *direct* relevance to the unemployment trend.

Although most unemployment is rightly called involuntary, the numbers unemployed are likely to be influenced by the level of unemployment benefit provided, and by the way in which entitlement to benefit is interpreted. Table 16.5 below shows the rise in the rate of unemployment benefit relative to prices and to average earnings.

The record of average benefits paid is considerably more complicated than this table suggests. Many of the unemployed depend on supplementary benefit (renamed as income support) rather than on unemployment benefit from the national insurance fund. Some will have been eligible for an earnings related supplement based on their contribution record. However, the general picture is unchanged: the real value of benefits paid to the unemployed did not rise much between the early 1970s and the late 1980s, and relative to average earnings most benefit rates fell behind. The financial incentive to become unemployed, or to stay unemployed, did not change greatly over the period, but for most groups it was reduced. Obviously, then, the explanation of the trend rise in unemployment must be sought elsewhere.

The way in which the benefit system is administered must influence the number of claimants. In the late 1980s the rules were tightened up, particularly to ensure that claimants really were available for work; about the same time the long-term unemployed were given a new kind of interview, Restart, which showed that some could be reclassified as sick or retired, and others were given counselling that helped them to find jobs. The result was a fall in the number of claimants, particularly in 1987. This fall may have reversed a rise in the early 1980s when the administration of

Table 16.5 *Unemployment benefit rates*

		Rate per week for single man (£)	Retail price index	Average earnings[a] (GB)	Rate per week	
					at 1974 prices	at 1974 earnings[b]
Oct	1973	7.35	96	100	7.66	7.35
July	1974	8.60	109.7	116.3	7.84	7.39
April	1975	9.80	129.1	138.3	7.59	7.09
Nov	1975	11.10	144.2	152.4	7.70	7.28
Nov	1976	12.90	165.8	171.3	7.78	7.53
Nov	1977	14.70	187.4	188.7	7.84	7.79
Nov	1978	15.75	202.5	217.7	7.78	7.23
Nov	1979	18.50	237.7	257.0	7.78	7.20
Nov	1980	20.65	274.1	298.9	7.53	6.91
Nov	1981	22.50	306.9	332.9	7.33	6.76
Nov	1982	25.00	326.1	358.7	7.67	6.97
Nov	1983	27.05	341.9	388.0	7.91	6.97
Nov	1984	28.45	358.8	415.0	7.93	6.86
Nov	1985	30.45	378.4	447.3	8.05	6.81
July	1986	30.80	384.7	473.9	8.01	6.50
April	1987	31.45	401.6	502.3	7.83	6.26

Sources: Annual abstract of statistics 1989 and 1983, *Economic Trends*, 1989 and 1983.
[a] 1973–80 the 'older series' for production industries and some services, now discontinued (*Economic Trends*, 1983).
  1980–87 the 'new series' for the whole economy (*Economic Trends*, 1989).
[b] Deflated by the index of earnings in column 3.

benefits was relatively slack. It is doubtful, however, whether changes in the administration of benefits ever made much difference to the number of unemployed as recorded by the Labour Force Survey on the search-based definition.

A much more difficult question concerns the attitude of the unemployed themselves to work and to dependency. Some changes *can* be identified. In the 1970s for example students in large numbers began to 'sign on' to the unemployment register during the long university vacation. This in itself had little effect on the overall numbers but it may have been indicative of a more general wish to participate in the labour market and also of a more general willingness to classify oneself as unemployed when unable to find a job. (There may also have been a greater eagerness to claim all the benefits to which one was entitled, but that should not strictly add to the search-based measure of unemployment. The change, if there was one, seems to be confined to unemployment benefit. The numbers claiming sickness or invalidity benefit do not show a comparable upward trend.)

The difficulty with this argument is that the experience of unemployment is itself likely to change attitudes. In a town where half or more of the population is unemployed, obviously the social stigma attached to that condition must weaken or disappear. Those who are frustrated in their search for work, may begin to think – or at least to say – that they do not really want it after all. If work were actually on offer such attitudes might quickly be reversed. Unfortunately this is a case where no very persuasive evidence is available either for or against the explanation.

The upward trend in unemployment may be accounted for by an increase in mismatch of some other kind between the supply of labour and the demand for it. The term is a very broad one, however, covering almost any explanation other than an overall deficiency in the demand for labour, or an increased reluctance to work in any occupation at all. It embraces three quite different kinds of explanation, Mismatch could have increased because the nature of the demand for labour was changing more rapidly than in the past, or because the kind of labour available was changing, or thirdly because the process of allocation of labour to jobs had become less efficient.

The structure of the British economy, and hence the pattern of demand for labour, has changed continuously throughout modern times. In the postwar years major changes took place, yet full employment was maintained continuously for about two decades. The changes in the industrial composition of employment during the 1970s and 1980s was not out of line with what had gone before, but the pace of change in some cases speeded up. Probably the most significant change at the industrial level was the more rapid decline in the share of manufacturing in total employment: this was 37 per cent in 1969, 34½ per cent in 1974, 31 per cent in 1979, but only 23½ per cent in 1987. The very sharp fall in the early 1980s presented an unusually severe problem of adjustment.

Other changes in the composition of the demand for labour, which are impossible to quantify, may have been more important. Many of the technical advances of the postwar years were based on large-scale production, often replacing skilled hand-craftsmen by semi-skilled machine operators. As output rose rapidly higher levels of productivity were achieved at the same time as an expansion of employment and growth in real wages. In the 1970s and 1980s the technical advances more often involved replacing semi-skilled or unskilled labour by sophisticated machines, which needed only a few highly skilled craftsmen or technicians to maintain them.

The new jobs required a higher level of basic education than the old ones, yet the standards of secondary education in the United Kingdom were not rising. Some would argue that they actually fell in the 1960s and 1970s. More confidently one can say that the achievement of the average school-leaver in this country was below that in Continental Europe. As education became more important to employment prospects, the disadvantage of the United Kingdom mattered more. It was not just a question of finding jobs for new school-leavers, although that certainly contributed to the special problem of youth unemployment mentioned above; the existing labour force of all ages was relatively inflexible because vocational training had been narrowly confined to particular occupations and not built on a very good foundation of education at school.

The situation required a large-scale investment in training, as part of the process by which workers were transferred from one job to another, or even from one occupation to another. But firms did not, individually, have the incentive to pay for training, except that of a specialised kind, because they had no means of preventing workers from shifting employment as soon as the training was completed. Moreover, trainee pay in Britain was unusually high in relation to the pay of skilled workers. It is likely in addition that firms under immediate financial pressure, as in the recession years of the mid-1970s, and again in the early 1980s, simply cut training as a way of meeting their immediate need for profits or for solvency.

The pressure on the corporate sector had another significant effect on unemployment, simply by forcing firms to shed labour which was not immediately paying its way. There is always some 'disguised unemployment', consisting of workers who are no longer needed, but who have no jobs to go to. In the climate of the 1970s and 1980s firms could no longer afford so easily to keep them on. Faced with the real prospect of plant closures, or the failure of strike action, unions in declining industries had to concede more rational attitudes to manning. Part of the so-called productivity miracle of the 1980s consisted simply of transforming concealed unemployment within firms into measured unemployment at the job centres.

One way in which mismatch can be reduced is by changes in relative wages making it easier to preserve the old jobs and making the workers more willing to take the new jobs. For the first five years of our period adaptation of this kind was made more difficult by the form of national incomes policy in place, which might have been designed specifically to keep differentials unchanged. But even in the 1980s relative pay was still determined by custom and practice as much as by market forces. Regional pay differentials in particular were non-existent in many occupations, so that the real value of pay (taking account of house prices) was actually *lower* in regions where labour was scarce.

The most worrying of all the obstacles to adjustment, however, was the reluctance of employers to recruit the unemployed. This must have slowed down considerably the turnover of labour of all kinds, and it resulted in the building-up of a pool of long-term unemployed, who accounted for an increasing proportion of unemployment in total. The longer a person had been unemployed, irrespective of all other characteristics, the worse the chances of that person getting a job. In effect employers were using their unemployment history as a way of eliminating candidates for jobs for which in many cases they were in fact quite well suited. The problem does not seem to have occurred on the same scale in other countries where unemployment rose. It would have required vigorous action by government to offset it, perhaps by giving a generous subsidy to firms who recruited benefit claimants.

To summarise: the upward trend may have resulted from a shift of labour demand from old, often unskilled, to new, more skilled, occupations and from the failure of the labour market to adjust to the new situation. Firms were quicker to shed redundant labour than they had been in the past, reluctant to train and reluctant to recruit the unemployed. Relative wages were inflexible. In the next section we ask how these factors may have been affected by the pressure of demand and by the macroeconomic policies which influenced it.

UNEMPLOYMENT AS THE RESULT OF
MACROECONOMIC POLICY

The pressure of demand in the labour market was low, or very low, for most of the period with which we are concerned. Thus much of the unemployment that was experienced during the period has a straightforward explanation along familiar Keynesian lines. But at the end of the period, or shortly after, demand pressure was relatively high and various explanations have been suggested as to how that can be reconciled with the persistence of unemployment rates far higher than those of the two postwar decades. The question remains whether the experience of relatively long and deep recessions, much longer and deeper than the cyclical downturn of the 1950s and 1960s, accounts for the structural changes which caused the upward trend in unemployment.

There are many reasons why the experience of relatively high levels of unemployment may of itself increase the level of unemployment that is subsequently sustainable. The idea was much discussed in the latter part of the 1980s, under the name of hysteresis (Chapter 9 above). It is easy to identity a number of ways in which it could work. When the pressure of demand is low, migration between regions slows down, training effort is reduced, fixed investment is low. The point to emphasise, however, is that all these difficulties could in principle be overcome by a sustained period of relatively high demand. They imply that it may take some time for full employment to be restored after a long recession; they do not imply that the sustainable level of unemployment is raised for ever. For example the widespread scrapping of plant and equipment during the early 1980s resulted in a severe shortage of capacity at the peak of the next boom. As a result unemployment did not fall as far as in the late 1980s as it otherwise could have done. But the shortage of capacity could have been made good had demand been sustained at a high level for a few years.

Discussion of hysteresis has not distinguished carefully enough between changes that are reversible and those that are not. It is quite possible that some of the changes brought about by low demand pressure in the 1970s and 1980s would take decades to reverse, if indeed they could be reversed at all.

If firms believe that full employment will be maintained more or less continuously, because the government is committed to that as a policy objective, then they will not be quick to shed labour when output contracts. They will be willing to hoard labour through a recession they believe will be short so as to avoid the costs of firing and rehiring. This will reduce the amplitude of swings in unemployment and probably its average level as well. Confidence in the maintenance of full employment depends on experience more than on policy commitments. Thus the loss of such confidence in the 1970s and 1980s might again take decades of full employment to make good.

It may be, as suggested above, that many workers in the 1950s and 1960s were reluctant to become unemployed because it carried some sort of social stigma. This attitude had to change when unemployment became the only way of life possible in some communities. Such a change of attitudes could well be irreversible.

The best time to train workers is when they first enter the workforce. But training is often neglected during a recession. Thus workers who entered the labour force during the 1970s and 1980s may never make up for the training they missed. This effect would last until that generation reached retirement age, a period of up to forty years.

A rather similar but shorter-lived effect results from older workers becoming unemployed in the recession. They may have felt that retraining or moving home was simply not worthwhile for the sake of the few years of working life left to them. In any case some firms were unwilling to recruit workers over the age of about 55.

More generally workers who become unemployed are regarded as less employable and experience difficulty in competing for jobs with those in other employment. Potentially this could result in a large number of workers becoming more or less permanently unemployed merely as a result of their previous unemployment history. It is possible that a long period of excess demand for labour would overcome the reluctance of employers to try them out, but there is a risk that this damage too is irreversible.

Enough has been said to suggest that demand deficiency could account, directly or indirectly, for much of the unemployment experienced in the 1970s and 1980s. The part that has been characterised as Keynesian must be counted as a waste of resources and therefore unambiguously regrettable. The rise in the *sustainable* level of employment, even if it *was* caused by the experience of weak demand may, or may not, represent a further waste of resources. It could be argued in particular that transferring workers from concealed to open employment actually improves the efficiency of the economy and results in a better allocation of resources.

The long-term unemployed are unfortunate as individuals, but the loss of their contribution to output may not be very damaging to the prosperity of the nation as a whole. Their place in the labour force may be taken by those on the margin of participation. The case for maintaining full employment is a social or a moral one, rather than simply an economic one.

The account given of the rise in unemployment implies that microeconomic policies as well as demand management would have been necessary to tackle it effectively. More attention was needed in particular to education and training, issues which only became the focus of attention in the later years of the period. It might also have been better if the administration of benefits had been tightened up much earlier, when unemployment first began to rise strongly in the mid-1970s. A case could be made out that such microeconomic policies work best when the pressure of demand is reasonably high. More government effort would have gone into training in the earlier part of the period if employers had been crying out for skilled labour. Benefit offices could have been tougher on claimants earlier on if there was a reasonable expectation that by moving to another area, retraining, or accepting a lower wage, they would in fact be able to get a job.

All in all there is little reason to change our initial judgement that macroeconomic policy was a failure so far as the maintenance of full employment is concerned. To understand the reasons for that failure we must consider its other objectives, notably the maintenance of price stability.

17

INFLATION

The price level has no significance for economic well-being or productive efficiency. This is one of the axioms of classical economics, familiar for several centuries and based firmly on deductive reasoning. There is a fundamental dichotomy between real variables, like output or relative prices, and nominal variables measured in current pounds whether they are prices, asset stocks or flows of income. The nominal variables could in principle all change in proportion by a factor of many hundred, leaving all the real variables unchanged. Nevertheless inflation, the rate of increase of the price level, is regarded, almost universally, as damaging to economic performance, socially disruptive and unfair. The reduction of inflation, ideally its total elimination, was the top priority, the most urgent concern, of policymakers in Britain in almost every year of the 1970s and 1980s.

It is notoriously difficult to demonstrate the damage that inflation does. Table 17.1 ranks inflation and economic growth in 24 OECD countries from 1968–87. Far from demonstrating that inflation reduced growth, the ranking shows a positive correlation, although not one which is statistically very significant. The United Kingdom was in fact unusual in combining rather high inflation with slow growth. The positive association between the rankings depends rather on cases such as that of Switzerland, with exceptionally low inflation and exceptionally low growth, or Turkey, which is almost at the top of both leagues. Of course tabulations of this kind do not demonstrate that inflation is beneficial, or even that it is harmless; but they serve to emphasise the point that inflation is unpopular and undesirable in its own right, not because it can be shown to hold back economic development or reduce average standards of living.

The classical dichotomy between real and nominal variables may hold as a description of long-run equilibrium, but inflation can nevertheless have real effects over periods of many years. These effects are not quickly eliminated even if the rate of inflation stays high for so long that its continuation at a brisk rate is universally expected. The experience of Britain in the 1970s was not a hyperinflation, in which the use of money values has to be suspended, but neither was the rate of inflation effectively negligible. It was an intermediate case, a gradual and incomplete adjust-

Table 17.1 *Inflation and growth in OECD countries, 1968–87* *Average percentage rate*

	Inflation	(rank)[a]	Growth	(rank)[a]
United States	6.36	17	2.71	19
Japan	6.18	18	5.49	1
Germany	3.95	24	2.82	18
France	8.35	12	3.09	15
United Kingdom	9.91	9	2.22	22
Italy	11.39	7	3.20	11
Canada	6.93	16	4.06	5
Austria	5.04	22	3.15	13
Belgium	6.14	19	2.86	17
Denmark	8.23	13	2.53	20
Finland	8.86	10	3.82	8
Greece	14.69	4	4.04	6
Iceland	33.98	1	4.57	3
Ireland	11.35	8	3.11	14
Luxembourg	5.56	20	3.17	12
Netherlands	5.41	21	2.90	16
Norway	8.12	14	3.89	7
Portugal	17.17	3	4.18	4
Spain	12.10	5	3.66	9
Sweden	7.88	15	2.34	21
Switzerland	4.12	23	2.04	24
Turkey	31.02	2	4.83[b]	2
Australia	8.66	11	3.60	10
New Zealand	11.52	6	2.16	23

Source: Arithmetic average of annual rates in OECD *Economic Outlook*, December, 1988.
[a] Coefficient of rank correlation is 0.43 (Critical values are 0.34 at 5 per cent level or 0.49 at 1 per cent level).
[b] 1973–87.

ment such that inflation continued to influence real variables, and hence to distort them. We shall consider first the effects of inflation on the economy at large, and then more briefly its effects on individuals.

Inflation that is perfectly anticipated in every way, according to classical theory, will affect the real economy only by increasing the cost of holding money balances. The yield on all interest-bearing nominal assets and liabilities will rise by the full amount of inflation, with non-interest-bearing money as the only exception. This is sometimes regarded as a sort of taxation, transferring real income from money holders to the monetary authorities. The scale of this transfer, however, was in practice rather small. When inflation was at its peak (26.9 per cent) in Britain in 1975, the monetary base was about £6 billion, implying an inflation tax at the rate of £1.6 billion a year. This compares with central government receipts and spending that year of £36.6 billion.

Larger transfers between sectors of the economy took place because interest rates did not rise nearly enough to compensate for inflation.

Treasury bill yields averaged 11.3 per cent in 1974 and 10.9 per cent in 1975, compensating for less than half of the inflation that actually occurred. Later in the period inflation again rose over 20 per cent, with short-term interest rates at 16.5 per cent on average in 1979, falling to 13.6 per cent in 1980.

We have considered at some length in Part 4 above how interest rates were set by the monetary authorities. The rate of inflation was one influence on their decisions amongst many; their response to an increase in inflation being much less than point-for-point. No doubt other indicators to which they also responded, including the exchange rate, gave them added indirect sensitivity to inflation. But the total effect was such that interest rates were low or negative when inflation was high, positive and sometimes large when inflation was low. The relative inflexibility of nominal interest rates was not due to a failure to foresee continuing inflation, but to a failure to respond with sufficient vigour.

Monetary authorities in most countries behaved in the same fashion, and nominal interest rates worldwide showed the same inflexibility of response. The authorities were not blind to inflation; they thought, however, that high nominal interest rates would have a powerful deflationary effect on the economy even if the rate of inflation was higher still. Nominal rates high enough to compensate in full for inflation would have risked 'overkill' and an unacceptably high rate of bankruptcy.

One effect of negative real interest rates was to transfer resources from the private sector to the government. The interest-bearing liabilities of the public sector are about six and a half times the size of the monetary base. Even if interest rates compensate for a half or three-quarters of the inflation rate, the 'tax' on holders of public sector debt was a more significant element in public finance than the 'seignorage' of the Bank of England. Moreover the rise in nominal interest rates reduced the market value of debt outstanding. As we saw in Chapter 14 above, inflation helped to keep the public sector's balance sheet reasonably healthy despite years of heavy borrowing in the 1970s.

This was not the only macroeconomic effect of inflation. To a surprising extent the financial effects which can be estimated in equations to explain savings and investment behaviour relate to *nominal* interest rates. Thus higher inflation, because it raises *nominal* interest rates may have reduced investment, even though *real* interest rates became negative. The situation may be similar to that faced by the ordinary homeowner with a mortgage. Inflation adds to the value of his asset, but it does not immediately provide him with the cash to pay a higher rate of mortgage interest. In the 1970s at least, building societies and banks were still reluctant to lend more to borrowers who were finding it difficult to meet their interest commitments, even if the value of the house or the factory they had bought had in the meantime increased. This was one area where the effective indexation of contracts was slow to develop.

There is ample evidence that inflation increased the personal sector savings ratio in the 1970s. This does not mean, however, that it made more resources available for investment. The main effect was to compensate for the loss of the real value of financial assets, the counterpart of the transfer of resources from the private to the public sector.

When inflation is described as neutral, that is, perfectly anticipated and without real effect, it is assumed that prices and wages can be changed costlessly and continuously. This was not literally true in the period with which we are concerned. Many prices and wages were, by convention, set once a year after due deliberation or negotiation. With infrequent price changes there was always an element of luck in the setting of individual prices. If they compensated only for past movements in the general rate of inflation, then the prices that were adjusted less frequently would fall in real terms when the rate of inflation became faster. If price-setters tried to anticipate future movements in the general rate of inflation they would often make mistakes.

During the 1970s and early 1980s the share of profits in national income (excluding oil) tended to fall. One reason for this may have been that firms failed to anticipate the extent to which costs would rise when they set their prices. No doubt in time they would have learnt to forecast better and to abandon conventional ideas of the appropriate mark-up on lagged costs. But in the meantime the distribution of income would have been distorted in favour of labour and against capital. Whilst it was in operation prices and incomes policy may have reinforced this effect. If this is correct then inflation was clearly having an important effect on the distribution of income at a macroeconomic level, and hence on the distribution of expenditure as between consumption and investment.

These macroeconomic effects may have been significant, but they were not the reason for the unpopularity of inflation. People disliked inflation because it upset their personal finances, adding uncertainty to any long-term calculation, producing a feeling of insecurity, and for many people a feeling that they were being cheated.

During the 1970s and 1980s the coverage of inflation indexation became more and more widespread. Public servants had enjoyed the security of index-linked pensions for many years, and some private sector funds began to imitate the public sector, making use of the index-linked securities issued by the government with this particularly in mind. The paying of interest by banks even on current account deposits was rather slow to develop, as competition concentrated rather on the services which were provided free; but here too the process had gone some way by the mid-1980s. Life insurance and property insurances were natural candidates for indexation, being long-term contracts where the penalties for underprovision could be very serious for the individual. Eventually, by the 1980s, insurance companies were ready to offer the service that was called for.

When inflation was particularly brisk accountants began debating the correct form for indexed company balance sheets. It was a slow and troublesome business securing agreement. By the time that many firms had begun to adopt the new procedures in the mid-1980s, inflation was again in single figures. 'Current-cost accounting' came and went in a few years, but in the process much had been done to raise the awareness of company directors of the potential pitfalls in conventional accounts.

Even in the late 1980s the process of adaptation to continuing inflation was far from complete. The taxation system still distinguished between income and capital gains, treating the two quite differently. When nominal interest rates rose in response to inflation the resulting transfer was treated as income, and taxed accordingly, even though it was in fact inadequate even to compensate for inflation. Capital gains tax by contrast had been so much reduced by indexation that there was talk of its total abolition. Despite two decades of moderate to high inflation, and despite the development of high speed computers, money values still played a pivotal part in contracts of every kind. Hence inflation was still unpopular, unfair and potentially damaging.

The tenacity with which the system has resisted indexation paradoxically bears witness to the damage which inflation can do. The advantage of money values is so great, it seems, that for many purposes they are retained even when inflation makes them unreliable. Moreover, the more general indexation becomes, the less the resistance to inflation and hence the greater the risk of faster, or more unpredictable, inflation. In the limit, there would be no friction at all in the inflationary process and money would cease to exist. In the 1980s the world, including Britain, stepped back from this frightening prospect and decided to give priority to price stability – or at least to a rate of inflation that was low and predictable. This fitted in well with the conservative turn in economic policy of all kinds at that time.

INFLATION AND THE MONEY SUPPLY

The classical view of macroeconomic policy, or rather of monetary policy since that is always the term preferred, is that price stability is its one and only aim. Good government means sound money. The way in which price stability is achieved is quite simply by control of the money supply. This account of macroeconomic policy never corresponded to reality in the period with which we are concerned.

In classical economic theory real variables and nominal variables are determined independently. The nominal variables all move proportionately, driven by the growth rate of the money supply, which is set exogenously by the monetary authorities, or by the quantity of gold in circulation. The authorities can control the money supply directly if they control the mint and the central bank's printing press. Monetary policy consists of deciding how many bank notes to print, allowing for some

Table 17.2 *The growth of the money supply*   *Per cent year-on-year*

	Narrow money (Mo)	Broad money (M3)	Inflation (RPI)
1971	8.1	12.1	9.2
1972	6.3	24.4	7.5
1973	13.0	25.6	9.1
1974	11.8	16.0	15.9
1975	14.3	8.3	24.1
1976	10.8	6.6	16.6
1977	10.7	7.6	15.9
1978	15.0	15.8	8.2
1979	13.1	12.8	13.4
1980	8.4	15.6	18.0
1981	4.5	16.7	11.9
1982	0.9	12.3	8.6
1983	5.8	12.9	4.5
1984	5.5	9.0	5.0
1985	4.7	12.5	6.0
1986	4.0	19.2	3.4
1987	4.7	20.7	4.2
Average 1971–87	(8.3)	(14.6)	(10.7)

Source: Economic Trends, 1989.

growth in the real economy and for some variation in the velocity of circulation. This is the classical model, but it does not correspond to monetary policy as it has in fact been operated.

Even in the period from about 1978–81, when the control of the money supply was given most weight in the conduct of monetary policy, interest rates and public sector borrowing were still being set judgementally. The target path for the monetary aggregate was not truly exogenous: it was changed in the light of experience, drawing on the behaviour of many different variables both nominal and real. Even in those most monetarist of years, the conduct of policy would be better described as demand management with the emphasis on price stability as the most important goal.

Table 17.2 shows the growth of the money supply on two alternative definitions. Narrow money (Mo) consists mainly of notes and coin, whilst broad money (M3) includes most of the liabilities of the banking system. Numerous other definitions have been proposed, but these will serve as representatives. The pattern of growth year-by-year is very different for narrow and broad money. On average the growth rate of narrow money was below the rate of inflation, the growth rate of broad money well above. Moreover the periods of relatively rapid growth of the two aggregates do not correspond. The correlation between the growth rates shown in the first two columns of table 17.2 is actually *negative* (minus 0.1).

In the early 1970s, narrow money never signalled in advance the scale of the inflation to come. The peak growth rate was in 1975, coinciding with the peak in the rate of inflation, and not nearly so high. In the late 1970s narrow money peaked two years in advance of inflation, but again the peak was relatively low. In the 1980s the growth rates of both Mo and the retail price index slowed down, although not closely in line. The correlation of growth in Mo with inflation is positive, 0.6 contemporaneously or 0.8 if inflation lags two years behind monetary growth.

The movements in broad money are quite different. It grew very rapidly in 1972 and 1973 following the removal of quantitative limits on bank lending, and then slowed down quite abruptly when the 'corset' was put in place. From 1978–81, it reaccelerated, even though it was the main focus of monetary policy, when quantitative control of lending was again abandoned. After a period of rather slower growth in the mid-1980s, broad money again reaccelerated to over 20 per cent growth right at the end of the period.

The peak of broad money two years before the peak of inflation in 1975 looks impressive, but otherwise the association is not at all close. Contemporaneously the correlation of broad money growth with inflation is negative (minus 0.4), but thanks mainly to the episode of the early 1970s the correlation with a two-year lag is positive (plus 0.5).

In a later section we attempt an econometric explanation of inflation over these years, using the monetary aggregates amongst other variables. But from the crude calculation of correlations, or just by looking at the figures in the table above, it is clear that the movements of the monetary aggregates on their own do not provide a consistent or accurate means of forecasting inflation. As aids to demand management they may have some small contributions to make, but they do not provide clear or unambiguous signals. Those with a practical interest in forecasting or demand management became disillusioned with them in the 1980s and increasingly impatient with the more doctrinaire monetarists who went on insisting that they had discovered the philosophers' stone.

The weakness of the time-series relationship between money and prices does not, however, dispose of monetarism altogether, or of the classical economics on which it is based. It remains true that direct control of the money supply, however defined, could in principle be used as a means of controlling inflation, provided that inflation need not be controlled with precision. The difference between the classical view of how monetary policy should be conducted and the way in which monetary policy was in fact conducted in Britain at this time turns on two related administrative or political institutions.

First, there was no acceptable or reliable means of controlling the money supply directly. The SSD scheme, or 'corset'; came closest to providing direct monetary control, but it was always viewed as temporary, and unsatisfactory in many ways. Since the money supply was not controlled directly the authorities might just as well have targeted their judgemental policy adjustments on inflation itself. The constant references to the money supply, qualified with talk of its changing velocity, served only to confuse the relationship between policy action and its ultimate goal.

Secondly the choice of monetary targets, and implicitly of inflation objectives, was made year-by-year in an informal way by Treasury ministers. Although they made some precommitments to a decelerating path, those commitments were not treated as binding in the event. Thus each year at budget time, if not more often, a judgement was made of the monetary growth rate for the period ahead and of the extent to which overshooting in the past should be corrected. That judgement inevitably involved the choice between a higher or a lower pressure of demand. A priority had to be established between more full employment or more price stability, at least so far as the year ahead was concerned. Monetarism seems to avoid that painful choice, but it does so only if the growth rate of the money supply is set independently of all consideration of the current economic situation. What happened in the late 1970s was that the priority given to full employment was reduced, and the priority given to price stability was increased. Monetarism provided a more acceptable way of describing what was happening than the blunt description which would have been given by a Keynesian.

THE ANATOMY OF INFLATION

The most commonly-used measure of inflation is the increase in the retail price index. This index is designed to show the rise in the cost of living for a typical household, and it is used for a variety of purposes as the basis for indexation. But its movements from year to year are subject to a number of influences, which would not necessarily be regarded as part of the general rate of inflation. It is raised, for example, by increases in indirect taxation or the cost of mortgage finance. The general rate of inflation should perhaps summarise only those influences which are general to all prices, or indeed to all nominal variables – that is variables expressed in terms of pounds and pence. Such a general inflation measure, however, does not in fact exist.

Table 17.3 shows five different indices of prices and costs. All are taken from the national accounts, so they have a well-defined relationship to one another. Some special factors influencing particular indices in particular years can be identified by reading this table methodically from left to right.

The first column shows the increase in employment income per unit of output, roughly equal to the difference between the growth in earnings and of productivity. This series shows very marked peaks in 1975 and in 1980, both being years when productivity was falling and wages accelerating. The troughs of 1977 and 1983 are also exceptionally prominent, so this column has a more pronounced cyclical pattern than most of the others. Moving from the first to the second column takes account of the movements in profit margins (broadly defined to include rent and self-

Table 17.3 *Indices of costs and prices* *Percentage increase*

	Employment income per unit of output	Total home costs per unit	Price index of GDP	Price index for imports of goods and services	Price index of domestic expenditure	Consumer price index
1972	10.2	10.8	9.0	3.0	8.1	6.3
1973	6.5	7.2	6.5	23.1	8.8	8.4
1974	23.5	17.1	15.0	42.2	19.8	16.7
1975	31.3	27.1	26.9	14.0	24.7	23.7
1976	11.0	14.7	15.0	22.2	15.7	15.9
1977	7.2	12.1	13.8	14.0	13.3	14.9
1978	11.4	12.0	11.5	2.9	9.9	9.1
1979	13.8	13.0	14.3	8.7	14.1	13.5
1980	21.4	18.5	19.7	9.7	18.3	16.3
1981	9.7	10.2	11.4	7.9	11.3	11.2
1982	3.7	6.9	7.6	7.2	7.8	8.8
1983	3.0	5.6	5.1	7.7	5.0	4.9
1984	5.0	5.7	4.8	8.8	5.1	5.1
1985	3.7	5.1	5.6	4.0	5.3	5.3
1986	4.2	2.6	3.6	−3.8	4.7	4.4
1987	3.6	5.0	4.8	2.8	4.7	3.8

Source: CSO, *Blue Book*, 1988.

employment income). This does not change the overall shape of the series very much, but it smooths out all the peaks and troughs. Margins seem generally to be cut at the peak of the inflation cycle, and subsequently rebuilt. (Exceptional movements in margins may be associated with changes in oil prices, most notably the fall that took place in 1986.)

Between the second and third columns indirect taxes are added and subsidies are subtracted. In some years the adjustment is considerable: in the early 1970s fiscal policy was used in this way to moderate the rise in consumer prices; subsequently there were several years when the need to improve the public sector finances was seen as an overriding consideration. Consequentially there were frequent complaints that the government itself was causing inflation.

The fourth column is a price index for imports. In 1973 world commodity prices exploded, whilst in 1974 oil prices quadrupled. These both added greatly to the prices of goods sold in Britain, much less to the prices of home-produced goods. The fifth column is a price index for the goods and services sold in Britain, whether imported or home produced.

Finally, the last column shows the deflator for consumer spending in the national accounts, an index which moves quite closely in line with the retail prices index (except when the cost of mortgages changes). The peaks of this series are not quite so high in 1975 and 1980 as those in column five, partly because it excludes the prices attributed to the output of the public sector. The main point to emphasise however is the similarity between the first and the last columns, and indeed all the columns in between. Inflation is a general phenomenon, affecting almost all prices or costs; the choice of index does make a difference to the story in particular years, sometimes turning an acceleration into a deceleration, but in the longer run the main message is always the same.

It would be tempting to treat table 17.3 not just as an anatomy of inflation but as a physiology as well – as an explanation of the way the system works, not just a description of its component parts. If wages were exogenous, then, as the table shows, they would almost completely determine prices. The fact that wages are largely determined as the outcome of a bargaining process reflecting the relative strength of employers and employees gives some support to this notion. Inflation is said to result from a shift in power towards employees, or from an increase in the militancy of unions. The weakness of the argument is that both employers and employees clearly take account of the prospects for price inflation when they bargain over wages. The process is undoubtedly a circular one, so that it is impossible to break into it at the point of a wage increase, and describe that event as exogenous. Even when incomes policy was in effect during the 1970s the figures for the norm were not plucked out of the air; they were based on a view of the speed with which a deceleration of inflation could in practice be imposed.

If we take this dynamic view of inflation, then the significance of the differences that appear in the columns of table 17.3 may be greater than they appear at first sight. Thus the rise in import prices in 1973 and 1974 may have added only a few percentage points to the prices of domestic sales *directly* in 1973 and 1974. But the fact that they raised consumer prices will have led to pressure for higher wages, which in turn will have added to inflation. The repercussions could grow indefinitely, unless there is some inertia in the process of inflation, or unless policy action is taken to slow it down.

There is no way that the degree of inertia or the importance of different shocks can be judged from the data in the table above. In the next section we shall try to model the inflationary process, but only a very simplified version of it. Our aim will be to explain why the spiral speeds up or slows down, not to describe the mechanism that tends to perpetuate it.

THE CAUSES OF INFLATION IN THE UNITED KINGDOM

The proximate cause of a rise in prices may be a rise in wages or the costs of raw materials, but to trace inflation to its root we need to find out the underlying causes of increases in both costs and prices. Theory gives some guidance as to the sort of relationship we ought to be investigating. It suggests that the determination of real and nominal variables may be (at least approximately) independent of each other. Thus the root cause of the price level (and of inflation) should be the level (and growth rate) of some nominal variable.

Under a gold standard in a closed economy the growth of the money supply would be (more or less) exogenous – that is independent of movements in prices. If so, growth in the quantity of gold is unambiguously the root cause of inflation. Similarly, in a small open economy with a fixed exchange rate, the main underlying cause of inflation must be the rate of inflation overseas.

It is quite possible to argue, however, that in practice there *is* no single root cause of this kind. If the money supply and the exchange rate both change to accommodate price increases then there may be no anchor to the price level at all. The rate of inflation at any point in time will depend only on what it has been in the past, and on the succession of impacts to which it has been subjected. In the 1950s and 1960s it is reasonable to treat inflation in the world economy as the main root cause of inflation in the United Kingdom. The purpose of this section is to see what nominal anchor, if any, was applied to inflation in this country in the 1970s and 1980s.

One view, already presented above, is that the behaviour of the monetary authorities is the root cause of inflation: that, by setting the growth rate of the stock of money, they determine how fast prices will rise. In this section some simple econometric equations based on that view will be presented. We shall *assume* for the sake of argument that the money supply is exogenous. As the earlier discussion has already suggested, these equations are not very successful as explanations of inflation. An alternative view will also be considered, that the root cause of inflation in this country is inflation abroad. Equations will be estimated to explore the way in which price rises here respond to those abroad, and to investigate the role played by the exchange rate. It is a familiar proposition that a small country imports the inflation rate of the world around it, if its exchange rate is held fixed. Perhaps a relationship still survives even when exchange rates are being determined by market forces.

The equations in Box 1 relate prices to the wide definition of the money supply, $M3$, using quarterly data for the period 1970–87. As equation (1) shows the coefficient on the money supply is actually negative, if it is unlagged and if a time trend is included. It becomes positive if the money supply is lagged two years as equation (2) shows. It becomes close to unity, which is the number that monetarist theory requires, if in addition a shift dummy is introduced to distinguish the period after the 1979 election. However, the relationship is totally changed if an index of world prices is added to it, as for example in equation (4). The coefficient on world prices is just over unity, whilst that on $M3$ is again negative, even though it is lagged two years. Some results using changes, or growth rates, instead of levels, are given as equations (5) and (6).

Obviously this is not an exhaustive test of the hypothesis that M3 is the cause of inflation (and we must remember that the exogeneity of M3 is

Box 1   *M3 1970(Q1)–1987(Q4)*

(1) $P = 7.089 +$ $0.04TIME -$ $0.473M3$ R^2 0.971 DF 0.869 DW 0.021
                  (6.52)   (2.34) SE 0.099 ADF −1.813

(2) $P = -4.100 +$ $0.003TIME +$ $0.742\,M3_{-8}$ R^2 0.975 DF 0.596 DW 0.035
                  (0.59)   (4.13) SE 0.091 ADF −0.889

(3) $P = -7.200 -$ $0.012TIME +$ $1.094\,M3_{-8}$ R^2 0.982 DF 1.643 DW 0.168
                  (2.10)   (6.49) SE 0.079 ADF −1.402
         $+0.208C$
         (5.12)

(4) $P = -0.108 +$ $0.011TIME -$ $0.101M3_{-8}$ R^2 0.995 DF −1.696 DW 0.163
                  (3.94)   (1.03) SE 0.042 ADF −2.369
         $+ 1.1495\,WP$
         (16.02)

(5) $\Delta P = 0.025 -$ $0.203\Delta M3 +$ $0.427\Delta WP$ R^2 0.355 DF −4.354 DW 0.857
                  (2.89)   (5.18) SE 0.011 ADF −2.492

(6) $\Delta P = 0.014 +$ $0.142\Delta M3_{-8} +$ $0.396\Delta WP$ R^2 0.315 DF −4.17 DW 0.801
                  (1.95)   (4.48) SE 0.012 ADF −2.41

P = CPI
WP = World price of manufactures in effective currency terms
Δ = Quarterly change
C = Shift dummy, 1 from 1979(Q2)
All values in logs (t statistics in parentheses)

assumed throughout). The results suggest however that any apparent empirical success of the hypothesis rests on the choice of a particular lag length, and on the exclusion of world prices as an additional independent variable. A narrow aggregate Mo fares rather better in a similar test, as can be seen in Box 2. In a simple regression, equation (1), of the level of prices on Mo together with a time trend, the coefficient is almost exactly unity. Adding world prices leaves Mo with a large and significant coefficient, but the coefficient on world prices is large and significant as well – see equation (2). Equation (5) shows that world prices on their own would have a coefficient a little in excess of unity and the equation has a standard error marginally lower than that of equation (1). The suggestion seems to be that *both* domestic and world variables influence the rate of inflation, a result intermediate between those expected for a fixed and a floating exchange rate system.

Static equations of the kind presented so far are perhaps too crude for the subtle distinctions we are concerned to make. The short-run response of inflation to world inflation or the growth of the money supply is likely to be smaller than the long-run response. The speed of response to the two

---

Box 2   *Mo 1970(Q1)–1987(Q4)*

(1) $P = -5.598 + \underset{(4.23)}{0.005TIME} + \underset{(17.55)}{1.032Mo}$ $R^2\ 0.994$ $DF\ -1.362$ $DW\ 0.130$
                                                                   $SE\ 0.044$ $ADF\ -2.131$

(2) $P = -3.762 + \underset{(5.15)}{0.005TIME} + \underset{(7.73)}{0.551Mo}$ $R^2\ 0.997$ $DF\ -1.946$ $DW\ 0.187$
     $+\underset{(8.32)}{0.633\,WP}$ $SE\ 0.031$ $ADF\ -2.772$

(3) $\Delta P = 0.016 + \underset{(3.41)}{0.402\Delta Mo}$ $R^2\ 0.142$ $DF\ -3.884$ $DW\ 0.719$
                                                                   $SE\ 0.013$ $ADF\ -2.051$

(4) $\Delta P = 0.013 + \underset{(2.40)}{0.263\Delta Mo} + \underset{(4.44)}{0.387\Delta WP}$ $R^2\ 0.333$ $DF\ -4.680$ $DW\ 0.963$
                                                                   $SE\ 0.012$ $ADF\ -2.626$

World prices 1970(Q1)–1987(Q4)

(5) $P = -0.818 + \underset{(18.32)}{1.110WP} + \underset{(7.58)}{0.008TIME}$ $R^2\ 0.995$ $DF\ -1.644$ $DW\ 0.152$
                                                                   $SE\ 0.042$ $ADF\ -2.286$

(6) $\Delta P = 0.018 + \underset{(5.18)}{0.447\Delta WP}$ $R^2\ 0.277$ $DF\ -4.056$ $DW\ 0.762$
                                                                   $SE\ 0.012$ $ADF\ -2.427$

P = CPI
WP = World manufacturing prices
All values in logs (t statistics in parentheses)

---

variables may be different. To investigate this a general dynamic equation was estimated, which simplified to give:

$$\Delta^2 P = 0.003 - 0.0002t - \underset{(3.2)}{0.33\Delta^2 WP_{-1}} - \underset{(1.7)}{0.17\Delta^2 WP_{-2}} - \underset{(1.6)}{0.14\Delta^2 WP_{-3}}$$

$$-\underset{(2.0)}{0.16\Delta^2 WP_{-4}} - \underset{(2.0)}{0.16\Delta^2 Mo_{-1}} - \underset{(2.0)}{0.13\Delta^2 Mo_{-3}} - \underset{(6.3)}{0.678\Delta P_{-1}}$$

$$+\underset{(4.5)}{0.489\Delta WP_{-1}} + \underset{(3.9)}{0.359\Delta Mo_{-1}}$$

$\bar{R}^2$ = 0.42
DW = 1.94

Data period 1970(Q4)–1987(Q4)

The short-run coefficients on world price inflation and on the growth of the narrow money supply are 0.16 and 0.20 respectively, whilst the long-run coefficients are 0.72 and 0.53 – not very different in fact from those shown in this static equation for the *level* of prices, equation (2) in Box 2.

This dynamic equation can be elaborated in all sorts of ways, subject only to the limitations of a short run of data. Additional terms can be added to take account of changes in indirect taxes and subsidies, but this does little to change the estimated responses to world inflation or to the money supply in the long run. The same is true if the *change* in capacity utilisation is included. The coefficient on this variable implies that a rising rate of capacity utilisation is associated with a *lower* rate of inflation. This apparently perverse result could be due to the association of a rising pressure of demand with increasing productivity at least in the short term.

The coefficients from a very general specification along these lines are tabulated in the first column of table 17.4. A simplification to eliminate small and insignificant coefficients could raise R^2 to 0.56 without changing the properties of the equation greatly. At this stage the place of the growth of the narrow money supply alongside world inflation as a root cause of United Kingdom inflation seems secure.

The second column of table 17.4 shows the effects of adding the *level* of capacity utilisation to this general specification. The fit of the equation is somewhat improved. The extra coefficient implies a long-run relationship, such that a higher *level* of capacity use is associated in this sample period with higher inflation. (The variable CU measures the proportion of firms in the CBI Survey reporting that they have some spare capacity, so as capacity utilisation rises this index falls.) The coefficient on Mo in the long-term solution is now negative and insignificant.

The natural conclusion to draw is that, in this sample period at least, the narrow money supply seems to have a significant effect on inflation only because its movements are associated with changes in the pressure of demand. Apart from that association the money supply contains no relevant information. This leaves open the possibility that the money supply has an effect, alongside other variables, on the pressure of demand, and would qualify for that reason as a cause of inflation. In that case, however, its effect would be confined to generating cyclical variations in the real economy. It would not be functioning as a nominal anchor.

The suggestion of a long-run relationship between the pressure of demand and the rate of inflation may seem like an attempt to resurrect the Phillips curve of the 1950s. That relationship, which seemed to fit the data, proved entirely unreliable when applied in the late 1960s or subsequently. No claim is being made in this study that a stable trade-off exists between inflation and unemployment. On the contrary it is argued elsewhere in this book that the nature of the trade-off depends on the way in which monetary policy is conducted, and a host of other things. Nevertheless an equation such as this provides an estimate of what the relationship was between inflation and the pressure of demand on average over a particular period of time, given the policies that were actually followed. The values of the coefficients indicate that, other things being equal, the range of variation in capacity utilisation between a high pressure of demand in 1979 and a low pressure of demand in 1981 would account for a difference in

Table 17.4 *Price equations with and without capacity utilisation*
(Coefficients with t-statistics in parentheses)

	Dependent variable is $\Delta^2 P$ Data $1971(Q1)$–$1987(Q4)$	
Constant	0.0012	0.0120
Time	+0.00002	−0.00003
$\Delta^2 P_{-1}$	−0.13 (0.59)	−0.27 (1.23)
$\Delta^2 P_{-2}$	−0.08 (0.43)	−0.37 (1.64)
$\Delta^2 P_{-3}$	−0.08 (0.55)	−0.30 (1.70)
$\Delta^2 P_{-4}$	+0.08 (0.60)	−0.08 (0.56)
$\Delta^2 WP$	0.00 (0.03)	+0.16 (1.28)
$\Delta^2 WP_{-1}$	−0.22 (1.47)	−0.29 (1.94)
$\Delta^2 WP_{-2}$	+0.02 (0.14)	−0.08 (0.54)
$\Delta^2 WP_{-3}$	−0.02 (0.17)	−0.11 (0.84)
$\Delta^2 WP_{-4}$	−0.19 (1.79)	−0.19 (1.91)
$\Delta^2 Mo$	+0.07 (0.72)	+0.03 (0.34)
$\Delta^2 Mo_{-1}$	−0.13 (0.81)	+0.02 (0.10)
$\Delta^2 Mo_{-2}$	−0.10 (0.09)	+0.08 (0.54)
$\Delta^2 Mo_{-3}$	−0.18 (1.15)	−0.01 (0.06)
$\Delta^2 Mo_{-4}$	+0.03 (0.24)	+0.15 (1.16)
$\Delta^2 TAX$	+0.06 (1.82)	+0.08 (2.44)
$\Delta^2 TAX_{-1}$	+0.07 (1.00)	+0.05 (0.75)
$\Delta^2 TAX_{-2}$	+0.08 (1.38)	+0.08 (1.45)
$\Delta^2 TAX_{-3}$	+0.07 (1.56)	+0.06 (1.46)
$\Delta^2 TAX_{-4}$	+0.01 (0.46)	+0.01 (0.36)
$\Delta^2 CU$	+0.01 (1.74)	+0.00 (0.85)
$\Delta^2 CU_{-1}$	−0.01 (1.14)	−0.01 (1.83)
$\Delta^2 CU_{-2}$	−0.01 (1.68)	−0.01 (2.31)
$\Delta^2 CU_{-3}$	−0.01 (2.55)	−0.02 (3.08)
$\Delta^2 CU_{-4}$	−0.01 (2.97)	0.01 (3.27)
ΔP_{-1}	−0.785 (3.61)	−0.722 (3.42)
ΔWP_{-1}	+0.543 (3.48)	+0.751 (4.13)
ΔMO_{-1}	+0.412 (2.59)	−0.113 (0.53)
ΔTAX_{-1}	+0.022 (0.26)	+0.096 (1.08)
ΔCU_{-1}	+0.015 (1.47)	+0.019 (1.98)
CU_{-1}	—	−0.0037 (2.02)
R^2	0.47	0.51

Notes:
P is the consumer prices index
WP is world prices of manufacturing
Mo is a narrow monetary aggregate
TAX is the ratio of the factor cost adjustment to GDP at current prices
CU is the CBI index of spare capacity

the rate of inflation of about 8 percentage points. The implication is that, within a given policy regime, demand management could have a very considerable impact on inflation.

A variety of equations was estimated in an attempt to identify the effects of incomes policy on inflation. The periods in which incomes policy was assumed to be in operation were 1972 (Q4) – 1974 (Q3), and 1975 (Q3) – 1978 (Q3), thus excluding both the social contract period under the Wilson government and the Winter of Discontent at the end of the Callaghan government. One of the equations estimated is shown below. The variable Z is equal to unity when incomes policy is in operation, and otherwise to zero. It is introduced multiplicatively so that the coefficients of the long-run relationship determining inflation can vary between policy-on and policy-off periods. Initially such multiplicative terms were attached to all the short-run adjustment terms as well as the terms describing the long-run equilibrium, but most of them were dropped during the process of simplification.

$$\Delta^2 P = [\text{various terms in second differences}] - 0.73\Delta P_{-1}$$
$$(4.1)$$

$$+ \; 0.39 \, Z.\Delta P_{-1} + 0.74\Delta WP_{-1} - 0.20 \, Z.\Delta WP_{-1} + 0.21\Delta Mo_{-1}$$
$$(2.1) \qquad\qquad (4.8) \qquad\qquad (1.2) \qquad\qquad (2.8)$$

$$+ \; 0.12\Delta TAX_{-1} + 0.02\Delta CU_{-1} - 0.004CU_{-1} - 0.005Z.CU_{-1}$$
$$(2.9) \qquad\qquad (2.9) \qquad\qquad (3.6) \qquad\qquad (2.1)$$

$R^2 = 0.63$
$DW = 1.7$
Data period 1970(Q4) – 1987(Q4)

The coefficient on ΔP_{-1} is considerably reduced during the incomes-policy periods, implying that inflation adjusted more slowly to economic conditions. That result is in line with expectations: the setting of a norm, based as it must be on recent experience of inflation, could well introduce inertia into labour market adjustment. The long-run coefficients on all the variables in the equation are increased, suggesting that incomes policy is a means of modifying the process of adjustment, not a way of avoiding the need for it. In particular the long-run trade-off with capacity utilisation seems to be *steeper* during incomes-policy periods, although too much importance should not be attached to detailed results of this kind. In some separate exercises a term was introduced modifying the constant in the regression during incomes-policy periods. Statistically the coefficient was never significant and its value was dependent on the other variables included in the regression. A typical result was that, all other things being equal, incomes policy reduced the rate of inflation by one or two percentage points.

Most modelbuilders now ignore incomes policy altogether when estimating structural models of prices or of wages. This may be inevitable given the shortage of observations. It presupposes, however, that incomes policy was a veil behind which labour market adjustment took place much as it always has done – a view which is difficult to reconcile with the history of the 1970s. Our own experience in this study suggests that taking special account of incomes policy effects does modify the results obtained for the period as a whole. Nevertheless, for the rest of this section, we shall adopt the usual practice and sweep the problem to one side.

The equation in the second column of table 17.4 can be simplified by dropping insignificant coefficients, including the one of the money supply. The long-run response of domestic to world inflation is then found to be greater than one-for-one. This is in line with the results from the static equations reported earlier, such as equation (5), in Box 2.

Two explanations could be offered for a long-run coefficient different from unity. The first would be based on the behaviour of the exchange rate. Under a fixed exchange rate system inflation at home should in theory respond in proportion to inflation abroad, all other things being equal. The foreign price level should be the nominal anchor of the system. It is possible, however, that inflation abroad might cause the sterling exchange rate to *fall*, thus amplifying the impetus to import prices and hence to domestic inflation. This rather surprising result could happen because of different monetary policy rules at home and abroad. If the response to inflation overseas was to tighten monetary policy and raise interest rates, the sterling exchange rate would probably fall in the absence of a similar tightening of policy in the United Kingdom.

It is interesting therefore to see what happens to the relationship between domestic and world inflation if the exchange rate (with a lag) is included as an explanatory variable. Experiments of this sort were tried, in combination with a variety of other explanatory variables. The coefficients on the exchange rate in the short run, and also in the long run, were always small and often statistically insignificant. For example adding the exchange rate to world prices and Mo produced the following result:

$$\Delta^2 P = 0.002 - 0.0002t - \underset{(3.4)}{0.35\Delta^2 WP_{-1}} - \underset{(1.9)}{0.19\Delta^2 WP_{-2}} - \underset{(1.4)}{0.12\Delta WP_{-3}}$$

$$- \underset{(2.0)}{0.16\Delta^2 WP_{-4}} - \underset{(1.9)}{0.16\Delta^2 Mo_{-1}} - \underset{(2.3)}{0.15\Delta^2 Mo_{-3}} + \underset{(1.5)}{0.04\Delta EX_{-1}} - \underset{(6.4)}{0.683\Delta P_{-1}}$$

$$+ \underset{(4.6)}{0.500\Delta WP_{-1}} + \underset{(3.9)}{0.367\Delta Mo_{-1}} - \underset{(1.1)}{0.035\Delta EX_{-1}}$$

$R^2 = 0.43$
$DW = 1.9$
Data period 1970(Q4) − 1987(Q4)
EX = Effective exchange rate

The exchange rate adds almost nothing to the explanation of inflation already given by the equation on page 275 above. Its coefficient in the short run has the wrong sign, and its coefficient in the long run is less than a tenth that of foreign prices. The conclusion seems to be that world inflation influences United Kingdom inflation by some route that does not involve the exchange rate. In other words United Kingdom inflation is related to foreign inflation in foreign currency terms, rather than after conversion into terms of sterling. It is as if firms in the United Kingdom for example, raise their prices in line with the *dollar* price of American goods, not with their sterling equivalent.

The second explanation of the estimated coefficients on overseas inflation in excess of unity is that similar circumstances in different countries produce different degrees of inflationary pressure. The regression estimates cannot distinguish between two different circumstances: between a causal connection linking inflation at home to inflation overseas, and a connection linking inflation, both domestic and foreign, to some other variable not included in the data set. An obvious possibility is that both world and United Kingdom prices are being driven by commodity prices and the price of crude oil. However, if these variables are included in the equation they do not change the coefficient on world prices of manufactures. It looks as if some other relationship is involved.

The time path of inflation through the 1970s and 1980s is indeed very similar for most of the major OECD countries. The table below shows the correlation coefficients for annual United Kingdom inflation with inflation in other countries over the period 1969–88 (using data from the OECD *Economic Outlook* statistical appendix.)

Correlation of United Kingdom inflation with:

United States	0.74
Japan	0.65
Germany	0.66
France	0.73
Italy	0.75
Canada	0.72
Minor OECD	0.77

Using the same data and regressing United Kingdom inflation on total OECD inflation gives:

$$UK\,Inf = -1.23 + 1.55\,OECD\,Inf$$

$R^2 = 0.76$
$DW = 1.5$

In this equation much of the variation in United Kingdom inflation can be explained as a reflection or amplification of inflation abroad. This suggests that a search for the root causes of inflation in this country must include a study of *world* inflation – a study which can be pursued no further in this book.

These investigations suggest that the idea of a single root cause of inflation, a single nominal anchor for the system, is not really applicable to the United Kingdom over this period. The simple relationship between money and prices (even when Mo is used rather than $£M3$) turns out to be illusory. (Moreover the exogeneity of the money supply over this period is implausible.) The world price level did not play the role of nominal anchor either, in that the estimated United Kingdom response to world inflation was more than proportionate. The correlation we observe may be due to common causes influencing inflation in all the major industrial countries, rather than due to the effects of world inflation on this country. In the absence of a nominal anchor the rate of inflation must be seen as the consequence of its own past values, the summation in effect of a series of shocks impacting on the process of cost and price increase. The role of exchange rate changes has not been successfully identified in this section, and our results here are at variance with those in other sections which use the National Institute Model. Nevertheless, some of the impacts on inflation can be identified: changes in world prices, changes in indirect taxes and changes in the pressure of demand for example. The last of these is especially important to macroeconomic policy as it lies at the heart of the problem of reconciling price stability with full employment.

18

OUTPUT GROWTH

ECONOMIC GROWTH AS A POLICY
OBJECTIVE

Economic welfare, as commonly understood, consists in the main of the consumption of goods and services rather than any enjoyment that goes with producing them. In that sense production is a means to an end, rather than something to be undertaken for its own sake. Much the same could be said of economic growth as an objective of government policy: it is a means to the end of raising living standards. The volume of gross domestic product is not (for this reason and for others) a satisfactory index of policy success or failure. These familiar points have some relevance to the important issue of the contribution which macroeconomic policy in particular might make to economic welfare by accelerating the process of growth.

Macroeconomic policy influences aggregate demand, and incidentally the composition of demand, but it does not directly influence aggregate supply. If changes in taxation and in public spending or in interest rates do have supply-side effects they become, to that extent, instruments of microeconomic rather than macroeconomic policy. All this is just a matter of terminology. The important questions concern the way in which aggregate demand and aggregate supply interact to determine output.

In the short term variations in the level of output are closely associated with movements in various measures of capacity utilisation. There is little doubt therefore that, over the trade cycle, output responds to demand. Equally there is evidence that the traditional instruments of demand management do influence output over a horizon of a year or more. The much more difficult questions concern the determination of output in the medium to long term. On this empirical evidence is relatively sparse, and one must give more weight to purely theoretical reasoning.

The notion of 'capacity' implies that the sustainable level of production in the economy as a whole can be deduced from the size of the capital stock and of the labour force in much the same way as it is for a single manufacturing plant. This is a useful simplification, although it is subject to many qualifications. It suggests that an increase in demand will raise output in the long run only to the extent that it raises either the size of the labour force or the size of the capital stock. If it has no effect on either factor of production (or the efficiency with which they are used) its influence on output is necessarily short-lived. If we were considering the output of a single firm or industry that would not be a reason for denying the influence of demand on output; a particular firm whose product is in demand can bid resources of capital and labour away from other uses. But how can this argument be applied at the level of the total national economy?

In the case of labour, an increase in demand for aggregate output may bid resources away from the enjoyment of leisure. In other words a higher pressure of demand in the labour market may increase participation rates. If so a higher level of aggregate demand will indeed raise output even in the very long term. We might question however to what extent such an increase in output constitutes an increase in economic welfare. Certainly the effect on gross domestic product will exaggerate the improvement, since it will ignore altogether the value of the leisure, or 'household production', that is foregone. A higher level of demand, if it is expected to persist, might also increase the total size of the capital stock. But, in a closed economy, if we make the strong assumption that possibilities for production now and in the future are given, increasing the rate of investment is not in general a way of raising economic welfare.

It seems from this purely theoretical argument as if there is very little that macroeconomic policy can contribute towards the objective of raising living standards. There are nevertheless several arguments suggesting that economic growth will either be promoted or held back by running the economy close to the limits of capacity. They are, in the main, arguments based on the interpretation of particular periods of history, not arguments at the very high level of abstraction which has characterised this section so far.

A high pressure of demand, for example the period of full employment in Britain for a generation after the war, could be *bad* for growth for the following reasons: firms become complacent if they think that there will always be demand for their products and do not bother to innovate; if there is no margin of slack, industry will be slow to respond to new markets; the export market will be ignored if the home market is always buoyant. More often the argument turns on the special position of trade unions: full employment, especially guaranteed full employment, encourages aggressive wage bargaining; if real wages rise too fast firms will be progressively driven out of business by foreign competition; the bargaining power of unions is higher when demand is buoyant and they may use that power to slow down innovation if it is against their members' interests.

Almost exactly the opposite arguments are also heard: when demand is buoyant firms have the incentive to innovate and invest; labour and capital respond better to the carrot than the stick and are therefore more mobile when the pressure of demand is high; unions are likely to be more co-operative if reorganisation of production does not mean the loss of jobs; rising real wages give firms the incentive to raise productivity; and so on.

Behind all these arguments, those for full employment and those against, is the assumption that growth is held back or accelerated mainly by the attitudes of management and labour, their willingness to accept change or to take risks. We are not now talking about increasing the resources of labour and capital, but rather of using existing resources more efficiently, overcoming inertia or conservatism.

The period of history covered by this study provides a good opportunity to distinguish between rival views of the relationship between the pressure of demand and growth. From the mid-1970s to the mid-1980s the pressure of demand in Britain was held relatively low. Did that reduce the sustainable growth rate of output, or increase it? If it ultimately increased it, did it do so on such a scale as to offset the cumulated value of all the output foregone by leaving resources idle, and workers unemployed? The question will be addressed in the sections which follow using both time series and cross-industry data.

THE ANATOMY OF ECONOMIC GROWTH

The measurement of output is governed by a set of conventions agreed by national income statisticians to make their job feasible. The volume of gross domestic product is an index number derived by adding up measures of the physical output of all industrial activities using weights that represent their relative market prices. Difficulties, both conceptual and practical, abound. New products are invented, existing products change in quality; for many service activities it may be well-nigh impossible to identify physical units of output at all; for public sector output there is no market price. Nevertheless the figures for gross domestic product are indispensable to any discussion of economic growth. They are the only benchmark we have.

Table 18.1 shows the growth rate of output since the 1950s, the periods being chosen to match the pattern of the trade cycle. From 1951–73 the trend growth rate of output was about 2½–3 per cent a year. At the time this was regarded as far from satisfactory. It was faster than prewar growth rates, but on the other hand it was slower than the rates being achieved in other advanced industrial countries.

After 1973 the growth rate was much reduced. In the latter part of the 1970s it was less than 1½ per cent a year, under 1 per cent a year if North Sea oil and gas production is excluded. The last period shown in the table, 1979–87, is longer than the others and includes both the recession years when output actually fell and the subsequent years of recovery. Moreover, 1987 was not a cyclical peak, and growth remained very fast in 1988. The figure of under 2 per cent for this period may do less than justice to the improvement as compared with the later 1970s.

The table also shows the growth of productivity over the same periods. Up to the mid-1960s the size of the workforce was rising. Thereafter it

Table 18.1 *Growth rates of output and productivity*   *Annual percentage change*

	Output		Output per person employed (excluding North Sea)
	Total	Excluding North Sea	
1951–55	2.7	2.7	2.1
1955–60	2.5	2.5	1.7
1960–65	3.1	3.1	2.2
1965–69	2.4	2.4	2.8
1969–73	3.0	3.0	2.7
1973–79	1.3	0.8	0.6
1979–87	1.9	1.8	2.4

Table 18.2 *Output by industry*   *Percentage increase*

	Weight in 1980	1961–74	1974–87
Agriculture forestry and fishing	22	42	32
Coal and coke	15	−54	−16
Other energy and water	31	84	46
Manufacturing	266	46	−2
Construction	63	17	16
Distribution etc.	128	31	24
Transport	46	44	14
Communications	26	92	62
Banking etc.	116	77	109
Public admin. and defence	69	17	2
Education and health	87	55	25
Other services	61	24	57
Total GDP[a]	1000	39	27

Source: CSO, *Blue Books*, 1983 and 1988.
[a] Includes the above plus oil and gas extraction, plus ownership of dwellings, minus adjustment for financial services. 1980 weights for the period 1961–77, then 1985 weights.

showed no clear trend; and it is estimated at 25.4 million in 1965 and 25.3 million in 1987. The numbers in self-employment rose substantially, whilst the number of employees fell. Table 18.2 shows the broad industrial breakdown of output growth over the thirteen years covered by this study, and over the preceding thirteen years for comparisons. The most striking contrast is for manufacturing industry. From 1974–87 the level of manufacturing output was virtually unchanged, although it had risen by 46 per cent between 1961 and 1974. The increase of total service output is estimated to be about the same in both periods, around a quarter. North Sea oil and gas production began in about 1975, and by 1987 it had added about 6 per cent to the value of GDP at 1985 prices.

The share of manufacturing in total output was falling substantially in the 1970s and 1980s. Was this a reason for special concern? Certainly some commentators took the view at the time that the poor performance of manufacturing counted for more than the good performance of services in the private sector.

The boundary between manufacturing and services is a hazy one for several reasons. A large manufacturing firm can choose between undertaking functions such as distribution, marketing or accounting in-house or buying them in; machines may be owned or leased. Some of the very rapid growth recorded for business services in the national accounts simply replaced value-added which would earlier have been credited to manufacturing industry. Thus some, but not very much, of the shift from manufacturing to services can be explained away as the result of statistical conventions.

It has long been recognised that demand tends to shift from goods to services as standards of living rise. There is a worldwide increase in the proportion of output accounted for by services. To that extent a relatively slow growth of manufacturing would be unremarkable; but for manufacturing to show no growth at all over thirteen years cannot be wholly explained in this way.

It would be a mistake to overvalue manufacturing, to regard it as in any sense a more real economic activity than services. Their relative value can only be estimated by what the market is prepared to pay for them. The development of manufacturing will be examined in more detail here, but it is not because the health of that sector matters more than the health of the rest of the economy. It is because the statistics are rather more reliable and because the problems that beset the British economy in the period of this study seem to have been felt in this sector more acutely.

Table 18.3 shows a decomposition of manufacturing into fifteen subsectors. There were large falls between 1974 and 1987, in mechanical engineering, in motor vehicles and in textiles. In all these industry groups output had been rising in the previous period. The only groups where output continued to rise significantly were chemicals and electrical engineering, and in both cases the growth rate slowed down markedly. Only in 'other transport equipment', a group including aircraft and shipbuilding, is the change in output more favourable in the second half of the table – it was unchanged between 1974 and 1987, having fallen in the previous period.

The relative growth rates of different groups within manufacturing probably owes little to changes in spending patterns. There was still a growing demand, at home and abroad, for cars, for textiles and some kinds of mechanical engineering. The fall in production in the United Kingdom resulted mainly from a loss of competitiveness either in price or in quality. We cannot hope to trace here the underlying reasons for the competitive success or failure of particular industries. Our concern rather is with the overall effects of macroeconomic policy, to see whether it helped or hindered industrial performance. To that end, the time profile of output

Table 18.3 *Manufacturing output*   *Percentage increase*

	Weight in 1980	1961–74	1974–87
Metals[a]	9	. .	−15
Other minerals and products	15	63	−13
Chemicals	24	125	27
Man-made fibres	1	233	−43
Metal goods n. e. s.[a]	16	. .	−25
Mechanical engineering	38	47	−27
Electrical and instruments	34	106	37
Motor vehicles and parts	15	47	−29
Other transport equipment	14	−11	nil
Food	24	23	11
Drink and tobacco	12	67	3
Textiles	9	24	−26
Clothing and footwear	10	14	nil
Paper, printing, publishing	24	38	3
Other manufacturing	21	67	8
Total manufacturing	266	46	−2

Source: CSO, *Blue Books*, 1983 and 1988.
[a] Metals and metal goods n.e.s. are not calculated before 1968.

and of productivity in manufacturing industry will be examined in more detail in the next section. After that we shall turn to the data on individual industrial activities, with a finer disaggregation than is shown in table 18.3 to see if that throws any light on the consequences of macroeconomic policy in the late 1970s or in the 1980s.

MANUFACTURING PRODUCTIVITY IN THE 1970S AND THE 1980S

Labour productivity in British manufacturing is substantially below that achieved in other major industrial countries. In the 1970s the gap was widening, and the performance of British industry generally was the subject of grave concern. Then came the recession of 1980–81 when the output of manufacturing industry fell by about 15 per cent. Soon thereafter there was evidence of a marked improvement in productivity growth which continued for the rest of the 1980s. It was variously described as a turnaround, a renaissance and an economic miracle. British experience was different in this respect from experience in most other industrial countries. In the 1970s even our *relative* performance was poor, but we made up for that by a much better relative performance in the 1980s. This section and the next will look at the record of productivity over this period and try to understand more precisely what happened.

The macroeconomic model already used in this study, that is the National Institute model in its 1989 version, pays special attention to the supply side of manufacturing industry. It uses the vintage approach to technical progress, that is to say it assumes that productivity depends on the year in which the capital stock was laid down. Machines of later vintage embody more advanced technology, and also reflect the relative costs of capital and labour at the date that they were installed. Once the machines are in place, it assumes that there is no scope for changing the labour required to operate them. Thus capacity can be measured simply by adding up the output which can be produced using all the machines in existence; and the demand for labour is the sum of the workforce needed to man the machines actually operating. Firms are assumed to use the latest, and most advanced, of the machinery in existence, keeping some reserve of capacity consisting of older machines soon to be scrapped. Investment and scrapping reflect the present relative prices of capital and labour as well as expectations about output, profits and the availability of finance.

Within this framework the model explains the path of manufacturing productivity through the 1970s and 1980s without recourse to any 'miracle' at all. The underlying rate of technical progress, reflected in the labour requirements of successive vintages of machines, is constant throughout. The equation for employment in manufacturing tracks the historical data well.

The explanation offered by the model for the acceleration of productivity in the 1980s is on the following lines. In the 1970s, especially the late 1970s, firms were expecting manufacturing output to go on rising. This is implied by the results of CBI surveys of expectations conducted at the time, and would be consistent with an extrapolation of manufacturing output growth from the 1960s. These optimistic expectations were proved wrong in the event, and industry found itself seriously overmanned. The recession of 1980 led to an abrupt reappraisal of labour requirements. The shakeout which followed was reinforced by financial stringency, and even in many cases by bankruptcy.

In the recession, as output fell, the older less advanced machines went out of use, and were in many cases scrapped. That in itself added to productivity in the 1980s. Although investment was low during the recession, the average age of the capital stock was shortening. Moreover the relative rise in real labour costs meant that the new machines being installed in the 1980s were designed especially to economise on labour. And the speed of adjustment of the labour force became faster because labour was a relatively expensive factor of production, which firms had to use efficiently. This leaves open the explanation of the rise in the relative price of labour. Perhaps the rise in real wages and the rise in productivity were *both* the result of changes in industrial relations. Other studies of productivity growth in the 1980s which do not include wages amongst the explanatory variables *do* identify an underlying improvement.

The account of productivity performance in the macroeconomic model may seem to miss out some factors which are known to be important for particular firms and industries. It is said that the changes made to trade union legislation in the 1980s contributed to a 'new realism' in the labour force about the need for higher productivity if British industry was to survive at all. It is said that the pressing need for external finance changed the attitudes of management as well, leading to a keener drive to raise the profitability of their firms. It is even said that the appreciation of sterling, which made firms uncompetitive on price, forced them to look harder for ways of saving on labour costs.

The account of events given by the macroeconomic model does not disprove these hypotheses. It suggests, however, that their effects may have been offset by other, equally unquantifiable, influences that tended to hold back productivity growth at about the same time. It is not difficult to think of examples. During the recession firms were obliged to cut back on expenditure which was not essential to their short-term survival. This included spending on research and development, and spending on training. The high level of unemployment all over the country in the early 1980s probably slowed down the normal migration of labour into the more prosperous regions. Some firms may have actually become more reluctant to lay their workers off, knowing that there were no jobs for them to go to. It is impossible, with a relatively short run of time series data to test all these plausible conjectures. They are in any case not of central concern to a study of macroeconomic policy. The 1980s may or may not have seen an improvement in the underlying growth of productivity in Britain. No reason has been found to attribute such an improvement, if it occurred, to the conduct of fiscal or monetary policy.

Higher productivity is not, of course, an end in itself. It is a means to achieving a better use of limited resources. As long as unemployment remained high the effort that went into improving the productivity of industry was, from a national point of view, largely wasted. However, by the end of the 1980s, it could be argued that much of the slack in the labour market had been taken up. Most of the new jobs had been found in the service sector, but the fall in manufacturing employment levelled off during 1987. By then manufacturing output had regained its 1979 level.

The recovery of manufacturing output after the recession owed much to a better export performance. Throughout the postwar period British manufactures had been losing share of world trade. A typical estimated elasticity of United Kingdom exports in response to market growth was about 0.6. In the 1980s there is evidence that the elasticity increased to about 1.0, so that the growth of United Kingdom export volume was in line with world trade. There is not, however, much evidence of a comparable improvement of competitiveness in the home market.

There is no doubt that the morale of management in manufacturing industry rose strongly during the 1980s. The better trade and productivity figures no doubt contributed, and profitability rose substantially. The share of profits (excluding stock appreciation) in the output of manufacturing rose from about 20 per cent at the beginning of the 1980s to about 30 per cent in 1987. In those terms, at least, there really was a renaissance.

COMPARING PERFORMANCE ACROSS
INDUSTRIES

In this section we make use of data for 94 individual industrial activities derived from successive annual census of production reports. The period covered is 1971–86 and, for each minimum list heading, comparable figures have been estimated for the annual change in employment and in the volume of output. Some extracts from that database are shown in table 18.4

The (unweighted) average of all 94 industries is shown at the foot of the table. Average productivity growth was over 5 per cent a year in the early 1970s, a time of cyclical expansion; but it was almost unchanged from 1974–9, falling in the recession and recovering only very slowly. During the early 1980s as output fell sharply, productivity on average accelerated to nearly 4 per cent in 1980-82 and 5½ per cent in 1983–6. This average performance is broadly consistent with the macroeconomic data used in the previous section, but it conceals a great deal of variation in the performance of individual industries. The extent of that variety is constant over the period, the standard deviation of productivity growth being 4–4½ percentage points.

Some industries attract more public attention than others, and their experience may be the basis for over-hasty generalisation. For example, the iron and steel industry is often quoted as demonstrating the economic miracle of the 1980s. In our sample its performance does indeed stand out as quite spectacular: a very rapid fall in productivity from 1974–9 is followed by an even more rapid rise in productivity from 1980–86. In a less dramatic, but still impressive, way the same story can be told about motor vehicles, another high profile industry. The contrast in this case between the 1970s and the 1980s was less marked, but an acceleration is still unmistakeable.

In both these cases it is difficult to doubt that the change of industrial policy after the 1979 election contributed to the change of productivity trend. But in this study we are concerned specifically with the effects of macroeconomic policy, which is more difficult to judge from individual instances. Moreover, as the table shows, it is easy enough to find industries whose performance followed a quite different time-path.

Brewing and malting, as it happens, performed very well in the late 1970s, and less well in the 1980s. For pharmaceuticals the acceleration in productivity came before the recession, and the same is true of soap and detergents, and of office machinery. Footwear is an interesting case in that productivity growth seems remarkably steady throughout the period.

Sixteen annual observations from 1971–86 are too few for time series

Table 18.4 *Growth rates of productivity by selected industries 1971–86*   *Per cent per annum*

Examples	MLH No.	1971–3	1974–6	1977–9	1980–82	1983–6
Brewing and malting	231	12.1	−1.6	5.2	−2.7	1.8
Tobacco	240	14.7	1.6	−2.1	6.0	−0.6
General chemicals	271	5.8	−4.7	−2.3	0.7	12.6
Pharmaceuticals	272	3.9	−0.5	7.9	4.8	6.1
Soap and detergents	275	−0.5	−1.9	13.0	5.2	6.8
Iron and steel	311	0.3	−13.2	−10.0	15.9	20.7
Office machinery	338	−2.6	2.5	10.3	3.9	12.6
Watches and clocks	352	6.0	1.8	−2.4	−1.9	16.4
Tractors	380	−4.2	−2.3	−3.9	−1.9	−1.0
Motor vehicles	381	2.9	−3.3	2.8	4.5	9.5
Man-made fibres	411	11.5	−10.4	−0.6	2.0	23.2
Footwear	450	3.8	3.3	2.3	2.2	3.4
Glass	463	10.5	−2.6	1.5	2.8	9.5
Timber	471	7.8	−1.6	0.7	4.7	3.1
Paper and board	481	9.0	−7.8	2.8	−0.3	6.2
Rubber	491	2.2	1.9	−5.1	3.6	6.8
94 Industries						
Mean		5.2	−1.8	2.3	3.8	5.5
Standard deviation		4.4	4.2	4.5	4.4	4.5

Source: NIESR Industrial Database, derived from Census of Production Reports.

analysis of individual industries. Instead we can look at the relationship between productivity growth and output growth across industries, and use the time series dimension to ask whether that relationship was changed in the 1980s as compared with the 1970s. This is important to a study of macroeconomic policy for two reasons. First we want to know whether buoyant demand helps or hinders the growth of productive potential, so we ask whether the industries in which productivity accelerated in a particular year were on average industries for which output growth was accelerating or decelerating. Secondly we want to know whether the changes in industrial policy after 1979 meant that the relationship between productivity and output was different. Did the changed climate mean, in particular, that firms responded to a fall in demand by cutting back their workforce more vigorously than they would have done in comparable circumstances in the past?

Table 18.5 shows regression coefficients calculated for each year across the 94 industries. The first two columns relate the change in productivity to the change in employment and the change in output. The third and fourth columns report similar results for second, instead of first, differences. In the event the results for changes and for accelerations are broadly similar.

Care is needed in interpreting cross-section relationships of this kind. For someone familiar with macroeconomic modelling based on time series the natural interpretation is that output responds to demand, and that

Table 18.5 *Productivity growth compared across industries: cross-section regression coefficients*

	Productivity growth[a]		Productivity acceleration[a]	
	Employment growth[b]	Output growth[b]	Employment acceleration[b]	Output acceleration[b]
1971	0.15	0.74		
1972	−0.03	0.59	−0.03	0.77
1973	−0.14	0.80	0.05	0.69
1974	0.42	0.75	0.15	0.80
1975	−0.22	0.90	0.42	0.86
1976	−0.22	0.86	−0.21	0.93
1977	−0.31	0.91	−0.65	0.95
1978	−0.33	0.85	−0.21	0.92
1979	−0.36	0.71	−0.39	0.85
1980	−0.13	0.67	−0.50	0.85
1981	−1.01	1.00	−0.59	0.92
1982	−0.11	0.73	−0.55	0.92
1983	−0.47	0.51	−0.39	0.70
1984	−0.04	0.58	−0.27	0.57
1985	0.03	0.68	0.02	0.66
1986	0.31	0.78	0.19	0.73
Averages				
Whole period	−0.15	0.75	−0.20	0.81
pre-1979	−0.12	0.79	−0.11	0.85
post 1979	−0.20	0.71	−0.30	0.76
1976−1984	−0.33	0.76	−0.42	0.85

[a] Dependent variable.
[b] Independent variable.

employment responds to output, although not fully in proportion. In cross-section, however, one might also observe a quite different relationship. Industries, like office machinery, in which technical innovation is rapid, show relatively good growth in both productivity and output, but this association is not caused by variations in aggregate demand and has nothing to do with macroeconomic policy. One reason for showing results in second differences, as well as first differences, is to reduce the likelihood of reporting correlations of this kind. The second difference regressions remove industry-specific factors like technical progress provided that they are constant from year to year.

The coefficients show that more rapid productivity growth was strongly associated with faster growth in output, and weakly associated with slower growth (or faster contraction) in employment. (This conclusion is not changed when lagged values of output growth are included in the regression as well as growth in the current period.) One interpretation would be that buoyant demand helps rather than hinders supply-side performance.

The variation in the regression coefficients from year to year is no doubt partly a matter of chance, but there is a suggestion of a systematic pattern as well. From 1976–84 the regression coefficients of productivity on employment are consistently negative, whilst both before and after that period they are often positive. This is not just a reflection of the trade cycle, since the years in question include the upswing at the end of the 1970s as well as the subsequent recession. There is no comparable pattern in the regression coefficients of productivity on output.

There are thus two ways of interpreting the productivity data. The first, treating employment as the independent variable, points to a shakeout of excess labour beginning in the mid-1970s, several years before the change of government, continuing until the mid-1980s and then coming to an end. Firms found that they could produce much the same level of output with fewer employees, irrespective of the level of demand.

The second interpretation, treating output as the independent variable, suggests that there was little or no systematic change in the determination of productivity during the period covered, although the results differ for individual years. It was true throughout the period that a rapid growth in demand tended to go with a rapid improvement in productivity, and falls in demand were closely associated with reduced productivity in the early 1980s recession, as at other times.

To sum up, there is no evidence here that demand deflation is good for the supply side of the economy, nothing to support the popular 'cold bath' theory. There may have been a 'new realism' in British industry from the mid-1970s to the mid-1980s, and it may have been reinforced by the industrial policy of the Conservative government (in the case of some industries we know that it was); but this tells us nothing about the effects of macroeconomic policy, acting on the aggregate pressure of demand. On the contrary the evidence from the 1980s, as from earlier periods, is that buoyant demand is associated with improved industrial performance.

PART 6

CONCLUSIONS

19

CONCLUSIONS

WHAT ACTUALLY HAPPENED

Since the fall of the Heath government in 1974, the philosophy and conduct of economic policy has been at the centre of party politics. As a result, the real issues have been clouded, as politicians and their supporters have sought to score debating points at each other's expense, and to gain popularity by a more skilful presentation of historical events. This party political debate is interwoven with the disputes between rival schools of economists which have on occasion been no less heated. This background of contention makes it difficult, but all the more necessary, to examine the policy changes which actually took place over a decade and a half, and to assess their likely effects on the economic performance of the country as dispassionately as possible. The picture that emerges is not quite what the accompanying controversy would lead one to expect.

In terms of party politics one of the main concerns underlying the controversy about economic policy was the proper role of trade unions, both in the management of firms or industries and in the formation of national economic policy. It was trade union power which brought down the Heath government, a fact which goes a long way to explain the bitterness of the division between the parties over the next ten or fifteen years. Wilson and Callaghan tried, at best with partial success, to harness the power of the trade unions; the Thatcher governments tried, with more success, to overcome it. By the end of the 1980s it again seemed obvious that the proper role of trade unions was to represent their members in bargaining with employers, not to dictate economic policy to the government. In those terms the defeat of the miners' strike in 1985 must be among the most important events of the period covered by this book. This is not, however, a book about politics, or indeed about industrial relations. From our point of view, events like the miners' strike which add drama, and heighten emotion, are a distraction from the main business. Our main business is to watch carefully what governments actually did by way of fiscal and monetary policy measures, and to see how that relates to subsequent economic performance.

Much the same could be said about the dogmatic arguments between the monetarists and the Keynesians, which took place in parallel with the political strife. The policy of the Labour government in the late 1970s was not textbook Keynesianism, neither would textbook monetarism be a fair description of the approach followed by the Conservatives in the 1980s. No doubt the theoretical framework within which policy is discussed, and the views of the economic advisers who have the ear of policymakers, both make substantial differences to economic policy. But they changed what was *said* more than they changed what was *done*.

The choices which policymakers have to take in respect of budget tax changes and the setting of interest rates are always of broadly the same kind. Should the pressure of demand be raised, risking more inflation? Or should demand be cut back, adding to unemployment? These choices were seldom made, or defended, explicitly; but they were made almost continuously nevertheless. Sometimes the choice took the form of setting a monetary target, sometimes of deciding whether to defend a particular exchange rate, sometimes of negotiating public expenditure plans with government departments, but the underlying need to decide between macroeconomic priorities was there all the time.

The really major upheaval for macroeconomic policy came shortly before our period begins. The floating of the exchange rate in 1972 changed the conduct of macroeconomic policy in a fundamental way and its implications were profoundly important for the whole period with which we are concerned. Movements in the exchange rate played a very important part in determining inflation year-by-year, and also had a significant effect on output and employment especially in manufacturing industry. But the monetary authorities were never able to control the exchange rate, or to predict its movements. The change from a fixed rate to a floating rate system was bound to make the economy more difficult to predict or to manage in the immediate aftermath. In fact, even with the passage of time, floating rates made forecasting and policy analysis much more difficult. These difficulties led to policy mistakes at a national level, and probably to wrong decisions by firms about investment and trade with consequences that were at least as serious. Some kind of economic explanation could sometimes be offered for appreciations and depreciations after the event, although often they seemed arbitrary or chaotic. All the major industrial economies were affected by turbulence of this sort, but the British economy more than most. Attempts to use the exchange rate as a policy instrument misfired; attempts to control it failed; attempts to ignore it were no more successful. The authorities never really got on top of the situation at all.

Against this background two major policy changes stand out during our period. The first was the ending of incomes policy; the second was the ending of direct controls on the banking system. Incomes policy was designed to check inflation by administrative control, in cooperation with trades unions. Even when it had legislative backing it could work only by consent, and it was abandoned because that consent was withdrawn. There were some years, 1977 for example, when incomes policy was very successful; but the success was short-lived. In a few countries, Sweden for example, this approach worked well throughout the 1970s and 1980s, but it did not work in Britain. In some years, 1975 for example, the form of policy adopted actually *raised* the inflation rate, making it higher than it would have been under free collective bargaining. It had been demonstrated in 1974 that incomes policy did not work under a Conservative government; then in 1979 it was demonstrated that it did not work under a Labour government either. The reaction against incomes policy, and against any involvement of trades unions in government, caused the Conservatives after 1979 to swing to the other extreme. It is doubtful, however, whether there would have been much prospect for an incomes policy in the early 1980s even if Labour had won the 1979 election. After several decades in which prices and incomes policies had been in effect more often than not, their complete abandonment was a step in the dark, and the uncertainty was reflected in the mistakes made in forecasting inflation over the next few years.

The demise of incomes policy would have necessitated a rethinking of macroeconomic policy more widely, even had monetarism never been invented. Ever since 1967 the policy combination to which successive Chancellors had aspired was in three parts: reflation to cure unemployment, depreciation of the exchange rate if necessary to protect the balance of payments; and incomes policy to hold back inflation. The whole package was unusable if incomes policy could not be negotiated. It does not follow, of course, that monetarism was the right alternative to adopt, but it *is* the case that some alternative had to be found. (It is perhaps just conceivable that by 1983 a much chastened trades union leadership would have agreed to make an incomes policy work had the Labour party won the election of that year, but that is not a 'counterfactual scenario' we can usefully explore now.)

The end of quantitative controls on the banking system was not forced in the same way; this second change was a deliberate choice. Direct controls inhibited competition between the clearing banks and perpetuated an effective cartel, which seemed increasingly unhealthy. The basis for quantitative control seemed to be undermined as international capital flows to and from London were growing in magnitude. It was thought that the abolition of exchange controls necessitated the abolition of the corset. Freeing the financial system from unnecessary restrictions was part of a wider initiative to encourage the free play of market forces. Certainly this deregulation was followed by a period of extraordinarily rapid growth in the measured output of financial services.

It would be wrong, however, to ignore the element of miscalculation in the decision to abandon direct controls. The authorities believed, mistakenly, that they could control the banks' balance sheets by varying the rate of interest. Their monetarist critics believed, also mistakenly, that the corset would in due course be replaced by monetary base control. The authorities were, in the event, seriously embarrassed to find that they could not maintain control of the money supply, on which the government had itself placed such extraordinarily heavy emphasis. The behaviour of consumer spending with unregulated credit markets was not understood and the buoyancy of demand in the latter half of the 1980s was consistently underpredicted. Again a change in the way policy was conducted led to subsequent forecasting errors.

One plausible explanation for the generally higher level of real interest rates ruling in the 1980s is that the higher cost of credit took the place of quantitative controls as a brake on spending. Even so the growth of credit, after the mid-1980s, was not held back by policy at all. Had quantitative restrictions still been available there is little doubt that they would have come into operation by 1987 at the latest. Having once dismantled the control system, it would have been difficult, as well as mortifying, to build it up again.

These were two major changes in the operation of macroeconomic policy, but most of fiscal and monetary policy, month-by-month and year-by-year, consisted, as it always has done, of small, routine adjustments to the traditional instruments of monetary and fiscal policy. The way in which this bread-and-butter business was conducted was not very different before or after 1974; neither was it very different under Labour and Conservative governments.

The scale of budget changes is often exaggerated in public debate. The tax measures announced with panache on budget day are usually small compared with the uncertainty of the revenue forecasts for the coming year at constant tax rates. They are also, as a rule, small relative to the problems of inflation or unemployment that they are supposed to tackle. If one wishes to allocate praise or blame to successive governments over this period it must be more often for what they failed to do than for the active measures they took. Nevertheless, taking several years together, and including changes in public spending as well as in taxation, fiscal policy has effects on demand which are significant relative to the amplitude of a normal trade cycle. In the late 1970s, in particular, following the sterling crisis of 1976, fiscal policy became a good deal tighter. The 1981 budget, famous for raising taxation in the depths of a recession, was a further step in the same direction.

We have tried in this study to judge the motivation of fiscal policy changes, not so much by the rhetoric that accompanied them, as by the circumstances in which they took place. The fact that budgets normally happen only once a year in the spring makes it difficult to do a satisfactory statistical analysis of fiscal policy over a limited period. Nevertheless, one could conclude that one consideration guiding fiscal policy in the 1970s and 1980s was still the state of the economy, including the level of real economic activity. The scale of the budget measures related mainly to the size of the public sector borrowing requirement expected on existing policy over the coming year. In addition to that, however, the judgements may have been influenced by the growth rate of the money supply or domestic credit, by inflation or even by unemployment.

To speak of the effects of fiscal policy changes on the economy one has to imagine an alternative course of policy which can serve as a benchmark. This choice of alternative is to some extent arbitrary, although clearly it should evolve, in some sense, smoothly over time. Thus one cannot say unambiguously whether policy was tighter or looser in 1987 than in 1974, but one can say with more confidence whether short-term changes in fiscal policy increased or decreased the amplitude of output fluctuations. In the calculations done for this study it appears that fiscal policy was on balance neutral in its effect, having a stabilising effect on output in some years (1977 for example) but a destabilising effect in others (notably 1981).

The conduct of monetary policy involves much more continuous decision taking, since interest rates could be changed on any day of the year. This provides much more data for statistical analysis. It seems that the main preoccupation of the monetary authorities was with international financial markets, with rates of interest abroad, with the movement of the sterling exchange rate and with the level of foreign exchange reserves. This was true under Labour and the Conservatives alike. Interest rate reactions to the state of the domestic economy were also significant, but they are less easy to sort out. The effect of inflation (and expectations of inflation) on interest rates is clearly much less than proportional, so real interest rates rise as inflation falls. In some periods inflation may have had no direct effect on nominal interest rates at all. A consistent effect of the output and employment cycle is also difficult to detect. The response to money supply figures ($M3$) also seems relatively weak, despite the great importance attached to them at times in the public presentation of monetary policy.

Two contrasts can be drawn between interest rate setting before and after 1979. The first is that, all other things being equal, interest rates were higher under the Conservatives. That may reflect different policy priorities, or a different view of the way the economy works. It could also, as suggested above, be the necessary consequence of deregulating credit. The second contrast is that under Labour there seems to be some effect on interest rates from unemployment, but not from inflation; under the Conservatives the reverse is true. This may reflect different priorities given to the two aims of policy, or else a different assignment of monetary policy as part of a different policy mix. This change of strategy, accompanied as it was by a profound change in the presentation of policy, may have had a profound effect on the behaviour of the economy.

Estimating the consequences of interest rate policy is difficult because one of its main influences is on the exchange rate. The exchange rate reacts to unexpected events, so the consequence of an interest rate change depends very much on whether it was expected or not. If interest rates followed a consistent rule, reacting in a set way to known indicators, then changes in interest rates would be associated with smooth and predictable changes in the exchange rate. But if the rule changed, the exchange rate would then jump to a new level consistent with the new rule. It is possible to interpret the appreciation of sterling in 1979 and 1980 as a response to such a policy shift brought in with the change of government.

The behaviour of the exchange rate is still deeply mysterious, one of the main obstacles to writing an analytical history of the period. Some plausible influences on the equilibrium real exchange rate can be identified, but they do little to explain the path followed by the nominal rate in fact. North Sea oil production, and the rise in oil prices in 1979, is often cited as an explanation for the most dramatic exchange rate movement of the period. This explanation would lead us to expect an almost equally dramatic fall in 1986, when oil prices fell back sharply; but that did not happen. Moreover, other identified influences on the real exchange rate, for example the outflow on capital account after the abolition of exchange control, should have offset most of the influence of oil production.

Sterling was exceptionally exposed to the effects of events abroad, since many other currencies at this time were protected by exchange controls. The ebb and flow of confidence in the dollar may have had an effect on sterling disproportionate to the importance of the United States and the United Kingdom to one another as trade partners or as competitors.

The most dramatic, and disruptive, episode in the history of sterling was the sharp appreciation in 1979 and 1980. Our preferred explanation of that event is a change in market expectations resulting from the shift in monetary policy already described. The market perceived, correctly, that interest rates would be higher under the Conservatives (other things being equal). As a consequence the exchange rate overshot and subsequently fell back for the rest of the decade.

The exchange rate, as already indicated, was a constant preoccupation of policymakers throughout the period. The current account of the balance of payments on the other hand was a problem that lay dormant. In the 1960s and early 1970s Britain had faced a balance of payments constraint. Right at the end of the 1980s the constraint was reimposed, but in between was a long period, the period of this study, when the balance was in small deficit or in large and comfortable surplus. The main reason was North Sea oil production, but the low pressure of demand in the rest of the economy was also important. In any event the oil wealth did not provide the opportunity, as had been hoped, for a rapid expansion of output or employment.

Compared with earlier years the economic performance of Britain in the 1970s and 1980s was generally disappointing. The same would be true of most other developed countries, but in terms of unemployment, of inflation and (in the 1970s) of output growth, the British figures compare badly.

The rise in unemployment to a million, two million and then three million horrified those who had come to accept full employment as a policy objective, and who understood full employment as meaning half a million or less unemployed, the level maintained without much trouble in the 1950s and 1960s. The consequences of abandoning full employment were not, as some expected, widespread riots or revolutions, but there can be no hiding the great personal hardship that was caused, or the social damage that was done. This explains, and even justifies, the tenacity of the Keynesians in pursuing their favoured policy mix long after the difficulties of implementing it had been fully exposed.

By the later 1980s it was clear that the pressure of demand in the labour market could be unsustainably high even when unemployment was as high as one and a half or two million. This suggests that the ambitions of the Labour government in the 1970s and later of the Labour Party in opposition, to return to the rates of unemployment seen in the 1960s could not be achieved by demand management alone. Even so the trend rise in unemployment may have been due in part to the low pressure of demand maintained in the late 1970s and especially in the early 1980s. The experience of sustained high unemployment may have brought about irreversible changes in the labour market, which would never have occurred if the pressure of demand had been maintained.

If this is true, the defeat of inflation, the outstanding achievement of the mid-1980s, was a very costly one. Clearly inflation had to be brought down from the very high rates seen in the 1970s which were frightening, unfair and socially divisive. The question is whether it could have been brought down at lower cost.

The fixed exchange rate regime of the postwar period had provided an anchor for the price level. Its importance was not fully appreciated in the years following the 1967 devaluation and the floating of sterling in 1972. The initial reaction was to welcome the freedom from an external constraint. But slowly it was realised that the need for financial discipline remained; the realisation took longer in the United Kingdom than in most countries. Even when monetary targets were adopted in the late 1970s they were always 'dragging anchors', that is to say they were targets that could always be revised or rebased if it proved impossible to hit them.

The experiments with monetary targets were not successful. With hindsight it is clear that the wrong definition of the money supply was adopted, a mistake due to a misreading of empirical evidence and to confused thinking about the role of credit and of public sector borrowing in the process of money creation. But the rival definition available, $M1$, would in the end have proved equally unsuitable had it been adopted.

More fundamentally the experiment failed because there was no effective means of controlling the money supply directly. The hit-and-miss approach using interest rates was altogether unpredictable. It is extraordinary, looking back, that so much reliance was placed on an untried instrument of policy.

The origins of faster inflation in Britian in the 1970s lay in developments which were shared by the whole world economy. The most obvious examples of inflationary forces of this kind are the oil price increases of 1974 and 1979, but this is not the whole of the story. Even after taking account of movements in oil or other raw material prices, the inflation rates of all major countries show a similar pattern through the 1970s and 1980s. The timing of inflationary pressure was much the same all over the world, but the scale was greater in the United Kingdom than in most other countries. Inflation in the United Kingdom was on average higher than world inflation – markedly so at its peak in the 1970s.

In the early 1970s, and again in 1980, particular policy mistakes exaggerated inflation in this country. In the first case the mistake was made when the incoming Labour government retained the threshold agreements which had been part of the Heath incomes policy. In a remarkably similar way the Conservatives in 1979 made the mistake of allowing the Clegg pay awards to go ahead – a commitment unwisely made in the course of the 1979 election campaign. Extra damage was done by the untimely increase in VAT in the 1979 budget.

The conquest of inflation in the early 1980s is credited to the firm stand of the Thatcher government, sometimes (implausibly) to the determination of the Prime Minister personally. But similar victories were being won all over the world by governments of very different complexions, operating different kinds of macroeconomic policies. If the battle was won more quickly in this country, it was won at an exceptionally heavy cost in terms of unemployment and of output lost. It was won in large measure by allowing the real exchange rate to rise, a route which did lasting damage to the manufacturing sector and its competitiveness, especially in the home market. It seems likely that the same effect on inflation eventually could have been achieved at lower cost by other means.

The growth rate of productivity was low by international standards in the 1970s, but during the 1980s performance in this respect improved. It seems that attitudes, both of management and labour, changed about this time, giving a higher priority to financial success and economic efficiency. On the other hand training was neglected and there was substantial scrapping of capital. There is no evidence that the acceleration of productivity growth was due to changes in the conduct of macroeconomic policy.

The suggestion of an 'economic miracle' is belied by experience at the end of the 1980s, just outside the period covered by this study. The euphoria of 1987 gave way to the qualified pessimism of 1988 and 1989. Inflation had not after all been laid to rest. The balance of payments reemerged as a preoccupation, and as a constraint.

THE LESSONS OF HISTORY

In Part 2 of this book the history of ideas about macroeconomics is related to the history of events. New experiences taught new lessons; views evolved about the way the world works as new evidence came to light. The shocks which hit the economy from abroad, and the changes made in domestic policy, could be regarded as experiments of nature. This section will highlight some of the conclusions that might be drawn.

Nothing happened to contradict the received opinion that short-term fluctuations in output are mainly caused by demand, and are subject in principle to control by demand management. There were two unusually deep cyclical downturns and one unusually long cyclical upturn, but the relationship between output, employment, investment, stocks and indices of capacity utilisation over the cycle broadly conformed to the usual patterns.

Further evidence accumulated that the rate of inflation accelerated as the level of capacity utilisation rose. The nature of the trade-off between inflation and unemployment had been in doubt in the 1960s, as the traditional form of Phillips curve proved unstable. There were many in the early 1970s who ventured to think that inflation was a purely cost–push phenomenon. By the end of the period that view was less widely supported. Experience in the 1980s showed first that wages were held back by recession, and subsequently that prices were accelerated by a boom. There were also many in the 1970s who believed that there was a stable relationship between the *change* in the rate of inflation and the level of unemployment, implying that a *temporary* rise in unemployment would be enough to secure a *permanent* fall in the rate of inflation. By the end of the period that proposition too was less easy to defend, as the rise in unemployment during the 1980s seemed unlikely to be reversed in full.

The theoretical case for an active macroeconomic policy was questioned by new classical economics. By the end of the 1980s a reasonable theoretical defence had been constructed. It rested on the observed fact that wages and prices are relatively inflexible, compared for example to exchange rates or the stock market, and on the supposition that they cannot (or should not) be made completely flexible. Thus, for example, when the Chancellor makes his budget judgement he has access to information about the economy which was not available to the private sector at the time when the latest annual wage bargain was struck. By using his judgement he can perhaps improve on the outcome for the economy that would result from market behaviour on its own. That now seems to be an acceptable defence of stabilisation in principle, but there are countervailing arguments in favour of precommitment. Moreover the conduct of discretionary policy in practice has never been easy.

The practical case for countercyclical demand management always rested on the technical feasibility of short-term macroeconomic fore-casting. It had been hoped in the 1960s that forecasting would improve, as estimated models were refined, and with experience in their use. In fact forecasting did not seem to get any easier: as the fluctuations in growth rates became wider, about the same proportion of their variation was successfully anticipated, leading to average forecasting errors which ten-ded if anything to increase.

Some advocates of demand management in the 1970s, went so far as to believe that the economy was not self-righting even in the long term. They said that a recession could *only* be brought to an end by fiscal reflation. The events of the years following 1981 showed that they were mistaken.

If some Keynesians were made to eat their words, the monetarists fared no better. In the 1970s it was quite widely believed that the course of inflation followed that of monetary growth in a well-defined pattern involving a lag of about two years. The 1980s showed that this was an *ignis fatuus*, or Will o' the wisp. Worse than that, it became clear that the relationship between the price level and any of the monetary aggregates was unstable and unpredictable. By the mid-1980s technical monetarism was in ruins.

Before the event, economists had little idea how a regime of floating exchange rates would work. They were anxious about its dynamic stability, but, provided that it did not actually explode, they believed it would in some ways make macroeconomic policy easier to conduct. It would make it possible for each country to decide its own rate of inflation independently of the rest of the world, and it would put an end to worries about the balance of payments.

The new system did prove sustainable, but it cannot be said to have worked well. The sterling exchange rate did not seem to be determined by fundamentals, that is to say by relative rates of inflation and the state of the trade balance. Instead, it took on a life of its own, responding to news and to changes in market sentiment, as well as to the signals sent out by the monetary authorities in a vain attempt to keep it under control. Far from easing the external constraint, free exchange rates meant that policymakers were obsessed by the need to please the markets.

It was thought by some economists in the 1970s that the domestic price level would respond so quickly to the exchange rate that the relative prices of traded goods would be held roughly constant. Experience showed that this was not true, and that exchange rate volatility was damaging to trade.

These are some of the lessons that were learnt about the behaviour of the economy as a result of experience in this country over a particular period of time. Not all of them will be of general application. Our experience does not prove for example that the velocity of monetary aggregates is always and everywhere unstable, or that there never have been recessions that only fiscal reflation could cure. With this warning in mind we may go on to ask what lessons from this history might be learnt about the best way of conducting macroeconomic policy. These lessons strictly apply to the retrospective assessment of policy. The choice of the right policy for the future is a related question, but a different one.

Macroeconomic policy was originally conceived as a means of influencing the overall level of economic activity without undue interference in the allocation of resources amongst competing users. It was not a kind of central economic planning, but rather a way of avoiding the need for such planning. In practice, by the 1970s, demand management was being supported almost continuously by incomes policies which did involve the government in detailed intervention in labour markets. Moreover, credit control in practice involved detailed intervention in financial markets.

It was largely for this reason that the Conservatives coming to power in 1979 felt the need to do away with demand management. This was part of a wider programme to reduce the extent of government involvement in the working of the economy. In any case relations of government with the trades unions had deteriorated to the point where their cooperation could no longer have been secured. Yet macroeconomic policy in some form is indispensable.

One attraction of monetarism was that it was a form of macroeconomic policy which required the cooperation of no-one, except of course the Bank of England. The monetary authorities set the growth rate of the money supply, and the rest could be left to market forces. It was economic policy at arms' length from the economy, with no need to interfere, or get one's hands dirty. If the market decreed that interest rates should rise, or the exchange rate should fall, that would not be the fault of the government, so long as they had done their duty by the money supply.

Even after it had become clear that monetarism did not work in practice, the hope remained that the government could keep its distance from events, that it would not need to take responsibility for every flurry in the market place. In particular changes were made in the way the Bank of England operated in the money markets designed to remove the impression that interest rates were simply set by government fiat. One reason for the change was the notorious difficulty of getting ministers to face the unpopularity of raising interest rates if they knew that they could be held directly responsible. But the substance of policymaking was not changed, and commentators continued to insist, rightly, that interest rates went up or down at the Chancellor's bidding.

The goverment also tried to distance itself from events in the labour market. The line they took was that unemployment rose because real wages were too high, not because the pressure of demand in the economy was too low. Yet, of course, after 1986 when unemployment started to fall rapidly they found it difficult not to accept the credit. They had, after all, provided the framework within which the economy was performing so well. In fact the government has the means to influence the pressure of demand, for some years if not for ever, and could reasonably be held responsible, both for the duration of the 1980s recession, and for the buoyancy of the eventual recovery. Their hands were not in fact tied. For much of the 1980s the authorities conducted, with reasonable success, a kind of demand management policy, emphasising nominal rather than real GDP.

It was widely believed in 1979, in 1983 and in 1987, that macroeconomic policy was used to stimulate demand to gain a short-term advantage ahead of general elections. The extent of the stimulus in all cases may have been exaggerated, but the possibility of a political business cycle of this kind is a real one, and it is a good argument for preferring some kind of rule to discretion that might be used unscrupulously.

Macroeconomic policy might have been more successful if the discretion of the authorities *had* been limited. It can in fact be helpful to have one's hands tied. Unfortunately, however, it may not suffice for the government to tie its *own* hands. If it can tie its own hands, it can also untie them. The only time in recent history when the British government really was subject to constraint of this kind was immediately after the 1976 Letter of Intent to the IMF. That constraint was not welcome at the time, and it was thrown off as soon as possible, but it clearly helped to get the British economy out of a crisis.

The constraint on macroeconomic policy from 1949–67 was the need to maintain a fixed exchange rate. The Bretton Woods system provided an international framework in which all major countries were mutually committed to preserving financial stability. It was recognised that sterling, as one of the two most widely held and traded of world currencies, had a special obligation to keep its parity fixed. To that extent the constraint of the Bretton Woods system was external, not self imposed.

In retrospect the Bretton Woods era looks like a golden age. The growth rate of output in Britain was higher than it had been before, and higher than it has been since; inflation was not zero, but it was always low; unemployment was virtually eliminated. No doubt there were many reasons why this performance could not be matched in the 1970s and 1980s, but the advent of floating exchange rates may well have had something to do with it.

Our early experience in the European 'snake' was an unhappy one; the attempt to follow a fixed exchange rate policy on our own in 1977 was also unsuccessful. It seems that the wrong lesson may have been drawn from these failures. The opportunity was missed in 1979 to accept the external constraint of full participation in the European Monetary System (EMS). At the time the constraint was not a very binding one, since realignments of exchange rates were frequent and quite large. It is impossible to know exactly what changes there might have been in the value of sterling, and hence what difference full membership would have made to output or to inflation. But Britain would have taken part in the evolution towards monetary union which began about the mid-1980s, with realignments less frequent, and with a convergence of rates of inflation. On balance it would have been better to have been in the exchange rate mechanism from the start.

The subsequent experience of other European countries suggests that Britain as a full member of the EMS would have benefited from the consistency of policy aims that would have been required by the system and from the credibility it would have conferred. We would have been spared some at least of the excessive appreciation of sterling in 1979–80, and the depth of the recession might have been moderated. Inflation would not have fallen so quickly in the early 1980s but it would probably have come down to about the rates experienced elsewhere in Europe by the mid-1980s.

The EMS is a monetary system, not a policy strategy. Even as a full member, the United Kingdom would have had to conduct its own monetary and fiscal policy. A full economic and monetary union of Europe may in the future remove responsibility for demand management from individual governments, but this was not true of the EMS as it operated in the 1980s. Full membership of the EMS might have improved the trade-off available, but the British government would have had in any event to decide what the relative priority was of full employment and price stability.

The issue is not just a technical one; it is mainly a political, and indeed a moral, one. On the one hand there is the duty of government to keep its implicit promise of price stability on which the market system rests; on the other hand there is the implicit right of each member of society to play an appropriate part in its economic life. One cannot, even with the wisdom of hindsight, see a way in which these two moral absolutes could have been fully reconciled in the 1970s or the 1980s.

We do know now, however, rather more of the nature of the trade-off than was known to those who had to decide policy at the time. By actively taking measures to depress demand (or by failing to take measures that would have increased it) the margin of slack in the economy was kept substantial for most of the period covered by this study. But it now seems that keeping the pressure of demand low for most of the period did not promote the growth of productive potential and almost certainly raised for the foreseeable future the sustainable level of unemployment. If this interpretation of the evidence had been available, and accepted by policymakers, at the time, it is possible that they would have opted for a higher pressure of demand, and a more gradual reduction in the rate of inflation.

That would be the natural conclusion to draw if one thinks of policy choices as resting ultimately on some utilitarian calculus of social welfare. If the 'price' of low inflation in terms of unemployment (over some finite period of time) is higher than one thought, one should 'buy' less of it. But no doubt there will be some who object to any such trading between political or moral absolutes.

APPENDIX

CALENDAR OF MAIN ECONOMIC EVENTS

1974

January 1	Libya increases posted price of oil from average $9 to $18 a barrel.
	Manpower Services Commission set up.
	3-day week for industry and commerce as a result of industrial action by coalminers.
January 19	French franc to float independently of EEC 'snake' for 6 months.
January 24	NUM decides to call strike ballot.
	Pay Board publishes *Problems of pay relatives (Cmnd* 5535).
February 5	NUM announces full-scale strike from 10 February.
February 8	Parliament dissolved.
February 11	Petrol price rises 8p a gallon to 50–52p.
February 28	General Election. Result indecisive. No overall majority although Labour has most seats (301 as opposed to Conservative 296).
March 1	First Unemployment Benefit Office opens, following the administrative separation of employment work from benefit payment.
March 4	Mr Heath resigns and Mr Wilson forms minority government: PM, H. Wilson; Chancellor, D. Healey; Employment, M. Foot; Industry, A. Wedgwood Benn; Trade, P. Shore; Chief Secretary to Treasury, J. Barnett.
March 5	New talks to begin to settle miners' dispute at Mr Foot's instigation.
March 22	Price Commission insists that major food retailers should have their gross margin reference levels cut by 10% to an average of 18%.
March 26	Chancellor announces budget measures. Net increase in expenditure of nearly £700 million planned for 1974/5, but £1,400 million increase in taxation estimated to reduce PSBR by £700 million to £2,700 million. Exchange controls tightened for financing direct and portfolio investment. Income tax rates: basic and higher rates to increase by 3%, top rate by 8%. New band introduced for incomes of £4,500 to £5,000 taxable at 5% above basic rate. Income tax allowances to be increased. Company taxation: rate of corporation tax for 1973/4 raised by 2% to 52% (42% for small companies). A Green Paper on an annual wealth tax to be published in the summer.
April 3	Treasury announces guarantees for official overseas sterling balances.
April 4	Bank of England announces 1% release of special deposits.

April 30	Government publishes the Trade Union and Labour Relations Bill to repeal the Industrial Relations Act.
	The supplementary deposits scheme, covering the growth of banks' interest-bearing eligible liabilities, extended from June to December.
May 16	Helmut Schmidt becomes Federal German Chancellor.
May 24	6–7 million workers to get immediate threshold pay increase of up to £1.20 a week following rise of over 3% in RPI in April.
June	Centre for Policy Studies founded.
June 12	Mrs Williams announces voluntary price agreement with food retailers to hold down price of some basic foods.
	TUC leaders back policy of voluntary wage restraint to follow lifting of statutory wage controls as contribution to 'social contract'.
June 26	TUC publishes 8–point wages policy guidelines.
July 1	Mr Douglas Wass takes up appointment as Permanent Secretary of HM Treasury.
July 22	Chancellor announces a mini-budget aimed to attack inflation and increase domestic demand. VAT reduced from 10% to 8%; rent, rates, rebates and rent allowances increased; £50 million food subsidy added to the £500 million in the March budget.
	Regional Employment Premium doubled to £3 a week.
July 26	Pay Board and National Industrial Relations Court abolished.
August 9	Mr Gerald Ford sworn in as President of United States.
August 15	Mr Wedgwood Benn, Secretary for Industry, outlines government plans for more state ownership and new system of planning agreements with companies in key sectors of industry in White Paper.
August 23	Royal Commission on the Distribution of Income and Wealth appointed under the chairmanship of Lord Diamond.
September	The Advisory, Conciliation and Arbitration Service begins work.
September 18	PM announces general election on 10 October.
October 1	Mr Healey proposes scheme for large extension of IMF's arrangements for recycling oil surpluses.
	Sir Bryan Hopkin takes up appointment as Head of the Government Economic Service.
October 2	EEC foreign and agriculture ministers agree to undertake fundamental review of CAP.
October 10	General election. Labour has 319, Conservative 276 seats.
November 12	Chancellor announces budget measures. Total financial benefits to companies estimated at about £1½ billion in 1975 but measures to restrict consumption will result in a slight weakening of aggregate demand. Stock appreciation for corporation tax purposes for 1973/4 limited to 10% of trading profits. Easing of price controls from December. Sterling guarantees will not be continued after 31 December 1974.
December 6	Government publishes TUC's wage guidelines for 'social contract'.
December 9	Mr Varley announces energy-saving proposals including higher petrol prices, lower speed limits and restrictions on heating in offices.

1975

January 28   Government announces first experiment in indexation of savings for people over pensionable age and small savers.

January 31   Industry Bill published, giving NEB £1 billion to invest in industry in return for state control.

February 11   Mrs Thatcher elected leader of Conservative Party.
GATT trade negotiations (Tokyo Round) begin in Geneva.

February 25   Government announces 45% rate for proposed Petroleum Revenue Tax on North Sea oil.

February 28   Bank of England drops Supplementary Special Deposits Scheme (the 'corset') introduced in 1973 and puts limit of 9½% on rate paid by banks on their small deposits.

March 18   Cabinet recommends that Britain should stay in the European Community.
OECD group approve a fund of SDR 2 billion to finance payments deficits.

April 14   32% pay rise announced for 500,000 civil servants.

April 15   Chancellor announces budget measures. Income tax: basic and higher rates raised by 2 percentage points. Single person's allowance up by £50 to £675, married allowance up £90 to £955. Value added tax: rate of 25%, previously applying only to petrol, to be levied on a wide range of 'luxury' goods. Excise duties on car tax raised. Public expenditure to be cut by £900 million (1974 prices) in 1976/7.

April 24   PM announces government to take majority shareholding in British Leyland.

April 30   BP accepts government demand for 51% state participation in North Sea oilfields.

May 1   Aircraft and Shipbuilding Industries Bill published, providing for the nationalisation of those industries.

June 5   Referendum on continued UK membership of EEC held.

June 6   Result of referendum:67.2% 'yes', 32.8% 'no'.

June 10   Cabinet reshuffle announced. Industry, E. Varley (formerly Energy); Energy, A. Wedgwood Benn (formerly Industry).

June 11   Britain's first oil from North Sea starts to flow.

July 10   France rejoins West European 'snake' system of floating currencies.

July 11   Government publishes White Paper, *The Attack on Inflation* (Cabinet Office, *Cmnd* 6151).

July 24   Unemployment figure (unadjusted) above one million for first time since 1940.

July 25   MLR raised from 10% to 11%.

August 5   Mr Foot, Employment Secretary, announces proposed Temporary Employment Subsidy.

September 4   *Report of the Inflation Accounting Committee* (Sandilands Committee) (*Cmnd* 6225) published.

September 24   Government launches £175 million scheme to create jobs including extension of employment subsidies and finance for industrial investment.

October 3	MLR raised 1% to 12% in move to aid pound.
	National insurance contribution rates increase by ¼%.
November 5	NEDC meeting at Chequers announces major shift of economic priorities away from public expenditure towards regeneration of Britain's industrial structure.
November 7	Government to apply to IMF for $2 billion loan; $1.2 billion under oil facility, $840 million as first tranche of normal IMF drawings.
November 12	Royal assent for Industry Bill which introduces planning agreements and establishes NEB, and includes the Bray amendment requiring the government to publish economic forecasts twice-yearly, and the Treasury to make its forecasting model available for public use.
November 15	Heads of governments of France, Germany, Italy, Japan, United Kingdom and United States have 3-day meeting at Rambouillet to discuss economic issues.
December 16	Industry Secretary announces government rescue of Chrysler UK.
	Central Policy Review Staff report, *The Future of the British Car Industry*, published.
December 17	Chancellor introduces series of new economic measures. HP down-payments reduced to 20% from 33⅓% and maximum repayment period increased to 30 months (24) for most consumer durables, but not cars; quotas on cotton yarn imports.

1976

January 8	IMF Committee on International Monetary System reaches agreement on major international monetary reform package providing for sale of one sixth of IMF's gold holdings, legalisation of floating exchange rates and average one third increase in IMF quotas.
January 16	Italy seeks IMF assistance.
January 22	Government announces selective voluntary price restraint scheme on 50 different product categories. Price rises to be kept to 5% for 6 months.
February 12	Chancellor announces £215 million programme to encourage investment and prevent unemployment rising.
February 19	White Paper published outlining government's expenditure programme to 1979/80. Volume of public expenditure estimated to grow by 3.9% in 1975/6 and a further 2.6% in 1976/7, representing upward revisions of £1.6 billion and £0.5 billion respectively.
February 28	Bank of England discontinues Supplementary Special Deposits Scheme.
March 5	Sterling falls below $2 for first time.
March 11	Government secures decisive vote of confidence for economic and financial policies after defeat at hands of left-wing Labour MPs on 10 March.
March 15	France leaves joint EEC currency float and franc falls by 2½%
March 16	Mr Wilson announces his resignation as PM.
March 23	Unemployment falls for first time in 2 years.
April 5	Mr Callaghan takes over as PM and leader of the Labour party.

April 6	Government publishes *Cash limits on public expenditure* (HM Treasury, *Cmnd* 6440), describing the arrangements which are being introduced in 1976–7.
	Chancellor introduces a 'conditional' budget. Income tax: changes in allowances conditional on a proposed pay limit of around 3% being agreed. Unconditional increases in age allowances and child tax allowances. Total cost in a full year about £1,300 million, of which £370 million is unconditional. Value added tax: higher rates on 'luxury' goods cut from 25% to 12½%. Temporary Employment Subsidy doubled to £20 a week and extended to end–1976.
	TUC leaders reject Chancellor's budget offer of 3% pay norm but Economic Committee agree to continue discussions with government.
April 23	MLR rises from 9% to 10½%.
May 5	Government and TUC agree on pay formula which is officially expected to add about 4½% to wages and up to 6½% to earnings in year beginning August, 1976.
May 19	CBI broadly accepts PM's proposals for modifying Price Code in July.
May 21	MLR rises by 1% to 11½%.
June 1	Most provisions of Employment Protection Act come into force.
June 7	Central banks in Group of Ten, Switzerland and BIS make standby credits of $5 billion available to Bank of England.
June 16	TUC supports government's pay policy, modified to 4½% limit.
June 30	Government publishes White Paper, *The Attack on Inflation: The Second Year* (HM Treasury, *Cmnd* 6507), limiting wage and salary increases to £2.50 for those earning up to £50 a week, to 5% for those between £50 and £80, and to a maximum of £4 a week at all higher levels of earnings.
July 24	The big clearing banks agree to take greater share of special medium-term lending for exports and shipbuilding as a contribution to cutting the PSBR in the next financial year.
July 28	TUC and Labour Executive formally endorse 'social contract', phase 2.
August 25	M Chirac resigns and is replaced as French PM by M. Barre.
September 10	MLR rises by 1½% to 13%.
September 16	Bank of England calls for extra £350 million of special deposits from banks and finance houses.
September 28	Record 4% fall in sterling to $1.64.
September 29	Chancellor to ask for $3.9 billion standby credit from IMF.
October 4	Conservative party publishes *The Right Approach to the Economy*.
October 7	MLR rises by 2% to record 15%, Bank of England suspending the market-related formula.
October 28	Sterling falls to record low of $1.57.
November 2	Mr J. Carter elected President of the United States.
November 5	HM Treasury presents IMF with short-term forecasts showing PSBR of £11 billion for 1977, £2 billion above July forecast.
	Chancellor states willingness of EEC Finance Ministers to help UK with aid beyond IMF's $3.9 billion.

November 12   Brent oilfield begins production.
November 18   Government imposes squeeze on bank lending. The 'corset' is reintroduced. Exchange control regulations tightened to prevent the sterling financing of third country trade.
November 19   Sterling stabilises at $1.65.
                MLR reduced by 1/4% to 14 3/4%.
November 29   Government withdraws from commitment to introduce a wealth tax in this parliament.
December 3   Government reaches agreement in principle on package cutting PSBR by £2 billion in next financial year.
December 9   Repayment announced of $1,545 million drawings on the $5.3 billion standby facility.
December 15   Chancellor announces mini-budget. It includes: letter of intent to the IMF, requesting loan of $3.9 billion over a two-year period; public expenditure to be reduced by a further £1 billion in 1978–9 (at 1976 survey prices); the reduction of the PSBR to £8.7 billion in 1977–8 and to about £8.6 billion in 1978–9. In 1976–7 the PSBR is expected to be £11.2 billion; future monetary targets to be expressed in terms of Domestic Credit Expansion rather than money supply. DCE to be kept to £9 billion in year ending 19 April, 1978 and further reduced to £6 billion in the following year; 10% increases in alcohol and tobacco duty from 1 January, 1977; sale of part of government stake in BP to raise £500 million; phasing out of such import controls as were imposed to protect sectors suffering temporarily from import competition; the 'corset' to be a key instrument in the short term. Following Chancellor's announcement the Treasury, for the first time, released economic forecast for 1977, as required under the Industry Act, 1975.
December 22   Regional Employment Premium abolished.
December 24   MLR cut by 1/4% to 14 1/4% as sterling rises and reaches $1.69.
December 30   Bank of England issues second tranche of £750 million of 15 1/4% Treasury Loan 1996, entirely allotted within the day.

1977
January 11   Chancellor underlines Britain's intention to reduce role of sterling as international reserve currency after Basle agreement on standby credit and a plan to encourage 'orderly' reduction in official sterling holdings by offering new form of UK government security denominated in US dollars or other foreign currencies and offered on market-related terms.
January 26   Department of Trade publishes report of Committee of Inquiry on Industry Democracy (*Cmnd* 6706).
January 27   Public Expenditure White Paper Volume 1 published (*Cmnd* 6721–I) showing decline of about 2 1/4% in total expenditure between 1976/7 and 1977/8.
January 28   MLR cut by 1% to 12 1/4%.
February 1   Further steps announced to encourage use of foreign currency for financing exports.

February 2	Record increase announced in official reserves by $3.07 billion to $7.20 billion, including $1.2 billion drawings on $3.9 billion IMF credit.
February 3	MLR lowered by ¼% to 12% and Bank of England suspends relationship of MLR to Treasury Bill rate.
March 23	Joint announcement by Mr Callaghan and Mr Steel of the 'Lib-Lab' pact.
March 29	Chancellor announces budget measures. Income tax: reductions totalling £2¼ billion in full year, £960 million of which contingent on negotiation of new pay policy; personal allowances raised. Level at which higher tax rates become payable raised by £1,000 to £6,000. Conditional change: basic rate of income tax reduced from 35% to 33%. Petrol, tobacco and excise duty raised. Temporary employment subsidy to continue for further year.
April 3	Month-long Geneva Conference, called to negotiate new common fund to stabilise commodity prices, ends in deadlock.
April 4	Child benefit replaces system of taxable family allowances.
April 6	National Insurance Surcharge introduced at rate of 2%.
May 4	Mr F. Atkinson appointed head of Government Economic Service.
May 5	Government decides to withdraw 5½p increase in petrol tax from 5 August (later changed to 8 August) due to parliamentary opposition.
May 7	Two-day summit in London begins for leaders of France, West Germany, Italy, Japan, UK, US and Canada.
May 12	Bank of England extends 'corset' controls on growth of banking system's resources for further 6 months.
June 14	Rooker-Wise amendment to Finance Bill requiring governments to raise personal tax allowances each year in line with inflation, except when specific exceptions are made in the Finance Act.
June 22	TUC publish guidance on strict maintenance of settlements made during the second phase (12-month rule).
June 29	Government approves Youth Opportunities Programme (YOP), based on MSC's Holland Report.
July 6	TGWU vote for return to 'unfettered collective bargaining' from end-July.
July 15	Chancellor announces government's guidelines for stage 3 of counterinflation policy. Income tax: basic rate cut by 1p to 34p in pound instead of conditional 2p cut announced in budget. Personal allowances raised. Child benefit: raised from April, 1978 to £2.30 for all children. Further step in phasing out child tax allowance. Petrol duty reduced by 5½p from 8 August. Price controls: companies which break 12-month rule on pay settlements to have statutory profit margin ceilings reduced by amount of offending pay rise.
July 27	PM and TUC General Secretary jointly present document entitled, *The next three years and into the 80s.*
	Bank of England switches from an exchange rate policy of $1.72:£1 to one of a fixed effective exchange rate as the dollar weakens.
July 28	Renewal of 'Lib-Lab' pact.

July 31	Phase 2 of government's pay policy ends (Labour government and TUC 'social contract' ends).
August 7	Finance ministers from 14 richest nations agree to provide IMF with extra $10 billion to help finance countries in difficulty.
August 11	Bank of England suspends 'corset' controls on growth of deposits.
September 7	TUC vote in favour of continuing 12-month rule between pay settlements.
September 22	Government to apply sanctions of withdrawing export credit guarantees from James Mackie and Sons because their pay settlement (22–23% increase) breached pay policy guidelines.
October 14	MLR cut by ½% to 5%, its lowest level since 1964.
October 26	Chancellor announces mini-budget costing £1 billion in current year and £2.2 billion next. Exchange control eased. IMF standby: government not to take up 310 million in SDRs available in November.
October 31	Bank of England announces that exchange rate will be allowed to float for the time being.
November 3	HM Treasury announces rise of $3.04 billion to $20.21 billion in official reserves in October. Nearly all increase reflected foreign exchange market intervention by Bank of England.
November 25	MLR raised by 2% to 7%.
December 14	Chancellor reconfirms government's determination to continue firm control of public spending and the counterinflationary thrust of its monetary policy in letter to IMF.

1978

January 12	Government White Paper on expenditure plans from 1978/9 to 1981/2 published: total spending to increase by nearly £1 billion in 1978/9 compared with previous White Paper.
February 7	Commons votes to include a clause in all future contracts between government and private companies ensuring rigid maintenance of 10% guidelines.
March 21	PM's Office publishes *The Challenge of North Sea Oil (Cmnd* 7143).
March 31	Policy Studies Institute set up.
April 1	Start of Youth Opportunities Programme and Special Temporary Employment Programme.
April 6	New state pension scheme begins.
April 11	Chancellor announces budget. Income tax: lower rate at 25% on first £750 of taxable income. Single person's allowance and wife's earnings allowance raised by £40 to £985 and married allowance by £80 to £1,535. Public expenditure: total additional expenditure of £550 million in 1978/9 (at 1977 prices) to be taken from £750 million contingency reserve. MLR increased from 6½% to 7½%.
April 19	Committee on Policy Optimisation chaired by R.J. Ball publishes report (*Cmnd* 7148) which considered 'the present state of development of optimal control techniques as applied to macroeconomic policy' and made 'recommendations concerning the feasibility and value of applying these techniques within Her Majesty's Treasury'.
May 5	MLR raised by 1¼% to 8¾%.

May 8	Opposition forces cut of 1p in standard rate of income tax in amendment to Finance Bill.
May 12	Bank of England abandons market-related formula for determining official MLR and pegs rate at present 9%. In future rate will be determined by administrative decision.
June 8	Government forced by market pressures and low level of gilt sales to introduce package of restrictive monetary and fiscal measures: MLR up by 1% to 10%; reactivation of 'corset' controls; 2½% increase in National Insurance surcharge from October.
June 28	Government decides to cut proposed increase in employers' National Insurance surcharge to 1½% because of Liberal pressure.
July 6–7	EEC summit in Bremen agrees in principle to set up a European Monetary System (EMS).
July 14	Government announces experimental small-scale job subsidy aimed at helping long-term unemployed.
	Bonn summit of world leaders ends in agreement on package of measures aimed at boosting economic growth, reducing inflation, cutting energy imports and warding off protection.
July 21	Government publishes White Paper, *Winning the Battle against Inflation* (HM Treasury, *Cmnd* 7293), which proposes: 5% for pay settlements, excluding productivity; productivity deals to be self-financing.
September 6	TUC annual conference rejects government's 5% pay policy.
October	National Insurance Surcharge rate increased to 3½%.
	Labour Party Conference carries overwhelmingly a motion rejecting any form of wage restraint and demanding an end to government intervention in pay negotiations.
November 9	Target for sterling M3 growth for year to October, 1979 announced to be 8–12%.
	MLR raised by 2½% to 12½%.
November 24	Government publishes Green Paper, *The European Monetary System* (HM Treasury, *Cmnd* 7405).
December 14	Government abandons discriminatory sanctions against private companies breaching 5% pay guidelines.
December 26	Oil exports from Iran cease after increase in intensity of anti-Shah strikes and go-slows by oil workers.
December 30	Start of EMS to be delayed by French refusal to begin because of dispute over monetary compensatory amounts.

1979

January 16	HM Treasury publishes *The Government's Expenditure Plans 1979–80 to 1982–83 (Cmnd* 7439) which puts forward relaxation of wages policy in bid to avoid series of crippling strikes in public services.
January 22	Ambulancemen and many other public service workers hold 24-hour strike.
January 28	Cash limits on public sector spending. Treasury ministers to minimise any adjustments in cash limits on public spending to accommodate increases in pay above official guidelines.
February 6	DES announces 1,150 schools shut due to industrial action.

February 7	Royal Dutch-Shell group to cut crude oil supplies to all customers by 15% from end-March because of loss of crude oil exports from Iran.
February 8	MLR rises by 1½% to 14%.
March 7	Professor Clegg appointed Chairman of Standing Commission on Pay Comparability.
March 12	EMS starts after 2½ month delay (without UK).
March 29	General election announced for 3 May.
April 2	Special surcharges introduced on almost half of OPEC's crude oil production, pushing up prices by 24–31% in 1979(2) over 1978(4).
April 3	Interim Finance Bill increases personal income tax allowances in line with inflation as required by Rooker-Wise amendment, to take effect in August.
May 3	Conservatives win general election with overall majority of 43.
May 4	Mrs Thatcher becomes PM.
May 5	Chancellor, Sir G. Howe; Foreign and Commonwealth Affairs, Lord Carrington; Industry, Sir K. Joseph; Trade, Mr J. Nott; Chief Secretary to the Treasury, Mr J. Biffen (1979–81).
May 6	Mr N. Lawson appointed Financial Secretary to the Treasury.
June 12	Chancellor announces budget. Income tax: basic rate down from 33p to 30p in the pound. All personal allowances raised. Higher rates: threshold for 40% rate up from £8,000 to £10,000 (taxable income). Top rate down from 83% to 60%. Investment income surcharge not payable below single new threshold, £5,000 of investment income. VAT raised to unified level of 15%. Petrol and derv duty raised by 7p a gallon and heavy oil other than derv by ½p. Petroleum Revenue Tax rate raised from 45% to 60%. MLR raised by 2% to 14%. Official 'corset' controls continued.
June 25	House of Commons Treasury and Civil Service Committee formed, chaired by Mr E. du Cann (25/6/79–9/12/83).
June 28	2-day summit in Tokyo of western leaders, who announced an agreement to curb oil imports. OPEC announces a 15% increase in crude oil prices.
July 5	UK removes exchange restrictions on non-bank use of sterling to finance third-country trade.
July 9	Employment Secretary, Mr J. Prior, presents consultative document on reform of trade union law to TUC and CBI.
July 12	Introduction of Competition Bill.
July 18	UK removes exchange restrictions on outward direct investment and on portfolio investment in securities in EEC currencies or from international organisations.
July 31	Price Commission abolished.
August 1	Clegg Commission recommends pay rises of up to 25.8%, half to be paid immediately, half from April 1980.
August 6	Mr P. Volcker takes over as Chairman of US Federal Reserve Board from Mr W. Miller.
August 30	French government announces 4½ billion franc reflationary programme.

October 23	Chancellor announces immediate removal of all remaining exchange controls, apart from those still needed in relation to Rhodesia.
November 1	HM Treasury publishes *The Government's Expenditure Plans 1980–81 (Cmnd 7746)*.
November 15	Chancellor announces measures aimed at controlling growth of money supply in statement on monetary policy: MLR increased to record 17%; collection of Petroleum Revenue Tax advanced 2 months to reduce this year's PSBR by £700 million; renewal of 'corset' for further 6 months; Bank of England and Treasury to issue discussion paper on techniques of monetary control; extension from 10–16 months of period covered by present target range for sterling M3 of 7% – 11% a year.
November 29	2-day summit of EEC heads of government in Dublin unable to agree on Britain's demands for budget relief of £1 billion.
December 5	Miners reject strike call in NUM ballot.
December 6	Mr Prior presents Employment Bill which makes provision for secret ballots and reimbursement of expenditure incurred by trade unions in holding secret ballots. Also states everyone should have the right 'not to be unreasonably excluded or expelled' from a union which operates a 'closed shop' agreement and picketing to be limited only to that 'carried out by a person attending at or near his own place of work . . .'.

1980

January 1	Mr T. Burns succeeds Sir F. Atkinson as Head of Government Economic Service.
February 7	BNOC to raise North Sea oil prices.
February 14	1980/1 special employment measures programme announced including expanded YOP.
March 21	HM Treasury and Bank of England publish Green Paper, *Monetary Control: a Consultation Paper (Cmnd 7858)*.
March 26	Chancellor announces budget. Announcement of MTFS. Income tax: personal allowances raised 18% in line with RPI increase. Lower band rate of tax of 25% on first £750 abolished. No change in basic rate of 30% or in higher rates but thresholds up by 11% on average. Excise duties and VAT raised. Target for growth of M3 for 14 months from February 1980 to mid-April 1981 set at 7–11% at annual rate. Target rate of 6% by 1983/4. Corset not to be extended beyond mid-June.
April	National steel strike ends with agreement on 16% pay increase.
April 3	Introduction of Competition Act.
April 29	Ending of mandatory foreign currency financing of export credit contracts.
May 13	Government announces target reduction of 630,000 persons or 10% in Civil Service staff by April 1984.
May 14	TUC day of action protest against government policies has limited effect.

June	Britain becomes net exporter of oil.
June 2	Cabinet accepts EEC budget deal.
June 18	'Corset' ends.
June 22	2-day economic summit of western leaders in Venice begins. They agree to fight inflation and cut dependence on oil.
July 16	Sterling M3 rises by £2½ billion, far in excess of target set at time of budget.
July 22	Report of Armstrong Committee on Budgetary Reform published. Government announces 7 enterprise zones.
August	House of Commons Treasury and Civil Service Committee, Session 1979–80, publishes *Third Report on Monetary Control*.
August 4	Standing Commission on Pay Comparability to be abolished at end–1980 but review bodies on top salaries, armed forces and doctors and dentists to be retained.
September 22	Iran and Iraq start war, threatening oil supply routes through Straits of Hormuz.
October	Sterling reaches peak exchange with dollar (2.43).
October 15	Mr Callaghan resigns Labour party leadership.
October 27	Government suspends civil servants' pay research arrangements.
November 4	Mr R. Reagan overwhelmingly defeats President Carter in US elections.
November 10	Mr M. Foot wins leadership of Labour party, defeating Mr D. Healey.
November 21	£250 million package of new measures to help unemployed announced by government. YOP doubled in size. Special Temporary Employment Programme dealing with long-term unemployed replaced by a larger Community Enterprise Programme. Changes in Temporary Short-time Working Compensation Scheme.
November 24	Chancellor announces new taxation and spending measures. Savings: eligibility for index-linked national savings certificates extended to raise £3 billion in 1981. National Insurance employees' contributions increased from April by 1% to 7¾%. Supplementary oil tax payable in addition to Petroleum Revenue Tax to be introduced in 1981. Monetary growth rate expected to slow down during remainder of 14-month period to April but likely to exceed 7–11%. Central government spending programmes, except health, cut by 2% in 1981 to produce savings of over £1 billion to offset additional expenditure on nationalised industries, employment measures and unemployment benefit. Reserve assets ratio to be phased out; money market to be allowed a greater role in determination of short-term interest rates, future of clearing banks' cash ratio to be considered and additional series for banking retail deposits to be collected. MLR cut by 2% to 14%.
November 25	Seasonally adjusted unemployment figures for UK adults rise above 2 million.

1981

January 5	Chief Secretary to the Treasury, Mr. L. Brittan; Trade, Mr. J. Biffen.

January 25	Mr D. Owen, Mr W. Rogers, Mrs S. Williams and Mr R. Jenkins announce inception of Council for Social Democracy, aimed at creating new party.
February 18	NCB withdraws plans to close 23 pits and government increases aid under threat of national coal strike.
	President Reagan's budget proposes a record number of measures on tax and expenditure cuts although it allows for a $90 billion increase in defence spending spread over 4 years.
February 24	House of Commons Treasury and Civil Service Committee, Session 1980–81 publishes *Third Report, Monetary Policy (HC* 163–I–II). Report examines government's monetary policy as it has evolved over last 18 months and considers how far theory on which MTFS was based seems to be valid.
March 3	Britain's net contribution to 1981 EC budget to be about £500 million instead of original estimate of £1.3 billion.
March 9	National 1-day strike by civil servants in protest against pay.
March 10	Chancellor announces budget. MLR down by 2% to 12%. Special tax on banks' windfall profits. New oil tax, Supplementary Petroleum Duty, imposed at 20% of North Sea oil and gas revenues, after 1 million tonne a year allowance for each field. No change in personal allowances and thresholds, resulting in an estimated 1¼ million more taxpayers in 1981/2. Alcohol, tobacco, petrol and derv and vehicle excise duty all up. New target range for M3 to be annual rate of 6–10% in 14 months to April 1982. Indexed securities to be sold to pension funds, life insurance companies and friendly societies. Public spending from 1982/3 onward to be planned in terms of cash available for each year.
March 22	Domestic rate bills in England and Wales to rise by just over 20% in April.
March 30	364 leading economists publish joint statement severely criticising the government's monetarist economic policies.
May 10	M.F. Mitterand elected as President of France.
June 22	All recognised banks and licensed deposit takers will have to place non-interest-bearing deposits equivalent to ½% of their eligible liabilities with the Bank of England.
June 25	Secretary of State for Defence announces government to honour NATO commitment of 3% real growth in defence expenditure each year until 1985–6.
July 2	Chancellor announces package of indirect tax increases to recoup loss of revenue resulting from reduction in derv duty proposed in budget.
July 20	2-day summit of 7 western leaders begins in Ottawa.
August 21	Changes in monetary control: publication of MLR discontinued; short-term interest rates kept within undisclosed band through open-market operations; abolition of requirement of banks to monitor minimum reserve asset ratio and of London clearing banks to hold 1½% of eligible liabilities with the Bank of England in non-interest bearing form; all banks and licenced deposit takers to hold ½% of eligible liabilities with the Bank of England.

September	Inflation-proofed national savings (granny bonds) made available to everyone.
September 16	Four main clearing banks raise base rates by 2% to 14%.
October 1	Base rates rise by 2% to 16%.
October 4	EEC Finance Ministers agree on currency realignment in EMS.
November 23	Mr Tebbit announces his department's consultative document, *Proposals for industrial legislation*.
November 26	Goverment to allow public spending for next year to rise by £5 billion above original planned total of £110 billion.
December 2	Government announces several measures on public expenditure in 1982/3 and on National Insurance contributions.
December 15	Green Paper on alternatives to domestic rates published.
	Government launches £1 billion a year programme to reform industrial training in Britain.

1982

January 4	Young Workers Scheme starts, giving subsidy to employers of young people under 18 earning less than £40 a week.
January 26	Unemployment figures pass 3 million.
January 28	Employment Bill published.
March 9	Chancellor announces budget. National Insurance Surcharge down by 1% to 2½% from 2 August. All income tax allowances and thresholds to rise by 2% more than required by indexation. Fuel, car, alcohol, tobacco and vehicle excise duty up. Threshold for capital transfer tax up. Capital gains (including those by companies) to be calculated after taking account of inflation. Indexed gilts no longer restricted to pension funds. Abolition of supplementary petroleum duty. Petroleum Revenue Tax raised from 70% to 75% with payments to be speeded up.
April 2	Argentina invades Falkland Islands.
May 4	MSC announces change of YOP into 12-month training programme for 16–17 year olds from September 1983.
June	House of Commons Treasury and Civil Service Committee, Session 1981–82 publishes *Sixth Report.. Budgetary Reform*. Report examines recommendations made by Armstrong Committee.
June 13	French government announces a 4-month prices and incomes freeze as part of stabilisation package to support devaluation of French franc by 10% against Deutschmark.
June 14	Ceasefire established in Falkland Islands. Argentina to negotiate surrender terms.
July 13	TUC and Labour party announce joint programme for 'social and economic reconstuction'.
July 27	Chancellor announces new measures aimed at alleviating unemployment.
	All government hire purchase controls on cars and other consumer goods abolished.
October 4	Dr H. Kohl of Christian Democrat Union becomes West German Chancellor after defeat of Dr H. Schmidt of Social Democrat party.
October 5	Government launches the Community Programme.

November 8	Chancellor presents autumn statement.

1983

January 11	Department of Employment publishes Green Paper *Democracy in Trade Unions (Cmnd 8778).*
February 18	NCB agrees to withdraw plans for 23 pit closures to avert a threatened coal strike.
March 6	Chancellor Kohl's centre-right coalition re-elected in West Germany.
March 15	Chancellor announces budget. Income tax personal allowances up by 14% but no change in basic rate of 30%. Fuel, alcohol, tobacco and vehicle excise duty up.
	EEC finance ministers agree comprehensive realignment of EMS with an effective 8% devaluation of French franc against Deutschmark.
April	National Insurance Surcharge rate reduced to 1½%.
	Youth Training Scheme (YTS) replaces YOP. Gives 1-year work experience and training for 16-year olds.
April 15	Sir P. Middleton succeeds Sir D. Wass as Permanent Secretary to the Treasury.
May 16	Labour party manifesto published proposing emergency programme of public expenditure to cut unemployment.
June 9	Conservatives win general election with overall majority of 144 seats.
June 11	Chancellor, Mr N. Lawson; Chief Secretary, Mr P. Rees.
June 12	DTI, Mr C. Parkinson.
June 19	Agreement reached on UK budget refund from EEC for 1983.
July 1	Mr R. Leigh-Pemberton succeeds Lord Richardson as Governor of Bank of England.
July 7	Government agrees to emergency package of £500 million in expenditure cuts in current financial year and to raising of an equal amount by extra sales of public assets.
August	Enterprise Allowance Scheme, launched in 5 pilot areas early in 1982, extended nationwide.
August 1	National Insurance Surcharge reduced to 1%.
August 16	Modified controls for London money markets come into force.
September 27	HM Treasury publishes *Financial Management in Government Departments (Cmnd 9058).*
October 2	Mr N. Kinnock becomes leader of Labour party and Mr R. Hattersley deputy leader.
October 16	DTI, Mr N. Tebbit.
	Building societies agree to end interest rate cartel and to set their own savings and mortgage rates.
October 26	Government publishes Trade Union Bill. Proposes large-scale expansion of union democracy; legislation to give all members right to elect leaders directly, to vote on any industrial action involving a breach of their contract of employment and to determine whether their unions should retain a political fund.
November 10	Agreement reached between US and Japan to bring about more realistic exchange rate between dollar and yen.

November 17	Chancellor announces autumn statement.
December 13	Mr T. Higgins succeeds Mr E. Du Cann as Chairman of Treasury and Civil Service Committee.

1984

January 12	NUM executive votes unanimously for continuation of ban on overtime working.
January 18	Proposals to overhaul regulation of Britain's financial organisations and to provide new powers for DTI published in Gower Report commissioned by government.
January 31	Department of Employment publishes *Training for Jobs (Cmnd 9135)*.
February 6	Review of housing benefits announced.
February 16	HM Treasury publishes White Paper, *The Government's Expenditure Plans (Cmnd 9143–I–II)*.
March 8	NUM leaders give official sanction to strikes planned in Scotland and Yorkshire and to similar action in any other area in protest at pit closures.
March 13	Chancellor announces budget. Income tax personal allowances to rise by about 12½%. Investment Income Surcharge abolished. Corporation tax cut from 52% to 50% this year, then to 45% in 1984–5, 40% in 1985–6, and 35% in 1986–7. Small companies rate down from 38% to 30% from year just ending. Stock relief abolished with effect from 13 March. National Insurance Surcharge abolished from 1 October.
	HM Treasury publishes Green Paper, *The Next Ten Years: Public Expenditure and Taxation into the 1990s (Cmnd 9189)*.
March 19	EEC summit conference in Brussels. No agreement reached on Britain's budget contribution.
April 2	Social Services Secretary, Mr N. Fowler, announces review of social security system.
June 8	Economic summit held in London between major western allies. Agreed proposals to combat international debt problem.
June 27	Agreement reached on UK's rebate on contributions to EEC budget, with continuing 66% refund of VAT share expenditure.
July 11	Britain's major banks announce a 2% rise in base lending rates to 12%, halting recent run on sterling.
July 23	HM Treasury publishes Green Paper, *Building Societies, a New Framework (Cmnd 9316)*, proposing measures to allow building societies to provide a wider range of services.
August 24	National dock strike called (ends 18 September).
September 3	At TUC Mr N. Willis succeeds Mr L. Murray as General Secretary.
October 1	National Insurance Surcharge abolished.
November 7	President Reagan wins second term in US elections.
November 12	Chancellor presents autumn statement.
November 20	British Telecom share issue 4 times oversubscribed.
November 28	Mr N. Lamont, Secretary of State for Industry, announces new regional industrial policy aimed at linking regional assistance more closely to job creation in order to achieve greater cost-effectiveness.

November 29   7 EEC member states, excluding Britain, Denmark and Greece, favour drafting Treaty of European Union to assist in economic integration.

1985
January 14   Sterling falls to $1.1105.
              Bank of England reactivates MLR, suspended in 1981, at 12%.
January 18   FT Ordinary Share Index exceeds 1,000 level for first time.
January 22   Government announces 3-year plans for public spending in White Paper, *The Government's Expenditure Plans, 1985/6 to 1981/8 (Cmnd 9428–I–II).*
March 3   NUM's delegate conference votes by 98 to 91 to return to work on 5 March (26.1 million days lost in year-long strike).
March 7   Sterling falls to $1.05.
March 13   Government announces abolition of BNOC.
March 19   Chancellor announces budget. Income tax allowances up. Alcohol, tobacco, fuel and vehicle excise duty up. Upper earnings limit on employers' contributions to national insurance abolished. Development Land Tax abolished.
March 28   Department of Employment publishes White Paper, *Employment: the Challenge for the Nation (Cmnd 9474).*
April 3   Department of Education and Science publishes White Paper, *Education and Training for Young People (Cmnd 9482),* linking the rationalisation of job qualifications with measures announced in the budget.
April 22   Creation of Employment Institute and Charter for Jobs announced.
May 2   7-day western nation economic summit begins in Bonn.
May 21   Government publishes Green Paper, *The Development of Higher Education into the 1990s (Cmnd 9524).*
May 29   President Reagan sends plan for extensive tax reform to Congress.
June   Securities and Investments Board set up under chairmanship of Sir K. Berrill.
June 20   Government announces reforms to strengthen supervision of UK banking system after last year's collapse of Johnson Matthey Bankers.
July 2   Government announces capital gains tax on gilt-edged securities and coporate bonds to be abolished from 2 July, 1986.
July 15   Cabinet Office publishes White Paper, *Lifting the Burden (Cmnd 9571),* on business deregulation.
July 17   Government removes wages council protection from about 500,000 under-21 workers and confines councils to setting minimum hourly and single overtime rates.
September 2   DTI, Mr L. Brittan; Chief Secretary to the Treasury, Mr J. MacGregor.
September 21 Plaza Agreement. Group of Five (US, UK, Japan, W. Germany and France) ministers meet in New York's Plaza Hotel to agree closer cooperation on stabilising world economy, particularly in halting rise in dollar and resisting protectionism.

October 15   Report by House of Lords Select Committee on Overseas Trade on the causes and implications of the deficit in the UK balance of trade in manufactures published.

October 17   Chancellor announces in Mansion House speech that sterling M3 target of 5–9% growth will be dropped for the rest of 1985/6 financial year but that sterling M3 target for 1986/7 will be set at time of next budget ('systematic overfunding would no longer be used').

November 12   Chancellor announces autumn statement. Public expenditure planning total to remain broadly unchanged in cost terms between 1985/6 and 1988/9.

December 12   President Reagan signs Gramm-Rudman-Hollings budget legislation, the Balanced Budget Act, which aims for elimination of deficit by 1991 through phased reductions.

December 16   DHSS publishes White Paper, *Reform of Social Security: Programme for Action (Cmnd* 9691), reprieving SERPS but curtailing benefits to cut costs. Supplementary Benefit and Family Income Supplement to be replaced by Income Support and Family Credit, most proposals to be implemented by April, 1988.

1986

January   Pilot scheme for Restart begins (scheme for long-term unemployed).

January 9   Mr Heseltine, Secretary of State for Defence, resigns from Cabinet over Westland affair.

January 15   Government publishes White Paper, *The Government's Expenditure Plans 1986–87 to 1988–89 (Cmnd* 9702), setting out plans for cuts in expenditure on defence and social security, and further asset sales, leading to public spending being roughly constant in real terms until 1988/9.

January 19   Finance ministers from Group of Five agree to suspend intervention in exchange rates in attempt to lower US dollar.

January 24   Mr Brittan, Secretary of State for Trade and Industry, resigns from Cabinet over departmental leak on Westland affair, and is succeeded by Mr P. Channon.

January 28   Department of Environment publishes Green Paper, *Paying for Local Government (Cmnd* 9714), detailing radical reform of rates system.

March 16   M. J. Chirac becomes PM of France.

March 18   Chancellor announces budget. Income tax basic rate down by 1% to 29%. Personal allowances indexed. Capital transfer tax abolished on lifetime gifts, sliding scale within 7 years of death, to be renamed Inheritance tax. Corporation tax down 5% to 35% for large firms, down 1% to 29% for smaller ones. Community Programme for long-term unemployed to be increased by 55,000 places. Job Start Scheme to be expanded from 9 pilot areas to nationwide. Enterprise Allowance Scheme to be expanded from 65,000 to 100,000 entrants a year. Business Expansion Scheme to be extended

	indefinitely. A New Workers Scheme to help young people during their first year into jobs by providing subsidy of £15 a week to employers recruiting 18–19 year olds.
April	The YTS expands to 2-year scheme for 16-year olds whereby the trainee has an opportunity to gain a vocational qualification.
April 1	North Sea oil falls below £10 a barrel following oil price slump.
April 15	DTI publishes White Paper, *Intellectual Property and Innovation (Cmnd* 9712).
April 18	Guinness wins £2½ billion takeover bid for Distillers against Argyll group opposition.
May 4	Annual economic summit of western leaders begins in Tokyo.
June 12	Unemployment count peaks, seasonally adjusted, excluding school leavers, at just over 3.2 million.
July	Following pilot scheme begun in January, Restart expands nationwide.
July 9	Oil prices fall to lowest level for 12 years, with spot Brent crude at $9.95 a barrel.
July 11	Annual rate of inflation in June fell to 2½%.
July 15	Department of Employment and DTI publish *Profit related Pay: a Consultative Document (Cmnd* 9835).
September 24	Flotation of Trustee Savings Bank.
October 27	London's Stock Exchange changes over to electronic trading and information systems – 'Big Bang'.
November 6	Chancellor announces autumn statement. Public spending up £4.7 billion in 1987–8 and £5.5 billion 1988/9.
November 7	Publication of Financial Services Act, 1986.
December 1	DTI initiates investigation into Guinness's affairs over question of insider dealing.
December 8	British Gas trading begins on Stock Exchange.
December 18	Local Government Finance Bill presented by Mr N. Ridley.

1987

January 14	HM Treasury publishes White Paper, *The Government's Expenditure Plans 1987–88 to 1989–90 (Cm.* 56–I–II).
January 25	Chancellor's Kohl's centre-right coalition retains power with reduced majority in West German general election.
February 5	Leaders of print union Sogat '82 vote to end strike at Wapping which began on 24 January 1986.
February 22	Louvre agreement between US, Japan, West Germany, France, UK and Canada made to stabilise exchange rate levels.
March 17	Chancellor announces budget. Income tax basic rate cut from 29% to 27%. Personal allowances increased in line with inflation. Changes announced to encourage the growth of profit-related pay. Encouragement for personal pension schemes. No change in taxes on oils, tobacco and alcohol implying cuts of about £7½ billion relative to an indexed base.
April 1	Chancellor describes targets for sterling of around DM 2.90 and US$1.60 in speech at NEDC meeting.

June 1	Halifax and Abbey National Building Societies join banks' centralised system for clearing payments such as standing orders and direct debits.
June 2	Dr A. Greenspan succeeds Mr P. Volcker as Chairman of US Federal Reserve.
June 7	Offer for shares in Rolls Royce closes, heavily oversubscribed.
June 9	Policy cooperation agreement between 7 major industrial countries at Venice economic summit meeting.
June 11	Conservatives win 101–seat majority in general election.

CHARTS OF MAIN ECONOMIC INDICATORS

Chart A.1 *Growth rates of GDP*

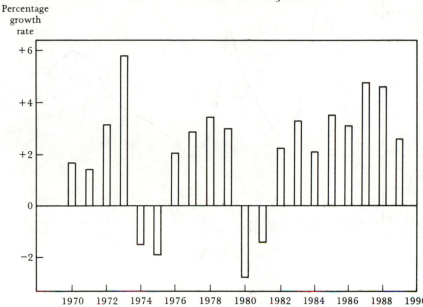

Source: Economic Trends Annual Supplement, 1990 updated from Economic Trends, July, 1990.

Chart A.2 *Unemployment*

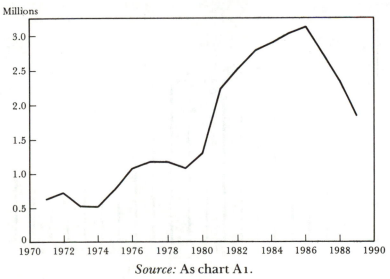

Source: As chart A1.

Chart A.3   *Vacancies*

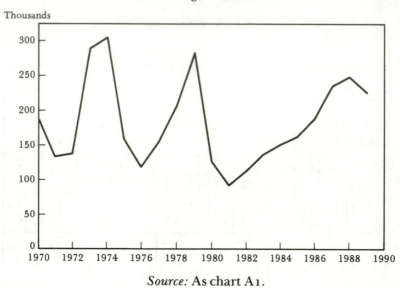

Source: As chart A1.

Chart A.4   *Inflation*

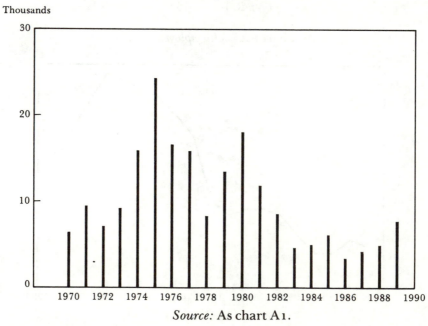

Source: As chart A1.

Chart A.5   *Balance of payments on current account*

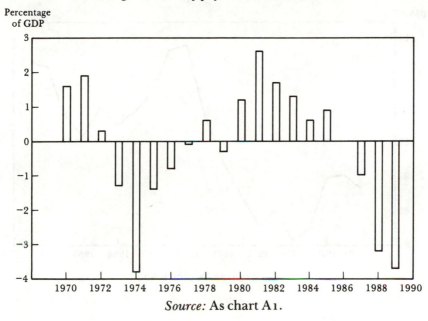

Source: As chart A1.

Chart A.6   *Exchange rate index*

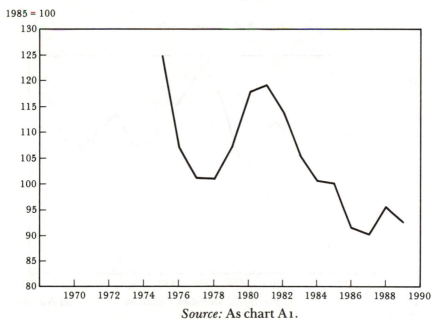

Source: As chart A1.

Chart A.7   *Relative export price index*

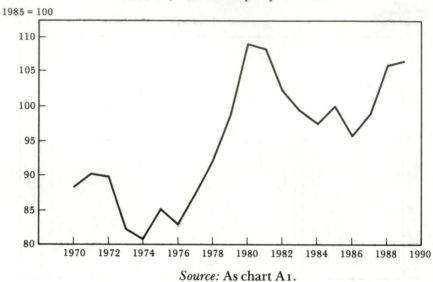

Source: As chart A1.

Chart A.8   *Interest rates*

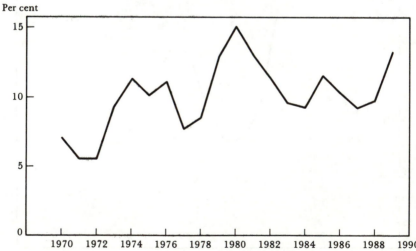

Source: IMF, *International Financial Statistics Yearbook, 1988*, and August 1990.

Chart A.9 *Monetary growth (M4)*

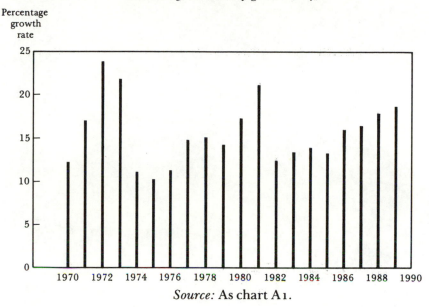

Percentage
growth
rate

Source: As chart A1.

Chart A.10 *General government financial balance*

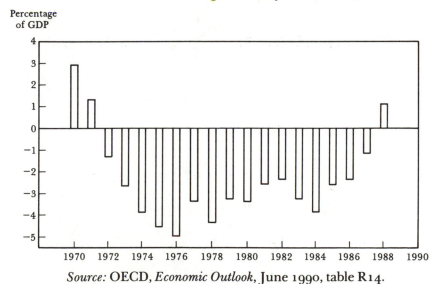

Percentage
of GDP

Source: OECD, *Economic Outlook*, June 1990, table R14.

BIBLIOGRAPHIC NOTES

PART 1

NARRATIVE OF EVENTS

We cannot hope in this note to provide a comprehensive list of all the written material referring to the events and issues that have been covered in the text. The economics profession has become too prolific for that. It may nevertheless be helpful to list some of the works which readers of this book may find it useful to consult, or to which this study is especially indebted. This first note concentrates on historical and descriptive studies, and official or semi-official publications, more analytical references being included with the part of this book to which they seem most relevant.

The development of the British economy year by year can be traced in the annual country studies published by the OECD Secretariat, in the account of recent events in the Treasury's Budget Reports, in the quarterly issues of the *National Institute Economic Review*, or in similar publications by other independent forecasters and commentators.

Postwar economic history up to 1960 is covered by Dow (1964) and from 1960–74 by Blackaby (Ed.) (1978). Assessments of the period of the Heath government are useful to understanding of subsequent events: see Harris and Sewill (1975) and Holmes (1982).

Books about economic policy during the period covered by this study by ex-officials include Browning (1986) on the period 1964–85, Gardner (1987) which begins in 1973 and Pliatzky (1989) which begins in 1979. Maynard (1988), which also concentrates on the period of the Thatcher government, is by an ex-Deputy Chief Economic Adviser to the Treasury. The authors of Donaghue (1987) and Ham (1981) were policy advisers to the Labour government, whilst the authors of Griffiths (1976) and Walters (1986) were both economic advisers to Mrs Thatcher during the period of this study. Those especially interested in the events of 1976 may wish to consult Burk (1989).

In addition to these accounts by 'insiders' there are numerous other studies. The period of Labour government is covered by Coates (1980) and by Holmes (1985a); a more analytical study by Artis *et al.* (1990) was in preparation at the same time as this book. The Conservative period is covered by Holmes (1985b) and in the context of a broader account of Thatcherism by Riddell (1983). Behrens (1980) gives one account of the origins of Thatcherism in the 1970s, Keegan (1984) another. Keegan (1989) takes the story up to the resignation of Nigel Lawson.

Official documents are indispensable to the study of economic policy; of special value are the papers collected together in Bank of England (1984b). On monetary policy the Green Paper on *Monetary Control*, Bank of England and HM Treasury (1980), repays very close scrutiny. From the same period, the report of the House of Commons Treasury and Civil Service Committee (TCSC) (1981) is of the first importance. For fiscal policy there is no substitute for the line-by-line study of successive issues of the Treasury's *Financial Statement and Budget Report*. Lawson (1981 and 1984) sets out the philosophy that was used to present macroeconomic policy at greater length.

Two lectures by Permanent Secretaries to the Treasury, when in office, Wass (1978) and Middleton (1989), form an interesting contrast. Wass (1983) is an example of a different genre, being reflections on policymaking after retirement. There are also a number of reflections by ministers after retirement, most notably Healey (1989), Callaghan (1987) and Barnett (1982).

There are many accounts for the general reader of how the Treasury and the Bank of England do their respective jobs. One of the more entertaining is Young and Sloman (1984) based on a radio programme.

This volume includes a Calendar of Main Economic Events, but it is only an abbreviation of Picton (1989), which has been published separately.

References

Artis, M. and Cobham, D. (Eds) (1990), *The Labour Government's Economic Record 1974–79*, Manchester University Press.

Bank of England (1982), 'The supplementary special deposits scheme', *Bank of England Quarterly Bulletin*, no. 1, March.

(1984a), 'Funding the public sector borrowing requirement: 1952–83', *Bank of England Quarterly Bulletin*, no. 4, December.

(1984b), *The Development and Operation of Monetary Policy, 1960–1983*, Oxford, Clarendon Press.

(1987), 'Measures of broad money', *Bank of England Quarterly Bulletin*, no. 2, May.

and HM Treasury (1980), *Monetary Control, Cmnd. 7858*, London, HMSO.

Barnett, J. (1982), *Inside the Treasury*, London, André Deutsch.

Behrens, R. (1980), *The Conservative Party from Heath to Thatcher; policies and politics 1974–79*, Saxon House.

Blackaby, F.T. (Ed.) (1978), *British Economic Policy 1960–74*, Cambridge University Press.

Browning, P. (1986), *The Treasury and Economic Policy 1964–1985*, London, Longman.

Burk, K. (Ed.) (1989), 'Symposium on the 1976 IMF crisis', *Contemporary Record*, November.

Callaghan, J. (1987), *Time and Chance*, Collins.

Coates, D. (1980), *Labour in Power? A Study of the Labour Government 1974–79*, London, Longman.

Donaghue, B. (1987), *Prime Minister*, Jonathan Cape.

Dow, J.C.R. (1964), *The Management of the British Economy 1945–60*, Cambridge University Press.

Gardner, N. (1987), *Decade of Discontent: The Changing British Economy since 1973*, Oxford, Basil Blackwell.

Griffiths, B. (1976), *Inflation. The Price of Prosperity*, London, Weidenfeld and Nicolson.

Ham, A. (1981), *Treasury Rules: Recurrent Themes in British Economic Policy*, Quartet Books.

Harris, R. and Sewill, B. (1975), *British Economic Policy 1970–74: Two Views*, London, Institute of Economic Affairs, Hobart Paperback no. 7.

Healey, D. (1989), *Time of My Life*, London, Michael Joseph.

HM Treasury (1975), 'The attack on inflation', Treasury Broadsheet no. 10, Britain's Economy no. 4, London, HM Treasury.

(1976), *The Attack on Inflation: the Second Year, Cmnd.* 6507, London, HMSO.

(1977), *The Attack on Inflation after 31st July, 1977, Cmnd.* 6882, London, HMSO.

(1978a), *The European Monetary System, Cmnd.* 7405, London, HMSO.

(1978b), *Winning the Battle against Inflation, Cmnd.* 7293, London, HMSO.

(1984), *The Next Ten Years: Public Expenditure and Taxation into the 1990s, Cmnd.* 9189, London, HMSO.

(1985), 'The relationship between employment and wages: empirical evidence for the United Kingdom.' Review by Treasury officials, London, HM Treasury.

(Session 1980–81) (1981), *3rd Report, Monetary Policy: Report, HC163–I–III*, London, HMSO.

Holmes, M. (1982), *Political Pressure and Economic Policy: British Government 1970–74*, London, Butterworth Scientific.

(1985a), *The First Thatcher Government 1979–1983. Contemporary Conservatism and Economic Change*. London, Wheatsheaf.

(1985b), *The Labour Government 1974–1979. Political Aims and Economic Reality*. London, Macmillan.

House of Commons Treasury and Civil Service Committee (Session 1979–80) (1980), *Memorandum on Monetary Policy* (Vols I and II), *MC* 720I–II, London, HMSO.

Keegan, W. (1984), *Mrs Thatcher's Economic Experiment*, Harmondsworth, Penguin Books.

(1989), *Mr Lawson's Gamble*, Hodder and Stoughton.

Lawson, N. (1981), 'Thatcherism in practice: a progress report', Speech to the Zurich Society of Economics, 14 January, HM Treasury press release.

(1984), 'The British experiment, the Fifth Mais Lecture', London, City University Business School pamphlet.

Leigh-Pemberton, R. (1987), 'The instruments of monetary policy', *Bank of England Quarterly Bulletin* no. 3, August.

Maynard, G. (1988), *The Economy under Mrs Thatcher*, Oxford, Basil Blackwell.

Middleton, P. (1989), 'Economic policy formulation in the Treasury in the post-war period', *National Institute Economic Review*, no. 127, February.

Nevin, M. (1983), *The Age of Illusions: the Political Economy of Britain 1968–82*, London, Gollancz.

Picton, H. (1989), 'Calendar of Economic Events 1984–87', mimeo, London, National Institute of Economic and Social Research.

Pliatzky, L. (1989), *The Treasury under Mrs Thatcher*, Oxford, Basil Blackwell.

Riddell, P. (1983), *The Thatcher Government*, Oxford, Martin Robertson.

Walters, A. (1986), *Britain's Economic Renaissance: M. Thatcher's Reforms 1979–1984*, Oxford and New York, Oxford University Press.

Wass, D. (1978), 'The changing problems of economic management', *Economic Trends*, no. 293, March.

(1984), *Government and the Governed: BBC Reith Lectures 1983*, London, Routledge and Kegan Paul.
Young, H. and Sloman, A. (1984), *But, Chancellor*, London, British Broadcasting Corporation.

PART 2

HISTORY OF IDEAS

This note will concentrate on the development of ideas described in the text, rather than attempt the impossible task of cataloguing all the literature relevant to macroeconomic policy written during the 1970s and the 1980s. For convenience it is in four parts, corresponding to the four chapters of this part of the book.

The 1970s: Developments in Keynesianism

At the beginning of the decade there was great interest amongst academic economists in this country in the reassessment of Keynes in Clower (1965) and in Leijonhufvud (1968). Another later line of development was represented by Barro and Grossman (1971 and 1976) in America, and by Malinvaud (1977 and 1982) in France. For the reflections at this time of one of the greatest of the Keynesians see Hicks (1974). Many of the greatest American Keynesians were devoting much of their attention to combatting the influence of monetarism – see, for example, Tobin (1972) (1977), Tobin and Buiter (1976, 1979 and 1980), Modigliani (1977) and Okun (1981). For another spirited counter attack see Kaldor (1982). The *General Theory* had a continuing fascination and various Keynesian anniversaries continued to be celebrated with conferences and conference volumes, as in Worswick and Trevithick (Eds.) (1983) and in Eltis and Sinclair (eds.) (1988). In 1982 the *National Institute Economic Review* celebrated its 100th number by publishing a series of articles by its previous editors, which now stand as a useful record of the controversies of the time, see Bispham (1982), Blackaby (1982), Mayes (1982), Minford (1982) and Surrey (1982).

Most of the literature of macroeconomic modelbuilding is also to be found in the conference volumes which typify the 1970s. The most important ones are Ormerod (Ed.) (1979), Holly, Rustem and Zarrop (Eds.) (1979), Hilton and Heathfield (Eds.) (1970), Posner (Ed.) (1978), Renton (Ed.) (1975), and Worswick and Blackaby (Eds.) (1974). The Treasury economists contributed to many of these conferences and also published a series of discussion papers, which are very useful as indicators of the way official thinking was developing. These include Bennett (1982), Odling-Smee and Hartly (1978), Lomax and Mowl (1978), Mowl (1980), Richardson (1981), Spencer and Mowl (1978), Shepherd (1978) and Shepherd *et al.* (1974). The Treasury also published the report of the Ball Committee, Ball (1978). The work of Jorgensen referred to in the text developed from Jorgensen (1963).

There was a substantial technical literature on optimal control which modelbuilders referred to extensively at this time. Especially relevant are Chow and Corsi (1975 and 1982) and Bray (1975).

The writings of the New Cambridge School can be found in the *Cambridge*

Economic Policy Review and in Godley and Cripps (1976 and 1983), Godley and May (1974), Featherstone and Godley (1978) and Coutts *et al.* (1981). There is further discussion of their ideas in Kahn and Posner (1974), in Bispham (1975) and in Blinder and Solow (1978).

The 1970s: The Monetarist Challenge

A useful point of entry into the monetarist controversies of the mid-1970s, as seen from this country, is the survey article by Laidler and Parkin (1975). From a world perspective the most influential monetarist writings included Friedman (1968 and 1970): also important were Brunner and Meltzer (1976), Lucas and Rapping (1969) and Andersen and Jordan (1986). Specially influential in the United Kingdom were Johnson (1971, 1972 and 1977); the work of the most significant of home grown British monetarists is typified by Laidler (1975).

The empirical studies of the Manchester monetarists, before they emigrated, are described in Parkin and Sumner (Eds.) (1975 and 1978) and in Parkin and Zis (Eds.) (1976). Studies of the demand for money in the United Kingdom include Goodhart and Crockett (1970) and Haache (1974) from the Bank of England, Artis and Lewis (1976) and Smith (1978) as well as Grice and Bennett (1981 and 1984) from the Treasury.

The ideas developed by the London Business School are set out in Ball and Burns (1976), Ball, Burns and Lowry (1977) and in Ball, Burns and Warburton (1979). International monetarism owed its inspiration in part to the economists of the International Monetary Fund, see IMF (1977) and Mundell and Polak (Eds.) (1977), and in part to Henry Johnson's time at LSE, see Frenkel and Johnson (Eds.) (1976).

The new classical economics was developed in the 1970s in articles such as Barro (1974 and 1976), Lucas (1972, 1976 and 1977), Lucas and Sargent (1981), Kydland and Prescott (1977), and Sargent and Wallace (1975 and 1976). It was later brought together in books, notably Sargent (1979 and 1987) and Barro (1984).

The British literature on new classical economics hardly begins until the end of the decade, with for example Begg (1980 and 1982), Attfield *et al.* (1981 and 1985) and Beenstock (1980). For an early application of rational expectations to the United Kingdom see McCallum (1975). For contemporary discussion of the issue see Mayes (1981). The modelbuilding work of the Liverpool new classical group can be found in their quarterly *Review* and in Minford and Peel (1983).

To understand how monetarism gained ground in Britain in the 1970s it is useful to refer to some of the influential writings of the time, for example, Brittan and Lilley (1977), Hayek (1975), Joseph (1978) and Jay (1976).

The 1980s: Monetarism in Practice

Much of the material discussed in this section can be found in official publications listed in the bibliographic note to Part I. The evidence submitted to the TCSC is especially valuable. Not to be missed (although difficult to find) is Niehaus (1981). Some of the ideas of Treasury officials on monetary control prior to the change of government can be seen in Middleton *et al.* (1981), another important text. For a Bank of England view on a related issue see Foot *et al.* (1979) and more generally Goodhart (1984). Another useful general reference is Griffiths and Woods (Eds.) (1981) reflecting the views of the influential City University economists. The views of the National Institute are set out in Savage (1979 and 1980). The evidence for monetarism in the United Kingdom was supplemented in the 1980s by Friedman and Schwartz (1982), which was criticised in Hendry and Ericsson (1983) and in Brown (1983). Evidence of the unique stability of the demand for Mo was provided by the Treasury in Johnston (1984). For the view that monetarism was really a kind of restrictive demand management see Fforde (1984), by a senior official of the Bank of England.

The 1980s: Alternatives to Monetarism

Useful surveys of the literature of the 1980s are Fischer (1988) on macroeconomics, Goodhart (1989a) on monetary policy and Wallis (1989) on macroeconomic forecasting. Responses to new classicism were made by Akerlof (1979), Buiter (1980) and collected usefully together in Davies (1989).

The New Keynesian school at Cambridge produced Meade (1982), Vines et al. (1983) and Weale et al. (1989) as well as Blake and Weale (1988). The idea of targeting nominal GDP is also discussed in Brittan (1981) and in Bean (1983). The output of the Centre for Labour Economics was especially prolific, and included for example Layard and Nickell (1985 and 1986), as well as Layard (1986). Hysteresis is discussed in Blanchard and Summers (1986) and in Cross (Ed.) (1988).

The literature on exchange rate determination and policy became voluminous in the 1980s. As examples we might take Dornbusch (1987), which is related to Dornbusch (1976), Eltis and Sinclair (Eds.) (1981), Artis and Currie (1981) and Brooks, Cuthbertson and Mayes (1986). A famous critique of exchange rate policy around 1979–80 is developed in Buiter and Miller (1981, 1982 and 1984); see also Sargent (1986).

The developments of macroeconomic modelbuilding in the 1980s were charted by the ESRC Modelbuilding Bureau at Warwick University in Wallis et al. (1985, 1986a, 1986b and 1987). National Institute work is reported in Britton (Ed.) (1983), and in Hall and Henry (1985 and 1988); work at the Treasury in Mellis (1984), Westaway and Whittaker (1986) and in Westaway (1986). The Bank of England model is described in Patterson et al. (1987); the City University new classical model in Beenstock et al. (1986). The LBS model is described in Budd et al. (1984) and the Liverpool model in Minford et al. (1984). The large disaggregated model built at Cambridge is described in Barker and Peterson (Eds.) (1987). All the main modelling teams came together at the end of the period for another conference, and another conference volume, Britton (Ed.) (1989). The use made of models and formal policy analysis in practice is usefully assessed in Currie (1985).

References

Akerlof, G.A. (1979), 'The case against conservative macroeconomics: an inaugural lecture', *Economica*, 46, no. 183, August.

Andersen, L.C. and Jordan, J.L. (1968), 'Monetary and fiscal actions: a test of their relative importance in economic stabilisation', *Federal Reserve Bank of St Louis Monthly Review*, 50, no. 11, November.

Artis, M.J. and Currie, D.A. (1981), 'Monetary targets and the exchange rate: a case for conditional targets' in Eltis and Sinclair, *Money Supply and the Exchange Rate*.

Artis, M.J. and Lewis, M.K. (1976), 'The demand for money in the United Kingdom 1963–73', *Manchester School*, no. 2, June.

Attfield, C.L.F., Demery, D. and Duck, N.W. (1981), 'A quarterly model of unanticipated monetary growth, output and the price level in the UK 1963–78', *Journal of Monetary Economics*, 8, no. 3, November.

(1985), *Rational Expectations in Macroeconomics: an introduction to theory and evidence*, Oxford, Basil Blackwell.

Ball, R.J. (1978), *Report of the Committee on Policy Optimisation*, Cmnd. 7148, London HMSO.

and Burns, T. (1976), 'The inflationary mechanism in the UK economy', *American Economic Review*, 66, no. 4, September.

Burns, T. and Laury, J.S.E. (1977), 'The role of exchange rate changes in balance of payments adjustment – the UK case', *Economic Journal*, 87, no. 1.

Burns, T. and Warburton, P.J. (1979), 'The London Business School model of the UK economy: an exercise in international monetarism' in Ormerod (Ed.), *Economic Modelling*, Heinemann/Gower.

Barker T.S. and Peterson, W. (Eds.) (1987), *The Cambridge Multisectoral dynamic model of the British Economy*, Cambridge University Press.

Barro, R.J. (1974), 'Are government bonds net wealth?' *Journal of Political Economics*, 82, no. 6, November/December.

(1976), 'Rational expectations and the role of monetary policy', *Journal of Monetary Economics*, no. 1, January.

(1984), *Macroeconomics*, New York and Chicester, Wiley.

and Fischer, S. (1976), 'Recent developments in monetary theory', *Journal of Monetary Economics*, no. 2, April.

and Grossman, H. (1971), 'A general disequilibrium model of income and employment', *American Economic Review*, no. 1, March.

and Grossman, H. (1976), *Money, Employment and Inflation*, Cambridge University Press.

Bean, C.R. (1983), 'Targeting nominal income: an appraisal', *Economic Journal*, 93, no. 372

Beenstock, M. (1980), *A Neoclassical Analysis of Macroeconomic Policy*, Cambridge University Press.

Warburton, P., Lewington, P. and Dalziel, A. (1986), 'A macroeconomic model of aggregate supply and demand for the UK', *Economic Modelling*, no. 4, October.

Begg, D. (1980), 'Rational expectations and the non-neutrality of systematic monetary policy', *Review of Economic Studies*, no. 147, January.

(1982), *The Rational Expectations Revolution in Macroeconomics*, Oxford, Philip Allan.

Bennett, A. (1982), 'Expenditure, wealth and the rate of interest, 1982', Treasury Working Paper no. 25, Government Economic Service Working Paper no. 59.

Bispham, J.A. (1975), 'The New Cambridge and monetarist criticisms of "conventional" economic policy-making', *National Institute Economic Review*, no. 74, November.

(1982), 'The nature of the inflation process', *National Institute Economic Review*, no. 100, May.

Blackaby, F.T. (1982), 'Forecasting and economic policy', *National Institute Economic Review*, no. 100, May.

Blake, A. and Weale, M. (1988), 'Exchange-rate targets and wage formation', *National Institute Economic Review*, no. 123, February.

Blanchard, O.J. and Summers, L.H. (1986), Hysteresis and the European unemployment problem, in *NBER Macroeconomics Annual 1986*, London and Cambridge, Mass, MIT Press.

Blinder, A.S. and Solow, R.M. (1978), 'What's "new" and what's "Keynesian" in the "New Cambridge" Keynesianism? in Brunner, K. and Meltzer, A.H. (Eds.), *Carnegie-Rochester Conference Series on Public Policy 9*, Amsterdam, North-Holland.

Bray, J. (1975), 'Optimal control of a noisy economy with the UK as an example' (with discussion), *Journal of Royal Statistical Society*, 138. A, part 3.

Brittan, S. (1981), *How to End the 'Monetarist' Controversy*, Hobart paper no. 9, London, Institute of Economic Affairs.

and Lilley, P. (1977), *The Delusion of Incomes Policy*, London, Maurice Temple Smith.

Britton, A.J.C. (Ed.) (1983), *Employment, Output and Inflation: the National Institute Model of the British Economy*, London, Heinemann.

(1989), *Policymaking with Macroeconomic Models*, Aldershot, Gower.

Brooks, S. Cuthbertson, K. and Mayes, D. (1986), *The Exchange Rate Environment*, Beckenham, Croom Helm.

Brown, A.J. (1983), 'Friedman and Schwartz on the United Kingdom, Bank of England', Bank of England Panel of Academic Consultants Panel paper no. 22, Monetary Trends in the UK.

Brunner, K. and Meltzer, A.H. (1976), 'An aggregate theory for a closed economy' in Stein, J. (Ed.), *Monetarism: Studies in Monetary Economics*, Amsterdam, North-Holland.

Budd, A.P., Dicks, G., Keating, G., Holly, S. and Robinson, B. (1984), 'The London Business School econometric model of the UK', *Economic Modelling*, no. 4, October.

Buiter, W.H. (1980), 'The Macroeconomics of Dr. Pangloss: a critical survey of the new classical macroeconomics', *Economic Journal*, no. 34.

and Miller, M.H. (1981), 'The Thatcher experiment: the first two years', Brookings Papers on Economic Activity no. 2.

and Miller, M.H. (1982), 'Real exchange rate overshooting and the output cost of bringing down inflation', *European Economic Review*, 18, no. 1/2, May/June.

and Miller, M.H. (1984), 'The macroeconomic consequences of a change of regime: the UK under Mrs Thatcher', LSE Centre for Labour Economics Discussion Paper no. 179, 1983.

Chow, G.A. and Corsi, P. (Eds.) (1975), *Analysis and Control of Dynamic Economic Systems*, Chichester and New York, Wiley.

and Corsi, P. (Eds.), (1982), *Evaluating the Reliability of Macroeconomic Models*, Chichester, Wiley.

Clower, R.W. (1965), 'The Keynesian counter-revolution: a theoretical appraisal' in Hahn, F.H. and Brechling F. (Eds.), *The Theory of Interest Rates*, Proceedings of a Conference held by the International Economic Association, London, Macmillan.

Coutts, K. *et al.* (1981), 'The economic consequences of Mrs Thatcher', *Cambridge Journal of Economics*, 5, no. 1, March.

Cross, R. (Ed.) (1988), *Unemployment, Hysteresis and the Natural Rate Hypothesis*, Oxford, Basil Blackwell.

Currie, D.A. (1985), 'Macroeconomic policy design and control theory – a failed partnership?', *Economic Journal*, 95, no. 378, June.

Davies, G. (1989), 'A critique of monetarism, old and new' in Shields, J. (Ed.), *Conquering Unemployment*, London, Macmillan.

Dornbusch, R. (1976), 'Expectations and exchange rate dynamics', *Journal of Political Economy*, no. 6, December.

(1987), 'Exchange rate economics: 1986', *Economic Journal*, 97, no. 385.

Eltis, W.A. and Sinclair, P.J.N. (Eds.) (1981), *Money Supply and the Exchange Rate*, Oxford University Press.

and Sinclair, P.J.N. (1988), *Keynes and Economic Policy*, London, Macmillan.

Fetherston, M.J. and Godley, W.A.H. (1974) 'Budget deficit and demand management', *London and Cambridge Economic Bulletin*.

and Godley, W.A.H. (1978), 'New Cambridge macroeconomics and global monetarism', Supplement to the *Journal of Monetary Economics*, Brunner and Meltzer (Eds), Carnegie-Rochester Conference Series on Public Policy 9.

Fforde, J.S., (1984), 'Setting monetary objectives' in Bank of England (Ed.), *The Development and Operation of Monetary Policy*.

Fischer, S. (1988), 'Recent developments in macroeconomics', *Economic Journal*, 98, no. 391.

Foot, M.D.K.W., Goodhart, C.A.E. and Hotson, A.C. (1979), 'Monetary base control', *Bank of England Quarterly Bulletin*, no.2, June.

Frenkel, J.A. and Johnson, H.G. (Eds.) (1976), *The Monetary Approach to the Balance of Payments*, London, Allen & Unwin.

Friedman, M. (1968), 'The role of monetary policy', *American Economic Review*, no. 1, March.

(1970), 'A theoretical framework for monetary analysis', *Journal of Political Economy*, no. 2, March/April.

(1975), *Unemployment versus Inflation*, London, Institute for Economic Affairs, Occasional Paper 44.

and Schwartz, A.J. (1982), *Monetary Trends in the United States and the United Kingdom: their relation to income, prices and interest rates, 1867–1975*, Chicago and London, University of Chicago Press.

Godley, W.A.H. and Cripps, F. (1976), 'A formal analysis of the Cambridge Economic Policy Group model', *Economica*, no. 172, November.

and Cripps, F. (1983), *Macroeconomics*, Fontana Books.

and May, F. (1974), 'Budget deficit and demand management', *London and Cambridge Economic Bulletin*.

Goodhart, C.A.E. (1984), *Monetary Theory and Practice: the UK Experience*, London, Macmillan.

(1989), 'The conduct of monetary policy', *Economic Journal*, 99, no. 396.

and Crockett, A.D. (1970), 'The importance of money', *Bank of England Quarterly Bulletin*, no. 2, June.

Grice, J. and Bennett, A. (1981), 'The demand for sterling M3 and other aggregates in the United Kingdom' with annex by Norman Cumming, Treasury, Government Economic Service Working Paper no. 45.

and Bennett, A. (1984), 'Wealth and the demand for M3 in the United Kingdom 1963–1978', *Manchester School*, no. 3, September.

Griffiths, B. and Wood, G.E. (Eds.) (1981), *Monetary Targets*, London, Macmillan.

Haache, G. (1974), 'The demand for money in the United Kingdom: experience since 1971', *Bank of England Quarterly Bulletin*, no. 3, September.

Hall, S.G. and Henry, S.G.B. (1985), 'Rational expectations in an econometric model: NIESR model 8', *National Institute Economic Review*, no. 114, November.

and Henry, S.G.B. (1988), *Macroeconomic Modelling*, Amsterdam, North-Holland.

Hayek, F.A. (1975), *Full Employment at Any Price?* London, Institute of Economic Affairs, Occasional Paper no. 45.

Hendry, D.F. and Ericsson, N.R. (1983), 'Assertion without empirical basis: an econometric appraisal of 'Monetary trends in . . . the United Kingdom' by Milton Friedman and Anna Schwartz', Bank of England Panel of Academic Consultants, Panel Paper no. 22, Monetary trends in the UK.

Hicks, J.R. (1974), *The Crisis in Keynesian Economics*, Yrjo Jahnsson lectures, Oxford, Basil Blackwell.

Hilton, K. and Heathfield, D.F. (Eds.) (1970), *The Econometric Study of the United Kingdom*, London, Macmillan.

Holly, S., Rustem, B. and Zarrop, M.B. (Eds.) (1979), *Optimal Control for Econometric Models: an approach to Economic Policy Formulation*, London, Macmillan.

International Monetary Fund (1977), 'The monetary approach to the balance of payments: a collection of research papers by members of the staff of the IMF', Washington, IMF.

Jay, P. (1976), *Employment, Inflation and Politics*, Institute of Economic Affairs.

Johnson, H.G. (1971), 'The Keynesian revolution and the monetarist counter-revolution, *American Economic Review*, 61, no. 2, May.

(1972), *Inflation and the Monetarist Controversy*, Amsterdam, North-Holland.

(1977), 'The monetary approach to balance of payments theory and policy. Explanation and policy implications', *Economica*, no. 175, August.

Johnston, R.B. (1984), 'The demand for non-interest-bearing money in the United Kingdom', HM Treasury Working Paper no. 28, Government Economic Service Working Paper no. 66.

Jorgensen, D.W. (1963), 'Capital theory and investment behaviour', *American Economic Review*, 53, no. 2, May.

Joseph, K.J. (1978), 'Conditions for fuller employment', Centre for Policy Studies.

Kahn, R. and Posner, M. (1974), 'Cambridge economics and the balance of payments', *London and Cambridge Economic Bulletin*, no. 85, July.

Kaldor, N. (1986), *The Scourge of Monetarism*, Oxford University Press.

Kydland, F. and Prescott, E.C. (1977), 'Rule rather than discretion: the inconsistency of optimal plans', *Journal of Political Economy*, no. 3, June.

Laidler, D.E.W. (1975), *Essays on Money and Inflation*, Manchester University Press.

(1982), 'On the case for gradualism' in *Monetarist Perspectives*, Oxford, Philip Allan.

(1985), 'Monetary policy in Britain. Successes and shortcomings', *Oxford Review of Economic Policy*, 1, no. 1, Spring.

and Parkin, J.M. (1975), 'Inflation: a survey', *Economic Journal*, 85, no. 741.

Layard R. (1986), *How to Beat Unemployment*, Oxford University Press.

and Nickell, S. (1985), 'The causes of British unemployment', *National Institute Economic Review*, no. 111, February.

and Nickell, S. (1986), 'Unemployment in Britain', *Economica*, 53, Supplement, no. 210(S).

Leijonhufvud, A. (1968), *On Keynesian Economics and the Economics of Keynes: a Study in Monetary Theory*, London, Oxford University Press.

Lomax, R. and Mowl, C. (1978), 'Balance of payments flows and the monetary aggregates in the United Kingdom Treasury', Government Economic Service Working Paper no. 5.

Lucas, R.E. (1972), 'Expectations and the neutrality of money', *Journal of Economic Theory*, 4, no. 2, April.

(1976), 'Econometric policy evaluation: a critique' in Brunner, K. and Meltzer, A.H. (Eds.), *The Phillips Curve and Labour Markets*, Amsterdam, North-Holland.

(1977), 'Understanding business cycles' in 'Stabilization of the Domestic and International Economy', Carnegie-Rochester Conference Series vol.5.

and Rapping, L.A. (1969), 'Price expectations and the Phillips curve', *American Economic Review*, 59, nos. 1/3/4/5.

and Sargent, T. (1978), 'After Keynesian economics', in *After the Phillips Curve: Persistence of High Inflation and High Unemployment*, Federal Reserve Bank of Boston.

and Sargent, T. (Eds) (1981), *Rational Expectations and Econometric Practice*, London, Allen and Unwin.

McCallum, B.T. (1975), 'Rational expectations and the natural rate hypothesis: some evidence for the United Kingdom', *Manchester School*, no. 1, March.

Melliss, C.L. (1984), 'Some experiments with optimal control on the Treasury model', HM Treasury Working Paper no 29, Government Economic Service Working Paper no. 67.

Malinvaud, E. (1977), *The Theory of Unemployment Reconsidered*, Oxford, Basil Blackwell.

(1982), 'Wages and unemployment', *Economic Journal* 92, no. 365.

Mayes, D.G. (1981), 'The controversy over rational expectations', *National Institute Economic Review*, no. 96, May.

(1982), 'Forecasting and economic policy', *National Institute Economic Review*, no. 100, May.

Meade, J.E. (1982), *Stagflation: Volume 1, Wage Fixing*, George Allen and Unwin.

Minford, P. (1982), 'The four ages of postwar British policy debate', *National Institute Economic Review*, no. 100, May.

Marwaha, S., Matthews, K. and Sprague, A. (1984), 'The Liverpool macroeconomic model of the United Kingdom', *Economic Modelling*, no. 1, January.

and Peel, D. (1983), *Rational Expectations and the New Macroeconomics*, Oxford, Martin Robertson.

Modigliani, F. (1977), 'The monetarist controversy or, should we forsake stabilization policies?' *American Economic Review*, 67, no. 2.

Mowl, C. (1980), 'Simulations on the Treasury model', HM Treasury Working Paper no. 15, Government Economic Service Working Paper no. 34.

Mundell, R.A. and Polak, J.J. (Eds.) (1977), *The New International Monetary System*, New York, Columbia University Press.

Niehaus, J. (1981), 'The appreciation of sterling – causes, effects, policies', SSRC Money Study Group (mimeo), Volkswirtschaftliches Institut (University of Bern) Discussion Paper, February.

Odling-Smee, J. and Hartley, N. (1978), 'Some effects of exchange rate changes', HM Treasury Government Economic Service Working Paper no. 2.

Okun, A.M. (1981), *Prices and Quantities. A Macroeconomic Analysis,* Washington, Brookings Institution.

Ormerod, P. (Ed.) (1979), *Economic Modelling,* Heinemann/Gower.

Parkin, J.M. and Sumner, M.T. (1975), *Incomes Policy and Inflation,* Manchester University Press and Toronto University Press.

and Sumner, M.T. (Eds.) (1978), *Inflation in the United Kingdom,* Manchester University Press.

and Zis, G. (1976), 'The determination of the rate of change of wages and prices in the fixed exchange rate world economy 1956–1970', in Parkin and Zis (Eds.), *Inflation in the World Economy,* Manchester University Press.

Patterson, K., Harnett, I., Robinson, G. and Ryding, J. (1987),'The Bank of England quarterly model of the UK economy',. *Economic Modelling,* no. 4, October.

Posner, M. (Ed.) (1978), *Demand Management,* London, Heinemann.

Renton, G.A. (Ed.) (1975), *Modelling the Economy,* London, Heinemann.

Richardson, P. (1981), 'Money and prices: a simulation study using the Treasury macroeconomic model', HM Treasury Working Paper no 17, Government Economic Service Working Paper no. 41.

Sargent, T. (1979), *Macroeconomic Theory,* London, Academic Press.

(1986), 'Stopping moderate inflations: the methods of Poincaré and Thatcher' in Sargent (Ed.), *Rational Expectations and Inflation,* New York, Harper and Row.

(1987), *Dynamic Macroeconomic Theory,* Cambridge, Mass and London, Harvard University Press.

and Wallace, N. (1975), 'Rational expectations, the optimal monetary instrument, and the optimal money supply rule', *Journal of Political Economy,* no. 2, April.

and Wallace, N. (1976), 'Rational expectations and the theory of economic policy', *Journal of Monetary Economics,* no. 2, April.

and Wallace, N. (1981), 'Some unpleasant monetarist arithmetic', *Federal Reserve Bank of Minneapolis Quarterly Review,* Fall.

Savage, D. (1979), 'Monetary targets and the control of the money supply', *National Institute Economic Review,* no. 89, August.

(1980), 'Some issues of monetary policy', *National Institute Economic Review,* no. 91, February.

Shepherd, J. (1978), 'Some problems in the development of the Treasury model', Economic Modelling Conference (Proceedings), July.

et al. (1974), 'The Treasury short-term forecasting model', Government Economic Service Occasional Paper no. 8.

Smith D. (1978), 'The demand for alternative monies in the UK, 1924–77', *National Westminster Bank Review,* November.

Spencer, P.D. and Mowl, C.J. (1978), 'A financial sector for the Treasury model. Part I. The model of the domestic monetary system. Government Economic Service Working Paper no. 17.

Surrey, M.J.C. (1982), 'Was the recession forecast?', *National Institute Economic Review,* no. 100, May.

Tobin, J. (1972), 'Inflation and unemployment', *American Economic Review,* 62, no.1, March.

(1977), 'How dead is Keynes?', *Economic Inquiry,* no. 4, October.

(1980), *Asset Accumulation and Economic Activity: Reflections on Contemporary Macroeconomic Theory,* Oxford, Basil Blackwell.

and Buiter, W. (1976), 'Long-run effects of fiscal and monetary policy on aggregate demand' in Stein. J. (Ed.) *Monetarism: Studies in Monetary Economics,* Amsterdam, North-Holland.

and Buiter, W. (1979), 'Deficit spending and crowding out in shorter and longer runs' in Greenfield, H.I. *et al.* (Eds.), *Theory for Economic Efficiency. Essays in Honor of Abba P. Lerner,* Cambridge, Mass, MIT Press.

Vines, D., Maciejowski, J.M. and Meade, J. (1983), *Stagflation Volume 2: Demand Management,* London, George Allen & Unwin.

Wallis, K.F. (1989), 'Macroeconomic forecasting: a survey', *Economic Journal,* 99, no. 394.

et al. (Eds.) (1985), *Models of the UK Economy. A Review by the ESRC Macroeconomic Modelling Bureau,* Oxford University Press.

et al. (Eds.) (1986), *Models of the UK Economy. A Second Review by the ESRC Macroeconomic Modelling Bureau,* Oxford University Press.

et al. (Eds.) (1986), *Models of the UK Economy. A Third Review by the ESRC Macroeconomic Modelling Bureau,* Oxford University Press.

et al. (Eds.) (1987), *Models of the UK Economy. A Fourth Review by the ESRC Macroeconomic Modelling Bureau,* Oxford University Press.

Weale, M., Blake, A., Christodoulakis, N., Meade, J. and Vines, D. (1989), *Macroeconomic Policy. Inflation, Wealth and the Exchange Rate,* London, Unwin Hyman.

Westaway, P. (1986), 'Some experiments with simple feedback rules on the Treasury model', HM Treasury Working Paper no. 40, Government Economic Service Working Paper no. 87.

and Whittaker, R. (1986), 'Consistent expectations in the Treasury model', HM Treasury Working Paper no. 39, Government Economic Service Working Paper no. 86.

Worswick, G.D.N. and Blackaby, F. (1974), *The Medium Term Models of the British Economy,* London, Heinemann.

and Trevithick, J. (Eds.) (1983), *Keynes and the Modern World. Proceedings of the Keynes Centenary Conference, Kings College, Cambridge,* Cambridge University Press.

PART 3

BRITAIN AND THE WORLD ECONOMY

Annual or quarterly economic surveys are produced by the OECD, the IMF, the European Commission, and the United Nations Economic Commission for Europe. The *National Institute Economic Review* has had a chapter on the world economy every quarter since 1959. The economic surveys of each member country prepared by the EDRC of OECD are especially useful to the historian. In addition the OECD Secretariat has published numerous reports and working papers and the IMF has published a regular series of studies and Staff Papers.

The McCracken Report (1977) is a useful starting point, reflecting the 'conventional wisdom' of the day. Nothing quite so ambitious has been attempted by the Secretariat since, but the development of thought as well as the course of events can be followed by reading the later OECD publications in the list of references below, and also Atkinson and Chouraqui (1984), Coe and Holtham (1983) and Llewellyn *et al.* (1988).

There is, of course, a great volume of other writings about the world economy as a whole. Bruno and Sachs (1985) bring together ideas which were influential from the end of the 1970s. Studies by British economists include Layard and Nickell (1985), Symons and Layard (1984), Grubb (1986), Maynard and van Ryckeghem (1976), Brown (1985 and 1988), Corden (1977), and Eatwell *et al.* (1974).

A group of papers appeared in this country in the early 1980s seeking to explain the slowdown in the growth rate of the world economy – see for example Matthews (Ed.) (1982), Prais (1983), Giersch and Wolter (1983), and Lindbeck (1983). Maddison (1982), supplemented by Maddison (1987), is especially useful on this question, as is also Englander and Mittelstädt (1988). The issue of high unemployment in the 1980s, which may or may not be related to slower growth, is addressed by Malinvaud and Fitoussi (Eds.) (1980), by Blanchard, Dornbusch and Layard (1986), by Cornwall (1990) and by McCallum (1986).

On the United States we should mention Eckstein (1978), Dennison (1980 and 1983), Allsopp (1987), Gordon (1982), Koromzay *et al.* (1987) and Oppenheimer and Reddaway (1989). On Europe we should mention Boltho (1982), Frowen *et al.* (1977), Layard *et al.* (1984) and Emersen (1984). On particular European countries see also Barker *et al.* (1984 and 1985), Courakis (1977 and 1981) and Hellwig and Neumann (1987). The quotation about Sweden in Chapter 11 is from Bosworth and Rivkin (Eds.) (1987).

Although it is not discussed at length in the text of this book, we should also mention here the growing academic literature on international policy coordination, to which British macroeconomists have made a particular contribution. Examples will be found in Bryant (1980), Oudiz and Sachs (1984), Bryant *et al.* (1988), Bryant and Portes (Eds.) (1987), Buiter and Marston (1985) and Currie and Levine (1985). Reference should also be made to the continuing debate over the related issue of world monetary reform. Two major British contributions to that debate are exemplified by Meade (1984) and by Williamson (1981 and 1983).

References

Allsopp, C. (1987), 'The rise and fall of the dollar: a comment', *Economic Journal,* 97, no. 385, March.

Atkinson, P. and Chouraqui, J–C. (1984), 'The conduct of monetary policy in the current recovery', OECD Economics and Statistics Department Working Paper no. 14, April.

Barker, K., Britton, A., Eastwood, F. and Major, R. (1985), 'Macroeconomic policy in Germany and Britain', *National Institute Economic Review,* no. 114, November.

Britton, A. and Major, R. (1984), 'Macroeconomic policy in France and Britain', *National Institute Economic Review,* no. 110, November.

Blanchard, O.J. (1987), 'Reaganomics', *Economic Policy,* no. 5.

Dornbusch, E. and Layard, R. (1986), *Restoring Europe's Prosperity,* Macroeconomic papers from the Centre for European Studies, Cambridge, Mass. and London, MIT Press.

Boltho, A. (1982), *The European Economy: Growth and Crisis,* Oxford University Press.

Bosworth, B. and Rivkin, A.M. (1987), *The Swedish Economy,* Washington DC, Brookings Institution.

Brown, A.J. (1985), *World Inflation since 1950. An International Comparative Study*, Cambridge University Press.

(1988), 'World depression and the price level', *National Institute Economic Review*, no. 123, February.

Bruno, M. and Sachs, J.D. (1985), *Economics of Worldwide Stagflation*, Oxford, Basil Blackwell.

Bryant, R.C. (1980), *Money and Monetary Policy in Interdependent Nations*, Washington, Brookings Institution.

and Portes, R. (Eds.) (1987), *Global Macroeconomics: Policy Conflict and Cooperation*, London, Macmillan.

et al. (1988), *Empirical Macroeconomics for Interdependent Economics*, Washington, Brookings Institution.

Buiter, W.H. and Marston, R. (1986), *International Economic Policy Coordination*, Cambridge University Press.

Coe, D.T. and Holtham, G. (1983), 'Output responsiveness and inflation: an aggregate study', OECD Economics and Statistics Division Working Paper no. 6, April.

Corden, W.M. (1977), *Inflation, Exchange Rates and the World Economy, Lectures on International Monetary Economics*, Oxford, Clarendon Press.

Cornwall, J. (1990), *The Theory of Economic Breakdown*, Oxford, Basil Blackwell.

Courakis, A.S. (1977), *Monetary Policy and Economic Activity in West Germany*, London, Surrey University Press.

(1981), *Inflation, Depression and Economic Policy in the West*, London, Mansell Publishing/Alexandrine Press.

Currie, D.A. and Levine, P. (1986), 'Macroeconomic policy design in an international world' in Buiter and Marston (1986) *International Economic Policy Coordination, op. cit.*

Denison, E.F. (1980), *Accounting for Slower Economic Growth: the United States in the 1970s*, Washington, Brookings Institution.

(1983), 'The interruption of productivity growth in the United States', *Economic Journal*, 93, no. 369, March.

Eatwell, J., Llewellyn, J. and Tarling, R. (1974), 'Money wage inflation in industrial countries', *RE Studies* 41(4), no. 128, October.

Eckstein, O. (1978), *The Great Recession. With a Postscript on Stagflation*, Amsterdam, North-Holland, Data resources series vol. 3.

Emerson, M. (Ed.) (1984), *Europe's Stagflation*, Oxford University Press.

Englander, A.S. and Mittlestädt, A. (1988), *Total Factor Productivity: Macroeconomic and Structural Aspects of the Slowdown*, OECD Economic Studies no. 10, Spring.

Friedman, B.M. (1982), 'Lessons from the 1979–82 monetary policy experiment', *American Economic Review*, May.

Frowen, S.F., Courakis, A.S. and Miller, M.H. (1977), *Monetary Policy and Economic Activity in West Germany*, London, Surrey University Press.

Giersch, H. and Wolter, F. (1983), 'Towards an explanation of the productivity slowdown: an acceleration-deceleration hypothesis', *Economic Journal*, 93, no. 369, March.

Gordon, R.J. (1982), 'Why US wage and employment behaviour differs from that in Britain and Japan', *Economic Journal*, 92, no. 365, March.

Grubb, D. (1986), 'Topics in the OECD Phillips curve', *Economic Journal*, 96, no. 381, March.

Hellwig, M. and Neumann, M. (1987), 'Economic policy in Germany: was there a turnaround?' *Economic Policy*, no. 5, October.

Koromzay, V., Llewellyn, J. and Potter, S. (1987), 'The rise and fall of the dollar: some explanations, consequences and lessons', *Economic Journal*, 97, no. 385, March.

Layard, R., Basevi, G., Blanchard, O., Buiter, W.H. and Dornbusch, R. (1984), 'Europe, the case for unsustainable growth', Centre for European Policy Studies Paper no. 8/9.

and Nickell, S.J. (1985), 'Unemployment, real wages and aggregate demand in Europe, Japan and the United States' in Brunner, K. and Meltzer, A.H. (Eds.), *The New Monetary Economics, Fiscal Issues and Unemployment*, Amsterdam, North-Holland, Carnegie-Rochester Conference Series on Public Policy vol 23.

Lindbeck, A. (1983), 'The recent slowdown of productivity growth', *Economic Journal*, 93, no. 369, March.

Llewellyn, J., Potter, S. and Samuelson, L. (1985), *Economic Forecasting and Policy: the International Dimension*, London, Routledge and Kegan Paul.

McCallum, J. (1986), 'Unemployment in OECD countries in the 1980s', *Economic Journal*, 96, no. 384, December.

McCracken, P. *et al.* (1977), *Towards Full Employment and Price Stability*, Paris, OECD.

Maddison, A. (1982), *Phases of Capitalist Development*, Oxford University Press.

(1987), 'Growth and slowdown in advanced capitalist economies', *Journal of Economic Literature*, June.

Malinvaud, E. and Fitoussi, J.P.(Eds.) (1980), *Unemployment in Western Countries*, Proceedings of a Conference held by the International Economic Association at Bischenberg, France, London, Macmillan.

Matthews, R.C.O. (Ed.) (1982), *Slower Growth in the Western World*, London, Heinemann.

Maynard, G. and van Ryckeghem, W.V. (1976), *A World of Inflation*, London, Batsford Ltd.

Meade, J.E. (1984), 'A new Keynesian Bretton Woods', *Three Banks Review*, no. 142, June.

OECD (1979), *Monetary Targets and Inflation Control*, Paris, OECD Monetary Studies Series.

(1982a), *Positive Adjustment Policies: Managing Structural Change: Summary and Conclusions*, Paris, OECD.

(1982b), *The Challenge of Unemployment: a Report to Labour Ministers*, Paris, OECD.

(1985), *Exchange Rate Management and the Conduct of Monetary Policy*, Paris, OECD.

(1986a), *Flexibility in the Labour Market: the Current Debate. A Technical Report*, Paris, OECD.

(1986b), 'The formulation of monetary policy: a reassessment in the light of recent experience', OECD Department of Economics and Statistics Working Paper no. 32.

(1988), *Why Economic Policies Change Course: Eleven Case Studies*, Paris, OECD.

Oppenheimer, P. and Reddaway, B. (1989), 'The US economy: performance and prospects', *National Institute Economic Review*, no. 127, February.

Oudiz, G. and Sachs, J. (1984), *Macroeconomic Policy Coordination among the Industrialised Economies*, Brookings Papers on Economic Activity, 1.

Prais, S.J. (1983), 'The recent slowdown in productivity growth. Comment on papers by Giersch and Wolter', *Economic Journal*, 93, no. 369, March.

Symons, J. and Layard, R. (1984), 'Neoclassical demand for labour functions for six major economies', *Economic Journal*, 94, no. 376, December.

Williamson, J. (1981), *Exchange Rate Rules: the Theory, Performance and Prospects of the Crawling Peg*, London, Macmillan.

(1983), *The Exchange Rate System*, Washington, The Institute for International Economics.

PART 4

THE CONDUCT OF POLICY

Many of the references already cited in the notes to Parts 1–3 are also relevant to the material in Part 4. Here we are concerned mainly with more technical literature related to the new statistical work that has been done for this study.

Fisher (1987) is an example of a recent text on macroeconomic policy which shows the uses and limitations of reaction functions as a method of analysis. See also the discussion of reaction functions in Anderson and Enzler (1987). Earlier and related ideas are developed in Alt and Chrystal (1981 and 1983) and in Pissarides (1972). On the merits of continuity in policy rules see Britton (1984). Other general references to both fiscal and monetary policy include (as well as those already cited) Allsopp (1985), Artis and Miller (Eds.) (1981), Chouraqui and Price (1983) and Dow and Saville (1988).

Not long before the beginning of the period covered by this study a conference was held bringing up to date an earlier review of economic policy in Britain by the United States Brookings Institution, which at that time meant mainly macroeconomic policy. The resulting conference volume is Cairncross (Ed.) (1970). Right at the end of the period another Anglo-American retrospective assessment of policy and performance was organised by a different group, and the papers were published as Dornbusch and Layard (Eds.) (1988), which included a useful coverage of both monetary and fiscal policy issues.

For a prototype of the interest rate equations estimated in Chapter 12 see Darby (1984). The ways in which policy might interact with economic behaviour to create a regular trade cycle is discussed in Britton (1986).

The effects of interest rates on the economy are discussed in Chouraqui *et al.* (1988), in Easton and Patterson (1987) and in Easton (1990).

On public spending see Pliatzky (1982), Likierman (1988), Levitt (1984) and Levitt and Joyce (1987). On fiscal policy more generally see Cook and Jackson (Eds.) (1979) and Chrystal and Alt (1979 and 1981).

There are many precedents for using macroeconomic models to assess the impact of policy in the past, for example Artis and Green (1982), Ball and Burns (1978) and Saville and Gardiner (1986). The pitfalls of these procedures in models with consistent expectations are discussed in Wallis (1988) and in Hall (1987). The version of the Institute's model which is used in the simulations for this book is described in Wren-Lewis (1988).

The literature on economic forecasting is surveyed in Wallis (1989), cited in Part 2 above. Of special interest here are Burns (1986) on the use of forecasting at the

Treasury, and Savage (1983) on the forecasts prepared by the National Institute. Keating (1985) provides another general survey.

The *National Institute Economic Review* published the papers from a conference on fiscal policy as seen in the mid-1980s. Budd, Dicks and Keating (1985) from the LBS, and Odling-Smee and Riley (1985) from the Treasury are especially relevant to this study. So is the Institute's own contribution by Biswas, Johns and Savage (1985), part of the literature on the measurement of fiscal policy.

Papers on that issue from the United States include Blinder and Goldfeld (1976), Fair (1978), Boskin (1988) and De Leeuw and Holloway (1985); some work for OECD can be found in Price and Muller (1984). Earlier work by the National Institute is in Savage (1982). The theoretical difficulties of measurement of this kind are emphasised in Buiter (1983). There is a useful survey in Miller (1985). For two constrasting papers by Treasury economists on this subject at different dates see Hartley and Bean (1978) and Bredenkamp (1987).

The compilation and uses of a public sector balance sheet are discussed in Bryant (1987), Britton (1987) and Chouraqui *et al.* (1986).

References

Allsopp, C. (1985), 'Monetary and fiscal policy in the 1980s', *Oxford Review of Economic Policy*, 1, no. 1, Spring.

Alt, J.E. and Chrystal, A.K. (1981), 'Some problems in formulating and testing a politico-economic model of the United Kingdom', *Economic Journal*, 91, Notes and Memoranda, no. 363, September.

and Chrystal, A.K. (1983), *Political Economics,* Brighton, Wheatsheaf Books.

Anderson, R. and Enzler, J.J. (1987), 'Toward realistic policy design: policy reaction functions that rely on economic forecasts' in Dornbusch, R., Fischer, S.W. and Bossons, J. (Eds.), *Macroeconomics and Finance,* Cambridge Mass, MIT Press.

Artis, M. and Green, C.J. (1982), 'Using the Treasury model to measure the impact of fiscal policy 1974–79' in Artis, M., Green, C.S., Leslie, D. and Smith, G.W., *Demand Management Supply Constraints and Inflation,* Manchester University Press.

and Miller, M.H. (Eds.) (1981), *Essays in Fiscal and Monetary Policy,* Oxford University Press.

Ball, R.J. and Burns, T. (1978), 'Stabilisation policy in Britain 1964–81', in Posner, M. (Ed.) *Demand Management,* London, Heinemann.

Biswas, R., Johns, C. and Savage, D. (1985), 'Government borrowing and economic policy: the measurement of fiscal stance', *National Institute Economic Review*, no. 113, August.

Blinder, A.S. and Goldfeld, S.M. (1976), 'New measures of fiscal and monetary policy 1958–73', *American Economic Review*, 66, December.

Boskin, M.J. (1988), 'Concepts and measures of federal deficits and debt and their impact on economic activity' in Arrow, K.J. and Boskin, M.J. (Eds.), *The Economics of Public Debt,* London, Macmillan.

Bredenkamp, H. (1987), 'Macroeconomic effects of changes in fiscal and monetary policy', HM Treasury Working Paper no. 51, Government Economic Service Working Paper no. 100.

Britton, A.J.C. (1984), 'Uncertainty, forecasting and budget changes', *National Institute Economic Review*, no. 107, February.

(1986), *The Trade Cycle in Britain 1958–1982,* Cambridge University Press.

(1987), 'Public sector borrowing and the public sector balance sheet', *National Institute Economic Review*, no. 121, August.

Bryant, C.G.E. (1987), 'National and sector balance sheets 1957–1985', *Economic Trends*, no. 403, May.

Budd, A., Dicks, G. and Keating, G. (1985), 'Government borrowing and economic policy: government borrowing and financial markets', *National Institute Economic Review*, no. 113, August.

Buiter, W. (1983), 'Measurement of the public sector deficit and its implications for policy evaluation and design', IMF Staff Papers vol. 30, no. 2, June.

Burns, T. (1986), 'The interpretation and use of economic predicting' in *Predictability in Science and Society*, London, The Royal Society and the British Academy.

Cairncross, A. (Ed.) (1970), *Britain's Economic Prospects Reconsidered*, London, Allen and Unwin.

Chouraqui, J–C, Driscoll, M. and Strauss-Kahn, M–O. (1988), 'The effects of monetary policy on the real sector: an overview of empirical evidence for selected OECD economies', OECD Working Papers no. 51, April.

Jones, B. and Montador, R.B. (1986), *Public Debt in a Medium-term Perspective*, OECD Economic Studies, Autumn.

and Price, R. (1983), 'Medium-term financial strategy: the co-ordination of fiscal and monetary policies', Paris, OECD Economics and Statistics Department Working Paper no. 9, July.

Chrystal, A. and Alt, J. (1979), 'Endogenous government behaviour: Wagner's Law or Götterdämmerung?' in Cook, S.T. and Jackson, P.M. (Eds.), *Current Issues in Fiscal Policy*, Oxford, Martin Robertson.

and Alt, J. (1981), 'Politico-economic models of British fiscal policy' in Hibbs, D.A. and Fassbender, H. (Eds.), *Contemporary Political Economy. Studies on the Interdependence of Politics and Economics*, Amsterdam, North-Holland.

Cook, S.T. and Jackson, P.M. (Eds.) (1979), *Current Issues in Fiscal Policy*, Oxford, Martin Robertson.

Darby, J. (1984), 'Fiscal policy and interest rates', *National Institute Economic Review*, no. 109, August.

De Leeuw, F. and Holloway, T.M. (1985), 'The measurement and significance of the cyclically adjusted Federal budget and debt', *Journal of Money, Credit and Banking*, no. 2, May.

Dornbusch, R. and Layard, R. (Eds.) (1988), *The Performance of the British Economy*, Oxford University Press.

Dow, J.C.R,. and Saville, I.D. (1988), *A Critique of Monetary Policy. Theory and British Experience*, Oxford, Clarendon Press.

Easton, B. and Patterson, K. (1987), 'Interest rates in five macroeconomic models of the UK: survey analysis and simulation', *Economic Modelling*, 4, no.1, January.

Easton, W.W. (1990), 'The interest rate transmission mechanism in the United Kingdom and overseas', *Bank of England Quarterly Bulletin*, 30, no. 2, May.

Fair, R.C. (1978), 'The sensitivity of fiscal policy effects to assumptions about the behaviour of the Federal Reserve', *Econometrica*, 46, no. 5, September.

Fisher, D. (1987), *Monetary and Fiscal Policy*, London, Macmillan.

Hall, S.G. (1987), 'Analysing economic behaviour 1975–85 with a model incorporating consistent expectations', *National Institute Economic Review*, no. 120, May.

Hartley, N. and Bean, C. (1978), 'The standardised budget balance', Government Economic Service Working Paper no. 1.

Keating, G. (1985), *The Production and Use of Economic Forecasts*, London, Methuen.

Levitt, M.S. (1984), 'The growth of government expenditure', *National Institute Economic Review*, no. 108, May.

and Joyce, M.A.S. (1987), *The Growth and Efficiency of Public Spending*, Cambridge University Press.

Likierman, A. (1988), *Public Expenditure*, Penguin Books.

Miller, M. (1985), 'Measuring the stance of fiscal policy', *Oxford Review of Economic Policy*, 1, no. 1, Spring.

Odling-Smee, J. and Riley, C. (1985), 'Government borrowing and economic policy: approaches to the PSBR', *National Institute Economic Review*, no. 113, August.

Pissarides, C.A. (1972), 'A model of British macroeconomic policy 1955–1969', *Manchester School*, no. 3, September.

Pliatzky, L. (1982), *Getting and Spending: Public Expenditure, Employment and Inflation*, Oxford, Basil Blackwell.

Price, R.W.R. and Muller, P. (1984), *Structural Budget Indicators and the Interpretation of Fiscal Policy Stance in OECD Economies*, OECD Economic studies no. 3, Autumn.

Savage, D. (1982), 'Fiscal policy, 1974/5–1980/81: description and measurement', *National Institute Economic Review*, no. 99, February.

(1983), 'The assessment of the National Institute's forecasts of GDP 1959–82', *National Institute Economic Review*, no. 105, August.

Saville, I.D. and Gardiner, K.L. (1986), 'Stagflation in the UK since 1970: a model based explanation', *National Institute Economic Review*, no. 117, August.

Wallis, K.F. (1988), 'The historical tracking performance of UK macroeconomic models 1978–85, ESRC Macroeconomic Modelling Bureau, University of Warwick Discussion Paper no. 17.

Wren-Lewis, S. (1988), 'Supply, liquidity and credit: a new version of the Institute's domestic econometric macromodel', *National Institute Economic Review*, no. 126, November.

PART 5

THE OUTCOME FOR POLICY OBJECTIVES

In this study we have not devoted a separate section to the effects of North Sea oil production on the British economy. It was however the subject of some interesting writings both before and after the event – that is before and after the exchange rate appreciation of 1979–80. *Ex ante* analysis can be found in Page (1977) and HM Treasury (1978); *ex post* analysis in Forsyth and Kay (1980), Eastwood and Venables (1982), Byatt *et al.* (1982), Spencer (1984), Bean (1987), Aktinson *et al.* (1983), Atkinson and Hall (1983) and in Bank of England (1980 and 1986).

Unemployment has been the subject of several major studies in Britain, and much controversy. A recent survey is Nickell (1990). Minford *et al.* (1983) presents the classical view. The difference between that and the views of the Centre for Labour Economics at LSE can be judged by reading Layard (1986), Nickell (1979, 1980, 1982 and 1984) and a book in preparation at the same time as this one, Jackman *et al.* (1990).

A study in preparation at the National Institute at the same time as this one will be Worswick (1991); see also Worswick (1976 and 1985). Other material relevant to this section of the book will be found in Atkinson, A.B. (1982), Metcalf (1984), Carruth and Oswald (1987), Sinfield (1981), Brittan (1975), Scott and Laslett (1978) and in the references on 'hysteresis' cited in Part 2 above. Budd *et al.* (1988) focusses attention on long-term unemployment. Special employment measures are discussed in Hart (Ed.) (1986), House of Commons (1986), Deakin and Pratten (1982), Layard and Nickell (1980) and Gregg (1990).

Some of the literature on inflation has been cited already. We should now add Hirsch and Goldthorpe (Eds.) (1978) for examples of the way in which the inflation problem was addressed in the late 1970s. Indexation is discussed in Fane (1974) and OECD (1975). Empirical studies particularly relevant to those reported here are Rowlatt (1987) reporting work at the Treasury, Whitley (1986) on incomes policy, Beckerman (1985) and Beckerman and Jenkinson (1986) on commodity prices, Matthews and Ormerod (1978) on the relationship of money and inflation in the United Kingdom, Paldam (1980) on international linkages of inflation and especially Wren-Lewis (1981 and 1984) from which the approach adopted in Chapter 14 was developed.

The standard work on the growth of the United Kingdom economy up to 1973 is Matthews, Feinstein and Odling-Smee (1982). Two of the same authors have also looked at growth in the 1980s in Feinstein and Matthews (1990). For an article on growth trends up to the early 1980s see Savage and Biswas (1986). Attention focused around the tenth anniversary of the 1979 election on the extent of, and also the reasons for, the improvement in economic performance in the United Kingdom – see for example Layard and Nickell (1989), Crafts (1988) and Landesmann and Snell (1989).

The reasons for the recession at the beginning of the 1980s were discussed at the Bank of England academic panel, and Bank of England (1981) includes a useful set of papers on the subject.

Chapter 15 draws on the work which went into the production of the 1989 vintage of the National Institute's macroeconomic model. It is reported more fully in Darby and Wren-Lewis (1989). A later section of that chapter is based on another project in progress at the Institute, using evidence from variations in performance across industries. Results from the work are reported in Oulton (1990).

References

Atkinson, A.B. (1982), 'Unemployment, wages and government policy', *Economic Journal* 92, no. 365.

Atkinson, F.J., Brooks, S.J. and Hall, S.G.F. (1983), 'The economic effects of North Sea oil', *National Institute Economic Review*, no. 104, May.

and Hall, S.G. (1983), *Oil and the British Economy*, Beckenham, Croom Helm.

Bank of England (1980), 'The North Sea and the United Kingdom economy: some longer-term perspectives and implications, *Bank of England Quarterly Bulletin*, 20, no. 4, December.

(1981), 'Factors underlying the recent recession', Papers presented to the Panel of Academic Consultants, no. 15.

(1986), 'North Sea oil and gas', *Bank of England Quarterly Bulletin*, 26, no.4, December.

Bean, C. (1987), 'The impact of North Sea oil' in Dornbusch, R. and Layard, R. (Eds.), *The Performance of the British Economy*, Oxford, Clarendon Press.

Beckerman, W. (1985), 'How the battle against inflation was really won', *Lloyds Bank Review*, no. 155, January.

and Jenkinson, T. (1986), 'What stopped the inflation? Unemployment or commodity prices?' *Economic Journal*, 96, no. 381, March.

Brittan, S. (1975), *Second Thoughts on Full Employment Policy*, London, Centre for Policy Studies.

Budd, A., Levine, P. and Smith, P. (1988), 'Unemployment, vacancies and the long-term unemployed', *Economic Journal*, 98, no. 393, December.

Byatt, I. *et al.* (1982), 'North Sea oil and structural adjustment', HM Treasury Working Paper no.22, Government Economic Service Working Paper no. 54.

Carruth, A. and Oswald, A.J. (1987), 'On union preferences and labour market models: insiders and outsiders', *Economic Journal*, 97, no. 386, June.

Crafts, N. (1988), 'British economic growth before and after 1979: a review of the evidence', CEPR Discussion Paper no. 292, November.

Darby, J. and Wren-Lewis, S. (1989), 'Manufacturing investment and labour productivity: an econometric analysis based on a vintage model', National Institute Discussion Paper no. 178.

Deakin, B.M. and Pratten, C.F. (1982), *Effects of the Temporary Employment Subsidy*, Cambridge University Press.

Eastwood, R.K. and Venables, A.J. (1982), 'The macroeconomic implications of a resource discovery in an open economy', *Economic Journal* 92, no. 366, June.

Fane, C.G. (1974), 'Index-linking and inflation', *National Institute Economic Review*, no. 70, November.

Feinstein, C. and Matthews, R. (1990), 'The growth of output and productivity in the UK' *National Institute Economic Review*, no. 133 August.

Forsyth, P.J. and Kay, J.A. (1980), 'The economic implications of North Sea oil revenues', *Fiscal Studies*, 1, no. 3, July.

Gregg, P. (1990), 'The evolution of special employment measures', *National Institute Economic Review*, no. 132, May.

Hart, P.E. (Ed.) (1986), *Unemployment and Labour Market Policies*, Aldershot, Gower.

HM Treasury (1978), *The challenge of North Sea oil*, Cmnd 7143, HMSO.

Hirsch, F. and Goldthorpe, J.H. (Eds.) (1978), *The Political Economy of Inflation*, Oxford, Martin Robertson.

House of Commons (1986), 'Special employment measures and the long-term unemployed', First report of the Employment Committee Session 1985/6, London, HMSO.

Jackman, R., Layard, R., Nickell, S. and Wadhwani, S. (1990), *Unemployment*, Oxford, Basil Blackwell.

Landesmann, M. and Snell, A. (1989), 'The consequences of Mrs Thatcher for UK manufacturing exports', *Economic Journal*, 99, no. 394, March.

Layard, R. (1986), *How to Beat Unemployment*, Oxford University Press.

and Nickell, S. (1980), 'The case for subsidising extra jobs', *Economic Journal*, 90, no. 357.

and Nickell, S. (1989), 'The Thatcher miracle?' CEPR Discussion Paper no. 315, April.

Matthews, K.G.P. and Ormerod, P.A. (1978), 'St Louis models of the UK economy', *National Institute Economic Review*, no. 84, May.

Matthews, R.C.O., Feinstein, C. and Odling-Smee, J.C. (1982), *British Economic Growth 1856–1973: the Postwar Period in Historical Perspective,* Oxford, Clarendon Press.

Metcalf, D. (1984), 'Full employment as a policy objective: On the measurement of employment and unemployment', *National Institute Economic Review,* no. 109, August.

Minford, P., Davies, P., Peel, M. and Sprague, A. (1983), *Unemployment – Cause and Cure,* Oxford, Martin Robertson.

Nickell, S.J. (1979), 'The effect of unemployment and related benefits on the duration of unemployment', *Economic Journal,* 89, no. 353, March.

  (1980), 'A picture of male unemployment in Britain', *Economic Journal,* 90, no. 360, December.

  (1982), 'Wages and unemployment: a general framework', *Economic Journal,* 92, no. 365, March.

  (1984), 'A review of *'Unemployment – Cause and Cure'* by Patrick Minford and others', *Economic Journal,* 94, no. 376, December.

  (1990), 'Unemployment: a survey', *Economic Journal,* 100, no. 401, June.

OECD (1975), *Indexation of Financial Assets,* Paris, OECD.

Oulton, N. (1990), 'Labour productivity in the 1970s and in the 1980s', *National Institute Economic Review,* no. 132, May.

Page, S.A.B. (1977), 'The value and distribution of the benefits of North Sea oil and gas, 1970–1985', *National Institute Economic Review,* no. 82, November.

Paldam, M. (1980), 'The international element in the Phillips curve', *Scandinavian Journal of Economics,* 82, no. 2 Part I Macro.

Rowlatt, P.A. (1987), 'Analysis of the inflation process', HM Treasury Working Paper no. 50, Government Economic Service Working Paper no. 99.

Savage, D. and Biswas, R. (1986), 'The British economy in the long term: an analysis of post-war growth rates and an illustrative long-term projection', *National Institute Economic Review,* no. 118, November.

Scott, M. and Laslett, R.A. (1978), *Can We Get Back to Full Employment?* London, Macmillan.

Sinfield, A. (1981), *What Unemployment Means,* Oxford, Martin Robertson.

Spencer, P.D. (1984), 'The effect of oil discoveries on the British economy – theoretical ambiguities and the consistent expectations simulation approach', *Economic Journal,* 94, no. 375, September.

Whitley, J.D. (1986), 'A model of incomes policy in the UK 1963–79', *Manchester School,* 54, no. 1, March.

  and Wilson, R.A. (1983), 'The macroeconomic merits of a marginal employment subsidy', *Economic Journal,* 93, no. 372, December.

Worswick, G.D.N. (Ed.) (1976), *The Concept and Measurement of Involuntary Unemployment,* London, George Allen & Unwin.

  (1985), 'Jobs for all?' *Economic Journal,* 95, no. 377, March.

  (1991), *Unemployment: A Problem of Policy,* Cambridge University Press.

Wren-Lewis, S. (1981), 'The role of money in determining prices: a reduced form approach', HM Treasury Working Paper no. 18, Government Economic Service Working Paper no. 42.

  (1984), 'Omitted variables in equations relating prices to money', *Applied Economics,* 16, no. 4, August.

INDEX

THE NATIONAL INSTITUTE OF ECONOMIC
AND SOCIAL RESEARCH
PUBLICATIONS IN PRINT

published by
THE CAMBRIDGE UNIVERSITY PRESS
(available from booksellers, or in case of difficulty from the publishers)

THE NATIONAL INSTITUTE OF ECONOMIC AND
SOCIAL RESEARCH

publishes regularly

THE NATIONAL INSTITUTE ECONOMIC REVIEW

A quarterly analysis of the general economic situation in the United Kingdom and overseas with forecasts eighteen months ahead. There are also special articles on subjects of interest to academic and business economists.

Annual subscriptions, £65.00 (home) and £80.00 (abroad), also single issues for the current year, £17.00 (home) and £25.00 (abroad), are available direct from NIESR, 2 Dean Trench Street, Smith Square, London, SW1P 3HE.

Subscriptions at a special reduced price are available to students and teachers in the United Kingdom and Irish Republic on application to the Secretary of the Institute.

Back numbers and reprints of issues which have gone out of stock are distributed by Wm. Dawson and Sons Ltd., Cannon House, Park Farm Road, Folkestone. Microfiche copies for the years 1959–88 are available from EP Microform Ltd., Bradford Road, East Ardsley, Wakefield, Yorks.

———

Published by
HEINEMANN EDUCATIONAL BOOKS
(distributed by Gower Publishing Company and available from booksellers)

DEMAND MANAGEMENT
Edited by MICHAEL POSNER. 1978. pp. 256. £18.50 net.

BRITAIN IN EUROPE
Edited by WILLIAM WALLACE. 1980. pp. 224. £12.95 (paperback) net.

THE FUTURE OF PAY BARGAINING
Edited by FRANK BLACKABY. 1980. pp. 256. £31.00 (hardback), £8.95 (paperback) net.

INDUSTRIAL POLICY AND INNOVATION
Edited by CHARLES CARTER. 1981. pp. 250. £26.50 (hardback), £9.95 (paperback) net.

THE CONSTITUTION OF NORTHERN IRELAND
Edited by DAVID WATT. 1981. pp. 233. £24.00 (hardback), £10.50 (paperback) net.

SLOWER GROWTH IN THE WESTERN WORLD
Edited by R. C. O. MATTHEWS. 1982. pp. 182. £26.50 (hardback), £10.95 (paperback) net.

NATIONAL INTERESTS AND LOCAL GOVERNMENT
Edited by KEN YOUNG. 1983. pp. 180. £25.00 (hardback), £10.95 (paperback) net.

EMPLOYMENT, OUTPUT AND INFLATION
Edited by A. J. C. BRITTON. 1983. pp. 208. £36.00 net.

THE TROUBLED ALLIANCE. ATLANTIC RELATIONS IN THE 1980s
Edited by LAWRENCE FREEDMAN. 1983. pp. 176. £25.00 (hardback),
£8.95 (paperback) net.

(Available from Heinemann and from booksellers)
THE UK ECONOMY
By the NIESR. 1990. pp. 96. £3.75 net.

Published by
GOWER PUBLISHING COMPANY
(Available from Gower Publishing Company and from booksellers)

ENERGY SELF-SUFFICIENCY FOR THE UK
Edited by ROBERT BELGRAVE and MARGARET CORNELL. 1985. pp. 224. £22.50 net.

THE FUTURE OF BRITISH DEFENCE POLICY
Edited by JOHN ROPER. 1985. pp. 214. £24.00 net.

ENERGY MANAGEMENT: CAN WE LEARN FROM OTHERS?
By GEORGE F. RAY. 1985. pp. 131. £22.50 net.

UNEMPLOYMENT AND LABOUR MARKET POLICIES
Edited by P. E. HART. 1986. pp. 230. £30.00 net.

NEW PRIORITIES IN PUBLIC SPENDING
Edited by M. S. LEVITT. 1987. pp. 136. £26.00 net.

POLICYMAKING WITH MACROECONOMIC MODELS
Edited by A. J. C. BRITTON. 1989. pp. 285. £29.50 net.

HOUSING AND THE NATIONAL ECONOMY
Edited by JOHN ERMISCH. 1990. pp. 158. £29.50 net.